# SOFTWARE PROJECT MANAGEMENT

6

# Software Project Management

Editor:

Prof. Dr. Zoran Gacovski, Ph.D.

ArclerPress

www.arclerpress.com

**Software Project Management**

*Editor: Prof. Dr. Zoran Gacovski, Ph.D.*



**708 3rd Avenue, 6th Floor**
**New York**
**NY 10017**
**United States of America**
**www.arclerpress.com**

ISBN: 978-1-68094-455-6

Library of Congress Control Number: 2016951150

# About the Editor

## Prof. Dr. Zoran Gacovski, Ph.D.

Dr. Zoran Gacovski has earned his PhD degree at Faculty of Electrical engineering, Skopje. His research interests include Intelligent systems and Software engineering, fuzzy systems, graphical models (Petri, Neural and Bayesian networks), and IT security. He has published over 50 journal and conference papers, and he has been reviewer of renowned Journals. In his career he was awarded by Fulbright postdoctoral fellowship (2002) for research stay at Rutgers University, USA. He has also earned best-paper award at the Baltic Olympiad for Automation control (2002), US NSF grant for conducting a specific research in the field of human-computer interaction at Rutgers University, USA (2003), and DAAD grant for research stay at University of Bremen, Germany (2008). Currently, he is a professor in Computer Engineering at European University, Skopje, Macedonia.

# Contents

## Section II: Program and Configuration Management



## Section III: Agile Methodology

## Section IV: Process Management and Tools

# List of Contributors

**Nazeeh Ghatasheh**
Department of Business Information Technology, The University of Jordan, Aqaba, Jordan

**Hossam Faris**
Department of Business Information Technology, The University of Jordan, Amman, Jordan

**Ibrahim Aljarah**
Department of Business Information Technology, The University of Jordan, Amman, Jordan

**Rizik M. H. Al-Sayyed**
Department of Business Information Technology, The University of Jordan, Amman, Jordan

**Vassilis C. Gerogiannis**
Department of Business Administration, Project Management Direction of Studies, Technological Educational Institute of Thessaly, 41110 Larissa, Greece

**Elli Rapti**
Centre for Research and Technology, Institute of Research and Technology of Thessaly, 38333 Volos, Greece

**Anthony Karageorgos**
Department of Wood and Furniture Design and Technology, Technological Educational Institute of Thessaly, 43100 Karditsa, Greece

**Panos Fitsilis**
Department of Business Administration, Project Management Direction of Studies, Technological Educational Institute of Thessaly, 41110 Larissa, Greece

**Dr Nasina Jigeesh**
IBS Hyderabad, IFHE University, India

**Peleg Yiftachel**
Caesarea Rothschild Institute for Interdisciplinary Applications of Computer Science, University of Haifa, Mount Carmel, Haifa 31905, Israel
Israeli Center of Excellence, EMC Cooperation, 7 Hamada Street, Herzelia 46733, Israel

**Irit Hadar**
Department of Information Systems, University of Haifa, Mount Carmel, Haifa 31905, Israel

**Dan Peled**
Department of Economics, University of Haifa, Mount Carmel, Haifa 31905, Israel

**Eitan Farchi**
Group of Software Performance Analysis Reviews and Quality (SPARQ), IBM Haifa Research Laboratory, Haifa University Campus, Mount Carmel, Haifa 31905, Israel

**Dan Goldwasser**
Department of Computer Science, University of Illinois, Urbana-Champaign, IL 61801, USA

**Beata Czarnacka-Chrobot**
Institute of Information Technology and Digital Economy, Warsaw School of Economics, Warsaw, Poland

**Jennifer Whyte**
School of Construction Management and Engineering, University of Reading, Whiteknights, Reading, RG6 6AY, United Kingdom

**Angelos Stasis**
School of Construction Management and Engineering, University of Reading, Whiteknights, Reading, RG6 6AY, United Kingdom

**Carmel Lindkvist**
School of Construction Management and Engineering, University of Reading, Whiteknights, Reading, RG6 6AY, United Kingdom

**Vijay Somanchi**
IBS Hyderabad, Hyderabad, India

**Ravikiran Dwivedula**
SKEMA Business School, Lille, France; IBS Hyderabad, Hyderabad, India

**Sheetal Sharma, Darothi Sarkar and Divya Gupta**
Amity School of Engineering & Technology Amity University Noida

**Jalil Abbas**
School of Computing and Information Sciences, Imperial College of Business Studies, Lahore, Pakistan

**Ratnesh Litoriya**
Department of Computer Engineering, JJT University, Rajasthan, India

**Abhay Kothari**
Department of CSE, SIMS, Indore, India.

**Rich C. Lee**
System Technology Group, IBM, Chinese Taipei
Department of Computer Science, National Taipei University of Technology, Chinese Taipei.

**Vipul Vashisht**
Quality Department, Polaris Financial Technology Limited, Gurgaon, India

**Hani Gharaibeh**
PMPC Consulting Inc., Amman, Jordan

**Leonidas Anthopoulos**
Business Administration Department, Technological Educational Institute of Thessaly, Larissa, Greece

**Iheb Abdellatif**
Department of Software Engineering and Information Technologies, Ecole de Technologie Supérieure, Montreal, Canada

**Alain April**
Department of Software Engineering and Information Technologies, Ecole de Technologie Supérieure, Montreal, Canada

**Lazaros Sarigiannidis**
Production & Management Engineering Department, Democritus University of Thrace, Xanthi, Greece.

**Prodromos D. Chatzoglou**
Production & Management Engineering Department, Democritus University of Thrace, Xanthi, Greece.

**Arti Rana**
Amity Institute of Information Technology, Amity University, Noida (UP), India

**S. P. Singh**
Birla Institute of Technology, Extension Centre, Noida, India

**Rachna Soni**
Department of Computer Science, DAV College for Girls, Yamuna Nagar, India

**Ashish Jolly**
Department of Computer Science, Govt. College, Bherian (Pehowa), Haryana, India

**David Hillson**
Risk Doctor & Partners, UK

**Ruth Murray-Webster**
Lucidus Consulting, UK

# Preface

Effective management of the software project management involves four P-s: People, Product, Process, and Project. The manager that forgets people's aspect of software engineering will never achieve success in the management of their projects. The manager who does not properly communicate with their clients, especially in the early stage of the product development, risks to create an elegant solution for a wrong problem (task). The manager who pays little attention to the process risks to apply state-of-the-art technical solutions in the wrong place and the wrong time. Today's software project management methods go well beyond the classical Waterfall approach, and typically involve the Unified process (including RUP), as well as the Agile methodology (including Scrum).

This book edition covers different aspects of the software project management process. It is divided in five Sections, described as follows.

Section 1 - Covers Management of People and Resources, describing the estimation of human resources needed in the software projects, their suitability for particular software development task, the impact of the people on the project, and the resource allocation among phases.

Section 2 - Covers Configuration and Program management, discussing about managing changes in complex and large scale IT projects, as well as the COSMIC methodology for work effort estimation per unit size.

Section 3 - Covers the Agile methodology focusing on the concepts of Agile, its comparison with the traditional approaches, the Scrum method explanation, and AgileMOW – a method for Agile web-based project estimation.

Section 4 - Covers Process management and Tools, describing internal controls in business processes, comparison between MS Project and Primavera using a scoring model, and the concept of Ontologies in the software project management.

Section 5 - Covers the Project Risk management, including categorization of software release risks, a new taxonomy for risk attitude estimation and a new methodology for the risk management.

**Editor**
**Prof. Dr. Zoran Gacovski, Ph.D.**

# SECTION I: PEOPLE AND RESOURCES MANAGEMENT

CHAPTER 1

# OPTIMIZING SOFTWARE EFFORT ESTIMATION MODELS USING FIREFLY ALGORITHM

Nazeeh Ghatasheh[1], Hossam Faris[2], Ibrahim Aljarah[2], Rizik M. H. Al-Sayyed[2]

[1]Department of Business Information Technology, The University of Jordan, Aqaba, Jordan

[2]Department of Business Information Technology, The University of Jordan, Amman, Jordan

## ABSTRACT

**Software development effort estimation is considered a fundamental task for software development life cycle as well as for managing project cost, time and quality. Therefore, accurate estimation is a substantial factor in projects success and reducing the risks. In recent years, software effort estimation has received a considerable amount of attention from researchers and became a challenge for software industry. In the last two decades, many researchers and practitioners proposed statistical and machine learning-based models for software effort estimation. In this work, Firefly Algorithm is proposed as a metaheuristic optimization method for optimizing the parameters of three COCOMO-based models. These models include the basic COCOMO model and other two models proposed in the literature as extensions of the basic COCOMO model. The developed estimation models are evaluated using different evaluation metrics. Experimental results show high accuracy and significant error minimization of Firefly Algorithm over other metaheuristic optimization algorithms including Genetic Algorithms and Particle Swarm Optimization.**

## INTRODUCTION

Effort estimation of software development has been a crucial task for software engineering community. Reliable effort estimation makes it more dependable to schedule project activities, allocate resources, estimate costs, and reduce the probability of project failures or delays. According to the survey in [1], most of the projects face overruns of effort or schedules. The survey also claimed that the lack of accurate estimation models is a main reason for project overruns.

**Citation:** Ghatasheh, N. , Faris, H. , Aljarah, I. and Al-Sayyed, R. (2015) Optimizing Software Effort Estimation Models Using Firefly Algorithm. Journal of Software Engineering and Applications, 8, 133-142. doi: 10.4236/jsea.2015.83014.

Usually projects seem to be vague at the beginning and become less vague as they progress. At the same time, each project has its special nature that makes it much harder to estimate the required effort for completion. Due to the uncertain nature of projects, authors in [2] [3] suggested developing models that can adapt to a wide range of projects. But for the fact that software project data sets are typically small and the underlying relations are inaccurate or missing, the task of prediction becomes more challenging.

Several effort estimation models have been developed and improved over time for better prediction accuracy and thus better development quality [1] [4] - [8] . Such models range from complex calculations and statistical analysis of project parameters, to advanced machine learning approaches.

Heuristic optimization [9] is a method that relies on several attempts to find an optimal solution. Heuristic optimizers have been used in software effort estimation [10] as the use of genetic programming in [11] for model optimization. Another example is the part that Particle Swarm Optimization took in [12] as a heuristic optimizer. Moreover, the hybrid approaches encompass a combination of heuristic algorithms like the use of Genetic Algorithm and Ant Colony [13] .

Despite a large number of experiments on finding the best prediction model, there is no clear evidence of a highly accurate or efficient approach. At the same time it is important to develop a prediction method that is less complex and much more useful. For instance, in some prediction models, a large number of variables that are used to construct the model do not reflect or improve the accuracy of the prediction model. Thus, collecting extra or unrelated variables is time-consuming with no significance. It would be more efficient to build a model with a minimum number of variables, hopefully finding the most important and common variables for generic project development efforts.

This work presents a study of how Firefly Algorithm improves the overall estimation of the software effort estimation. Where the main contributions are:

- Proving the suitability of Firefly Algorithm as predictor towards a generic prediction model for software effort estimation.
- The significant improvement in performance over previously reported methods.
- The suitability of machine learning approaches for effort prediction using a small number of input variables and data set instances.

## RELATED WORK

Many of Machine Learning (ML) approaches in the literature have been applied to improve the software effort estimation [2] . ML optimization algorithms that are inspired from nature have received much attention to find more accurate estimation for software effort. Nature-inspired ML algorithms include Cuckoo Search [14] , Particle Swarm Optimization (PSO) [15] , Bat Algorithm [16] , Firefly Algorithm [17] , and many others.

In [18] , the authors compared the performance of different soft computing techniques such as PSO-Tuned COCOMO, Fuzzy Logic with traditional effort estimation structures. Their results showed that the proposed model outperformed traditional effort estimation structures for NASAs software effort data set. In [7] , decision trees based algorithm was used to perform the software effort estimation. In addition, the authors presented an empirical proof of performance variations for several approaches that include Linear Regression, Artificial Neural Networks (ANN), and Support Vector Machines (SVM). Also the authors pointed to the suitability of the experimented ML approaches in the area of effort estimation. From their performance comparison results with other traditional algorithms, their results in terms of the error rate were better than other techniques.

A hybrid approach was adopted in [19] for parameter selection and model optimization. The authors used Genetic Algorithms (GA) for optimizing a Support Vector Regression model. The authors clarified the impact of using GA in feature selection and parameter optimization of the effort estimation model. The results of their approach showed that GA is applicable to improve the performance of the SVR model compared to other approaches. A generic framework is proposed in [20] for software effort estimation. The framework tries to simulate the human way of thinking to resolve the effort estimation by adopting fuzzy rules modeling. Therefore the generated models take advantage of experts knowledge, interoperable, and could be applied to various problems as risk analysis or software quality prediction. ANNs gained noticeable attention by researchers for effort estimation as illustrated by the review in [21] , but it is insufficient to generalize the applicability of ANN in effort estimation. The authors stated that it is required to have further thorough investigation. The authors in [22] relied on seven evaluation measures to assess the stability of 90 software effort predictors over 20 data sets. According to the empirical results it was found that analogy-based methods or regression trees outperformed in terms of stability. Such conclusions open the door for extensive research towards a superior and generic prediction approach regarding the software effort estimation issue.

## FIREFLY ALGORITHM

Firefly Algorithm (FA) is a multimodal optimization algorithm, which belongs to the nature-inspired field, is inspired from the behavior of fireflies or lightning bugs [17] . FA was first introduced by Xin-She at Cambridge University in 2007 [17] . FA is empirically proven to tackle problems more naturally and has the potential to over-perform other metaheuristic algorithms.

FA relies on three basic rules, the first implies that all fireflies are attracted to each other with disregard to gender. The second rule states that attractiveness is correlated with brightness or light emission such that bright flies attract less bright ones, and for absence of brighter flies the movement becomes random. The last main rule implies that the landscape of the objective function determines or affects the light emission of the fly, such that brightness is proportional to the objective function.

Algorithm 1. Pseudo-code of firefly algorithm.

Objective function $f(x)$
$x=(x1,\cdots,xd)T$
Generate initial population of fireflies $x_i\,(i=1,2,\cdots,n)$
Light intensity $I_i$ at $x_i$ is determined by $f(x_i)$
Define light absorption coefficient $\gamma$
**while** ($t$ < MaxGeneration) **do**
  **for** $i=1:\ n$ all $n$ fireflies **do**
    **for** $j=1:\ i$ all n fireflies **do**
      **if** ( $I_j > I_i$ ) **then**
        Move firefly $i$ towards $j$ in d-dimension;
      **end if**
      Attractiveness varies with distance $r$ via $\exp[\gamma r]$
      Evaluate new solutions and update light intensity
    **end for**
  **end for**
  Rank the fireflies and find the current best
**end while**
Post-process results and visualization

The attractiveness among the flies in FA has two main issues that are; the modeling of attractiveness and the various light intensities. For a specific firefly at location X brightness I is formulated as I(X) f(X). While attractiveness b is proportional to the flies and is related to the distance $R_{i,j}$ between fireflies i and j. Equation (1) shows the inverse square of light intensity I(r) in which $I_0$ represents the light intensity at the source.

$$I(r) = I_0 e^{-\gamma r^2} \tag{1}$$

Assuming an absorption coefficient of the environment g, intensity is represented in Equation (2) in which $I_0$ is the original intensity.

$$I(r) = \frac{I_0}{1+\gamma r^2} \tag{2}$$

Generally the Euclidean distance is illustrated in Equation (3), which represents the distance between a firefly at location $X_i$ and another at location $X_j$. In which $X_{i,k}$ is the $k^{th}$ component of the spatial coordinate $X_i$.

$$R_{ij} = \left\| x_i - x_j \right\| = \sqrt{\sum_{k=1}^{d} \left(x_{i,k} - x_{j,k}\right)^2} \tag{3}$$

A firefly i attracted to a brighter one j as illustrated in Equation (4) where attraction is represented by $\beta_{e^{\gamma r_{ij}^2}} \left(x_j - x_i\right)$, and $\alpha\left(rand - \frac{1}{2}\right)$ represents the randomness according to the randomization parameter α.

$$x_i = x_i + \beta_{e^{\gamma r_{ij}^2}} \left(x_j - x_i\right) + \alpha\left(rand - \frac{1}{2}\right) \tag{4}$$

Furthermore, variations of attractiveness are determined by γ which on its turn affects the behavior and convergence speed of FA.

## EFFORT ESTIMATION MODELS

One of the Famous and widely used effort estimation models is the Constructive Cost Models COCOMO and its extension COCOMOII. COCOMO is used as cost, effort, and schedule estimation model in the process of planning new software development activity, also known as COCOMO 81. COCOMO was defined between the late 1970s and early 1980s [23]. Where COCOMOII is a later extension of the previously defined model. This research work tries to optimize the parameters of three variations of the COCOMO model. The first is the basic COCOMO model which is represented in Equation (5).

$$E = a_i \left(\text{KLOC}\right)^{b_i} \tag{5}$$

E is the effort in person-months, KLOC represents the thousand (K) lines of code included in a software project. Typically, the coefficient $a_i$ and the exponent $b_i$ are chosen based on COCOMO pre-set parameters that depend on the software project details.

The other two models are extensions of the basic COCOMO model which are proposed by A. Sheta in [24]. Both models consider the effect of methodologies (ME) as supposed to be linearly related to the software effort. These models are represented in Equations (6) and (7) and named Model I and Model II respectively.

$$E = a_i \left(\text{KLOC}\right)^{b_i} + c_i\left(\text{ME}\right) \tag{6}$$

$$E = a_i \left(\text{KLOC}\right)^{b_i} + c_i\left(\text{ME}\right) + d_i \tag{7}$$

This work tries empirically to optimize the constants $a_i$, $b_i$, $c_i$ and $d_i$ using FA, GA and PSO.

## DATA SET AND EVALUATION MEASURES

This research considers a famous and public data set in order to produce comparable results; namely NASA projects' effort data set. The data set is challenging due to the small number of instances and limited number of analyzed variables. However, regarding the objectives of this research the data set is considered to be adequate. The data set is split into two parts; training set of about 60% and testing set of about 30% instances.

NASA data set [6] consists of 18 software projects for which this research considers three main variables that are the project size in thousand Lines of Code (KLOC), Methodology (ME), and Actual Effort (AE). Training data set has 13 instances and the records from 14 till 18 are for testing the model. Table 1 shows the actual values of the training and testing data sets.

In order to check the performance of the developed models, the computed measures are the Correlation Coefficient ($R^2$),

$$R^2 = \frac{\sum_{i=1}^{n}\left(y_i - \bar{Y}_i\right)^2 - \sum_{i=1}^{n}\left(y_i - \hat{y}_i\right)^2}{\sum_{i=1}^{n}\left(y_i - \bar{y}_i\right)^2} \tag{8}$$

the Mean Squares Error (MSE),

$$\text{MSE} = \frac{1}{n}\sum_{i=1}^{n}\left(y - \hat{y}\right)^2 \tag{9}$$

**Table 1**. NASA data set

| Project No. | KDLOC | ME | Measured Effort |
|---|---|---|---|
| 1 | 90.2 | 30 | 115.8 |
| 2 | 46.2 | 20 | 96 |
| 3 | 46.5 | 19 | 79 |
| 4 | 54.5 | 20 | 90.8 |
| 5 | 31.1 | 35 | 39.6 |
| 6 | 67.5 | 29 | 98.4 |
| 7 | 12.8 | 26 | 18.9 |
| 8 | 10.5 | 34 | 10.3 |
| 9 | 21.5 | 31 | 28.5 |
| 10 | 3.1 | 26 | 7 |
| 11 | 4.2 | 19 | 9 |
| 12 | 7.8 | 31 | 7.3 |
| 13 | 2.1 | 28 | 5 |
| 14 | 5 | 29 | 8.4 |
| 15 | 78.6 | 35 | 98.7 |
| 16 | 9.7 | 27 | 15.6 |
| 17 | 12.5 | 27 | 23.9 |
| 18 | 100.8 | 34 | 138.3 |

the Mean Absolute Error (MAE),

$$\mathrm{MAE} = \frac{1}{n}\sum_{i=1}^{n}\left|y_i - \hat{y}_i\right| \tag{10}$$

the Mean Magnitude of Relative Error (MMRE),

$$\mathrm{MMRE} = \frac{1}{n}\sum_{i=1}^{n}\frac{\left|y_i - \hat{y}_i\right|}{y_i} \tag{11}$$

and the Variance-Accounted-For (VAF).

$$\mathrm{VAF} = \left[1 - \frac{\mathrm{var}\left(y(t) - \hat{y}(t)\right)}{\mathrm{var}\left(y(t)\right)}\right] \times 100\% \tag{12}$$

These performance criteria are used to measure how close the predicted effort to the actual values, where y is the actual value, $\hat{y}$ is the estimated target value, and n is the number of instances.

## EXPERIMENTS AND RESULTS

The experiments apply FA, GA and PSO for optimizing the coefficients of the basic COCOMO model, COCOMO Model I and COCOMO Model II based on the training part of NASA data set. For FA, the Matlab implementation developed by X.-S. Yang [9] is applied. Number of flies, particles and population size is unified and set to 100 in all the algorithms. The number of iterations is set to 500. The rest of the parameters of FA, GA and PSO are set as listed in Tables 2-4. MAE criteria are used as an objective function which is shown in Equation (10). In order to carry out meaningful evaluation results, each algorithm is applied 25 times then the average of the evaluation results is reported. In each run, the optimized models are evaluated based on the testing data using VAF, MSE, MAE, MMRE, RMSE and $R^2$ evaluation metrics.

Carrying out the experiments, the average convergence curves for FA, GA and PSO are shown in Figures 1-3 respectively for the three variations of COCOMO model.

**Table 2**. Firefly algorithm parameter settings

| Parameter | Value |
|---|---|
| Maximum iterations | 500 |
| Number of fireflies | 100 |
| Alpha | 0.4 |
| Betamin | 1 |
| Gamma | 0.4 |

**Table 3**. GA parameter settings

| Parameter | Value |
|---|---|
| Maximum iterations | 500 |
| Population size | 100 |
| Selection method | Tournament selection |
| Crossover probability | 80% |
| Mutation probability | 5% |

**Table 4**. PSO parameter settings

| Parameter | Value |
|---|---|
| Maximum iterations | 500 |
| Particles | 100 |
| Acceleration constant | [2.1, 2.1] |
| Inertia weight | [0.9, 0.6] |
| Maximum velocity | 100 |

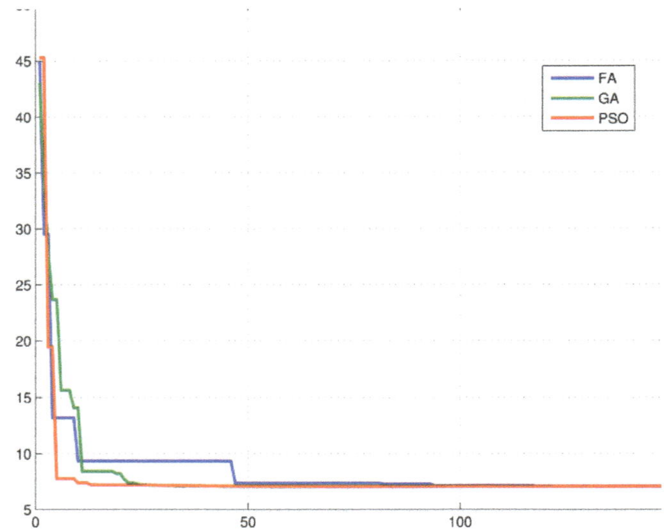


**Figure 1**. Convergence of FA, GA and PSO in optimizing the basic COCOMO model.

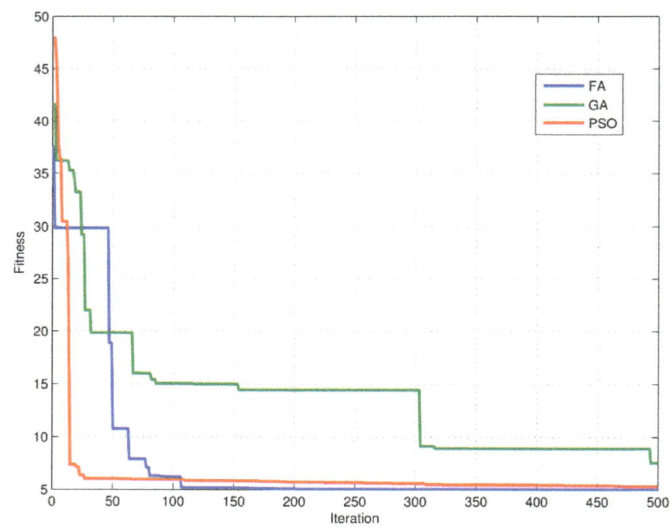


**Figure 2**. Convergence of FA, GA and PSO in optimizing Model I.

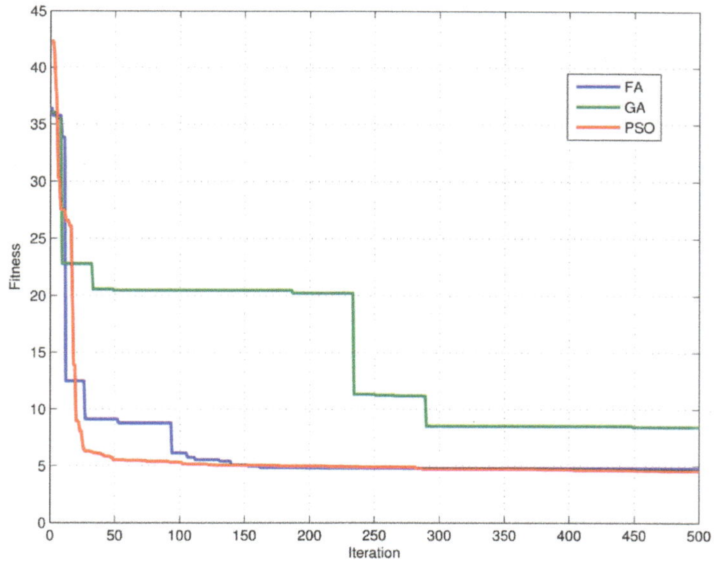


**Figure 3**. Convergence of FA, GA and PSO in optimizing Model II.

The evaluation results for training and testing cases are shown in Tables 5-7. Based on Table 5 andTable 6 it can be noticed that Firefly outperforms GA and PSO in optimizing the basic COCOMO model and the Model I by means of all evaluation metrics. For the Model II, Firefly and PSO are very competitive and have very close results. On the other hand GA has the lowest results and it has the slowest convergence.

In summary, FA as a metaheuristic optimization algorithm over-performs GA and PSO in terms of higher estimation accuracy for the software effort COCOMO based models.

**Table 5**. Basic COCOMO model

| | **Training** | | | **Testing** | | |
|---|---|---|---|---|---|---|
| | Firefly | GA | PSO | Firefly | GA | PSO |
| VAF | 93.82% | 93.72% | 93.73% | 98.16% | 97.97% | 97.98% |
| MSE | 104.88 | 107.28 | 107.15 | 59.14 | 63.96 | 63.68 |
| MAE | 7.04 | 7.03 | 7.03 | 5.65 | 6.06 | 6.04 |
| MMRE | 0.24 | 0.24 | 0.24 | 0.11 | 0.13 | 0.12 |
| RMSE | 10.24 | 10.36 | 10.35 | 7.67 | 8.00 | 7.98 |
| $R^2$ | 0.9367 | 0.9352 | 0.9353 | 0.9781 | 0.9763 | 0.9765 |

**Table 6**. COCOMO Model I

| | **Training** | | | **Testing** | | |
|---|---|---|---|---|---|---|
| | Firefly | GA | PSO | Firefly | GA | PSO |
| VAF | 96.78% | 92.94% | 96.96% | 98.62% | 97.97% | 98.52% |
| MSE | 56.05 | 127.70 | 54.16 | 47.74 | 98.17 | 60.07 |
| MAE | 5.42 | 8.94 | 5.16 | 5.56 | 7.70 | 5.63 |
| MMRE | 0.41 | 0.53 | 0.39 | 0.24 | 0.29 | 0.23 |
| RMSE | 7.48 | 10.95 | 7.36 | 6.82 | 9.39 | 7.72 |
| $R^2$ | 0.9662 | 0.9229 | 0.9673 | 0.9823 | 0.9637 | 0.9778 |

**Table 7.** COCOMO Model II

| | Training | | | Testing | | |
|---|---|---|---|---|---|---|
| | Firefly | GA | PSO | Firefly | GA | PSO |
| VAF | 96.95% | 92.42% | 97.48% | 98.63% | 97.60% | 98.70% |
| MSE | 53.74 | 129.37 | 45.28 | 45.02 | 114.79 | 52.85 |
| MAE | 5.36 | 8.20 | 4.43 | 5.57 | 7.83 | 5.29 |
| MMRE | 0.38 | 0.40 | 0.30 | 0.24 | 0.27 | 0.21 |
| RMSE | 7.26 | 11.05 | 6.72 | 6.62 | 9.86 | 7.19 |
| $R^2$ | 0.9676 | 0.9219 | 0.9727 | 0.9833 | 0.9575 | 0.9805 |

## CONCLUSION AND FUTURE WORK

Nazeeh Ghatasheh, Hossam Faris, Ibrahim Aljarah, Rizik M. H. Al-Sayyed This work investigated the efficiency of applying the Firefly Algorithm as a metaheuristic optimization technique to optimize the parameters of different effort estimation models. These models are three variations of the Constructive Cost Model COCOMO which are the basic COCOMO model, and other two extensions of the basic model that were proposed previously in the literature. The optimized models are assessed according to different evaluation criteria and compared with models optimized using other metaheuristic algorithms which are Genetic Algorithm and Particle Swarm Optimization. Evaluation results show that developed models using the Firefly Algorithm have higher accuracy in estimating software effort. Further future work is intended to overcome the instability issues, a more generic prediction model that is not highly affected by the size and the type of data set, and preferably an enhancement to the Firefly Algorithm itself. Moreover, it would be important to work towards a hybrid approach that encompasses the best characteristics of different prediction schemes.

## REFERENCES


1. Molokken, K. and Jorgensen, M. (2003) A Review of Software Surveys on Software Effort Estimation. 2003 International Symposium on Empirical Software Engineering, 30 September-1 October 2003, 223-230.
2. Song, Q. and Shepperd, M. (2011) Predicting Software Project Effort: A Grey Relational Analysis Based Method. Expert Systems with Applications, 38, 7302-7316.http://dx.doi org/10.1016/j.eswa.2010.12.005
3. Khatibi, V. and Jawawi, D.N. (2011) Software Cost Estimation Methods: A Review. Journal of Emerging Trends in Computing and Information Sciences, 2, 21-29.
4. Afzal, W. and Torkar, R. (2011) On the Application of Genetic Programming for Software Engineering Predictive Modeling: A Systematic Review. Expert Systems with Applications, 38, 11984-11997. http://dx.doi.org/10.1016/j.eswa.2011.03.041
5. Albrecht, A. and Gaffney, J.E. (1983) Software Function, Source Lines of Code, and Development Effort Prediction: A Software Science Validation. IEEE Transactions on Software Engineering, SE-9, 639-648. http://dx.doi.org/10.1109/TSE.1983.235271
6. Bailey, J.W. and Basili, V.R. (1981) A Meta-Model for Software Development Resource Expenditures. Proceedings of the 5th International Conference on Software Engineering, Piscataway, 107-116.
7. Ruchika Malhotra, A.J. (2011) Software Effort Prediction Using Statistical and Machine Learning Methods. International Journal of Advanced Computer Science and Applications (IJACSA), 2.
8. Yadav, C.S. and Singh, R. (2014) Tuning of Cocomo ii Model Parameters for Estimating Software Development Effort Using GA for Promise Project Data Set. International Journal of Computer Applications, 90, 37-43. http://dx.doi.org/10.5120/15542-4367
9. Wang, F.-S. and Chen, L.-H. (2013) Heuristic Optimization. In: Dubitzky, W., Wolkenhauer, O., Cho, K.-H. and Yokota, H., Eds., Encyclopedia of Systems Biology, Springer, New York, 885-885.
10. Uysal, M. (2010) Estimation of the Effort Component of the Software Projects Using Heuristic Algorithms. INTECH Open Access Publisher, Croatia.
11. Alaa, F. and Al-Afeef, A. (2010) A GP Effort Estimation Model Utilizing Line of Code and Methodology for NASA Software Projects. IEEE 10th International Conference on Intelligent Systems Design and Applications (ISDA), Cairo, 29 November-1 December 2010, 290-295.
12. Bhattacharya, P., Srivastava, P. and Prasad, B. (2012) Software Test Effort Estimation Using Particle Swarm Optimization. In: Satapathy, S., Avadhani, P. and Abraham, A., Eds., Proceedings of the International Conference on Information Systems Design and Intelligent Applications 2012 (INDIA 2012), Visakhapatnam, January 2012, Vol. 132 of Advances in Intelligent and Soft Computing, 827-835. Springer, Berlin and Heidelberg.
13. Maleki, I., Ghaffari, A. and Masdari, M. (2014) A New Approach for Software Cost Estimation with Hybrid Genetic Algorithm and Ant Colony Optimization. International Journal of Innovation and Applied Studies, 5, 72-81.
14. Yang, X.-S. and Deb, S. (2009) Cuckoo Search via Levy Flights. World Congress on Nature Biologically Inspired

Computing, NaBIC 2009, Coimbatore, 9-11 December 2009, 210-214.

15. Kennedy, J. and Eberhart, R. (1995) Particle Swarm Optimization. IEEE International Conference on Neural Networks, 4, 1942-1948.

16. Yang, X.-S. (2010) A New Metaheuristic Bat-Inspired Algorithm. In: Gonzlez, J., Pelta, D., Cruz, C., Terrazas, G. and Krasnogor, N., Eds., Nature Inspired Cooperative Strategies for Optimization (NICSO 2010), Vol. 284 of Studies in Computational Intelligence, 65-74. Springer, Berlin and Heidelberg.

17. Yang, X.-S. (2009) Firefly Algorithms for Multimodal Optimization. In: Watanabe, O. and Zeugmann, T., Eds., Stochastic Algorithms: Foundations and Applications, Vol. 5792 of Lecture Notes in Computer Science, 169-178. Springer, Berlin and Heidelberg.

18. Sheta, A., Rine, D. and Ayesh, A. (2008) Development of Software Effort and Schedule Estimation Models Using Soft Computing Techniques. IEEE Congress on Evolutionary Computation, CEC 2008 (IEEE World Congress on Computational Intelligence), Hong Kong, 16 June 2008, 1283-1289.

19. Oliveira, A.L.I., Braga, P.L., Lima, R.M.F. and Cornélio, M.L. (2010) GA-Based Method for Feature Selection and Parameters Optimization for Machine Learning Regression Applied to Software Effort Estimation. Information and Software Technology, 52, 1155-1166. http://dx.doi.org/10.1016/j.infsof.2010.05.009

20. Huang, X., Ho, D., Ren, J. and Capretz, L. (2006) A Soft Computing Framework for Software Effort Estimation. Soft Computing, 10, 170-177.http://dx.doi.org/10.1007/s00500-004-0442-z

21. Dave, V. and Dutta, K. (2014) Neural Network Based Models for Software Effort Estimation: A Review. Artificial Intelligence Review, 42, 295-307.http://dx.doi.org/10.1007/s10462-012-9339-x

22. Keung, J., Kocaguneli, E. and Menzies, T. (2013) Finding Conclusion Stability for Selecting the Best Effort Predictor in Software Effort Estimation. Automated Software Engineering, 20, 543-567. http://dx.doi.org/10.1007/s10515-012-0108-5

23. Boehm, B., Abts, C., Clark, B. and Devnani-Chulani, S. (1997) COCOMO II Model Definition Manual. University of Southern California, Los Angeles.

24. Sheta, A.F. (2006) Estimation of the COCOMO Model Parameters Using Genetic Algorithms for NASA Software Projects. Journal of Computer Science, 2, 118-123.http://dx.doi.org/10.3844/jcssp.2006.118.123

CHAPTER 2

# ON USING FUZZY LINGUISTIC 2-TUPLES FOR THE EVALUATION OF HUMAN RESOURCE SUITABILITY IN SOFTWARE DEVELOPMENT TASKS

Vassilis C. Gerogiannis[1], Elli Rapti[2], Anthony Karageorgos[3] and Panos Fitsilis[1]

[1]Department of Business Administration, Project Management Direction of Studies, Technological Educational Institute of Thessaly, 41110 Larissa, Greece

[2]Centre for Research and Technology, Institute of Research and Technology of Thessaly, 38333 Volos, Greece

[3]Department of Wood and Furniture Design and Technology, Technological Educational Institute of Thessaly, 43100 Karditsa, Greece

## ABSTRACT

**Efficient allocation of human resources to the development tasks comprising a software project is a key challenge in software project management. To address this critical issue, a systematic human resource evaluation and selection approach can be proven helpful. In this paper, a fuzzy linguistic approach is introduced to evaluate the suitability of candidate human resources (software developers) considering their technical skills (i.e., provided skills) and the technical skills required to perform a software development task (i.e., task-related skills). The proposed approach is based on qualitative evaluations which are derived in the form of fuzzy linguistic 2-tuples from a group of decision makers (project managers). The approach applies a group/similarity degree-based aggregation technique to obtain an objective aggregation of the ratings of task-related skills and provided skills. To further analyze the suitability of each candidate developer, possible skill relationships are considered, which reflect the contribution of provided skills to the capability of learning other skills. The applicability of the approach is demonstrated and discussed through an exemplar case study scenario.**

## INTRODUCTION

The problem of finding the "best" human resource in software projects is not always related to the optimal decision [1, 2]. For example, if a software programming task demands "high skill level for Java" and "low skill level for C++" then both of these requirements should be addressed by considering their respective levels of required knowledge. Thus, a human resource (i.e., a programmer in such a case) who meets both criteria is considered to be more suitable for the specific task, as opposed to another programmer with very high level skills in both Java and C++, since this resource could be assigned to a more demanding programming task. Moreover, human resource evaluation and allocation on software development projects are often based on experience, heuristic knowledge, and subjective judgments of experts (e.g., software team leaders and project managers). Although their judgments can be educated guesses that work in practice, managers lack appropriate tools to assess personnel and perform human resource allocation [3, 4]. Subjective decisions may result in selecting inadequate and unsuitable resources which require more time for training, a fact that consequently affects negatively the schedule of projects. In skill-based working environments, such as software development projects, where the objective of the development tasks is to provide customized and usually nonrepetitive solutions to end-users/customers, the risk of utilizing inadequate resources is high, which

**Citation:** Vassilis C. Gerogiannis, Elli Rapti, Anthony Karageorgos, and Panos Fitsilis, "On Using Fuzzy Linguistic 2-Tuples for the Evaluation of Human Resource Suitability in Software Development Tasks," Advances in Software Engineering, vol. 2015, Article ID 695873, 15 pages, 2015. doi:10.1155/2015/695873.

further causes excessive project costs and high probability for developing unsuccessful software products/services [5].

Therefore, a key problem in software project management is to achieve an, as much as possible, objective and documented assessment of knowledge and technical skills of available human resources, according to various task-related skill requirements needed by a software development organization to achieve its goals. Many approaches do not address efficiently this problem when it comes to human resource knowledge/skills representation and evaluation, by employing a conventional two-valued logic for characterizing required skill requirements, which proves to be very inefficient when dealing with the uncertainty and vagueness of this characterization. In dealing with the problem of knowledge/skills representation and evaluation in uncertain and imprecise settings, fuzzy logic [6] can be used as an efficient conceptual base, due to the fact that most human reasoning, evaluation, and assessment forms are qualitative and approximate by their nature [1, 2, 5].

In this paper, we use the fuzzy linguistic 2-tuple representation/computation model [7] to build an evaluation and selection approach for candidate human resources (developers) in software development tasks, according to provided/required technical skills/competencies. The proposed approach is based on a group-based fuzzy multicriteria method that applies similarity degree-based aggregation [8] to derive an objective assessment for provided/required skills/competencies. Since technical skills/competencies in software development are not often independent of each other (i.e., prior knowledge in various skills can contribute to learning of other skills) [2], an important contribution of the suggested approach is that it also emphasizes deriving objective assessments of developers matching skills by considering possible skill relationships and dependencies. The approach presented in this paper is an extension and followup of our previous work in human resource evaluation and selection as presented in [9, 10]. Compared to these previous works, in this paper, a more detailed description of the approach is given along with an extended literature review and a presentation of case study with analytical calculations showing the approach applicability. The approach has been developed in the context of the SPRINT SMEs project [11], an R&D project that aims to suggest techniques for software process improvement tailored to the needs of small and medium sized software development organizations.

The remainder of the paper is structured as follows. In Section 2, we provide the background behind our work and an overview on the related literature. In Section 3, we describe the proposed approach for the evaluation and selection of developers in software development tasks. In Section 4, we discuss how the outputs of the approach (estimations of resource-task suitability values) can be used as an aid to indicate proper allocations of each developer effort to each development task. In Section 5, we present an exemplar case study scenario with arithmetic results, followed by a brief discussion in Section 6 upon the usefulness of the provided results. Finally, in Section 7, we conclude the paper and present our future research plans.

## BACKGROUND AND LITERATURE OVERVIEW

Software process improvement (SPI) in small medium sized enterprises (SMEs) is gaining momentum in software research and industry. SPI is a challenging endeavour for most software SMEs aiming at preventing project failures and delivering high quality software products/services consistent with end-customer needs. The SPRINT SMEs project (research in software process improvement methodologies for small and medium sized software development enterprises) [11] is an ongoing R&D project in which the authors of the paper are involved with the objective to propose and develop a practical framework of methods for supporting the improvement of certain processes which take place in software SMEs. The framework of SPRINT SMEs methods focuses on suggesting rigorous decision making methods for supporting process assessment and improvement problems met by software SMEs. In particular, SPRINT SMEs methods concentrate on problems in selected process domains such as requirements engineering and prioritization and project planning and staffing [12, 13]. For project staffing problems, in particular, a systematic approach for evaluating the suitability of candidate human resources for each software development task is an imperative issue for a successful implementation of SPI [1, 2, 14]. While midsize to large companies are characterized by a large pool with a considerable number of available resources with different skills to choose from, small to midsize companies need to follow a tailored decision making process to effectively utilize the limited human resources available. The aim of SPRINT SMEs project is to take into consideration the particular needs of SMEs specializing in software development and propose easily applied and systematic approaches to help improve the domain of software project staffing processes. In the following, we present an overview of the research state of the art on resource evaluation, selection, and allocation in software projects focusing particularly on skill-based and fuzzy-based approaches. More interested readers are referred to [15] where a comprehensive literature review is presented on team composition criteria and team management approaches in software projects.

The problem of human resource allocation in a software project refers to the proper assignment of available human resources to the project tasks. The process usually followed by software development organizations concerns initially the division of project development effort into tasks, each one requiring specific skills, capabilities, competences, and previous experience. Once the various tasks to be performed have been defined, suitable candidates for each task need to be selected mainly according to skill-related requirements [1, 2, 16,17]. However, assignment of roles and consequent formation of project teams rely often on project managers' subjective judgments and experience, project constraints (e.g., project budget and timing constraints), resource constraints (e.g., availability of human resources), and skill-related requirements. All this information is not usually systematically recorded and handled [14]. Proper resource evaluation and selection of human resources is an important decision in software project management. This decision is not just crucial for the generation of efficient software teams, but it is also of strategic importance in software development organizations since it can support them for developing a competitive advantage by exploiting long term competences of available personnel and implement successful projects [18]. Many approaches discussed in the literature, regarding resource selection and allocation, handle resources in a quantitative manner, where all resources are treated as equally skilled [1]. However, in human and skill-centered working environments, such as software development projects, personnel selection and assignment decisions considering individual level of skills of each available human resource can clearly contribute to project success. For example, one expected benefit derived from improvements in a resource evaluation and allocation process is the decrease in project duration, an issue which further increases the organization productivity [2, 19].

Despite all research and advances in this research field, managing personnel in software projects still remains a very complicated problem due to the dynamic and complex context in which it takes place. Project managers/decision makers have to face a number of different possible staff combinations and many correlated and often conflicting decision variables, such as time, cost, and quality, and, respectively, make the best decision under pressure and high demands [16]. In addition, a major contributor to this complexity is the increased demand for specialized individual skills in the software development workforce, which results from high turnover rates and the fast pace at which new technologies and techniques are being developed. As a result of high demands, candidates with exact required skills to be allocated at software development tasks are usually not available [2].

Human resource evaluation is one critical task that determines to a large extent the organizational success, since the cost of human resources is usually the largest one in a software project [20]. The ability to properly evaluate the skill levels of available human resources is vital to achieve proper resource allocation in the development tasks comprising a software project. Besides skill-based assessment approaches, in the literature, there are also research works [3, 14] focusing on evaluations of various personality traits and different types of behavioral capabilities of candidate human resources, such as intrapersonal, organizational, interpersonal, and management capabilities. The main aim of these approaches is to properly assign available resources to project functional roles (e.g., project leader, analyst, designer, programmer, tester, etc.) and rather not to allocate resources to specific project development tasks, a decision that requires considering explicitly the capabilities of available resources regarding specific technical skills (e.g., level of knowledge in a particular programming language, expertise in applying an analysis/design methodology, competence in using a specific CASE tool, etc.). A central problem in software projects, in particular regarding the human resource allocation, is to evaluate accurately and objectively the capability of each developer/engineer with respect to required technical skills [5]. In the following, we review some representative approaches presented in the literature that attempt to manage the vague and imprecise problem of performing skill-based assessments to support resource allocation decisions in software projects.

For example, Tsai et al. in [21] proposed a method for selecting the most suitable set of human resources with the aim of completing a software project at minimum cost and duration. Their method adopts the critical resource diagram technique which focuses on resource, rather than activity scheduling, to represent task workflows and precedence relations. In addition, their method applies Taguchi's parameter design approach to optimize the selection of software engineers for tasks under dynamic/stochastic conditions. This approach considers technical skills (estimated as average numbers of lines of code per day) and tasks as controllable and uncontrollable factors, respectively, and Taguchi's parameter design is performed to select personnel who achieved high performance. However, this method cannot be easily applied by immature software SMEs since it requires detailed and systematic recording of personnel productivity (i.e., to keep records of average numbers of lines of code produced per day by each software engineer) and estimations of optimistic, normal, and pessimistic values of resource personal abilities for each task type.

Otero et al. in [2] presented a promising methodology, termed Best-Fitted Resource (BFR) approach, where human resource capabilities are evaluated by considering relationships between skills. According to BFR, skill-relationship tables are formed with the aim of describing how prior knowledge in various skills contributes to learning of other skills. BFR calculates the suitability of each resource with each task and, consequently, the allocation of resources to multiple tasks is solved as a simple linear programming problem with the aim of maximizing the overall resource suitability. While the consideration of required skills, provided skills, and skill relationships makes the approach similar to the one presented in this paper, BFR does not take into account vagueness issues in characterizing capabilities of candidate human resources and required levels of expertise and it does not result in a group-based objective assessment for the resources suitability. In the approach presented in this paper, objective skill assessments can be derived by aggregating evaluations from decision makers in a group decision making setting.

In practice, human resource evaluation and allocation are usually based on the experience, intuition, and expert judgments of project managers. Software development projects tend to become more complex in time requiring more diversified skills to carry them out and multiple constraints to be satisfied. These complexities raise the need for the introduction of advanced computation methods to assist decision makers to achieve best possible allocation of the available human resources [22]. To this end, a number of analytical approaches are proposed in the literature which apply powerful optimization techniques, such as constraint satisfaction [17, 23] and dynamic programming algorithms [18].

For example, Barreto et al. in [17] address project staffing as a constraint satisfaction problem [24], based on utility functions that should be maximized or minimized by the selected development team in order to provide greater value for a software development organization. Their approach takes as input the needs of the development tasks, the available human resources, and the constraints imposed by project managers. However, their approach does not consider differences in capability levels according to the required skills of different development tasks. Another constraint-based approach is the one proposed by Kang et al. in [23]. They identify human resources in software projects by individual and team-level constraints based both on the available literature and experts' judgment. Their approach estimates productivity of human resources by using the COCOMO II algorithmic effort estimation model and focuses on scheduling optimization of human resource allocations by applying accelerated simulated annealing. However, the major limitation of constraint-based approaches for software project staffing is their scalability, since these approaches become difficult to be implemented as the number of constraints increases. e Silva and Costa in [18] present another interesting optimization approach based on dynamic programming. Their method determines the fit between the complete set of skills available from a candidate member of a project team and the skills required from project resource requirements. Besides skills, they also identify interpersonality factors of human resource allocation to project management and judge the personality factors on the capability for project development. However, they also fail to address vagueness in skill evaluations and relationships between various skills that contribute to learning other skills.

Since human decision related to personnel evaluation and selection can be characterized as qualitative and highly imprecise, fuzzy logic techniques have been proposed as feasible methods to handle these issues [25, 26]. Fuzzy logic was first introduced by Zadeh [6] and has been widely recognized as a suitable tool to describe vague personnel capabilities as well as imprecise project requirements [27]. There are some interesting approaches in the literature which address human resource evaluation and selection in software projects using fuzzy logic. For example, Ruskova in [28] proposed a fuzzy logic-based model for human resource selection and evaluation which is divided into three modules. The first one describes the evaluation of job positions, where requirements for each job position are defined. The second module deals with candidates' appraisal, conveying a description for each candidate that includes candidate characteristics and competences possessed among others. The third module of the proposed system describes how the former two modules are combined to suggest a list of candidate professionals that better fulfil the requirements of available job positions. A tool that implements the model is also presented. While this model is also based on fuzzy logic as the one presented in the current paper, it does not explicitly address the fact that skills/competencies in software development are often not independent of each other.

Dodangeh et al. in [29] also developed a decision making methodology that integrates group decision making and fuzzy linguistic evaluation. Decision makers are able to evaluate candidates using linguistic variables. The proposed methodology applies aggregation for subjective evaluations provided by the decision makers with the aim of performing more robust human resource selection procedures. However, the authors do not consider skill relationships reflecting how prior knowledge in various skills can contribute to the learning of other skills.

Callegari and Bastos in [1] proposed a fuzzy rule-based approach for human resource evaluation in software projects while also considering dependencies between skills to extract objective evaluations of human resources. Their main assumption is that a software development organization maintains a knowledge base of fuzzy rules to describe, somehow arbitrarily, management knowledge about skill relationships and, consequently, follow a fuzzy inference mechanism to undertake human resource evaluation and decision. On the contrary, the approach presented in this paper is a group-based one that emphasizes deriving objective values for skill relationships and required/provided skill evaluations from corresponding subjective judgments expressed by decision makers/project managers. Another fuzzy rule-based approach is proposed in [5] by L. D. Otero and C. E. Otero. The authors propose a fuzzy rule-based expert system where personnel capabilities are modelled as fuzzy sets, relationships between skills are described as fuzzy rules, and capability assessments are computed by applying the Mamdani max-min method of fuzzy reasoning. However, the rules describing the skill relationships in the expert system knowledge base were developed in a rather ad hoc way by conducting experts/decision makers. This approach requires implementation and use of an expert system which cannot be easily adapted to the different skill-related requirements present in each development project that undertakes a software SME.

The underlying representation/computation of the approach presented in the current paper is the fuzzy 2-tuple linguistic model, presented by Herrera and Martínez [7]. Their model is based on the concept of symbolic translation and it is used to represent linguistic assessments in the form of 2-tuples composed of a linguistic term and a number. The main advantage of the fuzzy 2-tuple linguistic model is its continuity which overcomes the issue of information loss.

The fuzzy 2-tuple linguistic model has been compared with other symbolic linguistic computing models by Rodriguez and Martinez in [30]. It has been used in various application domains and in a number of approaches as a basis for experts to express their opinions [31]. Da and Xu in [32] introduced a proportional 2-tuple linguistic representation model and applied a group decision making/evaluation procedure in the context of complex construction projects. Dursun and Karsak in [33] proposed a fuzzy multicriteria decision making algorithm for personnel selection using the principles of fusion of fuzzy information, 2-tuple linguistic representation model, and the Technique for Order Preference by Similarity to Ideal Solution (TOPSIS). Raoudha et al. in [34] used the fuzzy 2-tuple linguistic representation model to determine appraisers' opinions about both acquired and required competence levels. Given the resulting 2-tuple assessments, they suggested an extended version of the TOPSIS method to get the candidates' ranking based on a similarity degree between required and acquired competence levels. In addition, Espinilla et al. in [35] presented an integrated model for a group-based, 360-degree performance appraisal process that manages heterogeneous assessments and computes a final linguistic evaluation for each employee. Their model applies effective aggregation by considering the interaction among criteria and reviewers weights. Assessment values are expressed in linguistic 2-tuples to deal with heterogeneous information and obtain linguistic results close to human cognitive model. However, while all of the above approaches are computationally practical, they do not explicitly consider skill relationships or the subjectivity in experts' opinion. Moreover, the use of the ordered weighted averaging (OWA) operator [33, 35] and the Choquet integral [35] increases the computation complexity of the respective approaches.

## DESCRIPTION OF THE PROPOSED APPROACH

In software projects, the resource selection process, where the resources considered are developers with a set of technical skills, typically involves decisions based on multiple criteria.

While the various choices are often distinct for each manager, the basis of selecting the most appropriate resources for each project and task is considered to have one common ground: the evaluation of each task's requirements aligned with the skills of the available resources. Thus, the problem is reduced to the proper assignment of resources to tasks, even when the most desirable skills are not available in the resource pool.

To address human resource evaluation and selection in software development tasks, we suggest a group-based fuzzy multicriteria approach using the fuzzy linguistic 2- tuple representation model. The proposed approach consists of 3 different stages, which further include nine distinct steps as presented in the flowchart of Figure 1. Specifically, in stage 1, consisting of Steps 1 to 5, the task profile (with respect to the required skills) is estimated using linguistic evaluations provided by experts on the skills required for the particular task. In stage 2, which includes Steps 6 to 7, the capabilities of the available human resources are evaluated using linguistic evaluations provided by experts on their skills. Last, in stage 3, consisting of Steps 8 to 9, the capabilities of the available human resources are reevaluated using linguistic evaluations of skill relationships provided also by experts/decision makers. Steps 2 to 4 are common to the three different stages of the algorithm to ensure the objectivity of the experts' evaluations. The nine steps of the approach are described in detail in the following subsections.

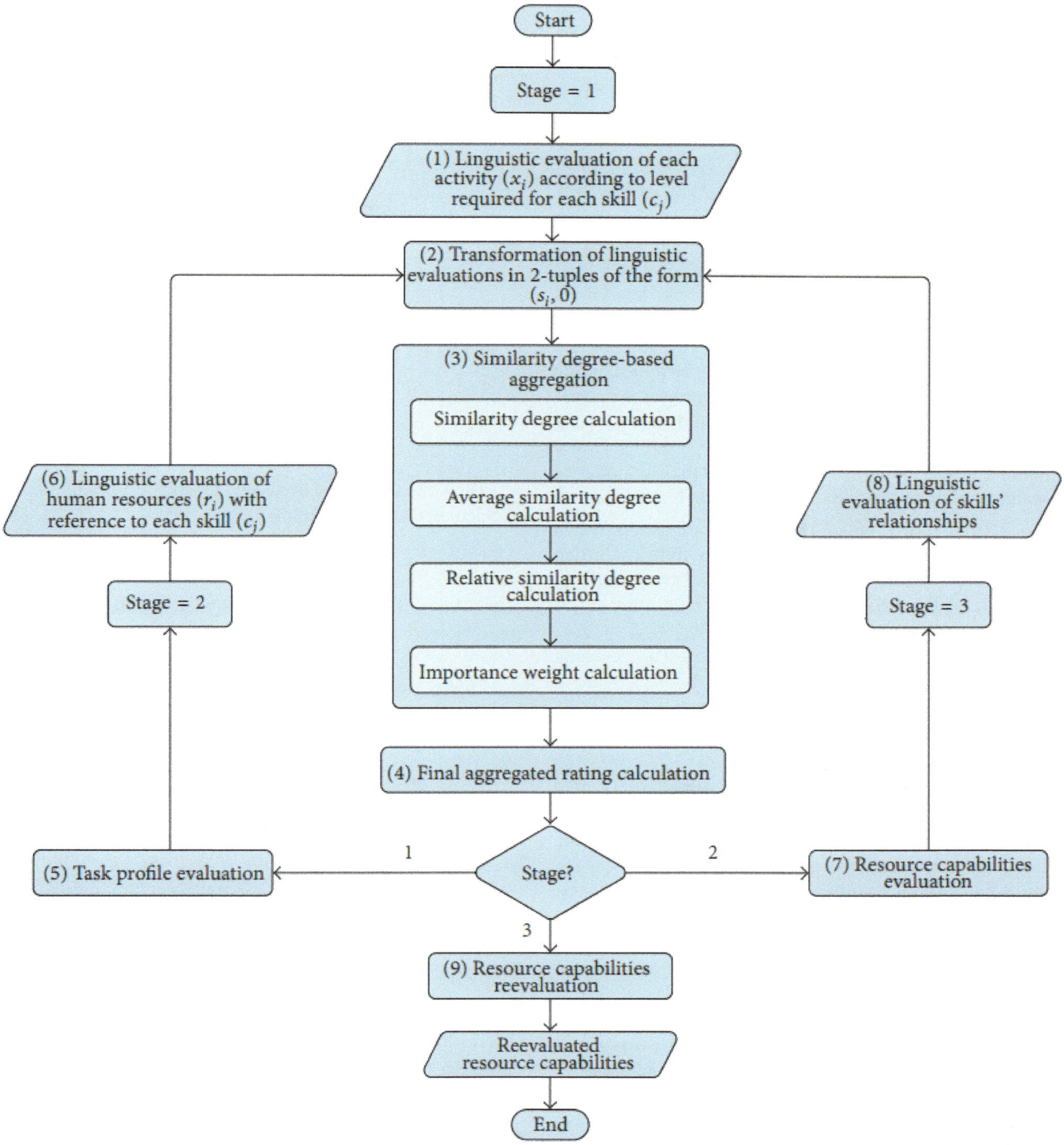


**Figure 1:** Flowchart of the proposed approach for the evaluation of human resources considering skill relationships.

*Step 1* (group-based linguistic evaluation of required skills). Let $T$ be a software development task in a software project. We assume that it is planned to be executed as a set of $N$ individual development activities $x$; that is, $T = \{x_1, x_2, \ldots, {}_N\}$. In total, the task activities require a set of $M$ technical skills/competencies $c$, such as knowledge in Java and/or C++, denoted as $C = \{c_j \mid j = 1, 2, \ldots, M\}$. The proposed approach applies a group-based decision approach by requiring from $K$ project managers/evaluators $e$, $E = \{e_k \mid j = 1, 2, \ldots, K\}$, to evaluate the level of each skill/competency required for each individual activity to be completed successfully. To express skill/competency requirements in a qualitative form we adopt the 2-tuple fuzzy linguistic terms approach [7]. Specifically, the 2-tuple linguistic representation/computation model was chosen as the underlying basis of the suggested approach, as it can effectively avoid loss/distortion of information, an issue typical with other fuzzy linguistic methods when dealing with fuzzification/defuzzification of available information [7, 36].

To express their evaluations, project managers use a linguistic label set $S = \{s_i \mid i = 0, 1, 2, \ldots, g\}$, where $g+1$ is the granularity of the selected linguistic term set. A 2-tuple linguistic variable is thus denoted as $(s_i, a_i)$, where $s_i \in S$ corresponds to the central value of the $i$th linguistic term in the term set and $a_i \in [-0.5, 0.5)$ is the distance from $si$. Project managers may also select different linguistic term sets (i.e., sets having different granularities or semantics) to express their assessments for the required skills. In this case, all heterogeneous linguistic assessments have to be transformed and expressed into a uniform linguistic term set by following the method proposed in [37, 38]. In addition, project managers may have different expertise and background in managing software projects and assessing the needs of software development tasks; therefore, a different relative importance level-weight $\varepsilon_k$ can be assigned to each project manager $e_k$.

*Step 2* (transformation of linguistic evaluations). Since project managers evaluate each development activity according to the required skills/competencies using linguistic terms from the term set $S$, the linguistic evaluation $X_{ij}$ for an activity $x_i$ ($i = 1, 2, \ldots, N$) with respect to the skill/competency $c_j$ ($j = 1, 2, \ldots, M$) is transformed into a 2-tuple of the form $(s_i, 0)$, according to the following transformation function [7]:

$$\theta : S \longrightarrow S \times [-0.5, 0.5), \quad \theta(s_i) = (s_i, 0), \; s_i \in S. \quad (1)$$

(1)

Step 3 (similarity degree-based aggregation). By performing group-based linguistic evaluation, all skills required to perform the software development task are characterized by the subjective judgments of project managers, which may be biased towards each required skill/competency. Thus, in order to derive a more objective assessment, we adopt a similarity degree-based aggregation technique similar to the one introduced in [8]. The final aggregated assessments consider not only the relative importance levels-weights $\varepsilon_k$ of project managers, but also similarities in their respective evaluations. Therefore, we expect the resulting assessments to reflect the collective judgments of project managers more reasonably and more objectively. The aggregation technique follows three distinct steps that are, respectively, presented in the following subsections.

## Similarity Degree Calculation

The similarity degree, denoted as $\text{sim}(X_{ij}^k, X_{ij}^l) \in (0, 1]$, is calculated for any two skill evaluations $X_{ij}$ provided by any two managers $e_k$ and $e_l$ ($k \neq l$, $k$, $l = 1, 2, \ldots, K$) for each development activity $x_i$ ($i = 1, 2, \ldots, N$) with respect to each skill/competency $c_j$ ($j = 1, 2, \ldots, M$). To calculate the similarity degree value, the distance $\delta$ between $X_{ij}^k$ and $X_{ij}^l$ evaluations is computed. To calculate this distance, the evaluations represented in 2-tuple linguistic form should be transformed into an equivalent numerical form. In particular, given a linguistic term set $S$, $\beta \in [0, g]$ is a number representing the aggregation result of a symbolic aggregation operation. Let $i$ = round ($\beta$) and $\alpha = \beta - i$ be two values such that $i \in [0, g]$ and $a \in [-0.5, 0.5)$, respectively. The number $a$ is called a symbolic translation. The 2-tuple that expresses the equivalent information with $\beta$ results from the translation function $\Delta(\beta)$ as follows [7]:

$$\Delta : [0, g] \longrightarrow S \times [-0.5, 0.5) \quad (2)$$

$$\Delta(\beta) = (s_i, a) = \begin{cases} s_i, & i = \text{round}(\beta) \\ \alpha = \beta - i, & a \in [-0.5, 0.5). \end{cases} \quad (3)$$

Therefore, a 2-tuple linguistic variable is transformed into an equivalent number $\beta \in [0, g]$ by using the reverse function $\Delta^{-1}$ as follows [7]:

$$\Delta : S \times [-0.5, 0.5) \longrightarrow [0, g], \quad (4)$$

$$\Delta^{-1}(s_i, a) = i + a = \beta. \quad (5)$$

Then, the distance $\delta$ between $X_{ij}^k$ and $X_{ij}^l$ evaluations can be calculated using the following formula:

$$\delta = \left|\Delta^{-1}\left(X_{ij}^k\right) - \Delta^{-1}\left(X_{ij}^l\right)\right|, \quad (6)$$

where $\Delta^{-1}$ is the reverse function that transforms a 2-tuple linguistic variable into its equivalent numerical value [7].

Finally, the similarity degree value $\text{sim}(X_{ij}^k, X_{ij}^l)$ is computed according to the following [8]:

$$\text{sim}\left(x_{ij}^k, x_{ij}^l\right) = 1 - \left|\frac{\Delta^{-1}\left(x_{ij}^k\right) - \Delta^{-1}\left(x_{ij}^l\right)}{g}\right|, \quad (7)$$

where $g+1$ is the granularity of the used linguistic term set. The closer the similarity degree is to 1, the more similar the evaluations of any two project managers are for the same activity with respect to a particular skill.

## Average and Relative Similarity Degree Calculation

The average similarity degree $SM_i(e_k)$ and the relative similarity degree $RSM_{ij}(e_k)$ are calculated for each project manager regarding the evaluation of each activity $x_i$ ($i = 1, 2, \ldots, N$) with respect to each skill/competency $cj$ ($j = 1, 2, \ldots, M$). These are, respectively, given by [8]

$$\mathrm{SM}_{ij}\left(e_k\right) = \frac{\sum_{l=1,l\neq k}^{K} \mathrm{sim}\left(x_{ij}^k, x_{ij}^l\right)}{K-1}, \tag{8}$$

$$\mathrm{RSM}_{ij}\left(e_k\right) = \frac{\mathrm{SM}_{ij}\left(e_k\right)}{\sum_{l=1}^{K} \mathrm{SM}_{ij}\left(e_l\right)}. \tag{9}$$

## Importance Weight Calculation

The importance weight $w_{ij}^k$ of the evaluation/assessment of project manager $e_k$ is calculated by considering his/her relative importance level weight $\varepsilon_k$ and the relative similarity degree of his/her evaluations, as follows [8]:

$$w_{ij}^k = \frac{\varepsilon_k \times \mathrm{RSM}_{ij}\left(e_k\right)}{\sum_{l=1}^{K}\left(\varepsilon_l \times \mathrm{RSM}_{ij}\left(e_l\right)\right)}. \tag{10}$$

*Step 4* (calculation of final aggregated ratings). The objective aggregation for all activities' ratings is computed by utilizing the weighted average operator, as it is defined for fuzzy linguistic 2-tuples in [7]. In particular, for a set of linguistic 2- tuples $\{(s_1, a_1), (s_2, a_2), \ldots, (s_n, a_n)\}$ and their corresponding weights $\{w_1, w_2, \ldots, w_n\}$, the 2-tuple weighted average operator $\overline{x}$ is computed as follows [7]:

$$\overline{x} = \Delta\left(\frac{\sum_{l=1}^{n}\left(\Delta^{-1}\left(s_i, a_i\right) \times w_i\right)}{\sum_{l=1}^{n} w_i}\right) = \Delta\left(\frac{\sum_{l=1}^{n}\left(\beta_i \times w_i\right)}{\sum_{l=1}^{n} w_i}\right), \tag{11}$$

where $\beta_i$ is calculated using the reverse function $\Delta^{-1}$ as defined in (5).

The final aggregated rating $\mathrm{FX}_{ij}$ of each activity $x_i$ ($i = 1, 2, \ldots, N$) with respect to each skill/competency $c_j$ ($j = 1, 2, \ldots, M$) can be computed by applying the weighted average operator (as it is given by formula (11)) on the linguistic evaluations of the activities and using as weights the previously calculated importance weights for the respective assessments. Thus, the final aggregated rating $\mathrm{FX}_{ij}$ is calculated as follows:

$$\mathrm{FX}_{ij} = \Delta\left(\frac{\sum_{l=1}^{K}\left(\Delta^{-1}\left(X_{ij}^l, a_{ij}^l\right) \times w_{ij}^l\right)}{\sum_{l=1}^{K} w_{ij}^l}\right). \tag{12}$$

*Step 5* (task profile evaluation). As stated above, a software development task is composed of a number of activities which result in the development of different software components. An overall "profile" can be created for the composite development task as a vector of linguistic 2-tuples. This profile represents the desired level of skills/competencies required for the task's successful implementation, based on the project managers' evaluations. The task profile vector, denoted as tp, with respect to each required skill/competency $c \in C$, can be calculated by applying the weighted average operator (11) to the previously calculated final aggregated ratings of skills (FX), using as weights the importance degree of each development activity $x \in T$ comprising the software development task. The importance degree $I_i$ of each development activity $x_i$, $i = 1, 2, \ldots, N$, may reflect the business value-criticality of the corresponding software component that is expected to result from the activity implementation. For example, we can assume that project managers agree that for the overall success of the software development task the development of the user interface component is an activity of higher business value compared to the development of the data base component. The task profile vector is calculated as follows:

$$\mathrm{tp}_j = \Delta\left(\frac{\sum_{i=1}^{N}\left(\Delta^{-1}\left(\mathrm{FX}_{ij}\right) \times I_i\right)}{\sum_{l=1}^{N} I_i}\right), \tag{13}$$

where $N$ is the total number of activities comprising the development task.

*Step 6* (linguistic evaluation of candidate human resources). Having calculated the task profile, we continue by evaluating candidate human resources (e.g., software programmers/ developers) according to their available skills/competencies with respect to the specific task required skills. To consider and evaluate objectively the capability/suitability of $Q$ candidate human resources $r$with respect to the task required skills $C$, Steps 2 to 4 are repeated. Specifically, each project manager evaluates, using a linguistic label set $S$, each candidate human resource $r$ according to his/her previous experience and/or his/ her level of knowledge in each required skill/competency $c \in C$. The linguistic evaluations of each resource according to each required skill are then transformed into 2-tuples in the form $(s_i, 0)$ according to (1). To derive an objective evaluation for these evaluations, the similarity degree value between any two project managers' evaluations is calculated using formula (7). The importance weights are calculated according to (10), using the average and relative similarity degree, as computed by (8) and (9), respectively. Then, a final aggregated rating $\mathrm{FR}_{ij}$ for each resource $r_i$ ($i = 1, 2, \ldots, Q$) with respect to each skill $c_j$ ($j = 1, 2, \ldots, M$) is calculated by applying the weighted average operator (11) on the linguistic evaluations of the resources using as weights the previously calculated importance weights for the respective assessments.

*Step 7* (capabilities evaluation). The capability (i.e., suitability) $\mathrm{cs}_i$ of each resource $r_i$ ($i = 1, 2, \ldots, Q$) is computed by applying the weighted average operator(11) on the final aggregated ratings $\mathrm{FR}_{ij}$, using as weights the previously calculated task profile assessments for each individual required skill. That is,

$$\mathrm{cs}_i = \Delta\left(\frac{\sum_{j=1}^{M}\left(\Delta^{-1}\left(\mathrm{FR}_{ij}\right) \times \mathrm{tp}_j\right)}{\sum_{j=1}^{M} \mathrm{tp}_j}\right), \tag{14}$$

where $\mathrm{cs}_i$ represents the capability of resource $r_i$ ($i = 1, 2, \ldots, Q$), $\mathrm{FR}_{ij}$ is the final aggregated rating for the resource $r_i$ ($i = 1, 2, \ldots, Q$) with respect to all skills $c_j$ ($j = 1, 2, \ldots, M$), and $\mathrm{tp}_j$ is the value in the task profile vector that corresponds to skill $c_j$ ($j = 1, 2, \ldots, M$).

*Step 8* (linguistic evaluation of skill relationships). Skills/ competencies in software development are not always independent of each other. On the contrary, prior knowledge in various skills contributes to the learning of other skills [2]. For example, prior knowledge in object oriented design can be considered helpful to develop skills in C++ programming. In this step of the approach we consider skill relationships, which represent the level to which capability in one skill/competency contributes to the improvement (via learning and/or practical experience) of another skill/competency. To this end, each manager evaluates subjectively skill relationships and a skill-relationships table is constructed, where relationships between skills/competencies are expressed in linguistic terms using a linguistic label set $S$. To evaluate objectively the skill/competency relationships with respect to the task required skills $c_j$ ($j = 1, 2, \ldots, m$), Steps 2 to 4 are repeated. Initially, the linguistic evaluations $c_{ij}$ of skill/competency relationships are transformed into 2- tuples in the form $(si, 0)$ according to (1). To derive a more objective assessment, the similarity degree values between the project managers' evaluations are calculated using formula (7). The importance weight is calculated according to (11), using the average and relative similarity degree calculated by (8) and (9), respectively. Finally, the objective skill/competency relationships are extracted through the final aggregated rating $\text{FSR}_{ij}$ of each relationship between any two skills/competencies $c_i$ and $c_j$ ($i, j = 1, 2, \ldots, M$). Specifically, $\text{FSR}_{ij}$ is calculated by applying the weighted average operator (11) on the linguistic evaluations of the skills/competencies using as weights the previously calculated importance weights for the respective assessments.

*Step 9* (reevaluation of the capability/suitability of candidate human resources). As a last step of the approach, the capabilities of human resources in each required skill/competency need to be reevaluated according to the final aggregated rating of skill/competency relationships, which were calculated in Step 8. A new value $\text{FR}^{\text{NEW}}_{ij}$ is computed for the capability of each human resource $r_i$ ($i = 1, 2, \ldots, Q$) with respect to each skill/competency $c_j$ ($j = 1, 2, \ldots, M$). This value is computed as the maximum value between the previously calculated capability in a skill and the weighted average contribution on that skill/competency from other skills/competencies, as follows:

$$\text{FR}_{ij}^{\text{NEW}} = \max\left(\text{FR}_{ij}; \frac{\sum_{h=1,h\neq j}^{m}\left(\text{FR}_{ih} \times \text{FSR}_{hj}\right)}{\sum_{h=1,h\neq j}^{m}\text{FSR}_{hj}}\right). \quad (15)$$

According to formula (15) the capability of a human resource in a specific skill is recomputed only when the contribution of other skills results in a greater value compared to the initial capability that was calculated without considering skill relationships.

Consequently, the reevaluated final aggregated rating $\text{cs}^{\text{NEW}}_i$ of each human resource $r_i$ ($i = 1, 2, \ldots, Q$) with respect to all skills/competencies $c_j$ ($j = 1, 2, \ldots, M$) is computed by applying the weighted average operator (11) on the reevaluated linguistic evaluations of the human resources, using as weights the previously calculated task profile assessments for each individual skill/capability. This final rating reflects the overall suitability of each resource to perform the software development task and it is calculated as follows:

$$\text{cs}_i^{\text{NEW}} = \Delta\left(\frac{\sum_{j=1}^{M}\left(\Delta^{-1}\left(\text{FR}_{ij}^{\text{NEW}}\right) \times \text{tp}_j\right)}{\sum_{j=1}^{M}\text{tp}_j}\right). \quad (16)$$

## ALLOCATION OF RESOURCES TO SOFTWARE DEVELOPMENT TASKS

Let us assume that a software company is undertaking $R$ development tasks $\{T_1, T_2, \ldots, T_R\}$ and at least one developer should be allocated to each task. Then, the above approach can be applied to calculate resource-task suitability values $\text{cs}_{ij}$ for each human resource (developer) $r_i$ ($i = 1, 2, \ldots, Q$) to perform each development task $T_j$ ($j = 1, 2, \ldots, R$). The use of these resource-task suitability values is helpful to indicate proper allocations of developers to tasks. For example, if one developer is needed for one task, then it might be a good decision to assign in this task the developer with the highest corresponding resource-task suitability. If two developers are needed for one task, then these developers may be the two developers characterized with two highest resource-task suitability values.

In the literature, we can find some rather strict assumptions regarding resource allocation in software projects. For example, it is assumed that all resources cannot be allocated at a single task [18] or a resource may be assigned to at most one task [2]. In a small software development company, however, due to limited number of developers it is often the case that all available developers should be involved in all running development tasks, in order to take full advantage of their competences and deliver fast paced projects. In such a case, the resource-task suitability values are useful to indicate proper allocations of each developer effort to each development task.

An estimation of effort allocation $\text{EEA}_{ij}$ (as a percentage % value) for each developer $r_i$ to each task $T_j$ can be calculated using formula (17) that divides the corresponding resource task suitability value $\text{cs}_{ij}$ by the sum of suitability values for all tasks in which the developer should be involved. We do recognize that this simple heuristic can be proven impractical to support complex resource allocation rules and availability constraints. In these situations the resource-task suitability values can be used as variables of a multiobjective optimization model, such as the one presented in [14]

$$\text{EEA}_{ij} = \frac{\text{cs}_{ij}}{\sum_{j=1}^{R}\text{cs}_{ij}}. \quad (17)$$

## EXEMPLAR CASE STUDY

Let us consider a scenario where a software development company needs to assign personnel to a software development task $T_1$, which is composed of four ($N$=4) individual development activities $x$; that is, $T_1 = \{x_1, x_2, x_3, x_4\}$. Thus, we assume that these four development activities lead, respectively, to the development of four software components of a software product; that is, the company follows a component based software development paradigm. It is also assumed that three project managers ($K$=3) are asked to evaluate the needs for four specific skills/competencies ($M$=4), namely, object oriented design, C++, Visual Basic, and Java programming, which are required to perform the activities of the software development task.

The linguistic term set $S$ used by project managers includes the following terms: $s_0$ = VVL (Very Very Low), $s_1$ = VL (Very Low), $s_2$ = L (Low), $s_3$ = M (Medium), $s_4$ = H (High), $s_5$ = VH (Very High), and $s_6$ = VVH (Very Very High). Table 1 presents the project managers' evaluations, in the form of 2-tuples, for the level of skills/competencies required for each one of the four development activities comprising the software development task $T_1$. For example, according to project manager $e_1$,a"Very Very High" level of competency in Java programming is required for activity $x_1$, expressed by the 2-tuple (VVH, 0). As shown in Table 1, we have assumed for simplicity reasons equal importance levels-weights for all three project managers (i.e., each $\varepsilon_k$ is equal to 1/3) involved in the case study example.

**Table 1:** Project manager evaluations on skill/competencies required for each activity x

| Activity ($x$) | Project manager ($e$)/weight of importance ($\varepsilon$) | Levels of skills required for a task ($c$) | | | |
|---|---|---|---|---|---|
| | | OO design ($c_1$) | C++ ($c_2$) | VB ($c_3$) | Java ($c_4$) |
| | $e_1$/(1/3) | (H, 0) | (L, 0) | (VL, 0) | (VVH, 0) |
| $x_1$ | $e_2$/(1/3) | (VVH, 0) | (VL, 0) | (M, 0) | (VH, 0) |
| | $e_3$/(1/3) | (VVH, 0) | (VVL, 0) | (M, 0) | (M, 0) |
| | $e_1$/(1/3) | (VL, 0) | (VL, 0) | (VH, 0) | (VL, 0) |
| $x_2$ | $e_2$/(1/3) | (VVL, 0) | (VL, 0) | (VVH, 0) | (L, 0) |
| | $e_3$/(1/3) | (VL, 0) | (L, 0) | (VH, 0) | (L, 0) |
| | $e_1$/(1/3) | (VH, 0) | (VH, 0) | (L, 0) | (L, 0) |
| $x_3$ | $e_2$/(1/3) | (VVH, 0) | (M, 0) | (L, 0) | (VL, 0) |
| | $e_3$/(1/3) | (VVH, 0) | (VVH, 0) | (L, 0) | (VL, 0) |
| | $e_1$/(1/3) | (L, 0) | (VVH, 0) | (VL, 0) | (VL, 0) |
| $x_4$ | $e_2$/(1/3) | (H, 0) | (VH, 0) | (VL, 0) | (VL, 0) |
| | $e_3$/(1/3) | (VH, 0) | (VH, 0) | (L, 0) | (VVL, 0) |

Considering the evaluations given by project managers $e_1$ and $e_2$ for activity $x_2$ with respect to skill $c_1$, that is, expertise in object oriented design (Table 1), the similarity degree between these two evaluations, according to formula (7), is

$$\operatorname{sim}\left(X_{21}^1, X_{21}^2\right) = 1 - \left|\frac{\Delta^{-1}\left(X_{21}^1\right) - \Delta^{-1}\left(X_{21}^2\right)}{g}\right|$$

$$= 1 - \left|\frac{1-0}{6}\right| = 0.833333. \tag{18}$$

The values of the similarity degrees between any two project managers' evaluations for the level of skills required for each activity are computed in the same manner and they are presented in Table 2.

**Table 2:** Similarity degree values between project manager evaluations

| | $e_1/e_2$ | | | | $e_2/e_3$ | | | | $e_1/e_3$ | | | |
|---|---|---|---|---|---|---|---|---|---|---|---|---|
| | $c_1$ | $c_2$ | $c_3$ | $c_4$ | $c_1$ | $c_2$ | $c_3$ | $c_4$ | $c_1$ | $c_2$ | $c_3$ | $c_4$ |
| $x_1$ | 0.666667 | 0.833333 | 0.666667 | 0.833333 | 0.666667 | 0.666667 | 0.666667 | 0.5 | 1 | 0.833333 | 1 | 0.666667 |
| $x_2$ | 0.833333 | 1 | 0.833333 | 0.833333 | 1 | 0.833333 | 1 | 0.8333333 | 0.833333 | 0.833333 | 0.833333 | 1 |
| $x_3$ | 0.833333 | 0.666667 | 1 | 0.833333 | 0.833333 | 0.833333 | 1 | 0.8333333 | 1 | 0.5 | 1 | 1 |
| $x_4$ | 0.666667 | 0.833333 | 1 | 1 | 0.5 | 0.833333 | 0.833333 | 0.833333 | 0.833333 | 1 | 0.833333 | 0.833333 |

Having calculated the similarity degrees for each activity with respect to each skill, we proceed to calculate the average and relative similarity degrees. For example, the average similarity degree for activity $x_2$ with respect to skill $c_1$ (object oriented design) is calculated by applying formula (8) as follows:

$$\mathrm{SM}_{21}\left(e_1\right) = \frac{\operatorname{sim}\left(X_{21}^1, X_{21}^2\right) + \operatorname{sim}\left(X_{21}^1, X_{21}^3\right)}{K-1}$$

$$= \frac{0.83333 + 1}{3-1} = 0.916667. \tag{19}$$

$\mathrm{SM}_{21}(e_2)$ and $\mathrm{SM}_{21}(e_3)$ are similarly calculated as 0.833333 and 0.916667, respectively. Thus, the relative similarity degree for project manager $e_1$ according to formula (9) is

$$\mathrm{RSM}_{21}\left(e_1\right) = \frac{\mathrm{SM}_{21}\left(e_1\right)}{\mathrm{SM}_{21}\left(e_1\right) + \mathrm{SM}_{21}\left(e_2\right) + \mathrm{SM}_{21}\left(e_3\right)}$$

$$= \frac{0.916667}{0.916667 + 0.833333 + 0.916667}$$

$$= 0.34375. \tag{20}$$

Applying these calculations we can compute all relative similarity degree values for each project manager (Table3).

**Table 3:** Relative similarity degree values for each project manager e

| | $e_1$ | | | | $e_2$ | | | | $e_1$ | | | |
|---|---|---|---|---|---|---|---|---|---|---|---|---|
| | $c_1$ | $c_2$ | $c_3$ | $c_4$ | $c_1$ | $c_2$ | $c_3$ | $c_4$ | $c_1$ | $c_2$ | $c_3$ | $c_4$ |
| $x_1$ | 0,285714 | 0,321429 | 0,285714 | 0,33333 | 0,357143 | 0,357143 | 0,357143 | 0,375 | 0,357143 | 0,321429 | 0,357143 | 0,291667 |
| $x_2$ | 0,34375 | 0,34375 | 0,34375 | 0,3125 | 0,3125 | 0,34375 | 0,3125 | 0,34375 | 0,34375 | 0,3125 | 0,34375 | 0,34375 |
| $x_3$ | 0,3125 | 0,375 | 0,33333 | 0,3125 | 0,34375 | 0,291667 | 0,33333 | 0,34375 | 0,34375 | 0,33333 | 0,333333 | 0,34375 |
| $x_4$ | 0,291667 | 0,3125 | 0,34375 | 0,34375 | 0,375 | 0,34375 | 0,34375 | 0,34375 | 0,33333 | 0,34375 | 0,3125 | 0,3125 |

Having assumed equal importance levels for all three project managers (i.e., each $\varepsilon_k$ is equal to 1/3, Table 1), we apply formula (10) to compute the weight of the assessments of each project manager. For example, the weight of the assessment of project manager $e_1$ for activity $x_2$ with respect to skill $c_1$ is computed as follows:

$$w_{21}^{1} = \frac{\varepsilon_1 \times \mathrm{RSM}_{21}(e_1)}{\varepsilon_1 \times \mathrm{RSM}_{21}(e_1) + \varepsilon_2 \times \mathrm{RSM}_{21}(e_2) + \varepsilon_3 \times \mathrm{RSM}_{21}(e_3)} = \frac{1/3 \times 0.34375}{1/3 \times 0.34375 + 1/3 \times 0.3125 + 1/3 \times 0.34355} = 0.34375. \quad (21)$$

The weights $w_{21}^{2}$ and $w_{21}^{3}$ of the assessments of project managers $e_2$ and $e_3$ are calculated in the same way and they are found equal to 0.3125 and 0.34375, respectively. It should be noted that assessment weights are found to be equal to the previously computed relative similarity degree values (Table 3) because we have assumed equal importance levels for all three project managers (i.e., each $\varepsilon k$ is equal to 1/3).

We continue by calculating the final aggregated rating for each activity with respect to each skill. For example, for activity $x_2$ with respect to skill $c_1$ using formula (12), the final aggregated rating is computed as follows:

$$\mathrm{FX}_{21} = \Delta\left(\frac{\Delta^{-1}(X_{21}^{1}) \times w_{21}^{1} + \Delta^{-1}(X_{21}^{1}) \times w_{21}^{2} + \Delta^{-1}(X_{21}^{3}) \times w_{21}^{3}}{w_{21}^{1} + w_{21}^{2} + w_{21}^{3}}\right) = \Delta\left(\frac{1 \times 0.34375 + 0 \times 0.3125 + 1 \times 0.34375}{0.34375 + 0.3125 + 0.34375}\right) = \Delta(0.68675) = (1, -0.31) = (\mathrm{VL}, -0.31). \quad (22)$$

The final aggregated ratings for all activities with respect to the various required skills/competencies are shown in Table 4.

**Table 4:** Final aggregated ratings for each activity FX and task profile TP

| Activity ($x$) | Importance degree ($I$) | Required skills ($c$) | | | |
|---|---|---|---|---|---|
| | | OO design ($c_1$) | C++ ($c_2$) | VB ($c_3$) | Java ($c_4$) |
| $x_1$ | VL (1, 0) | 5.4285/(VH, 0.43) | 1/(VL, 0) | 2.4285/(L, 0.43) | 4.75/(VH, −0.25) |
| $x_2$ | L (2, 0) | 0.6875/(VL, −0.31) | 1.3125/(VL, 0.31) | 5.3125/(VH, 0.31) | 1.6875/(L, −0.31) |
| $x_3$ | M (3, 0) | 5.6875/(VVH, −0.31) | 4.75/(VH, −0.25) | 2/(L, 0) | 1.3125/(VL, 0.31) |
| $x_4$ | VVH (6, 0) | 3.75/(H, −0.25) | 5.3125/(VH, 0.31) | 1.3125/(VL, 0.31) | 0.6875/(VL, −0.31) |
| Task profile (TP) | | 3.8638/(H, −0.13) | 4.1458/(H, 0.14) | 2.2440/(L, 0.24) | 1.3489/(VL, 0.34) |

Having calculated the final aggregated rating for each activity with respect to each skill, we proceed with the calculation of the task profile vector. For example, for skill $c_1$, namely, object oriented design (Table 4, column 3), the corresponding value in task profile vector is, according to formula (13), equal to

$$\mathrm{tp}_1 = \Delta\left(\frac{5.4285 \times 1 + 0.6875 \times 2 + 5.6875 \times 3 + 3.75 \times 6}{1 + 2 + 3 + 6}\right) = \Delta(3.8638) = (4, -0.13) = (\mathrm{H}, -0.13). \quad (23)$$

The resulting task profile for all individual required skills is, therefore, calculated as a vector of linguistic 2-tuples and it is shown in the last row of Table 4. From this task profile, we can conclude that, for this specific task, high level of competence in both C++ programming and object oriented design is required (i.e., the corresponding 2-tuples are equal to and , resp.) but a lower level of competency is required in Visual Basic and Java programming (i.e., the corresponding 2-tuples are equal to and , resp.).

Having calculated the task profile, we continue by evaluating candidate human resources (developers). Table 5 presents the judgments expressed by project managers for the level that characterizes each one of the four available developers ($Q$=4) with respect to each required skill. For example, according to project manager $e_1$, developer $r_1$ is characterized by a "Very Low" level of competence regarding object oriented design.

**Table 5:** Project managers' evaluation on skills/competencies of available human resources

| Resource ($r$) | Project manager ($e$)/weight of importance ($\varepsilon$) | Skills available from candidate resources ($c$) | | | |
|---|---|---|---|---|---|
| | | OO design ($c_1$) | C++ ($c_2$) | VB ($c_3$) | Java ($c_4$) |
| | $e_1$/(1/3) | (VL, 0) | (L, 0) | (H, 0) | (VH, 0) |
| $r_1$ | $e_2$/(1/3) | (L, 0) | (VL, 0) | (VH, 0) | (M, 0) |
| | $e_3$/(1/3) | (VL, 0) | (VVL, 0) | (VH, 0) | (L, 0) |
| | $e_1$/(1/3) | (VL, 0) | (VL, 0) | (VH, 0) | (L, 0) |
| $r_2$ | $e_2$/(1/3) | (VL, 0) | (VL, 0) | (H, 0) | (L, 0) |
| | $e_3$/(1/3) | (VVL, 0) | (VL, 0) | (VH, 0) | (L, 0) |
| | $e_1$/(1/3) | (M, 0) | (VH, 0) | (H, 0) | (L, 0) |
| $r_3$ | $e_2$/(1/3) | (H, 0) | (VH, 0) | (L, 0) | (VL, 0) |
| | $e_3$/(1/3) | (L, 0) | (VVH, 0) | (M, 0) | (VL, 0) |
| | $e_1$/(1/3) | (VH, 0) | (VVH, 0) | (VL, 0) | (VL, 0) |
| $r_4$ | $e_2$/(1/3) | (VVH, 0) | (VH, 0) | (VL, 0) | (VL, 0) |
| | $e_3$/(1/3) | (VH, 0) | (VH, 0) | (VL, 0) | (VVL, 0) |

Following the same procedure as above (i.e., Steps 2–4 of the approach), we get the final aggregated ratings of each candidate resource with respect to each skill, as shown in columns 2–5 of Table 6. The capability/suitability of each resource cs is calculated using formula (14) and the results are shown in the last column of Table 6.

**Table 6:** Final aggregated ratings for each resource FR and resource capabilities cs

| Resource ($r$) | Skills available from candidate resources ($c$) | | | | Resource capabilities (cs) |
|---|---|---|---|---|---|
| | OO design ($c_1$) | C++ ($c_2$) | VB ($c_3$) | Java ($c_4$) | |
| $r_1$ | 1.3125/(VL, 0.31) | 1/(VL, 0) | 4.6875/(VH, −0.31) | 3.25/(M, 0.25) | 2.0788/(L, 0.07) |
| $r_2$ | 0.6875/(VL, −0.31) | 1/(VL, 0) | 4.6875/(VH, −0.31) | 2/(L, 0) | 1.7253/(L, −0.28) |
| $r_3$ | 3/(M, 0) | 5.3125/(VH, 0.31) | 3/(M, 0) | 1.3125/(VL, 0.31) | 3.6301/(H, −0.37) |
| $r_4$ | 5.3125/(VH, 0.31) | 5.3125/(VH, 0.31) | 1/(VL, 0) | 0.6875/(VL, −0.31) | 3.9407/(H, −0.06) |

In the next stage of the approach we perform reevaluation of the resource capabilities. Project managers provide their judgments on skill relationships, that is, how prior knowledge in various skills contributes to the learning of other skills, as shown in Table 7. For example, according to project manager $e1$, existing competency in C++ programming contributes at a "Very Very High" level to improvement of skills in object oriented design. Following Steps 2–4 of the approach, as shown above, we get the final aggregated ratings FSR of skill relationships which are presented in Table 8.

**Table 7:** Project manager evaluations on skill/competency relationships

| Required skills/competencies ($c$) | Project manager ($e$)/weight of importance ($\varepsilon$) | Skills available from candidate resources ($c$) | | | |
|---|---|---|---|---|---|
| | | OO design ($c_1$) | C++ ($c_2$) | VB ($c_3$) | Java ($c_4$) |
| | $e_1$/(1/3) | — | (VH, 0) | (M, 0) | (VH, 0) |
| OO design ($c_1$) | $e_2$/(1/3) | — | (H, 0) | (L, 0) | (VH, 0) |
| | $e_3$/(1/3) | — | (VVH, 0) | (M, 0) | (VH, 0) |
| | $e_1$/(1/3) | (VVH, 0) | — | (L, 0) | (VH, 0) |
| C++ ($c_2$) | $e_2$/(1/3) | (H, 0) | — | (M, 0) | (H, 0) |
| | $e_3$/(1/3) | (VVH, 0) | — | (M, 0) | (VH, 0) |
| | $e_1$/(1/3) | (L, 0) | (M, 0) | — | (L, 0) |
| VB ($c_3$) | $e_2$/(1/3) | (L, 0) | (L, 0) | — | (VL, 0) |
| | $e_3$/(1/3) | (VL, 0) | (M, 0) | — | (VL, 0) |
| | $e_1$/(1/3) | (H, 0) | (VH, 0) | (VL, 0) | — |
| Java ($c_4$) | $e_2$/(1/3) | (H, 0) | (H, 0) | (M, 0) | — |
| | $e_3$/(1/3) | (VVH, 0) | (H, 0) | (M, 0) | — |

**Table 8:** Final aggregated ratings of skill/competency relationships FSR

| Skills/competencies ($c$) | Skills/competencies ($c$) | | | |
|---|---|---|---|---|
| | OO design ($c_1$) | C++ ($c_2$) | VB ($c_3$) | Java ($c_4$) |
| OO design ($c_1$) | — | 5/(VH, 0) | 2.6875/(M, −0.31) | 5/(VH, 0) |
| C++ ($c_2$) | 5.4286/(VH, 0.43) | — | 2.6875/(M, −0.31) | 4.6875/(VH, −0.31) |
| VB ($c_3$) | 1.6875/(L, −0.31) | 2.6875/(M, −0.31) | — | 1.6875/(L, −0.31) |
| Java ($c_4$) | 4.5714/(VH, −0.43) | 4.3125/(H, 0.31) | 2.4286/(L, 0.43) | — |

Having calculated the final aggregated ratings of skill relationships, we continue by reevaluating the resources' final aggregated ratings using formula (15). For example, we use the final aggregated rating $FR_{11}$ of resource $r_1$ with respect to skill/competency $c_1$ (object oriented design) that is found equal to (VL, 0.31) (see Table 6). $FR^{NEW}_{11}$ is then calculated by using formula (15) as follows:

$$FR_{11}^{NEW} = \max\left(1.3125; \frac{1 \times 5.4286 + 4.6875 \times 1.6875 + 3.25 \times 4.5714}{5.4286 + 1.6875 + 4.5714}\right) = \max(1.3125; 2.4124) = 2.4124. \quad (24)$$

The reevaluated final aggregated ratings of the resources are presented in Table 9.

## Table 9: Reevaluated final aggregated ratings of resources FR$^{NEW}$ and final values of resource capabilities cs

| Resource ($r$) | Skills available from candidate resources ($c$) | | | | Resource capability/suitability (cs) (reevaluated) |
|---|---|---|---|---|---|
| | OO design ($c_1$) | C++ ($c_2$) | VB ($c_3$) | Java ($c_4$) | |
| $r_1$ | 2.4124/(L, 0.41) | 2.7646/(M, −0.24) | 4.6875/(VH, −0.31) | 3.25/(M, 0.25) | 3.07569/(M, 0.08) |
| $r_2$ | 1.9235/(L, −0.08) | 2.0550/(L, 0.06) | 4.685/(VH, −0.31) | 2/(L, 0) | 2.5139/(M, −0.49) |
| $r_3$ | 3.4140/(M, 0.41) | 5.3125/(VH, 0.31) | 3.2712/(M, 0.27) | 3.9529/(H, −0.05) | 4.1274/(H, 0.13) |
| $r_4$ | 5.3125/(VH, 0.31) | 5.3125/(VH, 0.31) | 3.8731/(H, −0.13) | 4.6727/(VH, −0.33) | 4.9597/(VH, −0.04) |

Resource capabilities (i.e., resource-task suitability values) are computed using formula (16), as described in Step 9 of the approach, and the obtained results (final suitability values) are presented in the last column of Table 9. The comparison between the initial ratings (last column in Table 6) and the final ratings (last column in Table 9) of the candidate resources shows that definitely the most suitable candidate human resource to be involved in the activities of task $T_1$ is resource $r_4$.

By studying the results of the presented example, we can, for example, conclude that while in the initial evaluation the resources $r_3$ and $r_4$ are both highly suitable to cover the skill requirements of task $T_1$, with ratings (H, −0.37) and (H, −0.06), respectively (see Table 6, last column), considering skill-relationships (see Table 9, last column) $r_4$ ends up being more suitable (rated as (VH, −0.04)) with greater difference from $r_3$ (rated as (H, 0.13)).

Let us now assume that the current workload of the software company comprises two tasks $\{T_1, T_2\}$. This means that in parallel with $T_1$ the software company is undertaking the development activities of an additional task $T_2$. Performing the approach again results in resource-task suitability ratings of the available developers for the development activities of task $T_2$. These ratings are shown in Table 10 (third column) along with the ratings of developers for the activities of task $T_1$ (second column). It should be noted that there would be no need to ask project managers to express again their judgments for the skill level characterizing the developers in case that a required skill for task $T_2$ is the same as a skill required for task $T_1$. We can, therefore, apply formula (16) on these resource task suitability values to derive estimations of the allocation of each developer effort to tasks $T_1$ and $T_2$ (shown in the fourth and fifth column of Table 10, resp.).

**Table 10:** Resource capabilities cs to perform the development activities of two tasks and allocation of developers' effort EEA to tasks

| Resource ($r$) | Capability/suitability cs for task $T_1$ | Capability/suitability cs for task $T_2$ | Allocation of effort to task $T_1$ | Allocation of effort to task $T_2$ |
|---|---|---|---|---|
| $r_1$ | 3.07569/(M, 0.08) | 5.58151/(VVH, −0.42) | 35.53% | 64.47% |
| $r_2$ | 2.5139/(M, −0.49) | 4.42354/(H, 0.42) | 36.24% | 63.76% |
| $r_3$ | 4 1274/(H, 0.13) | 4.0976/(H, 0.10) | 50.18% | 49.82% |
| $r_4$ | 4.9597/(VH, −0.04) | 5.89241/(VVH, −0.11) | 45.70% | 54.30% |

Some useful assertions can be derived by observing and comparing these estimated effort allocations. For example, although resource $r_4$ is slightly more suitable for task $T_1$ (VH, −0.04), compared with the corresponding suitability of resource $r_3$ (H, 0.13), the allocation of $r4$ effort to task $T_1$ is lower (45.70%) than the corresponding value of $r_3$ (50.18%). This is because resource $r4$ should devote more time/effort (54.30%) to the development activities of task $T_2$ where the suitability resource $r_4$ (VVH, −0.11) is considerably higher than the corresponding suitability value of resource $r_3$ (H, 0.10).

## DISCUSSION

Since proper and systematic utilization of all available resources in a software development project is a vital issue, we proposed an approach that focuses on the efficient evaluation and selection of human resources in software development tasks. The approach contributes to and objectively supports project management in the difficult task of selecting and allocating human resources in software development tasks.

The proposed approach makes two important contributions to the literature. The first involves putting forward for use and development a framework for evaluating human resources to software development projects. We consider a group-based and multicriteria decision making mechanism for the assessment of human resources. We combine the 2-tuple fuzzy linguistic model with similarity degree-based aggregation to derive objective assessments for provided/required skills/competencies. The second contribution is that it emphasizes deriving objective evaluations of human resources matching skills required by software tasks by considering possible skill relationships and dependencies. Using subjective evaluations (expressed by project managers in qualitative linguistic forms) on skills/competencies required for specific task activities, available human resource skills/competencies, and relationships between the various skills/competencies, we are able to extract objective evaluation on resource capabilities and their suitability for the respective development task. Specifically, by considering skill relationships, which reflect the degree to which one skill contributes to the learning of other skills, the difference between the most suited human resource and the rest of the available resources for a specific task can be intensified, thus better indicating the most appropriate candidate for a specific task.

The above contributions are reflected through the results provided by the exemplar case study scenario. The results show that by using subjective evaluations provided by projects managers we can obtain objective results through the similarity degree-based aggregation technique. The reevaluation of human resource suitability through the consideration of skill/competency relationships can significantly enhance the differences between the available human resources. In addition, we have shown that suitability values are practically useful to estimate effort allocation of resources to development tasks.

We should finally mention that the computations underlying the approach are not apparent to the project managers/decision makers which only provide linguistic terms to state their evaluations. Actually, we implemented all required computations in a spreadsheet program that helps to effectively and practically apply the approach with a variety of inputs.

## CONCLUSION

A fuzzy linguistic description approach based on 2-tuple fuzzy linguistic terms to evaluate human resources involved in software development tasks is presented in this paper. The proposed approach follows a group and similarity degree-based aggregation method to obtain an objective assessment of the ratings of multiple required task-related skills and provided skills from the available human resources. In addition, we consider skill relationships, provided as 2-tuple fuzzy linguistic terms, to represent dependencies between the various task-related skills reflecting the contribution of one skill to the learning of other skills. Through the introduction of skill relationships we ensure the objective assessments of human resources matching skills required by software tasks.

To demonstrate the applicability of the proposed approach we presented an exemplar case study scenario with numerical results, which was implemented to assess the results obtained. The numerical results provide indications that the proposed approach can effectively support management decisions to objectively evaluate available human resources considering a set of skills and a set of project tasks. We are currently executing a case study in software SME with the aim of thoroughly validating the applicability of the proposed approach. In particular, since the approach utilizes and objectively aggregates multiple qualitative judgments for task-related and provided skills, our current interest is to apply the approach in the context of a software development company that follows 360-degree appraisal [35] to evaluate its personnel, where the judgment of each company employee about his/her level of competence is also considered.

Our future work aims at further improving the suggested approach by determining resource teams based on substitution and complementarity associations between candidate human resources. Another important issue to be addressed is the provision of appropriate support to the allocation of human resources to software development tasks by performing multiobjective optimization (e.g., according to budget and availability constraints).

## ACKNOWLEDGMENTS

This research has been cofinanced by the European Union (European Social Fund, ESF) and Greek National Funds through the Operational Program "Education and Lifelong Learning" of the National Strategic Reference Framework (NSRF), in the context of the research project "SPRINT SMEs," Act: "ARCHIMEDES III" in the Operational Program "Education and Lifelong Learning 2007–13."

## REFERENCES

1. D. A. Callegari and R. M. Bastos, "A multi-criteria resource selection method for software projects using fuzzy logic," in Enterprise Information Systems, J. Filipe and J. Cordeiro, Eds., vol. 24 of Lecture Notes in Business Information Processing, pp. 376–388, Springer, Berlin, Germany, 2009. ·
2. L. D. Otero, G. Centeno, A. J. Ruiz-Torres, and C. E. Otero, "A systematic approach for resource allocation in software projects," Computers and Industrial Engineering, vol. 56, no. 4, pp. 1333–1339, 2009. · ·

3. S. T. Acuña, N. Juristo, and A. M. Moreno, "Emphasizing human capabilities in software development," IEEE Software, vol. 23, no. 2, pp. 94–101, 2006. · ·

4. F. Padberg, "Scheduling software projects to minimize the development time and cost with a given staff," in Proceedings of the Software Engineering Conference (APSEC ‹01), pp. 187–194, 2001.

5. L. D. Otero and C. E. Otero, "A fuzzy expert system architecture for capability assessments in skill-based environments," Expert Systems with Applications, vol. 39, no. 1, pp. 654–662, 2012. · ·

6. L. A. Zadeh, "Fuzzy sets," Information and Control, vol. 8, no. 3, pp. 338–353, 1965. ·

7. F. Herrera and L. Martínez, "A 2-tuple fuzzy linguistic representation model for computing with words,"IEEE Transactions on Fuzzy Systems, vol. 8, no. 6, pp. 746–752, 2000.

8. X. Liao, Y. Li, and B. Lu, "A model for selecting an ERP system based on linguistic information processing," Information Systems, vol. 32, no. 7, pp. 1005–1017, 2007. · ·

9. V. C. Gerogiannis, E. Rapti, A. Karageorgos, and P. Fitsilis, "Human resource assessment in software development projects using fuzzy linguistic 2-tuples," in Proceedings of the 2nd International Conference on Artificial Intelligence, Modelling & Simulation (AIMS ‹14), pp. 217–222, IEEE, Madrid, Spain, November 2014. ·

10. V. C. Gerogiannis, E. Rapti, A. Karageorgos, and P. Fitsilis, "A fuzzy linguistic approach for human resource evaluation and selection in software projects," in Proceedings of the 5th International Conference on Industrial Engineering and Operations Management (IEOM› 15), pp. 1–9, Dubai, UAE, March 2015. ·

11. SPRINT SMEs Project, January 2015, http://sprint.teilar.gr/.

12. V. C. Gerogiannis, G. Kakarontzas, L. Anthopoulos, S. Bibi, and I. Stamelos, "The SPRINT-SMEs approach for software process improvement in small-medium sized software development enterprises," in Proceedings of the Scientific Workshop of R&D Projects in ARCHIMEDES III Research Programme, Technological Education Institute of Thessaly, Larissa, Greece, November 2013.

13. S. Bibi, V. C. Gerogiannis, G. Kakarontzas, and I. Stamelos, "Ontology based bayesian software process improvenent," in Proceedings of the 9th International Conference on Software Engineering and Applications (ICSOFT-EA ‹14), pp. 568–575, Vienna, Austria, August 2014. ·

14. M. André, M. G. Baldoquín, and S. T. Acuña, "Formal model for assigning human resources to teams in software projects," Information and Software Technology, vol. 53, no. 3, pp. 259–275, 2011. · ·

15. H. I. Ahmad, A systematic review of selection and management of a project team [M.S. thesis], Joensuu School of Computing, Faculty of Science and Forestry, University of Eastern Finland, 2013.

16. T. J. A. Santos, A. M. Lima, C. A. Reis, and R. Q. Reis, "Automated support for human resource allocation in software process by cluster analysis," in Proceedings of the 4th International Workshop Recommendation Systems for Software Engineering, pp. 30–31, Hyderabad, India, June 2014. ·

17. A. Barreto, M. D. O. Barros, and C. M. L. Werner, "Staffing a software project: a constraint satisfaction and optimization-based approach," Computers and Operations Research, vol. 35, no. 10, pp. 3073–3089, 2008.

18. L. C. e Silva and A. P. C. S. Costa, "Decision model for allocating human resources in information system projects," International Journal of Project Management, vol. 31, no. 1, pp. 100–108, 2013. · ·

19. R. Kolisch, "Resource allocation capabilities of commercial project management software packages,"Interfaces, vol. 29, no. 4, pp. 19–31, 1999. · ·

20. O. Zwikael and E. Unger-Aviram, "HRM in project groups: the effect of project duration on team development effectiveness," International Journal of Project Management, vol. 28, no. 5, pp. 413–421, 2010.

21. H.-T. Tsai, H. Moskowitz, and L.-H. Lee, "Human resource selection for software development projects using Taguchi›s parameter design," European Journal of Operational Research, vol. 151, no. 1, pp. 167–180, 2003. · · View at Zentralblatt MATH ·

22. M. Yoshimura, Y. Fujimi, K. Izui, and S. Nishiwaki, "Decision-making support system for human resource allocation in product development projects," International Journal of Production Research, vol. 44, no. 5, pp. 831–848, 2006. · ·

23. D. Kang, J. Jung, and D.-H. Bae, "Constraint-based human resource allocation in software projects,"Software: Practice and Experience, vol. 41, no. 5, pp. 551–577, 2011. · ·

24. W. W. Chu and P. Ngai, "A dynamic constraint-directed ordered search algorithm for solving constraint satisfaction problems," in Proceedings of the 1st International Conference on Industrial and Engineering Applications of Artificial Intelligence and Expert Systems (IEA/AIE ‹88), pp. 116–125, 1988. ·

25. W. Kwak, Y. Shi, and K. Jung, "Human resource allocation in a CPA firm: a fuzzy set approach," Review of Quantitative Finance and Accounting, vol. 20, no. 3, pp. 277–290, 2003. · ·

26. M. L. Hussein and M. A. Abo-Sinna, "A fuzzy dynamic approach to the multicriterion resource allocation problem," Fuzzy Sets and Systems, vol. 69, no. 2, pp. 115–124, 1995. · ·

27. D. Strnad and N. Guid, "A fuzzy-genetic decision support system for project team formation," Applied Soft Computing Journal, vol. 10, no. 4, pp. 1178–1187, 2010. · ·

28. N. A. Ruskova, "Decision support system for human resources appraisal and selection," in Proceedings of the 1st International IEEE Symposium on Intelligent Systems (IS ‹02), pp. 354–357, IEEE, Varna, Bulgaria, 2002. ·

29. J. Dodangeh, S. Sorooshian, and A. R. Afshari, "Linguistic extension for group multicriteria project manager selection," Journal of Applied Mathematics, vol. 2014, Article ID 570398, 8 pages, 2014. · ·

30. R. M. Rodriguez and L. Martinez, "An analysis of symbolic linguistic computing models in decision making," International Journal of General Systems, vol. 42, no. 1, pp. 121–136, 2013. · · ·

31. L. Martinez and F. Herrera, "An overview on the 2-tuple linguistic model for computing with words in decision making: extensions, applications and challenges," Information Sciences, vol. 207, pp. 1–18, 2012.

32. T. Da and Y. Xu, "Evaluation on functions of urban waterfront redevelopment based on proportional 2-tuple linguistic," International Journal of Computational Intelligence Systems, vol. 7, no. 4, pp. 796–808, 2014. ·

33. M. Dursun and E. E. Karsak, "A fuzzy MCDM approach for personnel selection," Expert Systems with Applications, vol. 37, no. 6, pp. 4324–4330, 2010. · ·

34. H. Raoudha, D. E. Mouloudi, H. Selma, and E. M. Abderrahman, "A new approach for an efficient human resource appraisal and selection," Journal of Industrial Engineering and Management, vol. 5, no. 2, pp. 323–343, 2012. · ·

35. M. Espinilla, R. de Andrés, F. J. Martinez, and L. Martinez, "A 360-degree performance appraisal model dealing with heterogeneous information and dependent criteria," Information Sciences, vol. 222, pp. 459–471, 2013. · · ·

36. F. Herrera and L. Martinez, "The 2-tuple linguistic computational model. advantages of its linguistic description, accuracy and consistency," International Journal of Uncertainty, Fuzziness and Knowledge-Based Systems, vol. 9, no. 1, pp. 33–48, 2001. · · ·

37. F. Herrera, E. Herrera-Viedma, and J. L. Verdegay, "A rational consensus model in group decision making using linguistic assessments," Fuzzy Sets and Systems, vol. 88, no. 1, pp. 31–49, 1997. · ·

38. F. Herrera, L. Martínez, and P. J. Sánchez, "Managing non-homogeneous information in group decision making," European Journal of Operational Research, vol. 166, no. 1, pp. 115–132, 2005.

CHAPTER 3

# WORKFORCE ISSUES AND THEIR IMPACT ON PROJECTS: STUDY ON THE INDIAN IT AND ITeS INDUSTRY

Dr Nasina Jigeesh

IBS Hyderabad, IFHE University, India

## ABSTRACT

**Today's information technology (IT) industry is facing challenges from different corners because of globalization, technological changes, market and economic fluctuations and dynamic changes in customer requirements. A new stream of jobs has been emerging from time to time in the IT and IT-enabled services (ITeS) industry. People management is gaining more concern compared with technology management. Recruiting the right people, motivating them to improve their productivity and retaining productive people are becoming additional challenges to the success of IT projects, and for enabling the IT industry to achieve steady growth and continue ongoing projects without any interruptions or constraints. This study focuses on the dynamics of the workforce in IT projects, and analyses the important issues of managing the workforce and its impact on time, cost and quality of the projects. From the analysis of data collected through surveys of some big IT and ITeS companies in India, it was found that the availability of human resources (HR) was the most significant issue, while the issue of employee-oriented programs was the least significant.**

## INTRODUCTION

Due to the competitive environment prevailing globally, every industry, for its survival, has been aggressively designing and implementing new business processes to produce better and innovative products or services. Rowden (2002) recommended several factors for organizational success which included the careful selection of employees, matching the employee's skills or skills development potential with the needs of the company, investment in training and employee-development activities, retention of employees by providing them with compensation and benefit packages, etc. Creation of high performance work environments within the organizations to fulfil human, social and psychological needs leads to increased productivity, product quality innovation and flexibility (Mirivis 1993; Schutz 1994). Rowden (2002) also added that, by allowing workers to influence their work activities, organizations can take competitive advantage of the human element. According to Pfeffer (1994), certain employment practices, including internal career ladders, workers discretion and extensive training, generally contribute to high levels of organizational performance. The information technology (IT) and IT-enabled services (ITeS) industry would also exhibit all these features.

In industries other than IT, but relying on IT applications, there would be a reduction of workforce in organizations (Jonscher 1994); Brynjolfsson et al 1994), hampering the motivation levels of employees. Continuing pressures associated with globalization, technological change and

**Citation:** Nasina Jigeesh, "Workforce issues and their impact on projects: study on the Indian IT and ITeS industry," ISSN: 1838-7845.

market deregulation suggest a continuing need for firms to use some form of downsizing and restructuring (Lawler et al 2000). But in the IT industry, the projects to bring up different IT applications/products/services have been growing day by day and this trend is creating a demand for a larger IT workforce. The reasons for and repercussions of the market forces reported by Lawler et al (2000) might be experienced in IT firms also. Maintaining innovation at all levels in products and services has been adding valuable support to competitive advantage of IT firms, which need to encourage creativity and innovation as part of the organisational mission. According to Galunic and Rodan (1998), the HR skills and motivation levels make it possible for creative suggestions, different proposals and research activities to foster innovation. According to PMBoK, the project HR management processes include HR planning and acquisition, development and management of the project team. HR planning deals with making different people accountable, authorized and responsible for different portions of the project. In the event of project team members not possessing the required competencies to accomplish the assigned project tasks, PMBoK recommends initiating proactive responses such as training, hiring, and schedule or scope changes. While acquiring human resources, their availability, ability, experience, interests and cost play an important role. The project team members should be properly trained to develop their general management skills, formal and informal communications, team-building attitude, etc. The skills and competencies would be improved to perform assigned activities more effectively with good team spirit.

## IT and ITeS Projects

The characteristics of IT projects are quite different from other projects. For example, the progress of IT projects is not visible immediately and per dollar or euro spent; software products contain more complexity than other engineered artifacts (Brooks 1987). Just like the invisible nature of status/progress of IT projects, the matching of skills of various project personnel with the project requirements will also become unclear in many cases. Therefore, the process of selection and recruitment of the right project staff in the IT industry is becoming increasingly complex, and the successful outcome of these processes is becoming vital for job performance, organizational success and competitive advantage. Jobs change accordingly as organizations respond to economic and technological pressures in the market and, similarly, skills vary accordingly as the jobs respond to the targets and demands of the market. Jobs and skills along with experience link up with the salary structures, which vary continuously based on different aspects like organizational capabilities, market demand, personal virtue and demands. When all these project and personal parameters are in place, there would be a right balance achieved between the employee's motivation levels and the organizational motivation exercises. Advanced economies has shown a trend of up-skilling and a remarkable variation in the skilled/unskilled composition of labor in the past few years (Machin and Van Reenen 1998; Spitz-Oener 2006). Knowledge workers as human capital can deal with what the target market accepts or expects as value, and are able to defend their companies against the aggressive movements of their competitors (Carneiro 2007). High-performance work practices assist people in the decision-making and problem-solving processes of their work activities (Rowden 2002) and thereby upgrading their motivation levels.

Poor strategic management and related human factors have been cited as a major cause of failures, which traditional techniques cannot incorporate explicitly (Rodrigues & Williams 1997). According to Tsai et al (2003), resource selection for choosing the best project team at the planning stage of a software development project is an important issue for reducing project cost, duration and risk. Several research studies (Boehm 1981; Brooks 1993, Krishnan 1998, Martz & Landof 2000) identified the importance of the team factor in software projects. Krishnan (1998) reported that the major categories of potential improvements in cost and quality of software are focused around technology, software development, process and product factors. Team and group work skills are necessary and increasingly important (Martz & Landof 2000), but human nature fights against collaboration as shared creation (Corbitt & Martz 2003).

This study focused on examining the importance and influence of various HR issues on IT project success from the developer's point of view, in terms of the traditional time–cost–quality "iron triangle" or "golden triangle" constraints (De Wit 1988; Hazebroucq & Badot 1996; Atkinson 1999; Cooke-Davis 2002; Westerveld 2003).

## Methodology

Various case studies or success stories of five top Indian IT firms were studied and analyzed to derive different challenging issues related to HR and project management. The views of IT professionals and recommendations of PMBoK were taken into account to analyze the issues. In this process, a list of six issues was prepared, excluding the issue of 'commitment'. This is because of the assumption that all the project team members have been working on the projects with commitment. These issues were then compared with the three major project management parameters of time, cost and quality.

The six HR-related issues that were dealt with in this study include:

- New resources operating new technology,
- Availability of resources,
- Skills of team members,
- Retaining talented people,
- Motivation, communication and coordination, and
- Employee-oriented programs.

These issues were then framed in the form of questions and a questionnaire was developed to gather quantitative data on the importance of each HR-related issue and its impact on the time, cost and quality of the project. The questionnaire consisted of four important questions relating to: (a) importance of the issue; (b) impact on quality; (b) impact on cost, and (c) impact on time span of the projects. The questionnaire was sent via email to about 100 IT professionals working in the selected IT companies situated in Bangalore (Karnataka), Chennai (Tamilnadu) and Hyderabad (Andhra Pradesh), which are the three southern Indian software clusters in terms of revenue generation. The feedback from various IT professionals, especially at the level of senior project team leaders and managers was gathered. A Likert scale of 1 to 10 was used to collect the feedback, '1' denoting "not at all important" or "not significant" and '10' representing "very important" or "very significant" and the remaining scores denoting relative importance or significance. Of a total of 100 questionnaires forwarded, 33 complete and reliable responses were received. This represents one-third or 33% response rate, which was treated as reasonable.

All six HR-related issues were analyzed together based on the collected feedback on the importance and impact of the HR issues on time, cost and quality of projects. For this purpose, testing of following null hypotheses was done:

- All six HR-related issues are important in the context of IT projects;
- All six HR-related issues show equal impact on the quality of IT projects;
- All six HR-related issues show equal impact on the cost of IT projects; and
- All six HR-related issues show equal impact on the time of IT projects;

One-way ANOVA (analysis of variance) was used with SPSS 16.0 software. Levene's test was used to test the homogeneity of variances. Post-hoc (Tukey HSD) tests with multiple comparisons among the issues were also performed to assess which issues differed from each other. After testing the above hypotheses, the data was further analyzed to assess the importance and type of impact of HR issues on time, cost and quality of IT projects, to make the research work beneficial for any IT project management process.

## Hypotheses Testing

The study took up different hypotheses to analyze the variance in the importance and impact of the six HR-related issues on IT projects.

### *Hypothesis $H_{01}$: All six HR Issues are Equally Important*

From the statistical analysis of the feedback data, it was found that the significance is 0.084 in the test of homogeneity of variance, which is greater than 0.05. Hence it passed Levene's test and all six HR issues have homogeneity of variances. In the case of ANOVA, the significance level, P = 0.000, is below 0.05 and therefore there is a statistically significant difference regarding mean importance between the different HR issues. Hence the null hypothesis can be rejected. The results showed that 'new resources operating new technology' has no significant difference from the remaining HR issues, except 'employee-oriented programs'. 'Employee-oriented programs' is significantly differenct from two other issues, namely, 'availability of resources' and 'retaining talented people'. 'Availability of resources' also differed in importance from 'skills of team members', 'motivation, communication and coordination', and 'retaining talented people'. Hence, there is significant difference in importance for all the HR issues concerned in IT projects.

In view of the above results, the null hypothesis can be rejected and can be reinterpreted as: Hypothesis $H_1$: All six HR issues have significant difference in their importance for IT projects.

### *Hypothesis, $H_{02}$: All six HR issues have equal impact on quality in IT projects*

From the statistical analysis of the feedback data, it was found that the significance is 0.671 in the test of homogeneity of variance, which is greater than 0.05. Hence the Levene's test is satisfied and all six HR issues have homogeneity of variances. In the case of ANOVA, the significance level, P = 0.082, which is above 0.05, and therefore, there is no statistically significant difference between the HR issues in the case of mean impact on quality of projects. Hence the null hypothesis cannot be rejected. But two issues, namely, 'availability of resources' and 'employee-oriented programs' showed some difference compared with the others.

In view of the above result, the null hypothesis cannot be rejected and can be interpreted as: Hypothesis, $H_2$: All six HR issues have no significant difference in their impact on quality in IT projects.

### *Hypothesis $H_{03}$: All six HR issues have equal impact on cost in IT projects*

From the statistical analysis of the feedback data, it was found that the significance is 0.882 in the test of homogeneity of variance, which is greater than 0.05. Hence it satisfied the Levene's test and all six HR issues have homogeneity of variances. In the case of ANOVA, the significance level, P = 0.000, which is below 0.05, and therefore, there is statistically significant difference between the HR issues regarding mean impact on cost of the projects. Hence the null hypothesis can be rejected. The issue of 'availability of resources' has significant difference compared with three other issues, namely, 'retaining talent people', 'motivation, communication and coordination' and 'employee-oriented programs'. Similarly, the issues 'skills of team members' and 'employee-oriented programs' have difference.

In view of the above results, the null hypothesis can be rejected and reinterpreted as: Hypothesis $H_3$: All six HR issues have significant difference in their impact on cost in IT projects.

### *Hypothesis, $H_{04}$: All six HR issues have equal impact on time in IT projects*

From the statistical analysis of the feedback data, it was found that the significance is 0.259 in the test of homogeneity of variance, which is greater than 0.05. Hence the Levene's test is satisfied and all the six HR issues have homogeneity of variances. In the case of ANOVA, the significance level, P = 0.313, which is greater than 0.05, and therefore, there is no statistically significant difference between the different HR issues in the case of mean impact on time of IT projects. Hence the null hypothesis cannot be rejected.

In view of the above results, the null hypothesis cannot be rejected and is interpreted as: Hypothesis, $H_4$: All six HR issues have no significant difference on their impact time in IT projects.

The above results are represented in Table 1.

**Table 1:** Significance values for test of homogeneity of variances and ANOVA of HR issues in IT projects

| Hypothesis | Levene's test of homogeneity – Significance value | ANOVA Significance value | Results |
|---|---|---|---|
| $H_{01}$: All six HR issues are equally important. | 0.084 | 0.000 | 1. There is homogeneity of variances.<br>2. There is statistically significant difference in the mean importance between the issues. |
| $H_{02}$: All six HR issues have equal impact on quality in IT project. | 0.671 | 0.082 | 1. There is homogeneity of variances.<br>2. There is no statistically significant difference in the mean importance between the issues. |
| $H_{03}$: All six HR issues have equal impact on cost in IT projects. | 0.882 | 0.000 | 1. There is homogeneity of variances.<br>2. There is statistically significant difference in the mean importance between the issues. |
| $H_{04}$: All six HR issues have equal impact on time in IT projects. | 0.259 | 0.313 | 1. There is homogeneity of variances.<br>2. There is no statistically significant difference in the mean importance between the issues. |

From the feedback, the mean values of the importance of each of the six HR issues were calculated along with their impact on time, cost and quality of projects. All these values are given in Table 2.

**Table 2:** Mean values of the importance and impact of challenging issues of human resources on time, cost and quality in IT projects

| HR issue | Feedback of respondents | | | |
|---|---|---|---|---|
| | Importance of HR issue | Impact on quality | Impact on cost | Impact on time |
| New resources operating new technology | 6.06 | 6.61 | 6.33 | 6.42 |
| Availability of resources | 7.27 | 6.91 | 7.18 | 6.79 |
| Skills of team members | 5.45 | 6.61 | 6.64 | 6.45 |
| Retaining talented people | 5.88 | 6.52 | 6.03 | 6.48 |
| Motivation, communication and coordination | 5.39 | 6.27 | 5.97 | 6.52 |
| Employee-oriented programs | 4.24 | 5.88 | 5.67 | 5.91 |

Based on the results of means and impact values of all six HR issues, as given in Table 2, four graphs were developed and compared with each other, as shown in Figure 1.

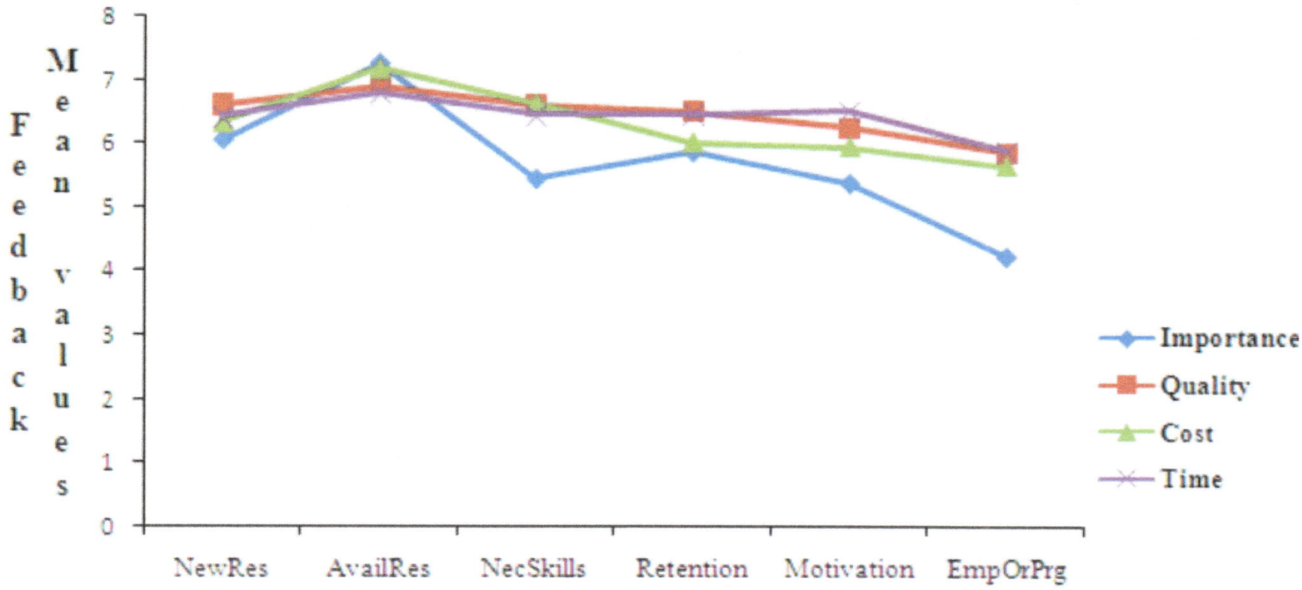


**Figure 1:** Importance and impact on quality, cost and time of six HR issues.

## RESULTS AND DISCUSSION

From the consolidated results, it was found that the HR issue of 'availability of resources' had the highest importance and the highest impact on time, cost and quality in IT projects. This was followed, in order of importance by the issue of 'new resources operating new technology', 'retaining talented people', 'skills of team members' and 'motivation, communication and coordination'. The issue of 'employee-oriented programs' was rated least important.

In the case of impact on quality in IT projects, after 'availability of resources', 'new resources operating new technology' and 'skills of team members' had equal importance, followed by 'retaining talented people', 'motivation, communication and coordination' and 'employee-oriented programs'.

Regarding impact on cost of IT projects, the issue of 'availability of resources' was followed by 'skills of team members', 'new resources operating new technology', 'retaining talented people', 'motivation, communication and coordination' and 'employee-oriented programs'.

In the case of impact on time in IT projects, 'availability of resources' was followed by 'motivation, communication and coordination', 'retaining talented people', 'skills of team members', 'new resources operating new technology', and 'employee-oriented programs'.

Since for all three cases, that is, importance and impact on time, cost and quality in IT projects, 'availability of resources' was given the highest significance in the feedback from the questionnaires, it was attempted to confirm this further through personal interviews with other project staff with more than 10 years of experience in IT projects. The majority reported many IT projects had been lagging because of non-availability of the right human resources. Some project staff have been working on multiple projects in parallel hence their availability is not properly maintained for some of these projects. In addition, in IT field, the project staff often switch over from one organization to another, in order to get more financial benefits, promotions and exposure to a variety of projects and environments. The project staff interviewed emphasized the significance of matching people skills with project requirements. They also attached the least importance to the issue of 'employee-oriented programs', pointing out that in the present competitive world, not only the market but also the IT staff are becoming more dynamic and are giving more importance to maintaining competence in the field. Hence IT organizations should recruit more skilled IT people and keep them on the projects. Proper loading and levelling of such resources should be done carefully, so that there is maximum availability of a particular resource for the relevant project.

## CONCLUSIONS

The success of any project depends mainly on three important parameters — time, cost and quality. Because of the entry of new technologies, applications and market demands, IT projects are becoming highly dynamic in nature. Accordingly, the workforce in such IT projects faces several challenges to produce the necessary output with the necessary quality while saving cost and time. The six major human resources-related issues analyzed in this study include 'new resources operating new technology', 'availability of resources', 'skills of team members', 'retaining talented people', 'motivation, communication and coordination', and 'employee-oriented programs'.

From the analysis of the data collected, all these six issues were assigned varying importance and priority in terms of their impact on improving quality and saving cost and time in projects. The issue of availability of resources was treated as the most important issue, whereas the issue of employee-oriented programs was rated least important. IT organizations should, therefore, give more importance in recruiting more skilled people and keeping them on projects and ensure their maximum availability to work on the assigned project.

## REFERENCES


1. Brooks, F.P. 1987, No silver bullet: essence and accidents of software engineering (Essay included in The Mythical Man-Month, Anniversary Edition, Addison-Wesley, 1995).
2. Brynjolfsson, E., Malone, T.W., Gurbaxami, V. & Kambil A. 1994, Does information technology lead to smaller firms?, Management Science, vol. 40, no. 12, 1628- 1644.
3. Carneiro A. 2007, "What is required for growth?", Business Strategy Series, 8(1), 51-57.
4. Duncan, W.R. 1996, A guide to the project management body of knowledge, Project Management Institute, USA.
5. Galunic, C.D. & Rodan, S. 1998, Resource recombination in the firm: knowledge structures and the potential for Schumpeterian innovation, Strategic Management Journal, vol. 19, no.12, 1193-1201.
6. Jonscher, C. 1994, An economic study of the information technology, in Allen, T.J., Scott Morton, M.S. (eds), Information Technology and the Corporation of the 1990s, Oxford University Press, New York, NY, 5-42.
7. Lawler, J.J., Chen, S. & Bae, J. 2000, Scale of operations, human resource systems and firm performance in East and Southeast Asia, Research and Practice in Human Resource Management, vol. 8, no. 1, 3-20.
8. Machin, S. & Van Reenen, J. 1998, Technology and changes in skill structure: evidence from seven OECD countries, Quarterly Journal of Economics, vol. 113 no.4, 1215-1244.
9. Mirvis, P.H. 1993, Building the Competitive Workforce: Investing in Human Capital for Corporate Success, John Wiley & Sons, New York, USA.
10. Pfeffer, J. 1994, Competitive Advantage through People: Unleashing the Power of the Work Force. Harvard Business School Press, Boston.
11. Rowden, R.W. 2002, High performance and human resource characteristics of successful small manufacturing and processing companies, Leadership & Organizational Development Journal, vol. 23, no. 2, 79-83.
12. Schutz, W. 1994, The Human Element: Productivity, Self-esteem and the Bottom Line, JosseyBass Publishers, San Francisco, CA, USA.
13. Spitz-Oener, A. 2006, Technical change, job tasks, and rising educational demands: looking outside the wage structure, Journal of Labor Economics, vol. 24 no 2, 235-270.
14. Tsai, Hsien-Tang, Moskowitz, H. & Lee, Lai-His. 2003, Human resource selection for software development projects using Taguchi's parameter design, European Journal of Operational Research, vol. 151, no. 1, 167.
15. Rodriques, A.G. & Williams, T.M. 1997, Software dynamics in software project management: towards the development of a formal integrated framework, European Journal of Information Systems, vol. 6, no. 1, 51-66.
16. Abdel-Hamid & Tarek K. 1989, The dynamics of software projects staffing: a system dynamics based simulation approach, IEEE Transactions on Software Engineering, vol. 15, no. 2,109-119.

CHAPTER 4

# THE STUDY OF RESOURCE ALLOCATION AMONG SOFTWARE DEVELOPMENT PHASES: AN ECONOMICS-BASED APPROACH

Peleg Yiftachel[1,2], Irit Hadar[3], Dan Peled[4], Eitan Farchi[5] and Dan Goldwasser[6]

[1]Caesarea Rothschild Institute for Interdisciplinary Applications of Computer Science, University of Haifa, Mount Carmel, Haifa 31905, Israel

[2]Israeli Center of Excellence, EMC Cooperation, 7 Hamada Street, Herzelia 46733, Israel

[3]Department of Information Systems, University of Haifa, Mount Carmel, Haifa 31905, Israel

[4]Department of Economics, University of Haifa, Mount Carmel, Haifa 31905, Israel

[5]Group of Software Performance Analysis Reviews and Quality (SPARQ), IBM Haifa Research Laboratory, Haifa University Campus, Mount Carmel, Haifa 31905, Israel

[6]Department of Computer Science, University of Illinois, Urbana-Champaign, IL 61801, USA

## ABSTRACT

**This paper presents an economics-based approach for studying the problem of resource allocation among software development phases. Our approach is structured along two parallel axes: theoretical and empirical. We developed a general economic model for analyzing the allocation problem as a constrained profit maximization problem. The model, based on a novel concept of software production function, considers the effects of different allocations of development resources on output measures of the resulting software product. An empirical environment for evaluating and refining the model is presented, and a first exploratory study for characterizing the model's components and developers' resource allocation decisions is described. The findings illustrate how the model can be applied and validate its underlying assumptions and usability. Future quantitative empirical studies can refine and substantiate various aspects of the proposed model and ultimately improve the productivity of software development processes.**

## INTRODUCTION

Fundamental disagreements often arise with regard to the "correct" allocation of resources to various software development phases (SDPs). For example, persuasive arguments are made for devoting substantial effort to requirements analysis and design, in order to avoid the costly consequences of modifications in later development stages [1–4]. However, the pressure to provide an executable product, which can be tested and presented to the customer sooner rather than later, can sometimes constitute a consideration for shifting resource allocation to implementation instead. Yet another approach can be seen in Test-Driven Development methods [5, 6], where much emphasis is placed on testing, both before and after implementation.

These tradeoffs are relevant when analyzing graphs showing the cost of detecting and correcting a fault as a function of the phase in which it is detected. Such graphs—prevalent in the literature—demonstrate the dramatic increase in cost when defects are detected later in the development process [7–9]. This observation is often used to support the claim that more resources should be allocated to early SDPs. Obviously, this claim can be pursued ad absurdum: dedicating all (or almost all) resources to the requirements and design phases would leave insufficient resources for implementation. Yet developers[1] cannot find any guidance as to how many resources should be allocated to the various SDPs.

**Citation:** Peleg Yiftachel, Irit Hadar, Dan Peled, Eitan Farchi, and Dan Goldwasser, "The Study of Resource Allocation among Software Development Phases: An Economics-Based Approach," Advances in Software Engineering, vol. 2011, Article ID 579292, 21 pages, 2011. doi:10.1155/2011/579292.

Why are such fundamentally different approaches being advocated for allocating resources to SDPs? Does a correct allocation for a given software project exist, and can it be identified?

Misallocating resources among SDPs can have serious consequences. Tens of billions of dollars are estimated to be spent annually in the US alone due to software faults or aborted projects [7]. Such huge costs may be attributed to various factors such as lack of understanding of the customer's domain or inadequate software development tools. The contention of this paper is that a large portion of these costs may result from incorrect allocation of software development resources among SDPs (see also [8]).

The most popular model dealing with economic perspectives of software development is the Constructive Cost Model (COCOMO) [2], which focuses on cost estimation. While its goal is not optimizing the allocation of resources among the SDPs, this model uses empirical data on software development costs to estimate the cost of any given project. The estimate is based on the project's characteristics and those of the developing environment. The COQUALMO model [10], which is based on COCOMO, discusses relationships between costs, schedule, and quality, but without addressing the resource allocation problem. Emam [11] emphasizes the importance of quality for profitability. Some works (e.g., [1, 7, 12]) present ex-post surveys of the actual resource allocation in different software projects. Heijstek and Chaudron [13] measure effort distribution among the SDPs according to the Rational Unified Process (RUP) hump chart. While much can be learned through hindsight from such cases, they do not provide a basis for a comprehensive method of up-front resource allocation planning. In contrast, Babu and Suresh [14] suggest how to allocate limited development resources across M development phases in order to maximize the average or the minimum of P quality factors, subject to various constraints. The problem is cast as a static nonlinear maximization problem, which assumes known functional forms and parameter values (not based on empirical data), but ignores crucial factors such as the iterative nature of modern software development processes, and omits various quality aspects from the objective function of the problem analyzed.

Value-Based Software Engineering (VBSE) [15] considers economic aspects within the entire software development lifecycle. It can be defined as a software development paradigm in which business value considerations are engineered into software processes, best practices, activities and tasks, management and technology decisions, as well as tools and techniques used throughout the software lifecycle.

Biffl et al. [15] surveyed different methods for solving multicriteria decision problems, presented them as constrained optimization models, and discussed their applicability to decisions in software engineering by analyzing, for example, whether a specific requirement should be included in a specific project/release. However, we did not find in the literature any empirically based decision making model that concretizes these generic optimization models to the specific problem of resource allocation across SDPs.

Some VBSE-related works address subproblems of the one we focus on. For example, Huang and Boehm [16] present a value-based approach for determining how much software assurance is enough before release. Jalote and Vishal [8] address the problem of allocating resources to different quality control stages, in order to minimize the (scalar) measure of the numbers of bugs to be removed during quality control.

To address the absence of guidelines on how to allocate resources to various SDPs, we propose here a conceptual framework for studying the problem of resource allocations among SDPs. While there are several types of resources, we refer here to the time invested by developers as a basic resource. Basing such a framework on scientifically sound principles while making it practical at the same time is a real challenge. In fact, well-known sources [17, 18] suggest that there are no silver bullet solutions to such essential software engineering problems.[2] Moreover, even if a solution does exist, it is likely to depend on specific product and developer characteristics and thus lack generality. Finally, studying this problem empirically poses many difficulties associated with defining, identifying, and measuring the variables. For example, how should we define and measure the output of the software development process, a necessary metric for comparing the consequences of alternative allocations of development resources?

The difficulties of the problem do not absolve us from recognizing its economic importance and should not curb efforts to resolve it. Our goal in this paper is to suggest an economics-based approach for studying the problem of resource allocation among SDPs.

A note on terminology: there is no common, standard terminology in the literature for the different activities and their classification according to what we call phases. For our purpose, it is important to distinguish between different activities, which are concrete instances of development work that need to be associated with one of the phases they belong to. Section 4 deals with this topic explicitly.

The rest of this paper is organized as follows. Section 2 provides a detailed overview of our research approach. Section 3 presents the economic model of software development, which captures the interplay between the allocations of development resources and resulting output. Section 4 proposes how to define and measure SDPs, and Section 5 proposes how to define and measure the resulting outputs. Section 6 analyzes the relationships among these variables. Section 7 illustrates how the model can be used to analyze incorrect resource allocation decisions when developing software in an empirical setting. We conclude and suggest how this research approach can be further developed in Section 8.

## AN OVERVIEW OF OUR APPROACH

Developing an appropriate analytical framework for optimizing resource allocations among SDPs should be based on a suitable formal theoretical model that can be evaluated empirically, as in other VBSE research [15]. In our case, the theoretical model should formulate the resource allocation problem in a manner that captures the consequences of alternative feasible allocations of resources among SPDs for given objectives of the decision maker.

Our approach for studying this problem is structured along two parallel axes:

- the theoretical axis consists of formulating the problem as an economic optimization model, based on characterizing the model components in a precise and measurable manner;

- the empirical axis is designed as an empirical environment in which case studies are used to explore and guide the construction of the theoretical structures and provide an empirical basis for refining the model and the characterization of its components.

Ultimately, the approach should generate a working model that can be used to prescribe the allocation of resources to the various SDPs in a manner that efficiently achieves the objectives of the software developer. This section provides a bird's eye view of our approach along these two axes.

## The Theoretical Axis

We present a novel formulation of an economic optimization model for software development and make some headway in characterizing its components. This model, allows us to analyze the problem of resource allocation among SDPs as a constrained value maximization problem.

For this conceptual model to be useful, its various components should be carefully characterized. In particular, (a) variables representing inputs should correspond to work performed in different development phases; (b) variables representing outputs should correspond to artifacts of the inputs; (c) the software production function should capture the relationships between inputs and outputs. Of course, the different variables, that is, the inputs and outputs of the model, must be measurable, which poses a challenge because software studies are known to suffer from non-standardized measurements [19].

## The Empirical Axis

We strive to create an empirical environment which will enable us to identify, quantify, and verify the key components of the economic model. That is, we develop an empirical research method and construct appropriate measurement tools, in order to obtain a quantitative representation of the variables in the model and the relationships among them. We demonstrate the feasibility of this empirical track and along the way develop solutions to some of the critical challenges involved in implementation of our model. For this aim we adopt the qualitative research approach and conduct an exploratory study. When aiming to explore and understand a phenomenon and its different aspects, rather than statistically corroborating a hypothesis or a theory, it is appropriate to use a qualitative research approach [20]. Qualitative research approaches have gained recognition in general in empirical research, and specifically in software engineering research (see [21], e.g.). These approaches are appropriate when studying software engineering aspects related to human behavior [21] as indeed is done in this research.

Employing qualitative research methods (see, e.g., [22]), we construct the first generation of research tools and illustrate how they can be used in the future for gathering the empirical data needed to complete the mathematical specification of the model and evaluate its usefulness. The data gathered in this study allows us to

- verify the model's utility in interpreting developers' actual conduct during the software development process:
- obtain some initial information about the general nature of the functional forms appearing in the model, and
- understand the possible reasons for observed deviations in software developers' conduct from the model's prescriptions.

Such an exploratory study is important for guiding further research activities [19] and towards future quantitative research.

Our approach emphasizes the need to base the precise specification of the software production function on empirical observations. Accordingly, as part of this research, we have developed an environment for empirical observation in which four subjects, each serving as a case study, worked independently on developing a software project, while we monitored and measured their activities during the entire software development process.

The participants in this study were undergraduate seniors in a management information systems (MISs) department, enrolled in the course "Human Aspects of Software Engineering." The students individually developed a product, called the taxi ordering server (TOS), based on identical requirements and constraints. We provided the participating developers an explicit profit objective, a function of the quality of their finished software product. We monitored and recorded the time allocated by each participant to the different development phases. For this purpose, we developed a tool, called Econometric, which automatically records the time spent in each development environment (e.g., SRS document, UML coding CASE tool, unit testing environment). Econometric also included a reflection document filled in by the students each time they moved between phases, explaining what they had accomplished in their recent activity, to which phase they planned to move next, and why. The students submitted intermediate versions of their work-in-progress every two weeks.

For evaluating the output of the students' work, we developed a Quality Checker (QC). The QC calculates several quality factors of the developed software. Given a prespecified objective function and based on these factors, the QC graded the students' projects. This grade was a significant component of the final course grade, hence served as a value for the students and provided them an incentive to optimize their output. Based on these evaluations, we analyzed the impact of the time allocated to each phase on the quality of the resulting software product. The economic model and its components' characterization were iteratively refined based on the data obtained during the empirical study.

This environment generated very detailed and multifaceted data, which allowed us to study the actual allocations of work time among SDPs and relate these allocations to developers' capabilities and expected personal reward.

While this observational environment is admittedly artificial, and unlikely to be available in real-life situations, it is highly informative and useful for constructing this custom-made research methodology for investigating the problem of resource allocation among SDPs. We view this study as the start of an ongoing effort to formalize the description of software development for the purpose of enhancing its productivity. As we accumulate more empirical data about resource allocations and their resulting output, the models and their components will be refined and perhaps customized to different types of software products. This interplay between theory and empirical findings will eventually lead to better utilization and productivity of software development resources.

## A VALUE-BASED MODEL FOR RESOURCE ALLOCATION AMONG SOFTWARE DEVELOPMENT PHASES

In this section we present a theoretical framework for modeling allocation of resources among SDPs. The model presents a desirable allocation of resources as a solution to a value-maximizing optimization problem, in the spirit of Value Based Software Engineering (VBSE). VBSE is a relatively young discipline, which has been successfully applied to various aspects of software design and management [15]. However, while VBSE has successfully integrated various theories such as utility theory, decision theory, and dependency theory to address particular software engineering problems, it has not yet applied elements from economic production theory, which this paper does. In fact this paper is the first to apply the VBSE approach to the study of resource allocation among SDPs.

The following two subsections describe two different versions of the model; the second one should be viewed as a dynamic extension of the first.

### Software Development as a Production Process: The Static Model

We borrow from economic theory the idea that any production process can be represented as a function which maps production factors (inputs) into producible output [24]. However, software development cannot be evaluated by physical produced units, as is typically done in economics. Instead, we consider software development output as consisting of a set of features, each with its own quality, and denote this output by Q. This notion of quality is external quality [25], as viewed from the customer's perspective, and is one of the main drivers of the developer's value from the product. For presenting the economic model in its simplest form in this section we treat Q as a scalar. In fact, this output has multidimensional structure. However, nothing in the model construction depends on this scalar representation.

Our model focuses on the case in which the resource is development time, to be allocated to work on four different development phases. A basic assumption underlying the model is that the same output can be developed with different combinations of inputs, albeit with different costs. Accordingly, we define $Q = f(t_1,t_2,t_3,t_4)$ as the software production function that maps work time inputs on development phases into the software development output

A general concept of software production function was used in its equivalent dual cost function form by several sources (e.g., Boehm et al. [2, 3], Hu [26], Pendharkar et al. [27]). They present the effort needed to develop software as a function of its size and possibly attributes of the developing organization. Since our focus is the impact resource allocation on software development output, we revert to the traditional economics concept of production function and extend it in two ways relative to these aforementioned references. First, we include both size and quality attributes in our characterization of software development output. Second, we distinguish between efforts extended on different development phases as distinct production factors. In order to capture the flow dynamics of inputs and output in software development, Madachy [28] presents a general dynamic software production function, without distinguishing input by development phases. The idea that the allocation of resources across development phases is linked to the quality of the resulting software was first presented by us in [29]. Heijstek and Chaudron [30] provide empirical evidence on the effects such allocations have on defect detection during development.

The inputs $(t_1,t_2,t_3,t_4)$, respectively, denote the time allocated to each of the following four development phases: Requirements, Design, Implementation, and Testing, respectively. The function f can also depend on additional developer-specific human and organizational factors. As explained in [23, Chapter 5.2], such factors can be based on COCOMO II scale factors and effort multipliers [2]).

The value of the output Q to the developer depends on how Q is perceived by the relevant stakeholder. The identity of the stakeholders can vary from customers purchasing the software to division managers in a large software development organization. We assume that the developer is trying to maximize a value function, denoted by V(Q), which is increasing in Q. This value function captures all the factors that constitute the developer's reward for the developed product. For instance, V(Q) could be the monetary income generated by selling a software product with properties represented by Q. Other factors affecting product demand, such as advertising and promotion, or deployment of the software product in the client organization, are currently ignored in this model, which focuses on the software development process. Alternatively, V(Q) can be the salaries, bonuses, and income equivalents of promotion opportunities enjoyed by a software developer working in a large organization.

The essence of the value-based software development optimization problem consists of maximizing V(Q) subject to a budget constraint on the total costs of the inputs chosen by the developer. While it is always possible to improve the resulting product along some dimension, the developer will seek to utilize the budget by choosing a combination of inputs that contributes the most to V(Q).

The relationship between the inputs and the resulting output is at the heart of this approach, and we elaborate accordingly on how it can be constructed. While the available resources can be allocated in different ways in the course of the development process, this will affect both the development output and its costs. To illustrate how one can capture the intricate relationship between work on different development phases and the resulting software product, we consider an alternative representation of the same software production function in terms of development phase artifacts. Let qi denote the quality of the artifact of phase i, $i \in \{1, 2, 3, 4\}$, and define the software development output as $Q = f(q_1, q_2, q_3, q_4)$.

These phase qualities correspond to internal quality as defined by [25]. Since the resulting output of each phase depends on the time allocated to that phase and may also be affected by the qualities of the artifacts of other phases, this alternative representation of the input-quality relationship is equivalent to the former in terms of working time on each of the four phases. The dependence among the artifacts of different phases is modeled by assuming that $q_1 = h_1(t_1)$ and $q_i = h_i(t_i, q_i-1)$; i = 2, 3, 4.

This formulation emphasizes the interdependence of the artifacts from different phases, as well as the fact that the resulting artifact of each phase depends on the resources allocated to it. With $w_i$ denoting possibly different costs associated with inputs to different phases, the budget-constrained value-maximizing problem is formulated as

$$\underset{t_1,t_2,t_3,t_4}{\text{Max}} \left\{ V(Q) \mid \sum_{i=1}^{4} w_i t_i = b \right\}, \tag{1}$$

where $Q = \hat{f}(q_1, q_2, q_3, q_4)$; $q_1 = h_1(t_1)$, $q_i = h_i(t_i, q_{i-1})$, $i = 2, 3, 4$, and $b$ is the given budget for the project.

The assumption that the project's budget will be exhausted holds whenever additional development work has a positive marginal effect on the product and an unused portion of the budget does not increase the developer's value. One can easily convert this constrained optimization description of the problem to an unconstrained problem, where no budget constraint is given to the developer and the inputs are chosen to maximize the value net of development costs. For such a version of the model, see [23].

The relationships between the different components of the model are summarized in Figure 1.

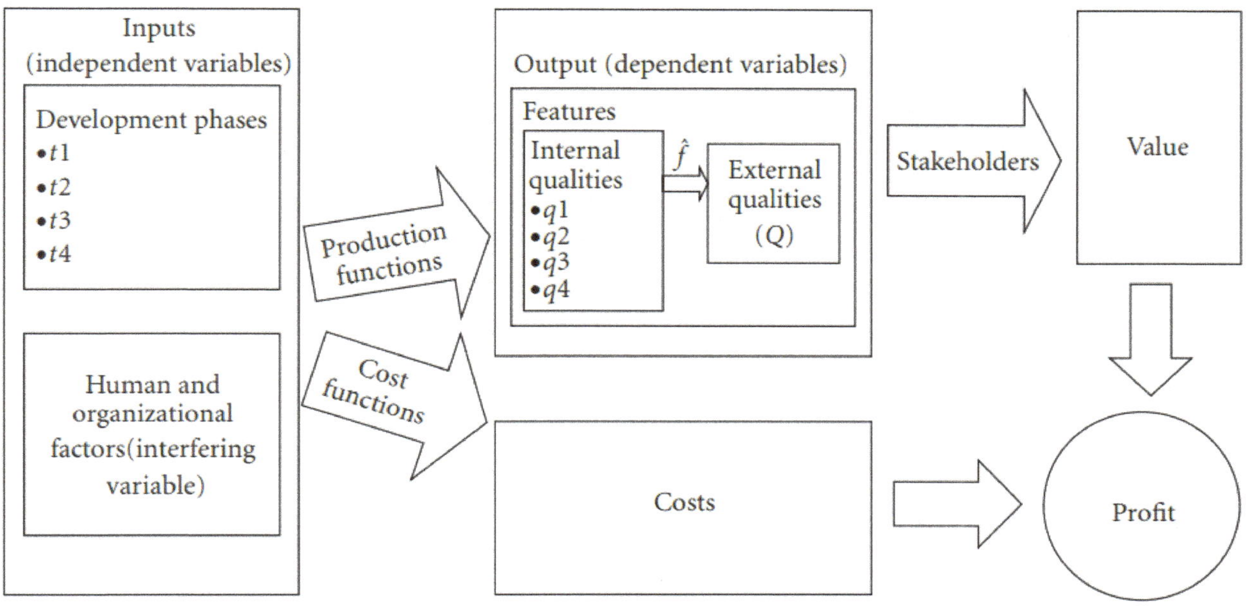


**Figure 1:** A schematic view of the economics-based approach to allocating software development resources among SDPs.

The schematic views presented in Figure 1, as well as its underlying economic model, are abstract and can be customized to suit any level of the software developing entity, by specifying appropriate rewards and cost functions.

For an individual developer or team leader, Q can include the amount of features under his responsibility and their quality. The value V(Q) will include the developer's salary and bonuses, which are assumed to be influenced by the work performed. The cost will include the alternative uses of the developer's time.

For a software developing firm, V(Q) will typically include the income generated by a development output Q, and possibly the indirect market positioning gained by having such a product available in the market at that time. The cost, at this level, is the budget devoted by the firm for developing the given product.

## The Dynamic Economic Model

Capturing the dynamic nature of software development is important for accommodating current iterative development methodologies, including incremental and even lean development such as in agile methodologies. The production function $\hat{f}$ presented in the previous subsection ignores the fact that the software development output is also influenced by the dynamic allocation of resources to different phases, rather than just by the aggregate amount of resources allocated to each phase. The richness of the dynamics of software development is explored in depth by Madachy [28]. The dynamic allocation of resources can be derived by solving a dynamic programming problem of allocating resources to development phases.

This dynamic allocation is based on an incremental quality improvement function, which describes the transformation of an existing software development output Q into its next state, Q', as a result of applying the subsequent unit of development resources to one of the phases, Q' = Q+g (Q, a). Here a ∈ {1, 2, 3, 4} indicates to which of the four development phases the next resource unit is allocated, and g (Q, a) is the change in the development output Q resulting from that allocation. Consequently, the output will be affected by the order in which subsequent resource units are allocated to the different phases, not just by the total allocated to each phase. Moreover, the dynamic allocation of development resources also allows us to stop the development process at any stage. As long as there are remaining resources available for further development, the optimal decision at each stage involves two choices: (1) to stop further development and release the product in its current form or continue the development process, (2) if development continues—to which phase to allocate the next unit of development time.

This dynamic allocation of resources to different development phases can be presented as a decision tree, as in Figure 2. The allocation of each subsequent unit of development resource to one of the phases depends on the current state of the development process, takes into account the implications of allocating the next unit to one of the phases, and recognizes that decisions on allocating subsequent resource units will be made in the future. This is the essence of the dynamic programming approach we propose for the dynamic model. The formal dynamic model can be viewed as an optimization formulation of a certain type of System Dynamics model advocated by [28].

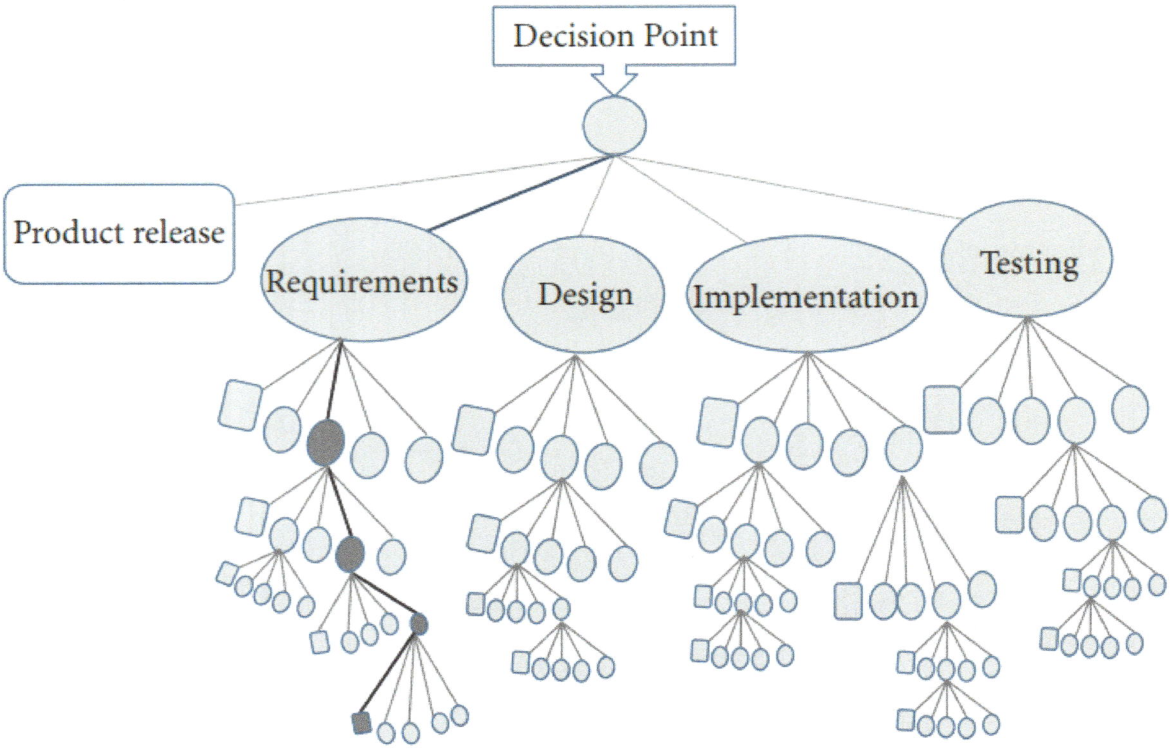


**Figure 2:** A schematic view of dynamic allocation of resources among development phases.

The main advantage of allocating resources dynamically is that it takes into account, by construction, the path of development work on each of the four phases, and not just the aggregate time spent on each phase. Furthermore, this dynamic model can be extended by including random effects that influence the transition of the development output Q or changes in available resources or the configuration of features to be included in the software product. However, in order to construct this dynamic programming formulation, one must have a valid description of the incremental quality improvement function, g, at each possible state of the software development output index.

## CHARACTERIZATION OF THE SOFTWARE DEVELOPMENT PHASES

This section characterizes the SDPs and suggests a procedure for associating each activity during the software development process with one of these phases. It further identifies two properties of the phases, which we assume to have influence on the process output.

Several well-known sources in the literature have categorized the software development phases in different ways (e.g., [2, 9, 31]). First, they have provided somewhat different lists of the phases participating in the software manufacturing process. Second, they have provided different definitions regarding which development activities belong to each phase. For example, the requirements and design phases are commonly distinguished based on viewing the requirements phase as dealing with what the software should do, while the design phase deals with how it should be done (IEEE definition, [32]). However, as pointed out by Berry [33], there are cases where it is not possible to precisely specify the what without going into the how. In such cases, attempts to measure work time allocated to each phase require a rule for determining whether a particular observed development activity should be considered as Requirements or Design. This problem is not confined to distinguishing between these two phases. It holds true as well for the Design and Implementation (e.g., writing pseudocode), Implementation and Testing phases (e.g., debugging/unit testing), and Testing and Requirements (e.g., writing tests prior to development, such as in XP methodology).

Our approach is based on identifying each atomic development activity and classifying it to one of the different development phases according to several criteria. To this end, we need a conclusive definition of the development phases and the boundaries between them, such that (1) each development activity can be classified to exactly one phase, (2) the time allocation for each phase can be measured, and (3) the quality of artifacts of each phase can be defined and measured.

To achieve this objective, each development activity was classified as belonging to a specific development phase according to the issue dealt with by the developer. We relied on the observation that each software development activity deals with one of the following four possible issues: what is to be done, how it should be done, carrying out the above how, and checking the results. Accordingly, every development activity can be uniquely mapped to one of the following phases:

- *Requirements*: the set of activities that result in a definition of what the software should do;
- *Design*: the set of activities that result in the definition of how the software should meet its requirements;
- *Implementation*: the set of activities that result in the computer program which is the physical, executable artifact that will eventually be delivered to the customer;
- *Testing:* the set of activities whose goal is to verify the implemented artifacts.

Note that activities aimed at validating the requirements or design, such as requirements review and design review, are included in the requirements and design phases, respectively.

The definitions aforementioned are based on known standards [32] and common knowledge.[5] However, as explained previously, it is still difficult to uniquely assign each activity to one of the phases. Some refinements are necessary to resolve this fuzziness and sharpen the boundaries between the phases. In what follows, we propose a direction for such refinements.

For example, with regard to the boundary between Design and Implementation, we classify everything that can be represented in the UML class diagram [9] semantics as Design, whereas anything more specific is part of the Implementation. More specifically, definitions of class hierarchy, method signatures, and class data members are classified as design, and more detailed code is classified as implementation. According to this distinction, if a piece of code is composed of one long method, for example, we assume that less design has been done than in a case in which the same functionality is composed of several shorter methods.

Unlike most works in the literature (e.g., [1, 2, 31, 32]), here we distinguish between coding and implementation. We see this distinction as the distinction between the working environments used and the actual phase to which the development activity belongs. For example, when coding a method signature, the classification of this activity to the relevant phase depends on the context. If this signature is coded according to a design document created earlier, the developer merely implements what has been defined in the design; hence this coding would be classified as an Implementation activity. However, if the developer codes the signature of a method without predetermining it in the Design, this activity should be classified as a Design activity.

This classification can be extended in light of Ralph and Wand [34], who suggest that the working phase is derived from the existing technology that can be used by the developer. If the developer deals with choosing between existing technologies, for example, implemented objects, it is considered Implementation. If the developer deals with technology that does not yet exist, for example, an object planned but still not implemented, it is considered Design. Furthermore, according to [34], we can view the collection of all the possible things we can do with the technology primitives as all the possible design alternatives, while the requirements are a constraint on this collection.

Another difficulty in associating activities with development phases stems from the developer's perspective. Consider, for example, the boundary between Requirements and Design. The requirements of a system component are actually part of the system level design. Similarly, the requirements of subcomponents constitute part of the component design. In the taxi ordering server (TOS) project used in our empirical study, for example, when thinking about how to build the system so it will meet the requirements, a decision to include a Parser component might be reasonably considered to be a part of this how, and hence a Design activity. The parser's responsibility is to check if a given text input is syntactically correct and, if it is, to build a data structure, namely, a logic representation of the text. Looking at the exact same activity when focusing on the Parser development leads to view it as requirements specification, since it deals with the capability required from this component.

In order to address this concern, we refine the above phase definitions by distinguishing between the developments phases with regard to a specific decomposition level of the system discussed. Decomposition, according to Paulson and Wand [35], is "the breakdown of a complex system into smaller, relatively independent units. It is the main tool available to simplify the construction of complex man-made systems." In our context, viewing the system as a whole, as required by the customer, defines the lowest decomposition level (level 0). Each successive breakdown, first to the system's direct components, then to their subcomponents, and so forth, defines a higher decomposition level. We define that each development activity is classified based on the issue it deals with, with respect to a specific decomposition level. Accordingly, for a given decomposition level, our definition resolves the fuzziness between the definition of what (Requirements) and how (Design). We can similarly use this decomposition analysis when assigning unit-testing activities. When considering checking of given software unit from the unit perspective, any test with regard to that unit is considered as Testing. However, viewing the same activity from the entire system's perspective will be considered as Implementation. This approach is similar to the one presented in [15, Page 160], where the analysis of project value requires multiple views that are painted using multiple measurement models. Each measurement model is like a lens, where each lens is used by an observer in order to make inferences about the properties of an object of interest.

After classifying the phases, we further characterize the development activities according to additional attributes. While there may be various such attributes, we find the following two to be the most relevant in terms of affecting the output:

- the environment in which the work is conducted. Word editor, UML tool, programming IDE, and so forth,
- latitude: the existence/nonexistence of choice regarding the next activity. Accordingly each activity can be described by one of the following:

- process-forced activity: a situation in which there is only a single choice for the next action at a given point; Such activities can be described in the context of our dynamic model (presented in Section 3) as contemporaneous choices that avoid obviously inferior outcomes;
- strategically chosen activity: the situation where there is more than one possibility for the next activity (that will positively affect the product's quality).

For example, at the beginning point of a project, the requirements phase is usually the only choice. This is a process-forced activity. However, after processing the first requirement, one has a choice to continue processing the next requirement or designing/implementing the system to meet the requirement already processed. A more common example is making Design/Requirements decisions during Implementation. This can be a process-forced activity if the developer gets stuck when writing the code, for example, when deciding what to write in the else condition of an if-else statement, or a strategically chosen activity when the developer decides in advance to leave a certain design decision to be made during Implementation.

In our empirical study, the above described attributes were identified and various combinations of them were found. In what follows we present several examples as written in the students' reflection documents (additional examples appear in [23]). Note that the emphasis in the texts was added by the authors. For each example we indicate the activity profile in the following template: [<issue>, <work environment>, <latitude>] according to the explanation above.

In the following example, a requirement activity is executed in the code environment, for the purpose of defining interfaces with an external system (activity profile: requirement, code environment, strategically chosen activity):

"I am reviewing the code in order to understand the system interface and the way it is supposed to serve the system requirements. This whole time is part of the requirements analysis. [Reflection document—John, May 15]".

In the next example, a strategic decision to design a specific element during Implementation is made, when more details are available (Activity profile: design, code environment, strategically chosen activity):

"I decided to design this [the class Configuration Manager] while dealing with the code, because this way I can think of more possibilities. For example, if I would design this using Paradigm [UML CASE tool], I would probably only think of the problems that may occur in reading the file (if it's damaged or empty) or problems in finding the file. Working with Eclipse I understand I need a class to hold parameters. There could also be a problem if one of the parameters is wrong. I didn't postpone it [the design] because of laziness; it's the dealing with the code that enables me to conclude the design required here. [Interview—Mary, August 30, regarding her May 29 Reflection]".

What follows is a different example for strategic work on Design (Activity profile: design, UML, strategically chosen activity):

"I am working on a Sequence Diagram for the process of reading data from file. The design documents are essential for understanding the code later. The code is quite complicated; it will be much easier to understand it using UML. I stopped coding in order to organize what already exists and document it in the code and the design documents. [Reflection document—Ann, July 2]".

The following example shows a requirements activity that is forcibly executed during Implementation, but not in the code environment (Activity profile: requirements, Software Requirement Specification document, forced):

"The coding phase of the requirement for order message processing and canceling, and their legality check according to certain parameters, obligates me to go back to the requirements document and understand these requirements better than I did in the initial stage of the project. [Reflection document—John, June 29]".

The importance of the solution presented in this section lies in reducing the fuzziness of the development phase definitions as they appear in the literature. We illustrated how each activity in the development process can be classified into one of the four phases according to the suggested definitions, employing a multidecomposition level structure. For a given decomposition level, activities can be allocated definitively to a development phase. Accordingly, it is now possible to produce a clear set of instructions for measuring time allocated to the different phases. Note that the guidelines presented in this section are not the only solution possible; their importance lies in their consistency. Whatever boundaries are defined to separate the phases, they should be consistent.

In addition, we suggest that the contribution of each time unit invested in a certain development phase is determined not merely by the issue dealt with by the developer but also by the specific profile of related attributes: environment and latitude. The possible combinations of these attributes may bring to numerous decision variables. Therefore, identifying which of these attributes substantially influences the output is helpful in quantifying the development effort.

## CHARACTERIZATION OF THE SOFTWARE DEVELOPMENT OUTPUT

This section proposes an approach towards a measurable definition of the software development output in a way that reflects what is produced and what will ultimately be used by the customer. This approach can be seen in contrast to, for example, an output measure based on the number of lines of code—which is of no interest to the customer.

Following the VBSE approach, note the distinction in our economic model between the definitions of software development output and the value derived from that output. The former is defined in terms of the product's properties, whereas the latter is based on how the output is perceived by the relevant stakeholder. This section deals only with defining the software development output. The output is a fundamental concept, whose definition must underlie any formulation and estimation of production, value, and cost functions.

Finding an appropriate output definition may also contribute to other areas of software engineering management [36]. Finding a way to measure how much software is produced will allow analyzing and comparing the productivity of different manufacturers, projects, development strategies, and invested resources. It will facilitate project planning, cost estimations, and so forth.

At the root of the difficulty in defining and measuring software output is the fact that software engineering deals with the development of a single prototype rather than mass production of identical goods. A basic and common approach for measuring output is the notorious lines of code (LOC) measure, which does not reflect the essence of the product, as noted previously. A more advanced approach is the function points (FPs) measure [2], reflecting the volume of the software functionality. The problem with this and similar approaches is that they do not take into account the quality of the product, as noted by Sommerville [31]. Recent approaches that do take quality into economic consideration (e.g., [8, 10, 11, 30]) deal only with specific aspects of quality, such as bugs per volume unit (as measured in LOC or FP terms), and do not deal with the problem of resource allocation among SDPs to improve this measure.

The output of the software manufacturer is defined here as a combination of software features and their qualities. We use the term feature to denote the software volume unit(s) that produces a particular functionality (note that this differs from the IEEE definition). Accordingly, a feature is an application capability that can be measured and weighted according to its importance for a representative user. Naturally, a feature may be decomposed into subfeatures. Although there are several ways to characterize a feature (volume unit), for example, the function points methodology [2], the object points methodology [2], or end-user features specified informally as "stories," [6], the characterization of the feature does not affect our approach to the resource allocation problem. For the sake of simplicity, we illustrate our approach for a single feature.

For quality modeling we use the notation of ISO 9126 [25, 37–39], which lists six main quality characteristics: Functionality, Reliability, Usability, Efficiency, Maintainability, and Portability. The quality is first examined from the customer's perspective, denoted as external quality. We assume that the customer combines the software features and the above six quality characteristics in what we call the software product matrix (SPM) presented in Figure 3.

| Features / Quality factors | Feature 1 | | Feature 2 | | | | Feature 3 | Feature 4 | | | . . . |
|---|---|---|---|---|---|---|---|---|---|---|---|
| | Feature 1.1 | Feature 1.2 | Feature 2.1 | Feature 2.2 | Feature 2.3 | Feature 2.4 | | Feature 4.1 | Feature 4.2 | Feature 4.3 | |
| Functionality | | | | | | | | | | | |
| Reliability | | | | | | | | | | | |
| Usability | | | | | | | | | | | |
| Portability | | | | | | | | | | | |
| Efficiency | | | | | | | | | | | |
| Maintainability | | | | | | | | | | | |

**Figure 3:** An example of the Software Product Matrix (SPM).

Columns in the SPM represent different functional features of the software product. Rows correspond to the external qualities of the above six characteristics.

Each numeric entry in the SPM represents the measure of the corresponding row's quality characteristic for a given column's functional feature. Each subfeature and each quality subcharacteristic can be further decomposed, with appropriate weights [37, 38]. Some quality attributes, for example, Portability, may not be decomposable for all software features. Some of the entries may be nonapplicable when a certain quality factor is irrelevant for a particular feature.

The output of each of the four main development phases contributes in a different way to the different factors of the external quality. We formalize these contributions in terms of phase artifact qualities, which can be presented along a third dimension of the SPM matrix. This quality definition fits the ISO 9126 notation of internal quality, which refers to static properties of software that are considered independently of its execution (see [25] for more details).

Figure 4 presents a schematic view of the interrelationships between the 2-dimensional SPM and the development work along the different phases. This relationship is presented as a 3-dimensional matrix, called the phase contribution box.

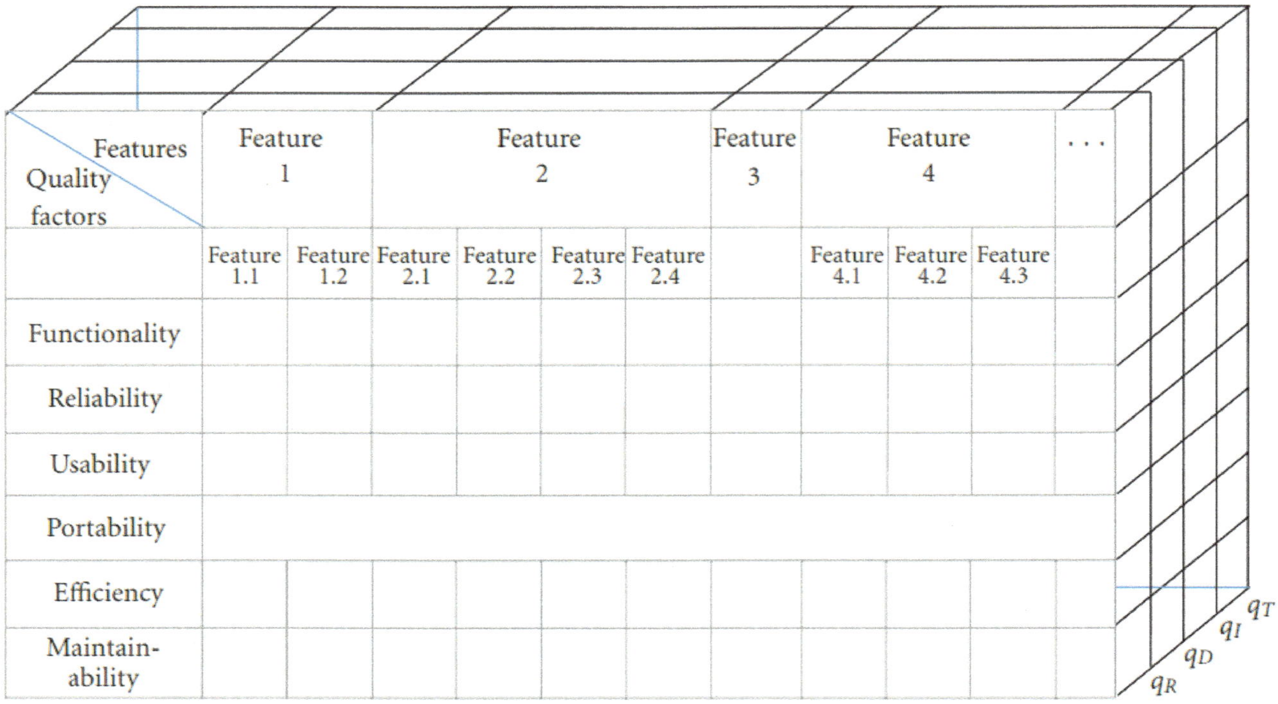


**Figure 4:** Example of the phase contribution box.

## External Quality Characterization

An external quality of a given software feature is defined by quality characteristics, which are used to evaluate the software behavior during execution from the user's point of view, with regard to this feature. The key to correct assessment of the quality factors is a comprehensive and properly weighted list of scenarios. This list should represent typical loads or stress tests under which the product should perform. The tests include running the software to obtain performance scores as well as experimenting with, for example, product modifications or portability to different operating systems.

A quality factor in general is a decomposable entity. It is composed of subfactors, each having a relative importance (weight). These subfactors, in turn, can be further decomposed. Thus, when discussing quality we refer to two elements: quality factors and their weighting [37, 38]. Weighting is largely affected by system usage, as illustrated in usage-based statistical testing techniques such as the Cleanroom approach [40].

A software developer is usually not explicitly aware of all the ISO quality characteristics or of their relative importance in the particular product being developed. However, given the accepted assumptions of the economics of uncertainty models, we assume that the developer behaves as if s/he does know them.

In our empirical study we created an artificial setting in which a taxi ordering server (TOS) application's quality factors and their weightings were explicitly defined to the students developing it. The factors and their weightings were handed to the developers only down to a certain level, below which they had to "guess" the relative weightings. Figure 5 illustrates this notion by means of a directed tree representing the artificial setting of the empirical study in terms of quality definitions. The nodes of the tree represent the quality factors. Descendants of a node in the tree represent its subfactors. The weightings on the arcs represent the relative importance of each quality factor.

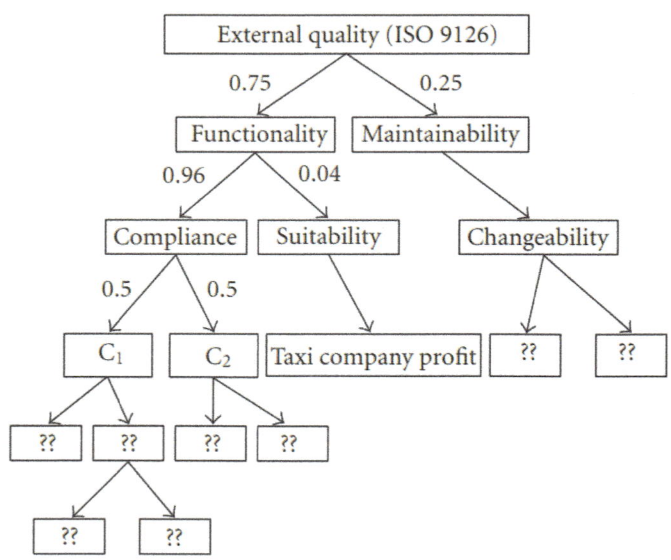


**Figure 5:** A directed tree representing the TOS external quality.

According to ISO 9126, the quality factor Functionality consists of the subfactors' Suitability, Accurateness, Interoperability, Compliance, and Security. In our study, only Compliance and Suitability have positive weights (0.96 and 0.04, resp.). Suitability is defined by ISO 9126 as "Attributes of software that bear on the presence and appropriateness of a set of functions for specified tasks" and Compliance is defined as "attributes of software that make the software adhere to application-related standards or conventions or regulations in laws and similar prescriptions" [25].

Using this general definition of Compliance, we divided the Compliance quality subfactors into two subfactors: $C_1$, the degree to which the application adheres to related standards in the case of correct inputs, and $C_2$, a similar measure of the application's response to incorrect inputs. We assigned equal weights to each of these subfactors

Thus far, we have seen the upper levels of external quality, explicitly defined for the students. Lower levels are assumed to have been defined by the students individually within the general definitions given for the upper levels. That is, in accordance with economic theory, we assume that the students make an educated guess regarding these subfactors and their weights or understand them without necessarily being aware of it.

Down the tree one can find quality subfactors relating to a more specific set of requirements. For instance, down the subtree spread under the subfactor $C_2$, one can find, for example, a quality factor at the (almost) lowest level, defined as the ability to adhere to the application-related standards in case of incorrect syntactic inputs originating from more than one space left between the words (tokens) in the passenger's message.

We assume that the relative importance of each of the external quality factors stems from the customer utility function and that they all "diffuse" into the developer's mind via the product demand function. We also assume that a rational software developer would try to make sure that his/her weighting evaluation is as accurate as possible. At the firm level, statistical testing techniques, such as in the Cleanroom approach [40], might be available. However, the individual developer tries to understand the importance of each quality subfactor using available means. This notion is well illustrated in an e-mail sent by one of the students, John, when trying to gather information from the "customer":

"[...] My question: is it critical to check that there is only a single space character between 2 words or is it less critical and therefore can be ignored, so I can move to implement other more critical functionalities? [Email—John, August 1st]".

In the above example, we see that John identified an implicit quality subfactor and tried to obtain information about its importance. That is, he understood that having more than one space between two tokens in the passenger's message is a syntax error; however, as he was very busy, he justly considered whether he should invest his time handling this error or continue to work on more important (i.e., more valuable) tasks. This example is consistent with our assumption that the software development process is a rational process of allocating resources for producing maximum quality units.

Generally, student behavior was consistent with the basic assumption that development resources are allocated primarily to achieve the highest possible quality measures. All students expressed time and again in their reflection documents their desire to increase (certain aspects of) quality when describing their decisions to move between development phases. This finding is consistent with [41], reporting that the external quality of software is the most important factor in the evaluation models of senior IS managers.

## Internal Quality Characterization

According to the ISO 9126 standard [25], internal quality is measured using internal metrics, which apply to static properties of software that are considered independently of its execution. Our approach associates internal quality with phase artifact quality. Internal quality measures quantify the artifacts produced by different development phases.

Our method for evaluating phase artifact quality is to do it feature by feature. We look at any particular feature and evaluate the contribution of each of the four development phase artifacts to each of its six external quality factors. This is analogous to slicing our phase contribution box along a fixed feature and extracting a 2-dimensional matrix. We call it the feature qualities matrix (FQM). A schematic view of this matrix is presented in Figure 6.

| | Functionality | Reliability | Usability | Portability | Efficiency | Maintain-ability |
|---|---|---|---|---|---|---|
| $q_R$ | | | | | | |
| $q_D$ | | | | | | |
| $q_I$ | | | | | | |
| $q_T$ | | | | | | |
| External quality (Q) | | | | | | |

**Figure 6:** A schematic view of the FQM.

In the upper four rows of the matrix, cell (i, j) contains the contribution of the artifact quality of the ith phase on the jth external quality factor. These four rows show artifact qualities of the four development phases with respect to the different quality factors. Naturally, for a given quality factor (column), the different qualities of each of the four phases are assumed to affect the external quality. The bottom row of the FQM holds the scores of the feature's external qualities.

The main challenge here is to devise sensible measures for each of the FQM internal quality cells, for measuring the contribution of each phase's artifact to the external quality. This will provide a practical means to estimate the assumed functional relation between the internal qualities and the external quality (see the definition of the function $\hat{f}$ in Section 3). These measures should be consistent with the phase definitions, so that it will be possible to estimate the functional relation between the resources allocated to a certain phase and the quality of this phase's artifact.

In what follows we illustrate how one can go about filling in the entries of the FQM. This illustration is based on the measurements taken in our empirical study [23].

In filling in the phase artifact cells for the Maintainability column, for example, one should consider how to define internal metrics for each of the four phases. The literature suggests many static evaluation methods for software Maintainability (e.g., [42–46]). Let us consider the effect of the quality of the Design phase artifact on Maintainability (the second cell of the Maintainability column in Figure 6). The metric to be selected should include factors such as documentation, modularity, and legibility, which will also be assigned weights.

Lindroos [42] summarizes several static metrics for the evaluation of Maintainability that seem highly connected with the external maintainability factor. Among the metrics listed by Lindroos, coupling between objects (CBOs) and response for a class (RFC) seem to be good candidates to be included in the evaluation metrics of modularity (via encapsulation), which bear high significance in maintainability.

The CBO score of a class is the number of classes to which the class under consideration is coupled. A high coupling measure has a detrimental effect on modularity and the ability to reuse the class in the future. The higher the coupling measure, the higher the sensitivity of the design to changes; that is, more effort is required for modification, fault removal, or environmental change (all ISO criteria for the evaluation of Changeability, which is one of the sub-characteristics of Maintainability). Therefore, the CBO measure is assumed to affect the external Maintainability score. In particular, CBO reflects the contribution of the design phase (as defined in Section 4) to Maintainability, as it refers to issues that can be represented by the class diagram semantics.

Other metrics for evaluating the contribution of the Design artifact to Maintainability may include the documentation of the design, that is, how exhaustive and well-written the software design document is, to what extent the design complies with the requirements, and how well the UML diagrams (if used) reflect the actual design as it appears in the code.

The cells reflecting the contribution of the three other phases on Maintainability can be examined in the same way. For instance, metrics for code modularity and documentation will probably be among the factors used to evaluate the effect of the Implementation's artifact on Maintainability (the third cell of the Maintainability column in Figure 6). Metrics such as the popular Maintainability Index (MI) [47], or metrics included in this index, such as the Halstead Complexity measures or the McCabe Cyclomatic Complexity measure, might be appropriate here since the aspects of Implementation they deal with do influence Maintainability. For example, a high value for the McCabe Cyclomatic measure indicates high code complexity, which makes the program less maintainable.

The challenge of finding metrics consistent with the definitions of development phases is indeed difficult to realize. One problem is developing metrics that strictly differentiate between Design and Implementation. The MI, for example, seems to evaluate elements linked to both Design and Implementation. However, given our suggested distinction between these two phases—everything that can be represented in the class diagram semantics is considered as part of the Design, whereas anything more specific in that context is part of the Implementation—the CBO indeed evaluates the quality of the Design, as it measures the relations among classes. Likewise, the McCabe index indeed evaluates Implementation. It should be emphasized, however, that the CBO cannot serve as the only metric for Design modularity and should be combined with other metrics.

Thus far we have examined the effect of the qualities of the artifacts of the different phases on Maintainability. For this purpose, we have not gone into the nuances of the distinctions between the various subfactors of Maintainability, since it is reasonable to assume a high correlation between the effect of an internal index on Analyzability, for instance, and its effect on Changeability or Testability. However, this is not necessarily the case for the other five ISO 9126 external quality factors. In the case of Functionality, for example, the distinction between the different subfactors is very important. For instance, the effect of the phase artifacts' qualities on Compliance is different from their effect on Suitability or Accurateness.

Let us consider the effect of the development phase artifacts on the Compliance factor. As suggested in the previous subsection, the external quality of this factor can be measured by the appropriate response of the software to different types of input. The metric evaluating external Compliance, therefore, examines the fulfillment of the external functional requirements. This examination results in a collection of test cases. For each of these test cases, the application can be operated under a quality checker to examine whether the required functionality has indeed been fulfilled. The external Compliance score consists of the weighted percentage of the cases that passed the test.

In order to fill in the four cells representing the effect of the different phase artifacts on the external Compliance, we have to statically evaluate the contribution of each phase to the external Compliance score, that is, to evaluate what percentage of the tests will pass. This can be done by defining the collection of required functions of the given feature.

The effect of the Requirements artifact on Compliance can be measured by examining what percentage of the required functions have been specified as functional requirements and their quality in terms of consistency, completeness, and unambiguity. The effect of the Design artifact on Compliance can be measured in part by examining what percentage of the required functions have been given solutions in the design documents. Similar metrics should be used for Implementation (by considering what percentage of the required functioned is actually implemented in the code) and Testing (by examining functional coverage).

The remaining cells in the FQM can be filled and applied for each feature of a given software product, gradually filling the entire phase contribution box for the output evaluation of the entire software, and thus quantifying the contribution of each phase to each of the external quality factors.

## Summary

This section characterizes software development output as a bundle of features, each of them provided at a certain quality level. We explained the principle of defining quality in the scope of a single feature, based on the ISO 9126 quality model. We emphasized the distinction between phase artifact quality (internal quality) and the quality as perceived by the customer (external quality). We exemplified this principle by presenting internal and external quality metrics for a small subset of ISO 9126 quality characteristics as measured in our empirical study (see [23]). We presented a workable framework, called the feature qualities matrix (FQM), which organizes all quality scores of a given feature.

Each cell in the FQM matrix holds a certain quality score of the feature, based on predefined heuristic. We demonstrated how to define measurable metrics for several cells in the FQM while focusing on Functionality and Maintainability. The demonstration was based on students' projects. However, in this specific sense we see no major difference from real, industrial projects. The practice of measuring coupling between objects (CBOs) as a metric for evaluating the effect of the design quality on maintainability or the Maintainability Index (MI) as a metric for evaluating the effect of the implementation is independent of the projects' scale. Thus we find the external validity intact in this context.

The evaluation of other cells in the FQM can in practice be done similarly, based on the presented guidelines. For example, consider the quality factor of Efficiency, which was not demonstrated. According to ISO 9126, "time behavior" is one of the subcharacteristics of Efficiency. In algorithmic oriented features, the external quality of time behavior is based on processing and response times. The effect of Design on time behavior will be measured by means of the algorithm's time complexity. The effect of Implementation will be measured by static code analysis metrics. As a simple example, consider a C++ metric that counts instances of function parameters, which are too big and would be better handled via references.

Having a metrics for all the cells of the FQM is not required for its practical use. Some software development teams receive the requirements specification as a mature and processed document. Such teams can ignore the Requirements row of the matrix. Likewise, for some software projects the Portability or the Usability factors may not be applicable. Focusing on the internal and external qualities of the ISO 9126 subfactors that are most relevant for the feature can make the FQM a practical tool for storing and organizing quality data. The output evaluation presented in this section can be extended beyond the scope of a single feature by incorporating into our framework a methodology for distinguishing between features and weighting them, using, for example, the function points methodology [2]. Accordingly, we believe that software development output can indeed be defined in sensible and measurable units. Building a CASE tool for handling output evaluation will undoubtedly help reduce the complexity of this evaluation process.

## PROPERTIES OF THE SOFTWARE PRODUCTION FUNCTION

The previous two sections dealt with the characterization of the economic model's variables. This section discusses the nature of the relationships between the dependent and independent variables. Since a comprehensive formulation of production functions should be based on a vast empirical basis which has yet to be built, this section only illustrates what can be learned about the theoretical model from empirical studies and how that model can help in interpreting the developers' observed conduct in experimental settings.

While the mathematical structures of these production functions were not fully characterized in this research, we maintain the assumption that such underlying functions do exist. The empirical study yielded some inferences about the functional forms of the relationships between work on development phases and the resulting development output. This section presents two key characteristics that emerged from this study regarding the nature of these functions: substitutability among development phases and decreasing marginal product.

### Substitution among Production Factors

The economic model proposed in Section 3 relies on knowing how different combinations of inputs, in the form of working hours invested in the Requirement, Design, Implementation, and Testing, affect the resulting software. More specifically, it is assumed that the software developer has the latitude to increase one of the inputs while decreasing the other or choose alternative sequences of time allocations among the phases, without changing the output index score of the produced software.

The curve in Figure 7 is a schematic picture of all combinations of two inputs, (holding the level of other inputs fixed), that yield the same output, known in economics as isoquant. Each isoquant is indexed by the constant level of output it represents, $Q_1 < Q_2$, and so forth. The existence of such a curve reflects the substitutability of production factors. Its downward slope indicates that if you scale down the use of one of the input factors, you need to scale up the use of another factor in order to preserve the same output. This ability to use alternative combinations of production factors allows the developer to choose the least costly combination of inputs that produces the desired output.

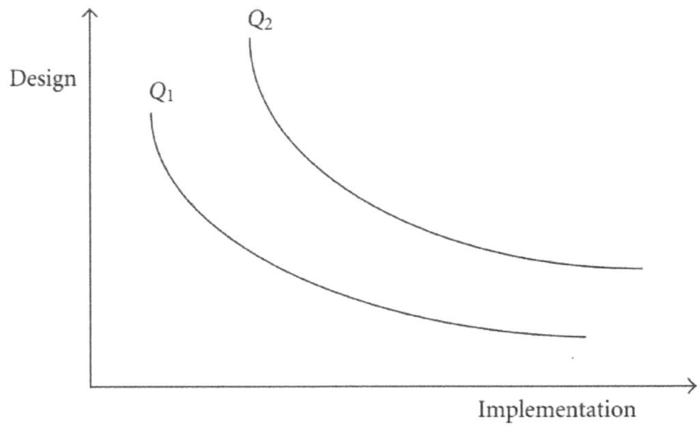


**Figure 7:** Schematic visualization of substitution in software production functions.

In the empirical study, we made two observations with regard to the nature of this substitution. One was the fact that developers chose vastly different input combinations and yet managed to produce similar outputs. This observation supports the general idea that one can produce a particular software product by different combinations of inputs. Thus, a nontrivial decision must be made here, namely, which input combination yields the highest return to the developer. The degree of substitution present among SDPs in performing a particular task depends on the aggregation level of the task. More elementary tasks allow less substitution among phases, down to, for instance, multiplying two numbers. Such a task still requires some requirement analysis, for example, whether the numbers are real, integers, or complex numbers, and some design work on alternative ways to carry out the requirement, with very limited substitution between them. On the other extreme, a large multifeatured software product admits a large degree of substitution among phases, including shifting among phases associated with different features or different quality characteristics.

Our second observation was that personal attributes of the developer can influence the degree of substitutability among the development phases.

Here is an example of how substitution is affected by Java development experience:

"In the beginning of the project I used to perform many tests, since I had no confidence in my programming. Now that I have more experience working with Java language, I don't perform as many tests as I used to; I know how to conduct Unit Testing more efficiently. [Interview—Mary, August 30]".

## Decreasing Marginal Product

Production processes having this property exhibit decreasing returns as one of the inputs is increased while holding other inputs constant. Such processes usually imply the desirability of an internal allocation of resources, with some positive amount of each input. As more and more resources are allocated to the same input, the improvement obtained becomes smaller, until at some point it pays off to shift resources to another input. This is known in economics as decreasing marginal product. In the context of a dynamic production process, this property determines when to shift the allocation of resources among inputs, and how much to allocate to each input.

In static optimization problems, the decreasing marginal product property is a necessary condition for concavity. Concave optimization problems can be solved by means of first order conditions. Moreover, their solutions are typically continuous functions of the parameters of the problem, allowing for straight forward sensitivity analysis of the solution with respect to parameters of the problem. Thus, to the extent that such functional structure is validated by empirical studies, the optimization model becomes a handy tool for extracting the optimal allocation of resources. The decreasing slope of the isoquants in Figure 7 reflects the decreasing returns property of each input in isolation.

In fact, availability of analytical solutions to the resource allocation problem is not essential given the advance of simulation-based models. Such models can be augmented by expanding the software production process module, according to the software production function proposed in this paper. Thus, the impact of alternative allocations of resources on various aspects of the developed output can be traced via simulations, along with its interactions with other aspects of managing the software project.

Our observations are consistent with the decreasing marginal product of working time allocated to each of the phases. Throughout the development process, the students usually moved from one phase to another when they felt that the previous phase's quality is satisfactory and their resources will have a higher contribution if applied to a different phase at that point. This notion is clearly exemplified in Ann's report on her shift from Design to Implementation:

"I moved to Implementation after achieving a reasonable level of the UML documents relative to the time I have left to complete the project. [Reflection document—Ann, May 26]".

In a follow-up clarification Ann was asked to explain what she meant by "reasonable level of UML documents," and this was her response:

"Reasonable level [of UML documents means]: a description of 2 basic functions and their sequence; which class performs which function; organizing the functionality according to a logical, sense-making, order. It's enough for me to describe the basic functions at this stage in addition to the main functions and not develop on paper [that is, in the UML diagrams as opposed to the code environment] all the functions, because I don't have enough time for it. [Ann, May 26]".

Ann clearly has a firm perception of what "reasonable level of design" means. She is also well aware of the time constraint. It seems that what she had determined as reasonable level of design is the design construction up to the point where the marginal product generated by an additional time-unit of Design is lower than the marginal product of Implementation. That is, given the current state of her development, her next working hour will yield higher return in Implementation than in Design, because she already made significant headway in Design.

This phenomenon was observed repeatedly with respect to all students in the study. Here is another example:

"Completed the Design of methods and parameters to be implemented to an adequate level and moved on to Implementation of methods' code [Reflection document—John, June 5]."

Nonetheless, we also observed shifts from one phase to the next, when the developer explicitly acknowledges that the previous phase is incomplete. For example,

"Due to time limitations I stopped at the stage of basic definition of the Requirements and did not go into its depth. I defined major functions and their respective tasks, and the data structures. If I had more time, I would have gone into more detail. [Reflection document—Ann, May 11]".

The shift from one phase to another despite recognized imperfections in the former, as opposed to completing one phase before moving to the next, is consistent with allocating development resources to activities that yield the highest marginal contribution.

## USING THE MODEL TO ANALYZE DEVELOPER DECISIONS

The model presented in this paper provides a framework within which we can analyze various developer decisions made at different points in the development process, identify the reasons for these decisions, and suggest how to improve them in future projects. We exemplify these capabilities of the model by analyzing suboptimal decisions made by the students developing the software in our empirical setting.

We have identified cases where the time allocation decisions made by the students were clearly not consistent with the model and indeed led to poor results in which students received zero scores on Functionality (during interim project submissions). In order to understand this result and the developers' conduct preceding it, we investigated the sources of the mistaken allocation decisions and arrived at the following possible reasons for them.

- The students failed to allocate sufficient time to Requirements and Testing. For example, mistakes in the format of the response message sent by the TOS to an incoming order request, a common reason for getting a zero score by the quality checker, could have been avoided by reading the requirements more carefully. Likewise, the software developed by some of the students failed to detect incorrect inputs despite our explicit instruction to detect them and respond with appropriate error messages. A main reason for this failure was that developers neglected to include appropriate tests of incoming orders.
- Given that the students had been informed that Functionality would account for 75% of their product's external quality (i.e., a major part of their course grade), they naturally tended to invest much effort in it. However, we found that some of them perceived Functionality improvement as stemming almost exclusively from time spent on Implementation, failing to appreciate the contribution of other development phases to this software quality factor. Thus, allocating time to Requirements and Design would have resulted, in their opinion, only in an increase of the Maintainability factor, which accounted for only 25% of the external quality. Moreover, we found that students invested time in infrastructural activities (e.g., writing a proper requirements document in the requirements phase, writing a UML diagram properly describing the design and other documents laying out the design rationale, and writing a test plan for the testing phase), mainly when forced to do so. For example, in an interview, Mary said "I considered writing a design document. Since you did not say it's a must, and I thought it will take me too much time, I decided not produce it after all."
- The students tended to overinvest in the Suitability aspect of Functionality at the expense of Compliance, though the latter had been defined as a much more important component of Functionality. Suitability was measured by the profits generated by the TOS scheduler, whereas Compliance was measured by the percentage of appropriate responses of the software to correct and incorrect sets of inputs. Not only was the weight of Compliance 24 times higher than that of Suitability (96% versus 4% of the Functionality grade, respectively, as was explicitly explained in the project description given to the students), but also the marginal impact of profits on Suitability was decreasing, thus resulting in very low profit in return for the time invested. After the development process was complete, we examined students' motivations while attempting to identify what caused such poor results. Our examination revealed that some students simply did not understand the quality definitions, while others did, but knowingly chose to operate differently. For example, in a follow-up interview Ann said "I was aware of the weights given to different quality factors, but personally the scheduling function was the one that challenged and interested me the most." This case exemplifies a developer maximizing her own individual objective function, which deviates from the objective function given.
- The students tended not to use helpful software tools with which they were not familiar. It appears that they ascribe more importance to evident time costs than to the unknown efficiency gains. Consequently, they may allocate too much time to developing new "tools" instead of using available ones, and this often distorts their decision as to how to allocate time among the development phases. For example, in order to apply syntax checking for incoming messages, some of the students chose to develop their own parser rather than use the existing software package supplied by Java (i.e., the regex package). This was a clear error, since using regex would have been more efficient.
- Cognitive aspects such as attention span, concentration ability, memory capacity, and diligence seem to have significant influence on the chosen allocation of time resources. For example, in many cases students chose their next activity according to how concentrated/tired they felt at that time or due to a concern that they might forget to conduct a certain activity at a later stage.

We believe that the relevance of the value-based underpinning of this work extends beyond the scope of the field-study presented in this paper. It is our working assumption that each software developer should operate to increase the product's external quality, since this is the factor that drives the demand for the product. Accordingly, development process decisions should be taken while considering their consequences in terms of external quality. In cases where external quality properties are practically not measurable, we suggest to use internal quality instead. Future research may estimate the functional relations between internal and external qualities, to yield proxies of the project's external qualities based on simple measurements of internal qualities.

## CONCLUSIONS AND FUTURE WORK

Optimal allocation of resources among software development phases is a complicated problem that has not been addressed systematically, despite its possible ramifications for software project quality and cost. The research framework presents two goals for addressing this problem. The first is to enhance our understanding of resource allocation decisions, their complex nature, and their influence on the output. The second goal, which will be handled in the long-term on the basis of this and future research, is prescriptive: proposing how to modify existing resource allocation approaches or develop new ones, in order to improve the productivity of the software development processes.

This paper presents an economics-based approach for studying this problem. The underlying assumptions of our work have been that it is feasible and useful to treat resource allocation among SDPs as rational decisions whose aim is to maximize a well-defined objective, and that these allocation decisions should be based upon measurable notions of inputs, outputs, costs, and resulting quality.

Our approach is structured along two axes: theoretical and empirical, building and refining a theoretical model based on empirical data. The paper presents the first steps conducted on these two axes. We have developed an economic model for analyzing the resource allocation problem as a constrained maximization problem and characterized its main building blocks: input in the form of work performed in different SDPs, software development output, and the software production function, which maps inputs into outputs. We have constructed an empirical environment for evaluating and refining the model, and conducted the first empirical study for examining software developers' time allocation decisions and their resulting output.

The empirical study was quite limited in its setting compared to typical projects in the software industry. First, our subjects were students rather than professional software developers, which was a limitation dictated by the need to let them all develop the same product (according to an identical set of customer requirements). However, Kitchenham et al. [19] argue that using students as subjects instead of software engineers is not a major problem (as long as the researchers are not specifically interested in experts). Second, the students worked individually, as 1-person teams, which is a limited simulation of real development teams in industry. However, our focus here is on variables and tradeoffs in decision-making processes at the individual level. Regardless of these limitations and the simplicity of the empirical setting, we have learned much about the nature of the variables and functions of the model as well as its practical application that could not have been obtained without the empirical evidence generated by this study.

To validate our approach and the proposed model, the following questions must be answered.

- Can each activity during the development process be appropriately classified into one of the development phases?
- Can the software development output be defined in measurable units which capture what the producer develops and what is consumed by the consumer?
- Is there a systematic relationship among the resources allocated to different SDPs and the resulting output?

We found positive answers to each of these questions, although more work is needed to refine the specifications of the model's components. These answers were spelled out in Sections 4, 5, and 6, where we characterized the model components and described the empirical study using the first version of the measurement tools we have developed.

We regard the work presented here as an illustrative first step. Its novelty lies in casting the resource allocation among SDPs as a familiar economic optimization problem, utilizing standard economic analytical tools, while developing the underlying concept of the software production function along with empirical methods for its evaluation. The usefulness of our approach will increase as we improve measurements of inputs and outputs and accumulate more reliable information about, and estimations of, the mathematical relationships among variables embedded in the software production function.

Even at this illustrative stage, our work demonstrates the usefulness of the model as an evaluation tool. For example, the feature qualities matrix (FQM), or even a subset of it, can be used as a practical tool for storing and organizing data regarding comprehensive aspects of the developed software quality.

The reasoning of the software production function can also be helpful in practice. Development organizations that will keep data of inputs and outputs across different versions of the same product, or across different features from the same family, may find systematic relations between them and improve their analytic capabilities.

We found in the developers' behavior within our study support for the underlying assumption of rational process for maximizing a quality-based goal function. On the other hand, we found significant and systematic deviations between actual allocations of resources among SDPs and those prescribed by the model and were able to use the model to identify some of the sources of these deviations.

In addition to indications supporting our model, we find that the model should be refined in several ways. For instance, more emphasis should be put on the allocation of resources to different features in the required application and on the order in which these features should be developed. We have observed that decisions regarding time allocation among features are made together with those regarding resource allocation among development phases. We can view each feature as having its own production function, and extend the model to include combinations of features and phases. Namely, each decision will refer to both: to which feature and to which phase to allocate the next time unit. Future work may use Function Points Analysis for deeper characterization of the term feature. Recent work such as the one by Batista et al. [48] can be helpful for this regard.

Our approach can also indirectly contribute to related fields in software engineering. For instance, phase-sensitive versions of the cost estimation model [3] will yield sharper and more accurate project effort and cost estimates, by adopting the phase characterizations presented in Section 4. A straightforward extension of our economic models can be used to model and analyze the optimal output level for releasing the software, thus contributing to the discipline of Release Engineering (e.g., [15, Chapter 9], and [49]). Future work should strive to further sharpen the characterization of variables in the model and estimate the relationships embedded in it, paying special attention to the incentive mechanisms under which software developers operate.

Additional work is needed to further formalize the characterization of the development phases and combine it with industrial development methods such as the RUP model (see [2, 13]). The characterization of the output should be concretized further by taking into account the different features embedded in a software product, using Function Point counting [2], and by developing a method for measuring and weighing subfeatures and their qualities. This will facilitate the comparison between different philosophies underlying alternative resource allocation strategies, even across different software projects.

Our proposed definition of internal qualities as phase artifact qualities should be augmented by metrics that capture the contribution of each development phase to each of the external quality characteristics. This can be accomplished, as illustrated in this work, by filling in more entries in the FQM, which organizes the quality scores in the context of a single feature.

We believe that a large part of software development consists of systematic work along well-defined routes, with measurable inputs and outputs. Our work demonstrates that that portion, at least, can be analyzed and improved upon as done for other production processes.

## ACKNOWLEDGMENTS

The authors gratefully acknowledge the financial support and encouragement of the Caesarea Rothschild Foundation Institute for Interdisciplinary Applications of Computer Science (C.R.I.) at the University of Haifa. The authors wish to thank Daniel Berry, Yair Wand, and Regev Porat for their contributions to this research.

## REFERENCES

1. S. R. Schach, Object-Oriented and Classical Software Engineering, McGraw-Hill, New York, NY, USA, 5th edition, 2002.
2. B. W. Boehm, C. Abts, A. W. Brown, et al., Software Cost Estimation with COCOMO II, Prentice-Hall, Englewood Cliffs, NJ, USA, 2000.
3. B. W. Boehm, Software Engineering Economics, Prentice-Hall, Englewood Cliffs, NJ, USA, 1981.
4. G. Smith and L. Wildman, "Model checking Z specifications using SAL," in the International Conference of Z and B Users (ZB '05), H. Treharne, S. King, M. Henson, and S. Schneider, Eds., pp. 87–105, Springer, 2005.
5. K. Beck, Extreme Programming Explained: Embrace Change, Addison-Wesley, Boston, Mass, USA, 2000.
6. H. Erdogmus, M. Morisio, and M. Torchiano, "On the effectiveness of the test-first approach to programming," IEEE Transactions on Software Engineering, vol. 31, no. 3, pp. 226–237, 2005.
7. G. Tassey, The Economic Impacts of Inadequate Infrastructure for Software Testing, National Institute of Standards and Technology, 2002.
8. P. Jalote and B. Vishal, "Optimal resource allocation for the quality control process," in Proceedings of the 14th International Symposium on Software Reliability Engineering, Denver, Colo, USA, November 2003.
9. S. R. Schach, Introduction to Object-Related Analysis and Design, McGraw-Hill, New York, NY, USA, 2004.
10. B. Steece, S. Chulani, and B. Boehm, "Determining software quality using COQUALMO," in Case Studies in Reliability and Maintenance, W Blischke and D Murthy, Eds., Wiley, Sidney, Australia, 2002.
11. E. K. Emam, The ROI from Software Quality, Auerbach Publications, Boston, Mass, USA, 2005.
12. Y. Yang, M. He, M. Li, Q. Wang, and B. Boehm, "Phase distribution of software development effort," inProceedings of the 2nd ACM-IEEE International Symposium on Empirical Software Engineering and Measurement, pp. 61–69, Kaiserslautern, Germany, 2008.
13. W. Heijstek and M. R. V. Chaudron, "Effort distribution in model-based development," in the 2nd Workshop on Model Size Metrics, and the 10th International Conference on Model Driven Engineering Languages and Systems, Nashville, Tenn, USA, 2007.
14. AJG Babu and N. Suresh, "Modelling and optimizing software quality," International Journal of Quality and Reliability Management, vol. 13, no. 3, pp. 95–103, 1996.
15. lS Biffl, A Aurum, BW Boehm, H Erdogmus, and P. Grünbacher, Value-Based Software Engineering, Springer, New York, NY, USA, 2005.
16. L. Huang and B. Boehm, "Determining how much software assurance is enough: a value-based approach," in the 7th Workshop on Economics-Driven Software Research, St. Louis, Mo, USA, 2005.
17. F. P. Brooks, "No silver bullet refired," in The Mythical Man-Month, pp. 207–226, Addison Wesley/Longman, Boston, Mass, USA, 1995.
18. D. M. Berry, "The inevitable pain of software development: why there is no silver bullet," in Proceedings of 9th International Workshop on Radical Innovations of Software and Systems Engineering in the Future, October 2002.
19. B. A. Kitchenham, S. L. Pfleeger, L. M. Pickard et al., "Preliminary guidelines for empirical research in software engineering," IEEE Transactions on Software Engineering, vol. 28, no. 8, pp. 721–734, 2002.
20. M. Bassey, "Methods of enquiry and the conduct of case study research," in Case Study Research in Educational

Settings, chapter 7, pp. 65–91, Open University Press, Buckingham, UK, 1999.

21. C. B. Seaman, "Qualitative methods in empirical studies of software engineering," IEEE Transactions on Software Engineering, vol. 25, no. 4, pp. 557–572, 1999.
22. N. K. Denzin and Y. S. Lincoln, Eds., Handbook of Qualitative Research, Sage, Thousand Oaks, Calif, USA, 2000.
23. P. Yiftachel, Resource Allocation among Software Development Phases, M.S. thesis, Computer Science Department, University of Haifa, 2006.
24. S. T. Hackman, Production Economics, chapter 2, Springer, Berlin, Germany, 2008.
25. ISO/IEC TR 9126, "Software engineering-product quality," 19-12-2000.
26. Q. Hu, "Evaluating alternative software production functions," IEEE Transactions on Software Engineering, vol. 23, no. 6, pp. 379–387, 1997.
27. P. C. Pendharkar, J. A. Rodger, and G. H. Subramanian, "An empirical study of the Cobb-Douglas production function properties of software development effort," Information and Software Technology, vol. 50, no. 12, pp. 1181–1188, 2008. ·
28. R. J. Madachy, Software Process Dynamics, Prentice-Hall/IEEE Press, Englewood Cliffs, NJ, USA, 2008.
29. P. Yiftachel, D. Peled, I. Hadar, and D. Goldwasser, "Resource allocation among development phases: an economic approach," in Proceedings of Economic Driven Software Engineering Research Workshop, the 28th International Conference on Software Engineering, pp. 43–48, Shanghai, China, 2006.
30. W. Heijstek and M. R. V. Chaudron, "On early investments in software development: a relation between effort distribution and defects in RUP projects," Tech. Rep., Leiden University, Leiden Institute of Advanced Computer Science, 2008.
31. I. Sommerville, Software Engineering, Pearson Education Limited, London, UK, 7th edition, 2005.
32. IEEE 610.12-1990, "A Glossary of Software Engineering Terminology," Institute of Electrical and Electrical and Electronic Engineers, Inc, 1990.
33. D. M. Berry, "What, Not How? When Is 'How' Really 'What'? and Some Thoughts on Quality Requirements," Tech. Rep., Computer Science Department, University of Waterloo, 2001.
34. P. Ralph and Y. Wand, "A proposal for a formal definition of the design concept," in Design Requirements Engineering: A Ten-Year Perspective, K. Lyytinen, P. Loucopoulos, J. Mylopoulos, and B. Robinson, Eds., pp. 103–136, Springer, Berlin, Germany, 2008.
35. D. Paulson and Y. Wand, "An automated approach to information systems decomposition," IEEE Transactions on Software Engineering, vol. 18, no. 3, pp. 174–189, 1992. ·
36. P. Yiftachel and I. Hadar, "Defining and measuring software development output: a light at the end of the tunnel for an essential problem. Presented at the workshop, No Silver Bullet: A Retrospective on the Essence and Accidents of Software Engineering," in the International Conference on Object Oriented Programming, Systems, Languages and Applications (OOPSLA ‹07), Montreal, Canada, October 2007.
37. M. King, "Living up to standards," in the 10th Conference of the European Chapter of the Association for Computational Linguistics (EACL ‹03), pp. 65–72, Budapest, Hungary, 2003.
38. V. Poladian, S. Butler, M. Shaw, and D. Garlan, "Time is not money: the case for multi-dimensional accounting in value-based software engineering," in the 5th Workshop on Economics-Driven Software Research, pp. 19–24, Portland, Ore, USA, 2003.
39. M. A. Côté, W. Suryn, C. Y. Laporte, and R. A. Martin, "The evolution path for industrial software quality evaluation methods applying ISO/IEC 9126:2001 quality model: example of MITRE›s SQAE method,"Software Quality Journal, vol. 13, no. 1, pp. 17–30, 2005. · ·
40. D. P. Kelly and R. S. Oshana, "Improving software quality using statistical testing techniques,"Information and Software Technology, vol. 42, no. 12, pp. 801–807, 2000. · ·
41. B. Anderson, A. Bajaj, and W. Gorr, "An estimation of the decision models of senior IS managers when evaluating the external quality of organizational software," Journal of Systems and Software, vol. 61, no. 1, pp. 59–75, 2002. ·
42. J. Lindroos, "Code and design metrics for object-oriented systems," in the Seminar for Quality Models for Software Engineering, Helsinki, Finland, 2004.
43. S. R. Chidamber and C. F. Kemerer, "Metrics suite for object oriented design," IEEE Transactions on Software Engineering, vol. 20, no. 6, pp. 476–493, 1994. · ·
44. Y. Wand and R. Weber, "An ontological evaluation of systems analysis and design methods," inInformation System Concepts: An In-Depth Analysis, E. D. Falkenberg and P. Lindgreen, Eds., pp. 79–107, North-Holland, Amsterdam, The Netherlands, 1989.
45. S. C. Misra, "Modeling design/Coding factors that drive maintainability of software systems," Software Quality Journal, vol. 13, no. 3, pp. 297–320, 2005. · ·
46. Y. Cai and K. J. Sullivan, "A value-oriented theory of modularity in design," in the 7th International Economics-Driven Software Engineering Research Workshop, St. Louis, Mo, USA, 2005.
47. K. D. Welker and P. W. Oman, "Software maintainability metrics models in practice," Crosstalk Journal of Defense Software Engineering, vol. 8, no. 11, pp. 19–23, 1995.
48. V. A. Batista, D. C. C. Peixoto, E. P. Borges, W. Pádua, R. F. Resende, and C. I. P. S. Pádua, "ReMoFP: a tool for counting function points from UML requirement models," Advances in Software Engineering, vol. 2011, Article ID 495232, 7 pages, 2011. ·
49. J. M. Akker, S. van den Brinkkemper, G. Diepen, and J. Versendaal, "Determination of the next release of a software product: an approach using integer linear programming," in Proceedings of the CAiSE ‹05 FORUM, pp. 119–124, 2005.

# SECTION II: PROGRAM AND CONFIGURATION MANAGEMENT

CHAPTER 5

# ANALYSIS OF SOFTWARE DEVELOPMENT AND ENHANCEMENT PROJECTS WORK EFFORT PER UNIT BASED ON THE COSMIC METHOD WITH REGARD TO TECHNOLOGICAL FACTORS—CASE STUDY

Beata Czarnacka-Chrobot

Institute of Information Technology and Digital Economy, Warsaw School of Economics, Warsaw, Poland

## ABSTRACT

**This paper aims to present a case study that consists in the analysis of work effort per unit of software systems Development and Enhancement Projects (D&EP) depending on technological factors. That analysis was commissioned by one of the largest public institutions in Poland. This is the COSMIC (Common Software Measurement International Consortium) function points method that is chosen by this institution as a point of reference for size of software systems developed/ enhanced for supporting its functions and therefore this method is the base for the analysis of D&EP work effort per unit with regard to technological factors.**

## INTRODUCTION

Software systems, like any other product, especially of engineering character, are characterised by certain attributes that should be subject to measurement. Basic attribute of each and every product is its size. Software engineering, however, cannot boast about being as mature in terms of units designed for size measurement (here: of software) as other engineering disciplines (e.g. construction engineering). This constitutes fundamental cause of the problems in reliable and objective estimation of such basic attributes of projects aimed at development, enhancement and maintenance of software systems as: total work effort and total cost, work effort per unit and cost per unit, project execution duration and project productivity. However, it is not possible to answer the question about the size of these attributes—particularly of the work effort per unit of software system Development and Enhancement Projects (D&EP)—without having previously assumed its appropriate size unit.

Among three measures of the software products size being used in practice, that is (for more details see e.g. [1]):

- programming units (e.g. source lines of code);
- construction complexity units (e.g. object points);
- functionality units, this is functionality units in the form of the so called Function Points (FP) that are now being recognized to the highest extent worldwide.

This has been proven by the fact of ISO (International Organization for Standardization) and IEC (International Electrotechnical Commission) having accepted them as the only adequate (i.e. sufficiently reliable and objective) units of software size—in the ISO/IEC 14143 norm [2], that standardizes the concept of the so called Functional Size Measurement (FSM).

**Citation:** B. Czarnacka-Chrobot, "Analysis of Software Development and Enhancement Projects Work Effort per Unit Based on the COSMIC Method with Regard to Technological Factors—Case Study," Journal of Software Engineering and Applications, Vol. 6 No. 11, 2013, pp. 597-609. doi: 10.4236/jsea.2013.611072.

As a result of many years' verification of reliability and objectivity of particular FSM methods, five among them (out of approx. 25) have been acknowledged by the ISO and IEC as conforming to the rules laid down in the ISO/IEC 14143 norm. They are the following (for more details see e.g. [3,4]):

A. First generation methods:

- International Function Point Users Group (IFPUG) method in its part limited to the so called unadjusted FP—normalized in the ISO/IEC 20926 standard [5]; in this method a measure unit is 1 IFPUG FP;
- Netherlands Software Metrics Association (NESMA) function point method in its part taking into account functional size—normalized in the ISO/IEC 24570 standard [6]; in this method a measure unit is 1 NESMA FP, which now is considered to be equivalent to 1 IFPUG FP;
- Mark II (MkII) function point method, having been developed by the United Kingdom Software Metrics Association (UKSMA) in its part taking into account functional size—normalized in the ISO/IEC 20968 standard [7]. B. Second generation methods:
- Common Software Measurement International Consortium (COSMIC) function point method—normalized in the ISO/IEC 19761 standard [8]; in this method a measure unit is 1 COSMIC Function Point (1 CFP);
- FSM method having been developed by the Finnish Software Measurement Association (FiSMA)—normalized in the ISO/IEC 29881 standard [9].

As indicated above, first generation methods have been accepted by the ISO/IEC in their part concerning only the functional size measurement, that is, further steps proposed by the organizations developing them (IFPUG, NESMA, UKSMA) have not been approved. On the other hand, second generation methods are accepted by the ISO/IEC in their full versions.

However, the IFPUG FP method continues to be the most popular FSM method—hence, for this very method, the largest resources of benchmarking data can be found [10], on the basis of which the above mentioned attributes of software systems D&EP, including work effort (total as well as per unit) and cost (total as well as per unit), are being estimated. On the other hand, for the past couple of years, this is COSMIC method that has been growing dynamically, however, the existing resources of benchmarking data for it are considerably scarce compared to such data available for IFPUG method as it is a much newer approach.

This paper aims to present a case study that consists in the analysis of work effort per unit of software systems D&EP depending on technological factors that is commissioned by one of the largest public institutions in Poland. This is the COSMIC method that is chosen by this institution as a point of reference for software size in case of development/enhancement of modules/applications of software system (being one of the largest in Europe) and therefore for the D&EP work effort per unit analysis.

Thus the structure of the paper reads as follows: after presented in Section 2, the assumptions are adopted in the considered case study and in Section 3, the resources of benchmarking data are worth using in the analysis of the issues considered; Section 4 will present selected data that are recommended to be used in direct calculation of the work effort per unit. Then Section 5 is devoted to major problems related to its indirect calculation. In Section 6, a synthesis of conclusions for the considered case study is presented while Section 7 features key conclusions resulting from all the considerations presented in the paper.

## ASSUMPTIONS FOR THE CONSIDERED CASE STUDY

Work effort per unit of software systems D&EP is difficult to determine since it depends on numerous factors, among others: on the type of software system, type of project, field of application, technological environment of project execution (mainly hardware platform and programming languages being used) as well as on many other factors affecting high differentiation in productivity of development/enhancement teams' work.

Thus, in addition to the assumption that analysis is to be based on COSMIC method, it should be also stressed that the subject matter being considered in this paper is work effort per unit of actions concerning applications dedicated to the needs of the considered institution (not commercial software packages) whereas these actions consist in development/ enhancement of such systems, in particular in development of new applications from scratch and in modification/enhancement of the existing ones, and not in their maintenance, in case of which work effort per unit requires analysis of different resources of benchmarking data. Moreover, client declares that all modules/applications considered should be treated as business applications (contrary to real-time projects). What's more, the purpose of the presented case study is to demonstrate how the effort per unit of software development/enhancement depends on several specific technological factors, i.e. technology of development/ enhancement (programming languages), hardware platform and processing mode—with the sizes of modules/ applications being taken into account. Information provided by client indicates that the considered modules/ applications are estimated to be within the following software size ranges: 1) less than 100 CPF—approx. 5% of the modules, 2) from 101 CFP up to 500 CFP—approx. 45% of the modules, 3) from 501 CFP up to 1000 CFP— approx. 40% of the modules, 4) over 1001 CFP—approx. 10% of the modules.

The above assumptions determine the use of specific benchmarking data resources.

## BENCHMARKING DATA RESOURCES FOR WORK EFFORT PER UNIT OF DEDICATED BUSINESS APPLICATIONS DEVELOPMENT/ ENHANCEMENT

Appropriate resources of own benchmarking data, which would allow to determine specific to a given software development organization work effort per unit or own productivity (being reverse of the work effort per unit) are owned by relatively few development organizations since owning such resources is conditioned not only by the effective implementation of measurement programmes for software products and processes, which in its own right does not occur often, but also by collecting such data for relatively many projects completed in the past, being similar in terms of application and technology, and additionally, referring them to the correct units of software systems size (for more details see [11]). This situation is all the more likely to happen in Poland where FSM methods, including COSMIC method, have been employed for a relatively short time now.

In the situation like that repositories with general benchmarking data prove useful. The largest, commonly known and widely available repository containing general benchmarking data for dedicated software systems D&EP, whose products are measured using the FSM methods, is managed by the International Software Benchmarking Standards Group (ISBSG). The ISBSG is a non-profit organization founded in the second half of the 1990s. with the purpose to enhance the processes of IT resources management both in business entities as well as in public administration institutions. This goal is being fulfilled by developing and maintaining several repositories with benchmarking data. One of them, the biggest one (current version of this repository contains data concerning more than 5600 projects from about 30 countries) includes data for software D&EP. It is normalized according to the ISO/IEC 15939 standard [12], verified and representative of the current technology.

Data gathered in the discussed repository have been classified by the ISBSG with regard to the following criteria (see [13,14]):

- country where a project was undertaken;
- context of a project, including: type of organization (including: developed for public institutions—approx. 750 projects) and area of business;
- type of project, including: type of actions (modification/ enhancement of a system—approx. 60%, development from scratch—approx. 40%), purpose of a project (internal needs—approx. 48%, external needs — approx. 52%) and size of development team;
- type of product, including: type of application (including business applications) and product size—for the most part expressed in IFPUG FP, however products measured in CFP are represented sufficiently too (approx. 400 projects);
- project execution environment, including: programming language (over 100 programming languages, among them 64% are 3GL languages, 33% - 4GL languages, while 3% are application generators; main programming languages include: COBOL, C/C++/C#, Java/J2EE/ Javascript, Visual Basic, PL/I, PL/SQL, Oracle, .Net, SQL, Natural, Access, PowerBuilder, ASP, and Lotus Notes) and hardware platform (approx. 40% are mainframe projects);
- development methods and tools being used.
- Using data gathered by this organization one should bear in mind that they are representative of rather above average projects which results from the following (for more details see [11]):
- criteria of gathering data in ISBSG repository take into account only those organizations that are using FSM methods while such organizations are considered more mature than others because they execute programmes concerning implementation of software measures;
- this is developers themselves that choose projects whose data they provide to the ISBSG repository—those may include projects that are typical of them as well as projects having best parameters;
- the ISBSG repository does not feature too many data about very large projects.

It should be stressed that ISBSG data are subject to rigorous process of verification with regard to quality. Hence they are appreciated in the IT industry while general conclusions coming from their analysis correspond with the conclusions coming from the projects of development/enhancement of software systems, including business applications.

Based on the data about dedicated software system D & EP the ISBSG produces cyclic analytical reports. From the perspective of the issues discussed in this paper the most important one is the report of March 2012 entitled, "The Performance of Business Application, Real-Time and Component Software Projects. An analysis of COSMIC-measured projects in the ISBSG database" [15], which the ISBSG made in collaboration with the COSMIC. It analyses the size of work effort per unit with regard to 1 CFP, that is the so called Project Delivery Rate (PDR), for various types of software systems depending on major impact factors. Thus PDR is the ratio of the work effort (expressed in work-hours) to the application size (expressed in function points—here in CFP). It is worth noting that this attribute is the inverse of other attribute that may be found more often both in the analyses as well in practice, namely productivity. In the discussed report total productivity (effort) is normalized on the so called first level, which means that it comprises all actions making up the project's life cycle: from specification to implementation. As indicated by the adopted assumptions, what is of interest here in this paper is PDR for development/enhancement of business applications.

## WORK EFFORT PER UNIT WITH REGARD TO 1 CFP—DIRECT CALCULATION

In the considered report, the analysis of PDR with regard to 1 COSMIC function point (CFP) is based on data coming from 314 business application projects (they were completed in 1999-2011), among them [15, p. 7]):

- 162 projects consisted in development of new business applications whereas:
  - their sizes ranged from 10 to nearly 2000 CFP,
  - their effort oscillated between 60 and 46000 workhours (i.e. approx. 30 work-years) with median3 amounting to 3289 work-hours (i.e. approx. 2.5 workyears).
- 152 projects consisted in enhancement of business applications whereas:
  - their sizes ranged from 3 to over 2000 CFP,
  - their effort oscillated between 24 and over 21000 work-hours (i.e. approx. 15 work-years) with median amounting to 3289 work-hours (i.e. approx. 2.5 workyears).

## Business Application Development Projects

Data presented in the report [15, pp. 8-13, 16-17] indicate that work effort per unit with regard to 1 CFP for business application development projects depending on the programming language generation reads as follows:

- For 3GL (82% of the projects under analysis), the PDR median is 24.5 work-hours/1 CFP, minimum value is 2.7 work-hours/1 CFP, while maximum value— as many as 330.6 work-hours/1 CFP, however 90% of the projects have PDR not higher than 64.8 workhours/1 CFP.
- For 4GL (18% of the projects under analysis—main programming languages include ASP. Net and Oracle), the PDR median is 9.2 work-hours/1 CFP, minimum value is 1.6 work-hours/1 CFP, while maximum value-82 work-hours/1 CFP, however 90% of the projects have PDR not higher than 31.2 work-hours/1 CFP.

The above indicates that application development projects using 4GL programming language on average are approx. 2.5 times more efficient comparing to application development projects employing 3GL languages.

More detailed analysis of specific 3GL programming languages that were analyzed allowed stating that:

- For programming languages: C, C#, C#.Net and C++, the PDR median is 14 work-hours/1 CFP, minimum value is 4 work-hours/1 CFP, while maximum value-52 work-hours/1 CFP, however 90% of the projects have PDR not higher than 43 work-hours/1 CFP.
- For programming language COBOL, the PDR median is 28 work-hours/1 CFP, minimum value is 8 workhours/1 CFP, while maximum value–as many as 330 work-hours/1 CFP, however 90% of the projects have PDR not higher than 110 work-hours/1 CFP.
- For programming language Java/J2EE, the PDR median is 23 work-hours/1 CFP, minimum value is 3 work-hours/1 CFP, while maximum value-139 workhours/1 CFP, however 90% of the projects have PDR not higher than 61 work-hours/1 CFP.
- For programming language Visual Basic, the PDR median is 23 work-hours/1 CFP, minimum value is 3 work-hours/1 CFP, while maximum value-57 workhours/1 CFP, however 75% of the projects have PDR not higher than 38 work-hours/1 CFP.

Thus, the PDR median for the analyzed 3GL programming languages differs significantly. Hence it is important to take into account the influence that factors such as hardware platform or size of delivered application may have on it.

For 3GL programming languages the PDR with regard to hardware platform reads as follows:

- Mainframe–median is 29 work-hours/1 CFP, with minimum value being 8 work-hours/1 CFP, and maximum value being 330 work-hours/1 CFP, however 90% of the projects are characterized by PDR not going higher than 101 work-hours/1 CFP.
- Mid-range–median is 36 work-hours/1 CFP, with minimum value being 10 work-hours/1 CFP, and maximum value being 65 work-hours/1 CFP, however 75% of the projects are characterized by PDR not exceeding 38 work-hours/1 CFP.
- PC—median is 23 work-hours/1 CFP, with minimum value being 3 work-hours/1 CFP, and maximum value being 139 work-hours/1 CFP, however 90% of the projects are characterized by PDR not going higher than 55 work-hours/1 CFP.
- Multi-platform–median is 21 work-hours/1 CFP, with minimum value being 3 work-hours/1 CFP, and maximum value being 66 work-hours/1 CFP, however 90% of the projects are characterized by PDR not exceeding 52 work-hours/1 CFP.

As indicated by the above, mainframe application projects are characterized by visibly lower productivity/ higher work effort per unit as compared to PC projects and multi-platform projects.

Conclusions coming from the influence of particular 3GL programming languages and hardware platform on the PDR median are displayed in Table 1.

The PDR varies also with regard to the software size. Relevant data for 3GL and 4GL languages (of all business application development projects under analysis) are displayed in Figure 1, showing productivity (instead of PDR) calculated as the ratio of CFP value to the workmonth, with the assumption taken that work-month consists of 120 work-hours on average.

As indicated by the chart shown in Figure 1, economies of scales may be noted for business application development projects since median of their productivity goes up with the increase of software size (at least up to the size of over 1000 CFP). This is a conclusion of great significance as it contradicts the hitherto numerous studies of economies/diseconomies of scale in software engineering that as a rule provide quite the opposite conclusion (for more details see e.g. [16]). In the opinion of the author of this paper, fundamental cause for this status quo is referring, in this very case, work effort to appropriate units of software systems size (CFP), whereas other works take into account units of software size that hardly may be considered as appropriate (e.g. source lines of code).

**Table 1.** Business application development projects–PDR median by programming language and hardware platform

| | Mainframe | Multi-platform | PC |
|---|---|---|---|
| All C type | - | 16 | 11 |
| COBOL | 28 | - | - |
| Java | 33 | 19 | 25 |

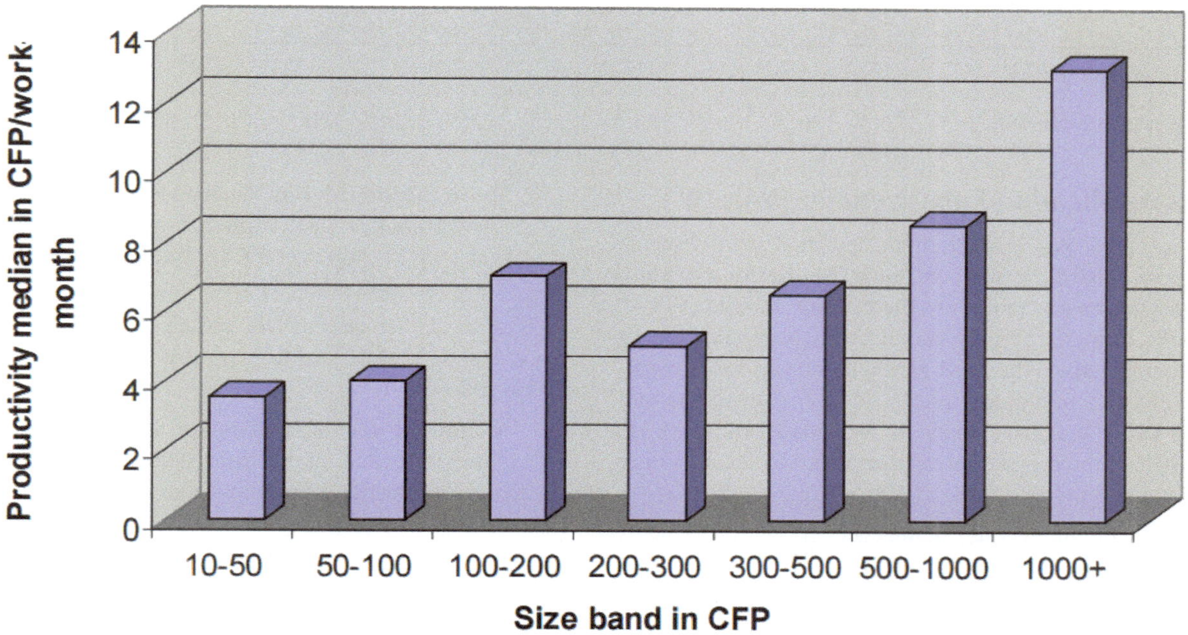


**Figure 1.** The productivity median by the size of business applications development. Source: [15, p. 10].

Taking into account the described observations it is suggested for business application development projects to use such PDR values as those displayed in Table 2, which is showing how PDR depends on programming language and hardware platform in the situation where PDR median is normalized for the application size of 100 - 200 CFP range.

On the other hand if this is possible to consider all 3 key impact factors (or rather a combination of them) being analyzed by the ISBSG and COSMIC, that is programming languages, hardware platform and software size, then the data from Table 2 are suggested to be treated as initial data for which correction coefficients shown in Table 3, taking into account the influence of application size on PDR, should be applied.

Thus if we want to determine work effort per unit with regard to 1 CFP for example for a project of development of business application whose size is estimated to be 400 CFP, using Java language on multi-platform, then from Table 2 we choose normalized PDR median taking into account combination of programming language and hardware platform, which equals 20, and next we multiply it by coefficient for estimated application size, in this case being 0.8, as a result getting PDR amounting to 16 work-hours/1 CFP.

It should be stressed that in the discussed report it is stated explicitly that factors having strongest influence on PDR include (following the order given): 1) application size, 2) generation of programming language being used, and next 3) hardware platform, whereas specific language of given generation shows relatively lower influence on the work effort per unit4 [15, p. 12].

Other technological factors are considered as having less significant impact on PDR; among them the processing modes-divided into batch, online and mixed mode, may be regarded as worth noting. Data contained in the ISBSG and COSMIC report indicate that batch application development projects are characterized by 1.7 times higher work effort per unit (PDR median equalling 30 work-hours per 1 CFP) than projects consisting in development of online application (PDR median equalling approx. 18 work-hours per 1 CFP) while in the case of projects developing software working in a mixed mode, the PDR is 2.2 times higher (PDR median equals approx. 40 work-hours per 1 CFP) than that noted for online application projects. Explanation of such relative results is as follows:

- technology designed for online software development provides functionality (e.g. GUI interfaces) particularly easily comparing with technology used to develop batch software;
- development of batch software requires negotiating of interfaces with other systems which decreases productivity (increases PDR).

However, using these median values as well as specific conversion rates one should bear in mind that size of the sample on which their calculation was based was small: 23 projects in total, among them there were 15 batch, 4 online and 4 mixed projects therefore these data can hardly be regarded as representative. There is no doubt, however, that in case of batch processing the PDR value will be higher than that of online processing and this being due to the above mentioned reasons.

**Table 2.** Business application development projects–normalization of PDR median with regard to programming language and hardware platform for the application size of 100 - 200 CFP range

| | Mainframe | Multi-platform | PC |
|---|---|---|---|
| All C type | - | 17 ± 7 | 20 ± 10 |
| COBOL | 25 ± 9 | - | - |
| Java | 25 ± 9 | 20 ± 7 | 20 ± 10 |
| 4GL | - | 9 ± 4 | 9 ± 4 |

**Table 3.** Business application development projects–PDR correction coefficient for data shown in Table 2 by application size

| Application size in CFP | 10 - 50 | 50 - 100 | 100 - 200 | 200 - 300 | 300 - 500 | 500 - 1000 | 1000+ |
|---|---|---|---|---|---|---|---|
| PDR correction coefficient | 1.2 | 1.1 | 1.0 | 0.9 | 0.8 | 0.65 | 0.5 |

## Business Application Enhancement Projects

The report [15, pp. 17-22] indicates that for projects consisting in enhancement of business applications (adding new, modifying and/or removing the existing functionality—approx. 75% of total 152 projects under analysis included all those actions together) the PDR median amounts to 27 work-hours/1 CFP, with minimum value being 1.5 work-hours and maximum value being as many as 315 work-hours/1 CFP, however 90% of the projects are characterized by the effort per unit being up to 81 work-hours/1 CFP.

What seems interesting is that enhancement projects show little differentiation in PDR median with regard to programming language, respectively:

- For COBOL language, the PDR median amounts to 27 work-hours/1 CFP (thus it is almost identical as in case of business application development projects), minimum value is 3 work-hours/1 CFP while maximum value-187 work-hours/1 CFP, however 90% of the projects prove having PDR not higher than 84 work-hours/1 CFP.
- For Java language, the PDR median amounts to 26 work-hours/1 CFP (similar to that of business application development projects), minimum value is 5 work-hours/1 CFP, while maximum value—as many as 326 work-hours/1 CFP, however 90% of the projects prove having PDR not higher than 188 workhours/1 CFP.
- For VB and VC++ languages, the PDR median amounts to 21 work-hours/1 CFP, minimum value is 1.5 work-hours/1 CFP, while maximum value-52 work-hours/1 CFP, however 90% of the projects prove having PDR not higher than 38 work-hours/1 CFP.
- For 4GL languages, the PDR median amounts to 29 work-hours/1 CFP (note: value higher than that for the above mentioned 3GL languages), minimum value is 3 work-hours/1 CFP, while maximum value- 68 work-hours/1 CFP, however 90% of the projects prove having PDR not higher than 41 work-hours/1 CFP.

With similar situation (PDR median slightly differentiated) we are dealing with regard to hardware platform, where PDR reads as follows:

- Mainframe–median amounts to 27 work-hours/1 CFP (similar to that of business application development projects), while minimum value equals 3 work-hours/ 1 CFP, and maximum value-316 work-hours/1 CFP, however 90% of the projects are characterized by PDR not higher than 80 work-hours/1 CFP.
- PC—median amounts to 30 work-hours/1 CFP, while minimum value equals 2 work-hours/1 CFP, and maximum value-248 work-hours/1 CFP, however 90% of the projects are characterized by PDR not exceeding 149 work-hours/1 CFP.
- Multi-platform–median amounts to 29 work-hours/1 CFP, while minimum value equals 17 work-hours/1 CFP, and maximum value-49 work-hours/1 CFP, however 75% of the projects are characterized by PDR not higher than 38 work-hours/1 CFP.

In case of the considered projects this is also productivity that grows as the size of business application enhancement increases, which may be seen in the chart in Figure 2.

As indicated by the data displayed in Figure 2 being compared to the data shown in Figure 1, productivity growth in case of business application enhancement projects is very similar (at least for the values up to 750 CFP) to productivity growth characteristic of business application development projects. What's more, it is stated in the report explicitly that large projects of business application enhancement (above 1000 CFP) should be treated as projects of their development (see Section 4.1).

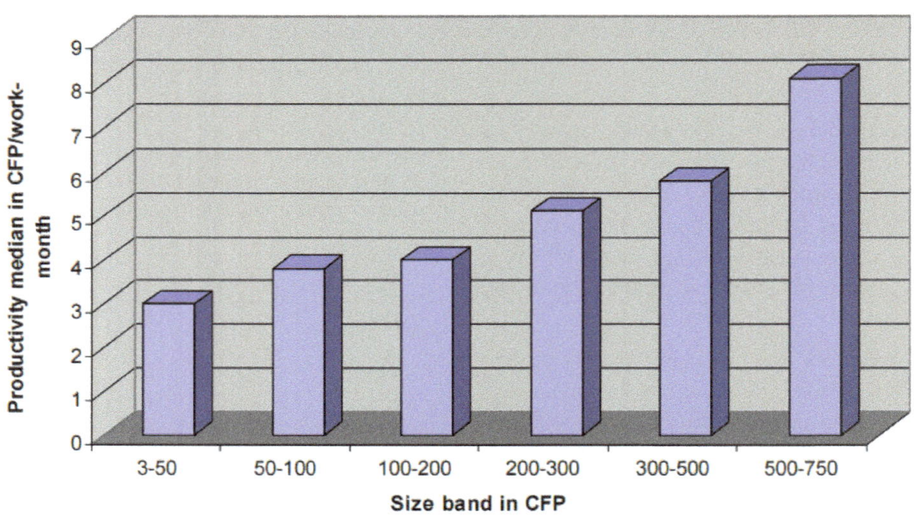


**Figure 2.** The productivity median by the size of business application enhancement. Source: [15, p. 19].

## SUMMARY

Generalizing the above presented results it should be stated that (see [15, pp. 42-44]):

- For 4 basic categories of business application projects the PDR median reads as follows:
  - development, 3GL languages, multi-platform/PC: 20 work-hours/1CFP,
  - development, 3GL languages, mainframe: 25 workhours/1CFP,
  - development, 4GL languages: 9 work-hours/1CFP,
  - enhancement: 27 work-hours/1CFP.
- Thus business application enhancement projects require more work-hours per 1 CFP than business application development projects do. On the other hand, business application development projects employing the 4GL languages are characterized by significantly higher (more than double) productivity (lower PDR) comparing with business application development projects based on 3GL—assuming, of course, that product size is the same. What seems interesting, however, is that such differences with regard to the generation of programming language employed do not occur in case of business application enhancement projects (lack of significant difference in terms of productivity).
- Productivity median for business application development projects increases (and PDR median decreases) as the application size grows—more than double for projects having product of the 500 - 1000 CFP range comparing to those with product below 50 CFP.
- Productivity median for business application enhancement projects increases (and PDR median decreases) as the size of application enhancement grows—more than double for projects having product of the 500 - 750 CFP range comparing to those with product below 50 CFP.
- Due to small sample of projects differentiated with regard to the processing mode the ISBSG data cannot be regarded as representative although they do confirm the assumption that batch processing decreases productivity (increases PDR).

It is also worth noting that both in business application development as well as in business application enhancement projects the following regularities were observed (see [13, pp. 33-34]):

- PDR is low (productivity is high) if 20% to 40% of the total work effort is allocated to the stage of specification and design in project's lifecycle;
- PDR is high (productivity is low) if:
  - less than 20% of the total effort is allocated to the stage of specification and design—since part of the actions need to be undertaken in further stages of project where they require higher expenditure;
  - more than 40% of the total effort is allocated to the stage of specification and design—since this as a rule implies difficulties with determining specification and/or with design.

Undoubtedly, the presented benchmarking data are valuable to an organization that wants to compare its effectiveness against its environment as well as for the estimations of the future projects.

## WORK EFFORT PER UNIT WITH REGARD TO 1 CFP—POSSIBILITY OF INDIRECT CALCULATION?

### COSMIC Method versus IFPUG Method—Differences Being of Significance in the Context of Work Effort per Unit Calculation

Current benchmarking data of the ISBSG are based on the analysis of approx. 4500 business application development or enhancement projects, among them approx. 4000 are projects in which software products were measured using the IFPUG/NESMA FP method. Thus they constitute decidedly larger group of projects than those whose products were measured in CFP. What's more, these are business applications, which the IFPUG and NESMA methods were intended for. Hence one may consider using benchmarking data also for IFPUG/NESMA methods in order to determine work effort per unit with regard to 1 CFP indirectly that is taking into account conversion rates for IFPUG/NESMA function points and COSMIC function points. However one should bear in mind that (see [15,17]):

The COSMIC method is a significantly younger method therefore data pertaining to it concern other time than that of data for IFPUG/NESMA methods, what also entails change of productivity of developing/enhancing software products over the years, e.g. due to the emergence of new programming languages, new types of products, etc.

- Any comparisons should be made only with regard to unadjusted IFPUG/NESMA function points [18], on which the latest ISBSG calculations are based.
- It has been proved that there is certain correlation for the sizes of the same fragment of software expressed in IFPUG/NESMA FP and COSMIC FP.
- Due to significant differences in both discussed approaches, in case of measurement of software modification size it is rather not possible to correctly compare PDR for enhancement projects versus PDR for development projects being calculated using those two different methods.

All methods of software functional size measurement originate from A. Albrecht's concept of Function Point Analysis (FPA) hence there are some similarities between them. For IFPUG and COSMIC methods, such similarities include most of all the same concept of software functional size measurement, based on similar understanding of measurement's purpose, measurement's range and definition of application boundaries (see e.g. [19]). Both approaches, although differently, meet also the requirements that the ISO/IEC 14143 norm imposed on FSM methods therefore both were recognized as international standards for such measurement (the IFPUG method, however, not in the full version yet in its most important part) (for more details see [3]).

However there are features these two methods differ with and which are of significance from the perspective of calculation of software development effort per unit (see e.g. [4], [20, pp. 270-280]):

- The rules of both methods are based on similar yet not identical meaning of terms linked with data where such key notions of IFPUG method as: entity, file and data element type (DET) have the following equivalents in COSMIC method: object of interest, data group and data attribute.
- What's also similar yet not identical is the concept of data transformation, that is of elementary processes/ transactional functions (IFPUG) and functional processes (COSMIC) as well as the users viewed generally —as recipients of functionality of the measured software.
- Phases of measurement—both approaches make similar but again not identical assumption on the occurrence of the elements identification phase on the basis of which functional size is being determined, and of the phase of proper measurement where those elements are conveyed on that size expressed numerically [21]. In the IFPUG method, however, the first phase is not described explicitly as a part of measurement process although it assumes that measurement is based on the specification of functional user requirements (FUR). In the phase of proper measurement, with regard to these elements the explicitly described rules of this method are being used. On the other hand, the measurement phase in the COSMIC method is based only on the FUR specification which leads to the separation of various layers of software. Next, upon identification of appropriate boundaries, functional user requirements are being decomposed into a set of functional processes, each of them consisting of the set of data movements. In the phase of proper measurement each movement must be identified as the functional size is being determined based on them.
- Different way of expressing functional user requirements—in both methods they are being expressed with the use of the so called basic functional components (BFC); these components however differ. In the approach having been developed by the IFPUG, the following 5 types of BFC are singled out: internal logical file, external interface file, external input, external output, and external inquiry, while in the COSMIC method there are 4 BFC types that were isolated: entry, exit, read and write. There is no simple analogy between them since in the COSMIC method data are not measured explicitly and they are not distinguished as type of BFC although in both methods logical transactions are being measured (somewhat differently), which may be proved by the schematic comparison of both methods displayed in Table 4.
- Rules of measurement. Fundamental difference in this area is the fact that the IFPUG method takes into account General System Characteristics (GSC), expressing the impact of technological and quality requirements on the functional size. This is the reason why this approach has not been fully approved by the ISO/IEC, however including GSC to the calculations is not necessary (when skipping them we obtain unadjusted number of function points). Characteristics of this type do not exist in COSMIC method where the measurement is based solely on FUR.
- Boundaries of process sizes. In the IFPUG method, the size of all five BFC is arbitrarily limited therefore the size of software depends on the number of those components. In the COSMIC approach, on the other hand, there is no upper limit for the size of functional process as the size of process is determined by the number of data movements. Besides, from the perspective of the level of measurement, this is data movements of COSMIC method rather than its functional processes that correspond with elementary processes of the IFPUG method (i.e. inputs, outputs and inquiries) while their size is 1 CFP and does not depend on the number of attribute data nor files to which they pertain as it is the case of the IFPUG method.
- Way of including data stored in a system. In the method having been developed by the IFPUG, data are included to the calculations in two ways: separately as internal/ external files as well as referenced files affecting the size of elementary process. In case of the COSMIC method, data stored in a system are included into calculations at each movement of data of read or write type. Thus using IFPUG method requires constructing of data model which is not necessary (yet useful) in the COSMIC approach [22, p. 145]. In the IFPUG method, data model provides also base for early estimations whereas in the COSMIC approach this is process model that is more often used for approximation.
- Different perspective of measurement. With the use of IFPUG method, functional size is being measured from the perspective of the end user while using COSMIC method—from the point of view of functional user that comprises, next to end user, also developers, and they give notice to other applications and devices that interact with the measured software (see [21, p. 115], [23]). Perspective limited to the end user only carries danger of missing out in the calculations such functionality that is not visible to a user human, on the condition however that we assume that only user being human may be recipient of functionality.

**Table 4.** Comparison of basic functional components of the methods: IFPUG vs. COSMIC

| FSM method | Data | Data size | Transactional functions | Transactions | Transaction size |
|---|---|---|---|---|---|
| IFPUG | *internal file*<br>*external file* | - number of data element types (DET)<br>- number of record element types ( RET) | *external input*<br>*external output*<br>*external inquiry* | | - number of data element types (DET)<br>- number of file type referenced ( FTR) |
| COSMIC | transient<br>persistent | part of functional process | functional process | *entry*<br>*exit*<br>*read*<br>*write* | number of data movements |

Thus it is not possible–at least for the time being—to make exact conversion of the results of the two methods. When using mathematical formula for this purpose, main reason for this status quo is the fact that basic functional components of the IFPUG method cannot be mapped accurately into BFC of the COSMIC method, and vice versa (see Table 4), however differences in the rules of measurement are of significance here too. This first of all concerns:

- different understanding of file and its influence on size in the IFPUG method as compared with object of interest in the COSMIC method,
- different calculation rules for elementary process of the IFPUG method as compared with functional process of the COSMIC method,
- the fact that in the IFPUG method the influence that number of attribute data has on the size is taken into account whereas in the COSMIC method this is only number of objects of interest that is taken into account,
- the fact that in the IFPUG method all types of BFC have their upper limit of the size which does not exist for functional processes in the COSMIC method,
- concept of software layers existing in the COSMIC method, contrary to the IFPUG method,
- different way of measuring software modifications, which has been already mentioned and which results in a situation where for projects consisting in modification of the existing software conversion of sizes, even approximate one, is practically impossible.

## COSMIC Method versus IFPUG Method—Attempts on Approximate Conversion of Functional Sizes

There are, however, three potential approaches to approximate conversion of results obtained with the use of IFPUG (or NESMA) method into the results expressed in COSMIC function points—for more details see [17, pp. 22-25, 28-29]. One of them is conversion based on statistical formula. Numerous studies had been undertaken that aimed to obtain adequate statistical formula expressing the correlation between the sizes obtained with the use of both methods, their results, however, significantly differ (see Table 5). Thus it is recommended that an organization facing the need of conversion of sizes of its applications undertakes its own analyses using the regression method in order to derive equation being specific to itself, based on adequate size of the sample of benchmarking data concerning measurement as well as on examples that are representative, typical of given organization.

The above indicates that the issues of conversion of business application functional sizes obtained with the use of both analyzed methods require further investigation therefore-despite significantly larger resources of benchmarking data existing for the IFPUG method– when determining effort per unit of business application development with regard to 1 CFP it is recommended to use direct calculation (see Section 4).

**Table 5.** Examples of statistical formulas for the conversion of the IFPUG method results into COSMIC method results[a]

| No. | Author (year) | Sample size | Formula (regression analysis) | $R^2$ |
|---|---|---|---|---|
| 1. | Fetcke (1999) | 4 | $CFP = 1.1 \times UFP - 7.6$<br>($UFP$ – number of unadjusted function points IFPUG) | 0.97 |
| 2. | Vogelezang, Lesterhuis (2003) | 11 | $CFP = 1.2 \times UFP - 87$<br>$CFP = 0.75 \times UFP - 2.6$ ($\leq 200$ $UFP$)<br>$CFP = 1.2 \times UFP - 108$ ($>200$ $UFP$)<br>($UFP$ – number of unadjusted function points NESMA) | 0.99 |
| 3. | Abran, Azziz, Desharnais (2005) | 6<br>(public organisation applications) | $CFP = 0.84 \times UFP + 18$<br>($UFP$ – number of unadjusted function points IFPUG) | 0.91 |
| 4. | Desharnais, Abran (2006) | 14 | $CFP = 1.0 \times UFP - 3$<br>($UFP$ – number of unadjusted function points IFPUG) | 0.93 |
| 5. | Van Heeringen (2007) | 26<br>(business applications) | $CFP = 1.22 \times UFP - 64$<br>($UFP$ – number of unadjusted function points NESMA) | 0.97 |
| 6. | | 21 | $CFP = 0.83 \times UFP - 36.6$<br>($UFP$ – number of unadjusted function points IFPUG) | 0.7 |
| 7. | Cuadrado-Gallego *et al.* (2008, 2010) | 14 | $CFP = 0.85 \times UFP + 0.2$<br>($UFP$ – number of unadjusted function points IFPUG) | 0.86 |
| 8. | | 35<br>(combination of the previous ones) | $CFP = 0.73 \times UFP - 4.5$<br>($UFP$ – number of unadjusted function points IFPUG) | 0.9 |
| 9. | C. Jones (2007) | no data available | $1\ UFP = 1.15\ CFP$<br>($UFP$ – number of unadjusted function points IFPUG) | no data available |
| 10. | Cuadrado-Gallego *et al.* (2010) | no data available | $1\ UFP \approx 1\ CFP$<br>($UFP$ – number of unadjusted function points IFPUG) | no data available |

[a] $R^2$ is a coefficient of determination describing degree to which the model explains the shaping of the variable being explained–in this case expressing the proportion of deviation in the COSMIC size (in CFP) being explained by the change in the IFPUG/NESMA size. Significant difference in constants between the functions of linear regression as a rule results from the influence of logical files on the functional size in the IFPUG method, which in case of small products causes it to grow faster than in the COSMIC method. Source: author's own analysis based on: [17, p. 26], [22, p. 147], [24, pp. 347-357], [25, pp. 427-432], [26, pp. 170-177], [27, p. 242].

## WORK EFFORT PER UNIT FOR BUSINESS APPLICATION DEVELOPMENT/ENHANCEMENT—CASE STUDY

The above conclusions were reflected in the proposed specific values of the median of the work effort per unit (PDR) of software development and enhancement being calculated with regard to 1 CFP which was recommended to the Polish public institution commissioning this analysis. The main obstacle to providing accurate values in many cases turned out to be lack of information about application/module/modification size.

Depending on benchmarking data available and on data acquired from the client, both the projected and existing applications/modules of the system were divided into 8 groups for which relatively accurate (as far as possible) or just minimum values of the work effort per unit with regard to 1 CFP depending on main technological factors were determined. The synthesis is displayed in Table 6. It also shows relative differences in work effort per unit, assuming value 1 for the highest effort per unit median—separately for development and for enhancement.

## CONCLUSIONS

The presented data above are differentiated to a large extent—there is no possibility to derive accurate values for the effort per unit with regard to 1 CFP without taking into account specificity of widely understood development organization. As this effort, per unit is influenced by a number of factors, including those such as experienced and stable development team, experienced project manager, stable requirements, and many others. However, lack of own (organizational) resources of adequate benchmarking data continues to be common situation—not only in Poland but worldwide as well. Hence necessity to use general benchmarking data and the best source in this case is undoubtedly the ISBSGN data repository.

**Table 6.** The work effort per unit with regard to 1 CFP depending on main technological factors–case study for Polish public institution (the synthesis)

| Group of applications/modules | Development | | Enhancement | |
|---|---|---|---|---|
| | **Effort per unit median** | **Relative value of median** | **Effort per unit median** | **Relative value of median** |
| Applications/modules for which the size of application/module is known | at least 11.3 | at least 0.61 | 23.5 | 0.84 |
| **Applications/modules for which the size of application/module is known plus upward correction was made due to batch processing** | at least 6.3 | at least 0.34 | as for development | |
| Applications/modules for which the size of application/module is known plus sum of the sizes of modules making up an application is taken into account | at least 6.0 | at least 0.32 | at least 18.2 | at least 0.65 |
| Applications/modules for which the PDR median is a very approximate value in case of development, and this being due to possibility of including differentiated programming languages only (without the size of application and hardware platform). In case of enhancement, on the other hand, the PDR median is an approximate value due to differentiated programming languages only (for it does not take into account the size of enhancement and hardware platform-however application enhancement is not significantly sensitive to hardware platform) | approx. 18.5 | 1 | approx. 27 | approx. 0.96 |
| Applications/modules for which the PDR median is an approximate value in case of development and this being due to possibility of including 4GL language only (without the size of application) and lack of benchmarking data for 4GL and mainframe. However, because of platform, PDR will probably be significantly higher. In case of enhancement, on the other hand, the PDR median is an approximate value taking into account 4GL language and hardware platform, not including though the size of enhancement | at least 9.2 | at least 0.5 | approx. 28 | 1 |
| Applications/modules for which the PDR median is a very approximate value in case of development, and this being due to possibility of including differentiated programming languages only (without the size of application). However, because of platform, PDR will probably be significantly higher. While in case of enhancement the PDR median is an approximate value taking into account differentiated programming languages and hardware platform, not including though the size of enhancement | at least 12.6 | at least 0.68 | approx. 26 | approx. 0.93 |
| Applications/modules for which the PDR median is a very approximate value in case of development, and this being due to possibility of including programming environment only (without the size of application and hardware platform). While in case of enhancement the PDR median is an approximate value taking into account a programming environment only (not including though the size of enhancement and hardware platform-however application enhancement is not significantly sensitive to hardware platform) | approx. 16 | approx. 0.86 | approx. 27 | approx. 0.96 |
| Applications/modules for which the PDR median is a very approximate value in case of development, and this being due to possibility of including 4GL language only (without the size of application) and lack of benchmarking data for 4GL and mainframe. However, because of hardware platform and batch processing, PDR will probably be significantly higher. In case of enhancement, on the other hand, the PDR median is an approximate value taking into account 4GL language and hardware platform, not including though the size of enhancement. Due to batch processing, PDR will probably be higher | at least 9.2 | at least 0.5 | approx. 28 | 1 |

The ISBSG and COSMIC report indicates that the factor having strongest impact on PDR is first of all size of software product, next generation of programming language employed, and then hardware platform while specific language of given generation shows relatively low influence on the work effort per unit. Other factors, also technological ones, including processing mode, are regarded as having less significant influence.

In the situation where there are no data concerning COSMIC method available for specific factors, one may try using data for the IFPUG method—this, however, should be done with great caution. It results from the fact that the issues of the conversion of business application functional sizes obtained with the use of both analyzed methods require further investigation. Thus, despite significantly larger resources of benchmarking data existing for the IFPUG method, it is recommended to use direct calculation when determining effort per unit of business application development/enhancement with regard to 1 CFP. This calculation was used in the analysis of the effort per unit of software systems development/enhancement projects based on the COSMIC method, depending on main technological factors and by taking into account software product size, having been carried out for one of the biggest public institutions in Poland, having in its disposal software system that was listed among the largest ones in Europe.

## REFERENCES

1. B. Czarnacka-Chrobot, "The Economic Importance of Business Software Systems Development and Enhancement Projects Functional Assessment," International Journal on Advances in Systems and Measurements, Vol. 4, No. 1-2, 2011, pp. 135-146.

2. ISO/IEC 14143, "1998-2011 Information Technology—Software Measurement—Functional Size Measurement—Part 1-6," ISO, Geneva.
3. B. Czarnacka-Chrobot, "The ISO/IEC Standards for the Software Processes and Products Measurement," Frontiers in Artificial Intelligence and Applications, Vol. 199, 2009, pp. 187-200.
4. B. Czarnacka-Chrobot, "The Effectiveness of Business Software Systems Functional Size Measurement," Proceedings of the 6th International Multi-Conference on Computing in the Global Information Technology (ICCGI 2011), Luxemburg City, Luxemburg, 2011, pp. 63-71.
5. ISO/IEC 20926, "2009 Software and Systems Engineering—Software Measurement—IFPUG Functional Size Measurement Method," 2nd Edition, ISO, Geneva, 2009.
6. ISO/IEC 24570, "2005 Software Engineering—NESMA Functional Size Measurement Method Version 2.1. Definitions and Counting Guidelines for the Application of Function Point Analysis," ISO, Geneva.
7. ISO/IEC 20968, "2002 Software engineering—Mk II Function Point Analysis—Counting Practices Manual," ISO, Geneva.
8. ISO/IEC 19761, "2011 Software Engineering—COSMIC: A Functional Size Measurement Method," 2nd Edition, ISO, Geneva.
9. ISO/IEC 29881, "2008 Information Technology—Software and Systems Engineering—FiSMA 1.1 Functional Size Measurement Method," ISO, Geneva.
10. C. Jones, "Sources of Software Benchmarks, Version 13," Capers Jones & Associates LLC., Narragansett, 2011.
11. B. Czarnacka-Chrobot, "The Role of Benchmarking Data in the Software Development and Enhancement Projects Effort Planning," Frontiers in Artificial Intelligence and Applications, Vol. 199, 2009, pp. 106-127.
12. ISO/IEC 15939, "2007 Systems and Software Engineering—Measurement Process," ISO, Geneva.
13. International Software Benchmarking Standards Group, "Data Demographics-Release 11," ISBSG, Hawthorn, VIC, 2009.
14. International Software Benchmarking Standards Group, "Release 10 Repository Demographics," ISBSG, Hawthorn, VIC, 2007.
15. H. Heeringen and Ch. Symons, "The Performance of Business Application, Real-Time and Component Software Projects. An Analysis of COSMIC-Measured Projects in the ISBSG Database, COSMIC and ISBSG," 2012.
16. B. Czarnacka-Chrobot, "(Dis)economies of Scale in Business Software Systems Development and Enhancement Projects," Computer Technology and Application, Vol. 3, No. 1, 2012, pp. 88-97.
17. Common Software Measurement International Consortium, "The COSMIC Functional Size Measurement Method, Version 3.0, Advanced and Related Topics," COSMIC, Québec, 2007.
18. International Function Point Users Group, "Function Point Counting Practices Manual, Release 4.3, Part 0-5," IFPUG, NJ, 2010.
19. J. Cuadrado-Gallego, D. Rodríguez, F. Machado and A. Abran, "Convertibility between IFPUG and COSMIC Functional Size Measurements," Proceedings of 8th International Conference on Product-Focussed Software Process Improvement (PROFES 2007), Riga, 2-4 July 2007, pp. 273-283.
20. B. Czarnacka-Chrobot, "Functional Measurement of Management Software Systems Development and Enhancement Projects," Warsaw School of Economics, Warsaw, 2009.
21. G. Xunmei, S. Guoxin and Z. Hong, "The Comparison between FPA and COSMIC-FFP," Proceedings of Software Measurement European Forum (SMEF) Conference, Rome, 10-12 May 2006, pp. 113-114.
22. H. Heeringen, "Changing from FPA to COSMIC. A Transition Framework," Proceedings of Software Measurement European Forum (SMEF) Conference, Rome, 9-11 May 2007.
23. Common Software Measurement International Consortium (COSMIC), 2013. http://www.cosmicon.com/advantagecs.asp
24. J. Cuadrado-Gallego, L. Buglione, M. Domínguez-Alda, M. de Sevilla, J. Gutierrez de Mesa and O. Demirors, An "Experimental Study on the Conversion between IFPUG and COSMIC Functional Size Measurement Units," Information and Software Technology, Vol. 52, No. 3, 2010. http://dx.doi.org/ 10.1016/j.infsof.2009.12.001
25. J. Cuadrado-Gallego, L. Buglione, R. Rejas-Muslera and F. Machado-Piriz, "IFPUG-COSMIC Statistical Conversion," Proceedings of the 34th Euromicro Conference on Software Engineering, Parma, 1-5 September 2008.
26. C. Gencel and C. Bideau, "Exploring the Convertibility between IFPUG and COSMIC Function Points: Preliminary Findings," Proceedings of Joint Conference of the 22nd International Workshop on Software Measurement and the 7th International Conference on Software Process and Product Measurement, Assisi, 17-19 October 2012.
27. C. Jones, "Estimation Software Costs," McGraw Hill, New York, 2007.

CHAPTER 6

# MANAGING CHANGE IN THE DELIVERY OF COMPLEX PROJECTS: CONFIGURATION MANAGEMENT, ASSET INFORMATION AND 'BIG DATA'

Jennifer Whyte, Angelos Stasis, Carmel Lindkvist

School of Construction Management and Engineering, University of Reading, Whiteknights, Reading, RG6 6AY, United Kingdom

## ABSTRACT

**As we enter an era of 'big data', asset information is becoming a deliverable of complex projects. Prior research suggests digital technologies enable rapid, flexible forms of project organizing. This research analyses practices of managing change in Airbus, CERN and Crossrail, through desk-based review, interviews, visits and a cross-case workshop. These organizations deliver complex projects, rely on digital technologies to manage large data-sets; and use configuration management, a systems engineering approach with mid-20th century origins, to establish and maintain integrity. In them, configuration management has become more, rather than less, important. Asset information is structured, with change managed through digital systems, using relatively hierarchical, asynchronous and sequential processes. The paper contributes by uncovering limits to flexibility in complex projects where integrity is important. Challenges of managing change are discussed, considering the evolving nature of configuration management; potential use of analytics on complex projects; and implications for research and practice.**

## INTRODUCTION

Digital technologies radically transform project delivery. Twenty years ago, Morris described the evolution of project management as closely related to developments in systems engineering, modern management theory, and the evolution of the computer (Morris, 1997: p.2). Today, mobile hardware, cloud computing and integrated software are becoming used for storage and retrieval, automated search, and prototyping and simulation functions. As such technologies are adopted in project-based industries, their use is breaking the mould of established approaches to project management, enabling more rapid and agile forms of organizing (Levitt, 2011 and Whyte and Levitt, 2011). Up-front project planning, using multiple layers of work breakdown structures, became established by the 1960s in the management of large complex projects (Morris, 1997: p.44). New digitally-enabled approaches are emerging in industries, such as consumer electronics, software development, biotechnology and medical devices, that operate in dynamic and less predictable situations in which plans need to be updated and modified during project delivery (Whyte and Levitt, 2011). In these, data analytics and visualization using large digital data-sets – along with rapid, informal interaction and exchanges of information – provide the basis for more responsive, flexible and real-time decision-making (Levitt, 2011).

**Citation:** Jennifer Whyte, Angelos Stasis, Carmel Lindkvist, "Managing change in the delivery of complex projects: Configuration management, asset information and 'big data,'" International Journal of Project Management 34 (2016) 339–351. doi:10.1016/j.ijproman.2015.02.006.

The information used to make decisions in the management of complex projects is generated and stored digitally. Complex projects are a set of projects that share particular defining characteristics: they are high-tech, capital intensive engineering projects that are of a significant scale, relatively long duration, and require firms to work collaboratively across firm boundaries in project delivery (Davies and Hobday, 2006, Hobday, 1998 and Miller et al., 1995). Such projects deliver complex product systems, such as aircraft, experimental facilities and railways. Their delivery requires systems integration capabilities, as complex product systems are designed and integrated through a network of component and sub-system suppliers (Davies and Mackenzie, 2014, Davies et al., 2009 and Hobday et al., 2005). Within these projects information about complex product systems is developed across multiple firms, involving diverse professions and trades, as these organizations interact through the digital systems.

A starting point for our work is the observation that, as we enter an era of 'big data', asset information is becoming a project deliverable. *Data* are unprocessed, often described as "unorganized facts" (e.g. Faucher et al., 2008: p. 55), while *information* is interpreted and presented to inform in a given context. Owners seek to use asset information to achieve sustainable and safe performance of complex systems through the life-cycle. An asset may be an assembly, sub-assembly, or component, but is the smallest unit maintained by an owner. The term 'asset information' is used to describe information about an asset, which may include the provenance, part types and serial numbers, design life, maintenance schedule, and design rationale for sub-systems or components. As data gets reused across the life-cycle, sets of data and information become combined and can be mined, interpreted and used in new ways. The UK government, for example, is, as a client for built infrastructure, requiring project teams to deliver asset information through building information modelling ( BIS/ Industry Working Group, 2011); and seeks to aggregate and combine data-sets, connecting them with Smart City and Smart Grid initiatives as part of a strategy for Digital Built Britain (UK Government, 2013).

Established approaches for managing change on projects use configuration management, a systems engineering approach with origins in the mid-20th century. In its original form, configuration management is characteristics of what Levitt (2011) describes as 'project management 1.0.' It involves hierarchical, sequential and asynchronous processes; managing change against a baseline. Its use focuses attention on assets as *configuration items*: sub-systems or components that have value to the organization, in which changes will often have systemic consequences on the function or layout of other items within the product structure and hierarchy. The baseline is an agreed description of one or a number of assets at a point in time, where the current configuration of a complex product system is described by the latest baselines plus approved changes.

New practices of managing change in complex projects might be expected as we enter an era of 'big data', in which internal and external data-sets become linked and asset information becomes a project deliverable. Morris argued that: "*rigorous change control is fundamental to good project management*" ( Morris, 2013: p.126). Poor change control is one of the issues that limits managers' ability to execute viable project plans (Pinto, 2013). Others see projects, themselves, as information processing systems (e.g. Winch (2010)drawing on Galbraith, 1973 and Galbraith, 1977). As project management information systems (Braglia and Frosolini, 2014) are increasingly used, altering the pace and complexity (Shenhar and Dvir, 2007) of projects, there are challenges to the: "*heavy formality of several of the techniques to manage large-scale, one-time, non-routine projects*" ( Morris, 2013: p. 133). Here, Morris, like Levitt, points to software projects, in particular, as rebelling, using agile forms of management, through small projects with close developer-customer relationships.

The aim of this research is to articulate how changes in assets and the associated asset information are managed in the delivery of complex projects as we enter the era of 'big data.' This is done by analyzing leading practices in three organizations: Airbus, CERN and Crossrail. Each of these organizations delivers complex projects; relies on digital technologies to manage a large volume of information; and uses configuration management to establish and maintain the integrity of the complex product system and associated information (see Table 1). Airbus is an aircraft manufacturer, operating in the aerospace industry and engaged in production of commercial and military aircrafts, with long-term projects to design and develop new aircraft designs and bring them into operation. Its headquarters are in France but the supply-chain is global, with the assembly of each plane involving thousands of companies and millions of parts. CERN is the European organization for nuclear research and the largest particle physics research establishment in the world, with 21 member states, 6 observer states and more than 80 collaborating countries. Its mission is to provide scientists from all around the world with tools to study the building blocks of matter and the origins of the universe. Crossrail is the largest construction project in Europe, with 14.8bn funding, delivering a new 100 km rail route with 10 new stations and a tunnel through central London connecting 40 stations. It has a complex supply-chain involved in delivery with more than 1,300 contracts.

The next section outlines extant research on managing change in delivery, before the following sections describe our research methods and findings. It outlines the development of configuration management techniques; characteristics of an era of big data; and relevance configuration management and big data to Morris' interest in 'reconstructing project management.'

**Table 1.** Background of organizations studied, and their industries.

| | Airbus | CERN | Crossrail |
|---|---|---|---|
| Industry | Aerospace design and manufacturing | Nuclear research infrastructure | Civil engineering and railway infrastructure |
| Background | Leading aircraft manufacturer of commercial and military aircrafts, with a substantial international supply-chain. | Largest particle physics research establishment in the world with tunnels and particle accelerators | Design and construction of new railway across London with tunnels and 37 stations |
| Relationship to projects | Long term internal projects to design and manufacture new additions to the fleet, such as the A380, integrating sub-systems and components and delivering to customers. | Experienced project owner, managing supply-chain delivering accelerators such as the Large Hadron Collider (LHC) | Delivery client for a mega-project, the duration of which is 2008–2018, interfacing with future operators of the railway. |
| Location | France | Switzerland | UK |

# MANAGING CHANGE IN PROJECT DELIVERY

## Development of Configuration Management Techniques to Manage Change

Configuration management was developed in the 1950s by the US military to control documentation in the manufacture of missiles (Brouse, 2008, Burgess et al., 2005 and Gonzalez, 2002). Early documentation on engineering change control, released by the military, clarifies the contractual obligations and role of suppliers. It refers to a product baseline describing the functional, physical and interoperability characteristics of components for testing and operations (DOD, 1978 and Military, 1988). Two example change processes, used in the commercial arrangements of acquisition and supply, are provided by the Department of Defense guidance issued in 2013 (see Fig. 1 for one of these, where the other is a variant). As well as change control, the classic approach to configuration management involves the identification of the product structure and configuration items; *status accounting* to determine the configuration of the system at any stage of the lifecycle ( Burgess et al., 2003 and Kidd and Burgess, 2010) and report on the availability and retrievability of data; and *audit* to verify the consistency of the information ( Kidd and Burgess, 2010). The approach has become extensively used in the software industry ( Bersoff, 1984, Estublier, 2000 and Williams, 2009), and in safety critical systems such as nuclear and aerospace ( Burgess et al., 2005 and Williams, 2009). It became recognized as an ISO 10007 quality management process in 1995 (ISO, 2003). The presentation, with a man at a drawing board, shows the heritage of this approach in the paper-based processes of the late 20th century; though in the 21st century such processes are supported by digital systems.

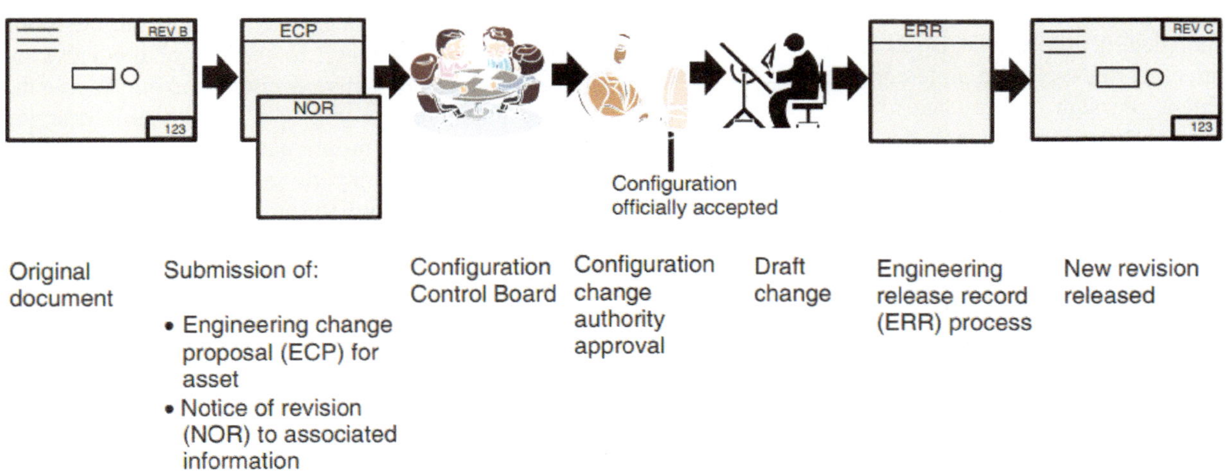


**Figure 1.** Standard change process (redrawn from source: DOD, 2013: p. 33, to clarify and explain acronyms, same images of documents and clip art used).

The US military describes configuration management's overarching goal as: "*to ensure there is documentation which completely and accurately describes the intended design, the actual product matches the documentation, and there are processes in place so this continues throughout the product's life*" (DOD, 2013: p.10). The ambition is to address the problems which occur in projects due to unchecked changes in one sub-system having wider consequences for other sub-systems of a product (Hameri, 1997); and due to scope creep, where requirements change during the process of delivery (Williams, 2009); providing traceability of product data to understand where problems occur, diagnosing and contributing to recovery (Burgess et al., 2003). A configuration is: "*a generic term for anything that has a defined structure or is composed of some predetermined pattern*" (Kidd and Burgess, 2010: p. 109). An authorization approach is used to control change and there are different hierarchy levels depending on the use of configuration items (Billingham, 2008). A baseline is established: "*wherever it is necessary in the product life cycle to define a reference for further activities.*" ( ISO, 2003: p. 4). From an approved baseline, a configuration change authority assesses the recommendation of other representatives to approve, approve with modifications, or disapprove submitted changes based on the: "*total lifecycle impact of the action to include cost, schedule, performance and logistics impact*" ( DOD, 2013: p. 27).Thus the processes, procedures and users of the configuration management system play an integral role in maintaining the integrity of information throughout the life-cycle by controlling changes. If users do not follow the process, errors can occur which can cause problems to the product in production and to related information dissemination ( Hameri, 1997 and Hameri and Nitter, 2002). Researchers of configuration management constantly find the benefits of such a controlled process of change are not always understood or realized by users ( Ali and Kidd, 2014, Burgess et al., 2003, Kidd, 2001 and Kidd and Burgess, 2010).

The upsurge in the use of digital technologies and flexible team-working bring into question configuration management practices based on documents rather than information (Burgess et al., 2005). Characteristics of 'configuration management' are not stable and fixed but are themselves evolving, to include the life-cycle, agile approaches, and changes to strategy as well as project. For example, after cancelling its configuration management standard MIL-STD-973 in 2000, the US Department of Defense found that it continued to be used in non-standard ways. From 2010 they developed a new standard for configuration management to changes through life using digital systems (Windham, 2012). The interim standard mentions three baselines, with a functional baseline giving system level requirements; allocated baseline giving subsystem or configuration item level requirements; and product baseline giving detailed definition (DOD, 2013: p. 18). There are recent attempts to develop an agile approach to configuration management through a system to accommodate small continuous changes and manage the additional complexity across dispersed teams (Moreira, 2010); and reports suggesting an expanded scope of configuration management, to include enterprise as well as product baselines (Wozny et al., 2014).

## Reuse of Information and Data Linkages in the Era of 'Big Data'

There are rapid developments in digital technologies and an extensive growth in the volume of data stored digitally that affects project delivery. The term 'big data' indicates the use of large heterogeneous data-sets that can themselves be aggregated, and subjected to various forms of analytics to enable patterns in the data to be visualized. While there is not agreement on a precise definition, many writers, across both information science and social science literatures, draw on Laney (2001) to refer to data volume, velocity and variety. *Volume* of data is implied by the term 'big data' and is an issue because there is an increasing extent of data available ( Wu and Wu, 2014), with 2.5 exabytes of data created globally each day in 2012 and expectations that the rate of data production will double every 40 months (McAfee and Brynjolfsson, 2012: 62). Yet recent work emphasises characteristics other than volume ( Boyd and Crawford, 2012 and Kitchin, 2014). *Velocity* relates to the speed of production and of access of data. Advances in computing processing capacity enable data-sets to be engaged with in real-time, or near real-time, rather than 'freeze framed' ( Kitchin, 2014) or processed offline. *Variety* refers to the diverse range of data sources and types of data that are combined (Viitanen and Kingston, 2013 and Wu and Wu, 2014). On projects this variety can include hierarchically structured data such as models, and unstructured data such as laser scans, videos, sensor data, photos and experimental data. While volume, velocity and variety are generally characteristic of the applications described as 'big data', these applications vary in the extent to which they emphasise one or the other of these characteristics.

Big data represents a paradigm shift, where "*most of our attitudes and behaviors still reflect hierarchical and sequential processing of data*" ( Galbraith, 2014). Information is no longer created and used for a single purpose (Constantiou and Kallinikos, 2015). As we enter an era of 'big data', information from projects becomes seen as a project deliverable and used throughout the lifecycle. Organization scholars observe how: "*organizations are swimming in an expanding sea of data that is either too voluminous or too unstructured to be managed and analyzed through traditional means*" ( Davenport et al., 2012: p. 22). Different professional users bring their own way of organizing data to understanding it, so early work highlighted a need for indexing strategies that were agnostic to these structures (Laney, 2001: p. 1). Big data is different from 'lots of data' as it is: "*those data that disrupt fundamental notions of integrity and force new ways of thinking and doing to reestablish it*"( Lagoze, 2014: p.4-5). It thus raises a conundrum for science (Lagoze, 2014): how to utilize the benefits of 'big data' while maintaining the validity of data.

Despite ongoing concerns about integrity, many organizations are moving away from asynchronous and reactive decision-making; to the use of predictive analytics for real-time and proactive decision-making. Within the social science literatures on 'big data', analytics is described as a differentiator of organizational performance (LaValle et al., 2011); a source of competitive advantage (Barton and Court, 2012 and McAfee and Brynjolfsson, 2012); or new frontier of competition (Floridi, 2012). Here, the challenge of big data has been reframed as one of identifying small patterns (Floridi, 2012) within immense databases, and the use of these to create new value and knowledge. Emerging technologies are associated with this business analytics (Chen et al., 2012); and the way that information is considered is different, as analytics may be used to seek insights from the flow of information as well as its content (Williams et al., 2014). Various text and web mining as well as social network analysis techniques are becoming used to organize and visualize information to understand performance in organizations (Chen et al., 2012 and Williams et al., 2014). The many-to-many non-linear data relationships that arise in large and evolving data-sets (Wu and Wu, 2014) lead to challenges in ensuring reliability, which has implications for decision making. Different preferences in recording data can result in diverse representations and relationships that makes it difficult to discover useful patterns (Wu and Wu, 2014). Synthesized information may thus need to be situated in a broader historical context to be used in a predictive manner (Boyd and Crawford, 2011).

The power of flexibly linking asset information with other data-sets is beginning to be realized by owners of complex product systems such as infrastructure. Transport for London has, for example, made data available to customers, and also to engineers, to combine data in new ways to develop new applications.[1]Williams et al. (2014) point to the potential for a census rather than sampling approach to organizational data to be used to assess organizational maturity in the use of project-management. Recent industry reports envision a future in which data-sets are linked and analytics are used predictively, for example to precompute scenarios and inform decision-making (e.g. BIM 2050 Group, 2014). There may be latent applications in complex projects, for example in the use of dashboards as an interface to whole data-sets to evaluate supply-chain performance.

## 'Reconstructing' Project Management: Configuration Management in an Era of Big Data

Morris (2013) has an ambition to 'reconstruct' project management by shifting attention from the execution of projects to the management of projects – which includes the definition of the project, the role of the owner or sponsor, and the project context. This wider view is necessary to investigate how change is managed in an era of 'big data' where asset information has becomes a project deliverable. The complex project delivers an asset that is used in operations. As asset information becomes a deliverable, Fig. 2shows how data-sets become increasingly aggregated and linked in the delivery of the project, with links to external sources of data (e.g. from suppliers, manufacturers and maintainers), and the complex project responsible for managing change in an increasing volume, velocity and variety of data in project digital systems. This anticipates potential new connections, for example between information used in the project and reference schedule and cost data; and between asset information and the owner's enterprise resource planning system.

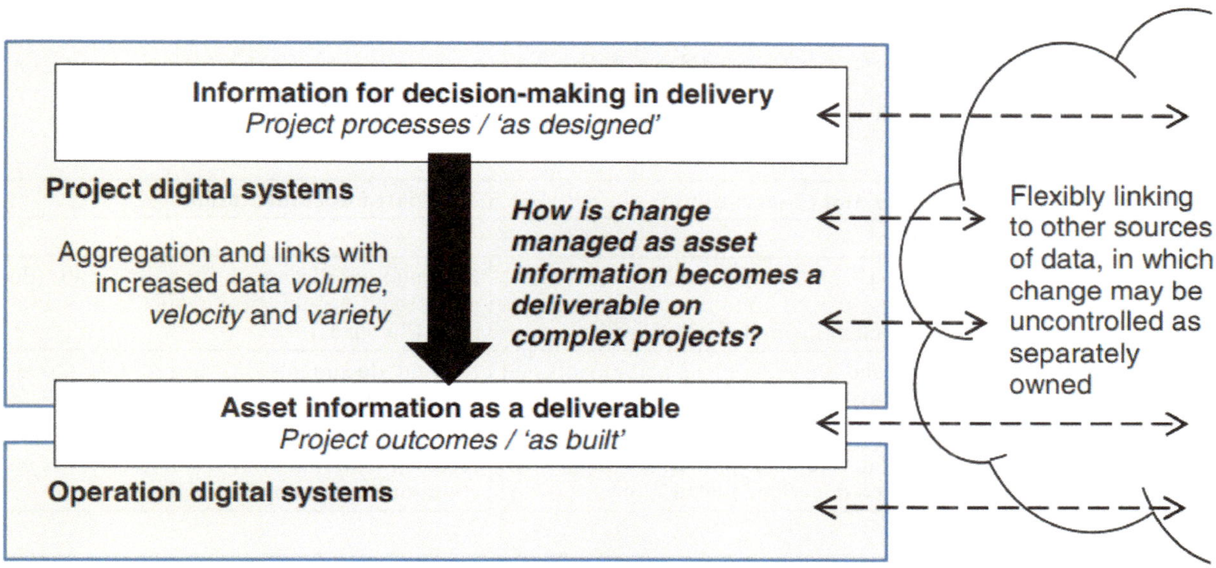


**Figure 2.** Context for our research question on managing change as asset information becomes a deliverable on complex projects.

Digital systems are not homogeneous, but combine networks, servers, and computers with software for different purposes, and from different vendors. They are used in the storage, retrieval, management and manipulation of data; with data management software used to upload, integrate, structure, index and search data, and to manage remote access, security, versions and workflows. Stored data includes files, folders and meta-data; held in a range of specialist software. In projects most of this data is classified and structured, though it can be combined with a variety of sources of unstructured data in projects, which have previously been ignored (Boyd and Crawford, 2011). Where organized for a particular purpose we describe it as information, hence asset information as a deliverable is managed digitally, and reuses the same data-sets that have been used to inform decision-making in delivery.

A major question, raised by the era of 'big data' relates to control and the management of change as digital data-sets cross organizational boundaries; particularly as information about assets gets re-used in operations. In manufacturing and construction industries the use of information through the life-cycle is often referred to as Product Life-cycle Management (PLM) and Building Information Modeling (BIM) respectively. The practical concerns of project managers about control in this context are reflected in the report of a meeting of the Major Projects Association, which in summary notes that: "*Manual uploading of data between software programmes allows better understanding of progress and visibility*" ( MPA, 2013: p. 3). In this report there are concerns that project managers feel swamped as the project controls themselves produce massive data-sets. The solutions proposed are manual interventions, to identify key information or manually transfer data.

Configuration management is discussed little in the project management literatures, and where it is mentioned, notably in Morris' work, it is as implemented through the digital systems used on projects. In the move toward the "era of the paperless project", Morris describes configuration management: "*extended to include the configuration of the total project documentation handling process.*" ( Morris, 1997: preface, note 4); noting increasing focus on information rather than documents. The Project Management Body of Knowledge Guide likewise refers to the configuration management system as a component of the project management information system, containing versions and baselines for all project documents (PMBOK guide, 2013: p. 28). Standards for asset management likewise indicate this need to manage changes to assets assessing risks and consequences of change. While we know that users resist configuration management processes and these are not fully implemented (e.g. Ali and Kidd, 2014), we know little about how change is managed on complex projects, as we move into an era of 'big data, and asset information becomes used as a project deliverable. We approached our empirical work with a question about how changes in assets and asset information are managed in this context as summarized in Fig. 2.

## METHODS

Using a case study methodology (e.g. Eisenhardt and Graebner, 2007, Stake, 1995 and Yin, 1994), we analyzed change management practices in the three separate organizations as cases, and then compared and contrasted the findings across cases to develop further insight. The organizations were selected as leading organizations that deliver complex product systems using digital technologies to manage the large volumes of associated information. Data was collected from the three organizations, and their interactions with each other as summarized in Table 2. Our initial contact with participants indicated our interest in examining the transition from an "as-designed" configuration baseline to an "as-built" configuration baseline; as information was delivered to owners and operators. The preliminary analysis was based on a desktop review of leading configuration management activity in through-life engineering and scoping interviews with 1–2 personnel from the CAD management and/or configuration management teams from Airbus, CERN (online) and Crossrail (in-person) as well as a visit to Airbus premises. The scoping interviews used a protocol with starter questions including: How is configuration management defined? What are the processes involved in setting up this configuration management? What is the approach to configuration control? What are the challenges in terms of integration of data from as-design configuration baseline to the as-built configuration? At the end of projects did you find differences between the as-built with the as-designed?

**Table 2.** Sources of data for the individual cases and the comparison across cases.

| Organization | Interactions and observations | Associated documentation |
|---|---|---|
| ***Data on each individual case*** | | |
| Airbus | Online call (2 participants and 2 researchers) and day-long visit to Toulouse (10 participants and 2 researchers); email clarifications. | Presentation discussed in online call (20 pages) and 3 publically available presentations (79 pages). |
| CERN | Online call and presentation (2 participants and 2 researchers); email clarifications. | Internal documents (23 pages, QA procedure; status report); 2 conference papers (6 pages); and presentation (29 pages). |
| Crossrail | In person interview (1 participant and 2 researchers) and ongoing collaboration. | Access to internal system and documents on configuration management. |
| | | |
| *Comparison across cases* | | |
| Airbus; CERN and Crossrail | 3 hour workshop with 20 participants, recorded in 49 photographs (some video) and notes; email correspondence. | Presentations from the workshop (94 slides). |

The comparison across cases was facilitated by an afternoon workshop hosted in the Crossrail offices in London. The workshop in Crossrail offices involved twenty participants, with at least two participants from the CAD management and/or configuration management teams within each organization studied. This day was recorded with video; 49 photographs and notes as well as through the distribution of presentation from each organization afterwards (totaling 94 slides from the 3 companies). It was an opportunity for presentations about the context for the research; for feedback of preliminary findings; presentations on configuration management from the three companies and discussion of key theoretical challenges.

Following the workshop we analyzed and iterated a detailed table that compared configuration management practices in the three collaborating organizations, in relation to topics that had arisen in the discussion at the workshop: 1) *background* (e.g. overview, infrastructure type, scope of works, budgets); 2) *lifecycle* (e.g. typical lifecycle duration; development time); 3) *complexity* (e.g. physical assets; asset information); 4) *configuration management motivation* (corporate motivation, industry guidance, teams); 5) *approach and systems* (e.g. lifecycle breakdown, approach, data management, information systems and supporting tool, structure of configuration items; 6) *managing change and change control process* (e.g. change perspective, change control process, conformances and non-conformances); 7) *risks*; *cultural and social issues* (e.g. language, culture). The table we generated was used to visualize the data for discussion in the research team ( Miles and Huberman, 1994), to identify salient similarities and differences, and to check details with the collaborating firms. We discussed the findings in this table, which was seven pages long, to identify why all three firms had a strong interest in configuration management and to highlight the similarities and differences. To develop our argument we reorganized our data, bringing it into dialogue with the existing literatures on the management of projects.

## FINDINGS

The three organizations studied have different levels of experience of configuration management. Airbus has mature processes and systems, with interest in leading development of future systems to manage and control the growing amount of data produced in the delivery of complex products. CERN introduced configuration management in the 1990s (Bachy and Hameri, 1997, Hameri, 1997, Hameri and Nitter, 2002 and Hameri and Puittinen, 2003) and are reflecting on their approaches to configuration management, challenges and areas for improvement. As a major project, Crossrail is a temporary organisation, established in 2008. It has a configuration management team and has drawn on industry standards (e.g. ISO, 2003) to rapidly embed configuration management processes in the delivery of asset information. Motivations given for using configuration management in managing change in these settings include the complexity of complex product systems, operational constraints, and the need for valid asset information. The regulated nature of each of the industries (aerospace, nuclear research and civil engineering), mean these organizations all need to be able to track configuration items to be able to revisit designs and comply with future regulation on safety-critical facilities. In Airbus, configuration management is a strategic priority. In CERN and Crossrail, it is an explicit activity that is addressed in organizational strategy using the language of managing change.

### Configuration Management in Airbus

As an aircraft manufacturer, Airbus employs around 63,000 people in France, Germany, Spain and the United Kingdom. It has subsidiaries in the United States, Japan, China and India; and the final assembly of aircraft is in France, Germany, Spain, and through a joint venture in China. Customers include commercial airlines. Satisfying their evolving needs requires the design and manufacture of new additions to the fleet. Airbus invests about two billion euros annually in research, development and technology activities. It operates in the highly regulated aerospace industry, in which each aircraft manufactured requires an individual certificate of airworthiness showing it conforms to the approved design, and has the relevant documentation, inspections and tests to ensure it will be safe in operations. Aircraft components have strict definitions that include architectural nature and materials. There are rules on how components are aggregated into sub-assemblies and assemblies to ensure the correct serviceable part is available for every configuration and operating condition.

Configuration management is one of the 14 Airbus key competences, considered in procurement of the supply-chain and included as a requirement in contracts. It is well established in Airbus. There is a Centre of Competence where 80 internal employees and 70 external consultants work to edit methods, process and tools; and a significant broader capability, with more than 8000 professionals with related tasks, including 800 internal and 500 external configuration management professionals.

A motivation for configuration management is the product complexity. It can take more than a decade to develop a new aircraft design. Airbus produces several aircraft families, each with members and versions. No two aircraft are the same as customers can select between variants and the production standard evolves continuously. The number of parts and combinations of solutions grow with product complexity along with the combination of configurations to be managed. Product architecture includes component parts, numbering and links; with 500–1000 concept definitions, with associated solutions and ways to restore previous solutions.

There is a significant *volume* of data, where each aircraft has millions of parts. The Airbus A380 plane has, for example, about 4 million parts, with 2.5 million part numbers produced by 1,500 companies from 30 countries around the world. There is a growing *velocity*, with increasing production rates, and shorter product development lead times. As aircraft design requires careful analysis of performance data, there is also significant *variety*, with product information linked to structured and unstructured data-sets with test results, electrical bonding calculations, requirements from economic analyses, weight distribution, and weight calculations, etc. Configuration management processes have substantial digital support, with six preferred suppliers for configuration management services. However, as the number of data-sets has increased, some information related to the aircraft is no longer well linked. For example, the functional baseline with the initial specifications is not well linked with the technical baseline, within which change is managed once requirements are approved. Instead these are synchronized at a particular point and reset.

In Airbus, a configuration item is seen as "an invariant item in the product structure", where each configuration item is linked to a design solution. While configuration items stay the same, the engineering baseline, used to design, gives a different view of the product architecture from the manufacturing baseline, which is used to install things, and both are different from the data needed in customer services. It can be difficult to recover a technical functional baseline when a big evolution is done to a standard aircraft, where the interface between different data-sets are not linked which means the source of data is not easily known. A significant milestone is the move between concept and definition phases, where data is moved from a development environment to a production environment, which often involves different data structures. At this point, engineers may be involved in manually updating data, re-numbering data-sets as well as re-defining links.

Before product evolution can take place in the concept stage there is an important "congruency process", through which engineering and manufacturing agree on product architecture and terminology. A request for a product evolution then involves four stages: *initialization*, which is the change request; *evaluation*, which involves an evaluation study; *investigation*, which involves a modification proposal and consideration of technical, cost, embodiment and production repercussions; and *implementation and closure*, in which there is a full technical repercussions sheet, technical dossier and modifications approval sheet. There are also processes for managing change in product identification, and releasing information from engineering and manufacturing information in the definition stage. All these process involve a final step that verifies the implications of change to the product structure at higher levels within this complex product system; and ensures consistency across all domains (including systems, electrical, test and technical data).

Airbus wants to improve efficiency of the product data management by achieving: *scalability*, through reuse of data; *agility*, through integration of data, and *adaptability*, through flexibility in integrating data changes. Configuration management challenges include:

- *Different product architectures* – Developing agreement between stakeholders in engineering, management and customer services takes a long time. In Airbus' experience, developing a complete architecture can take up to three years to agree. After the congruence process, the product architecture is the same in both engineering and manufacturing and a bill of materials is produced.
- *A desire to be agile in a highly controlled environment.* The strict and rigid system developed through the congruency process lacks flexibility. Yet, even after the congruency process is complete there are still changes that need to take place based on technology developments and the changing competitive environment that may not have been included in the congruency process.

Other challenges include the increase of product and process complexity; variety of software vendors and their lack of support for the interfaces between systems; heavy load of changes to manage; communication to a growing configuration management community; and shorter product development lead time.

## Configuration Management in CERN

To achieve its mission of providing scientists from around the world with tools to study the building blocks of matter and origins of the universe, CERN builds and operates huge particle accelerators on the border between Switzerland and France, close to Geneva. It has approximately 2,350 staff, 2,000 contractors and 10,000 visiting scientists, with an annual budget of about 800 million EUR. As an integrated owner-operator, it has responsibility for the full asset life-cycle. Development and delivery of each particle accelerator is a major project. The Large Hadron Collider (LHC), for example, involved millions of high-tech components installed in a 27 km long circular tunnel, 100 meters below ground, with particles accelerated to 99.999999% of the speed of light, corresponding to over 11,000 revolutions per second. The design phase took approximately 20 years, and the work was globally distributed with collaborators in more than 80 countries across five continents. The material cost was approximately 3.7 billion EUR.

While a lot of the design work and drafting is sub-contracted, there are about 150 full time designers using CAD, who are engaged in designing in 2D and 3D, updating information, and upgrading designs on the different projects. A digital system for data management has been used since the late 1990s, with 5,700 active users registered on the system. The volume of data is significant: The whole complex involves 100 million components; with about 1.5 million documents and drawings; 1.6 million individually registered assets; and almost 2 million equipment interventions logged. The velocity of information involves about 3,000 new pieces of equipment a month, and 7,000 new documents and drawings created a month. In work on an accelerator in 2009 there were approximately 12,500 equipment interventions per month. This data is of significant variety, it includes physics parameters, technical specifications, layouts and equipment codes (in specification); simulations, bill of materials, documents and drawings, (in design); manufacturing processes and test procedures and results (in manufacturing); installation and safety procedures; and "as-installed" documentation (in installation); and radiation measurements, material composition, recycling procedures; and waste management (in dismantling).

There is substantial interest in configuration management within CERN with an ongoing initiative to update processes of change control. The manufacturing team has a mature understanding of configuration management, and uses the work breakdown structure to manage assets through the supply-chain, and follow up changes. Manufacturing software is linked to the digital system for data management, where manufacturing data on critical equipment can be entered. There is interest in improving this for the design data including production drawings; and a desire to formalize the feedback from operation and maintenance teams as input for new designs and standardizing of parts. Challenges include the:

- *Extended life-cycles* – Installations have lifecycles of more than 50 years, so they use historical data and formats, such as microfilm drawings, and collect missing information by scanning and photographing the system. New asset information will be relied on by operators in the mid-to-late 21st century, so needs to be self-explanatory and complete.
- *Large, complex and advanced installation* – Many pieces of equipment unique, designed specially, and the result of many years of research and development. New accelerators and experiments must be installed into the overall system of tunnels and facilities, for example a new accelerator reused the main part of an old tunnel, with some interventions such as ground construction work to upgrade it.
- *Support for a scientific culture* – The nature of the science means tolerances may be measured in microns (one micron is a thousandth of a millimeter) in an installation of several kilometers. Yet unlike the military context in which configuration management was developed, there is not a centralized command and control culture. The ethos is based around international research collaboration.
- *Major operational constraints* – There is no access to tunnels and equipment when scientific experiments are in progress. There is a long shut-down for maintenance work every 1–2 years, with a short technical stop every 1–2 months. Even then access is curtailed by the need to limit installers and maintainers exposure to radiation; and to cool-down and warm-up equipment after and before experiments.
- *Regulations for nuclear installations* – Installers and maintainers have to wait to enter certain zones because of the radiation generated. Radiation effects are calculated for each material. Where equipment or components are installed or removed, these have to be tracked. CERN is classified as a nuclear installation,

so regulations are similar to a power plant, requiring traceable documentation of equipment, interventions and procedures.

- *Parallel design work* – Upgrades are managed by machine versions (2007, 2009, 2012, 2015 etc.) as different accelerator configurations are worked on in parallel. Changes include planned configuration changes across versions; and interventions to fix things. When equipment is installed, it needs to fit with what is there. Where there have been unexpected changes, installers have had to cut and weld equipment when installing it, modifying it on the spot to make it fit.

There is particular focus on managing such 'non-conformities', where changes happen to the design during the using, testing, installing or modifying the equipment. Such changes may result in a design not being exactly within the specification. How the equipment does not conform to specification is documented. Checks are made to establish whether equipment can be used, accepted as it is, or corrected, and how it might be corrected. Some equipment is bespoke and extremely expensive, so it may be accepted despite not conforming to specification if it can be adapted on site. 'As-built' information is required for maintenance and disposal, as well as the next generation design, so test data and new versions of the drawings need to be entered into the systems, along with the location of the installed equipment in the tunnel.

## Configuration Management in Crossrail

Crossrail acts as the delivery client for a new railway, which is due to begin operation in 2018. This £15.8 billion complex project aims to hand-over a physical and digital railway. It involves upgrading existing rail networks; building new stations; boring 42 km of new tunnels across central London from Paddington Station to Liverpool Street Station; installing, extending and commissioning a wide array of underground electrical and mechanical systems; and delivering the associated asset information to owners and operators. Contracts with the supply-chain require delivery of asset information as well as assets. There is a program of briefing the supply-chain on how to deliver this; and the quality of received information is benchmarked, initially every quarter, and now every 2 weeks. High quality asset information is required as the railway is expected to operate for over 100 years.

Configuration management is important in ensuring a consistent, validated set of asset information as a project deliverable. Through delivery there has been a small team focused on configuration management in a broader information management team. They are involved in developing processes for establishing and maintaining the integrity of configuration items in the preparation for hand-over. Digital system is used to manage data, where the project manages a significant volume of data, expecting to generate 2–3 million records in asset databases, 1 million model and drawing records; and quarter of a million GIS records. Asset information is stored within a repository, which is managed by data management software, with document, model and geographic information linked to this, but requiring different software to be viewed and edited. There is hence a significant variety of linked data in the form of asset information (and all the associated variables, such as author, approver, dates and versioning); digital *documents*, such as operational and maintenance manuals, plans, requirements, 2D designs; parametric building information *models*; and *geographic information*, such as asset locations.

Physical assets include rail-tracks, trains, shafts and buildings. The contractor is responsible for providing labels to identify assets as configuration items where practical, as well as equipment/serial number labels on all equipment, unless the size restricts application. The labelling of assets enables tracking of these items. Assets are also related to other assets to represent vital 'powered by' or 'controlled by' relationships. The associated information is controlled by contractors until they deliver 'as-built' information to Crossrail. From there onwards in the lifecycle, Crossrail locks down information associated with configuration items, equipment/serial number labels, and controls any further changes internally, to ensure the integrity of asset information in their digital system. The delivery client can introduce configuration items when design has matured, from detailed design onwards. Crossrail applies configuration control at the 'as-built' stage so changes to the configuration before handover are consistently maintained for the owner. There are currently around 155 thousand client configuration items, and by March 2016 the number is expected to rise over 600 thousand. Challenges include:

*Rapid deployment in a temporary organization* – International standards for configuration and asset management were important, where obtaining the 'buy-in' to establish and maintain integrity is hugely challenging in the middle of a complex mega project.

- *Complexity and culture of delivery* – There are conflicts and interfaces among the many processes and procedures currently used in the industry for changes in programme baseline, design management, red-line (marked-up) and as-built drawings. There are challenges in understanding these and creating the culture that get managers and engineers to understand and use these existing change processes.
- *Multiple change processes* – the configuration management team has concluded that having multiple change processes, as is currently the case within the industry is not ideal, particularly where each change process may differ slightly and in some the same person is assessing the impact of change and making the decision of whether it should or shouldn't be rejected.
- *Establishing a requirements-led orientation* – There is a need for a change from typical methods in the industry to mitigate the risk of scope creep, by having assets that conform to asset information, which in turn conform to requirements. The red-line procedure, for example, covers the process of annotating changes to drawings after they have been released for construction. The task, which is conducted by the site contractor, is intended to highlight approved, post-design changes from the original drawings, as reflected by an inspector of the built asset. The annotated drawings are then transferred to Crossrail. These records are used to later update the as-built drawings prior to data handover to the operator.
- *Determining operational requirements* – There are ongoing discussions with the future owners and operators regarding the type and format of asset information that will be used in operations; and a need

to future-proof this information because of the long operational life.

An interface to the digital system has been reconfigured to facilitate this delivery of the large volume of asset-specific information. This specifies how asset information is to be identified, named, labelled, stored, synthesized and managed. Additional rules for numbering and naming complement the use of international configuration management standards to provide robust methods of maintaining asset information. By following a standard structure, and definitions, the aim is to organize asset information within the digital system and to hand it over to operators in ways that will be useful to future operation and maintenance. The interface helps users to transfer asset requirements to contractors, as well as capture the configuration items that those contractors return. Asset labels, equipment labels and serial numbers are used to represent configuration items, as defined in three different hierarchies based on location, function and classification. The system allows metadata searching; and provides the ability to explicitly link groups of assets to form a single system.

## Approaches to Managing Change

While each organization, Airbus, CERN and Crossrail, operates in a different industry, similarities in their approaches and experience of using configuration management reveal shared characteristics and challenges of managing change in complex projects as asset information becomes a deliverable. Table 3 summarizes and compares the relationship between project delivery and operations; the data aggregation and connections in project delivery; and approach to managing change to provide asset information as a deliverable; and these topics are discussed in turn below.

**Table 3.** Comparing how change is managed as asset information becomes a deliverable.

| | AIRBUS | CERN | CROSSRAIL |
|---|---|---|---|
| *Relationship between project delivery and operations* | | | |
| Organization type | Service provider, with multiple customers. | Integrated owner-operator | Delivery client, handing over infrastructure provider(s). |
| Responsibility | Design, manufacturing, and servicing in operation. | Full life-cycle. | Design, construction and handover. |
| Information as a deliverable | For customer services to monitor operational aircraft. | For maintenance and upgrades to accelerators. | For station and railway operators and maintainers. |
| Responsibility for operation information | Final configuration of customer's aircraft; updating servicing information. | Asset tracking; work management information; disposal information. | Asset information at hand-over; not responsible for updating and maintaining. |
| | | | |
| *Data aggregation and connections in project delivery* | | | |
| Interfaces in digital systems | Between the development environment and the production environment. | Across machine version; and between manufactured and installed equipment. | Between the delivery client's design and as-built asset information. |
| | | | |
| *Approach to managing change* | | | |
| Configuration management | Used in the concept, product identification and definition stages. | Principles most familiar in manufacturing; initiatives to reduce non-conformities. | Used to manage and control as-built information; principles used in design. |
| Configuration items | Agreed by manufacturing and engineering through a 'congruency process.' | Different configurations of the machine managed in parallel. | Identified by the delivery client and labelled by contractors. |
| Complex product system – hierarchy and baselines | Functional baseline for requirements; engineering baseline for design; manufacturing baseline for production and installation; Customer service baseline for technical information. | Different generations of machines have baselines that are managed in parallel, making it important to get information about unplanned changes back into the design information. | Configuration items first identified at detailed design stage. Contractors manage the information up to an as-built baseline. |

In summary, each of these organizations is interested in configuration management in operations as well as delivery, though they vary in the extent to which they have lifecycle responsibilities. Because Airbus has service contracts it retains an interest in aspects of configuration management, such as conformity, throughout the lifecycle for aircraft that it has designed and manufactured. CERN is an integrated owner-operator, with responsibility for the whole lifecycle. As the delivery client, Crossrail hands over asset information for operation and maintenance. For each organization, the complex products – aircraft, particle accelerators and railways – have a long operational life (more than 20, 50 and 100 years) so information on assets, such as material, provenance, and design rationale, need to be available to enable efficient and safe operation.

Project delivery involves managing change in asset information as data-sets are aggregated and re-used through life. The volume, velocity and variety of data bring new challenges of version control, linkages across project stages and with other data-sets; and ways of structuring and organizing. While there is increasing integration between data-sets in project delivery, digital systems are not seamlessly integrated, but heterogeneous, with major transitions in the use of data through the project life. For example, in Airbus, there is a significant transition between the development and the production environment, in which there is manual work to restructure and re-link data (there may be instances where the product does not change, but connections between configuration items is different in engineering and production). All three organizations carefully manage the upload of information to their digital system because of the importance of its integrity. Where equipment providers have relevant asset information, these organizations will often duplicate that information in their own systems rather than link to it, because they need to ensure it will still be available in decades to come, when the manufacturer may have different equipment for sale and may not maintain legacy information.

Change is managed through the digital system, with configuration management software providing workflows for defining baselines for particular assets and asset systems; and for assigning roles and responsibilities for approving changes. This use of configuration management starts earlier in Airbus, than in Crossrail, where the use of configuration management is most pronounced in the control of as-built information. Each organization has a substantial and distributed supply-chain that has access to input relevant information, and to be involved in the approval of change within project digital systems. Design globally distributed in both Airbus, with 4 million parts supplied from 30 countries for A380, and CERN, with 80 countries across 5 continents involved in the LHC design. Crossrail has a substantial supply-chain of contractors involved in construction. Contractors within this supply chain have permissions to input 'as-built' asset information into Crossrail's digital systems, with information approved for purpose before it is made available.

Baselines are sometimes interpreted as an agreed description of the complex product system at a point in time. This study has clarified the types of baselines now used in Airbus, CERN and Crossrail increasingly focus on assets or groups of assets. This is most clearly articulated in Airbus, which uses functional, engineering, manufacturing and customer service baselines to manage related changes in relevant stages of the life-cycle. Thus there is no longer a simple baseline, but functional, product and other baselines managed on different timescales. Although in the 1950s configuration management enabled a move backwards to the baseline, in the era of big data this is not straight forward. Re-baselining may not account for different evolutions in data unless these are all linked; and there is significant work in industry to achieve this.

## DISCUSSION: RENEWED IMPORTANCE OF CONFIGURATION MANAGEMENT IN AN ERA OF 'BIG DATA'

For managers in these organizations that deliver complex projects, configuration management has become more, rather than less, important as we enter an era of 'big data'. New challenges arise as asset information has become a project deliverable; as data increases in volume, velocity and variety; and as it is aggregated and re-used; with connections (and potential connections) across internally and externally held data-sets. The organizations perceive a greater need for control through configuration management. The analyses suggest the need for integrity, in assets and in asset information, is a reason for this renewed emphasis on and interest in the associated control processes, as complex projects manage a significant volume and variety of asset information and hand this on to owners and operators. Ensuring integrity in operations is essential in industries that are regulated and safety-critical but organizational complexity, large distributed supply-chains and time-pressures increase the challenge of projects delivering the asset information to support this.

Configuration management has its origins in the mid-20th century. However, what is meant by configuration management has changed significantly. There has been a shift from relatively slow paper-based processes to faster database oriented practices; and extension of configuration management practices to cover the life-cycle through articulation of multiple baselines and aspects of the product. It is through such changes that configuration management has increased in importance as an approach to managing change in the delivery of complex projects, in an era of big data, rather than left behind with the paper-based processes of the late 20th century. There is some evidence that the speed of interaction with this data is growing, with for example Crossrail increasing the frequency with which it benchmarks its supply-chain from every three months to every two weeks. This is not just about doing change control better, but also about providing more visibility of quality of change control by different parts of the supply-chain. Such changes are within the paradigm of configuration management: they are beginning to be reflected in related standards and guides, with configuration management described as a component of the project management information system (PMBOK guide, 2013); and, during the timeframe of our study, the military developing and releasing a new interim standard (DOD, 2013), having considered the use of a 3D model, definition of as-designed, as-built and as-maintained baselines, and definition of the product (Windham, 2012). Thus change management is no longer a paper-based process, as implied by Fig. 1, but it is predominantly concerned with digital data. Digital workflows become important to manage the integration of information; and conformity between requirements, specifications and asset information.

As previous research has shown that users often don't follow the prescribed processes involved in configuration management (Ali and Kidd, 2014, Burgess et al., 2003, Kidd, 2001 and Kidd and Burgess, 2010), there are opportunities to consider whether new digital technologies might enable other approaches to managing change. Airbus, CERN and Crossrail all face challenges in implementing control processes; and are actively engaged in developing new strategies. In complex projects, we anticipate limits to the extent to which 'big-data' will break the mould of established approaches to enable radically new, rapid and flexible form of organizing envisioned by Levitt (2011). However, we recognize the possibility of a broader shift away from baseline planning, as has occurred in software projects (Levitt, 2011); or a complete transition away from principles such as decomposition and hierarchy, as advocated by the military (Alberts and Hayes, 2003). Other approaches to managing change might be to mine data-sets to identify information relevant to the operational performance of assets; or to seek new scalable approaches to managing change in non-critical documents, where Wikipedia, might suggests a model in which changes are made, and then corrected; which contrasts with the more bureaucratic, pre-authorization approach of configuration management.

While managing change is important to project management, configuration management has had limited attention in literatures on complex projects. Research on complex projects has instead discussed how systems integration capabilities are mobilized in innovation in construction (Gann and Salter, 2000); and in manufacturing settings such as aircraft engine control system (Brusoni et al., 2001) and flight simulation (Miller et al., 1995). This research on systems integration, like the work on configuration management, traces its history to the USA missile programme in the 1950s (Sapolski, 2003). Change management through 'configuration management' relates to systems integration, as it involves the decomposition of the complex product system to identify assets, and then manage change within these assets and their associated asset information.

## CONCLUSIONS

While prior research has argued that digitally-enabled approaches break the mould of established approaches to project management, enabling rapid, flexible forms of project organizing; in this study we find Airbus, CERN and Crossrail, using relatively hierarchical, asynchronous, sequential processes to manage change. We conclude that the unstructured, uncontrolled nature of 'big data' presents challenges to complex projects that deliver assets. Thus this paper contributes by uncovering limits to flexibility where integrity is important. The potential to use 'big data' in these contexts presents a conundrum, similar to that discussed by Lagoze in science. While there is the potential for analytics to provide commercial advantage by revealing small patterns, 'big data' represents a paradigm shift that disrupts notions of integrity and force new ways of thinking and doing to re-establish it. It challenges the existing approaches to ensuring the integrity of assets in regulated and safety critical environments.

There are practical implications. The first is that as managers in complex projects begin to deliver asset information, as well as assets, they should expect changes in both assets and associated asset information, and plan to manage this change. The second is that managers should be aware of the challenges that an 'era of big data' presents to this process of managing change. Configuration management provides a set of tools for maintaining integrity in this context, and implementation of configuration management has changed and is changing as a result of digital technologies. As well as using these processes, there may be contexts in which there are opportunities for managers to seek new proactive approaches to using data from projects to understanding future scenarios. Managers seeking to benefit from 'big data', must do this while maintaining the validity of the information on which the delivery and maintenance of complex product systems rely.

There are also implications for research. This study returns attention to Morris' interests in the history of project management; the centrality of change control to good project management; and the shift from project execution to broader questions of management of projects. There are a number of directions for further research. First, more needs to be done to understand the idea of a baseline. Morris critiques the ethos of important guidelines, such as the PMBOK Guide as to: "*plan and then put on cruise control*" (Morris, 2013: p. 282), where this misses the challenges at the front-end of projects; and the constant need for updating and modifying plans during project delivery. We need to understand more about the process of agreeing baselines; how baselines are used to managing changes in the configuration of assets, and how they are controlled across complex supply-chains. Second complex product systems may have different hierarchical descriptions and hence more needs to be done to understand how configuration items are identified. There are questions about when and how the complex product system becomes decomposed into assets that are then controlled, and also what information needs to be known about assets. Mapping different approaches might lead researchers to set out frameworks for understanding the kinds of change management that are most effective in different circumstances. Third, more needs to be understood about the process of ensuring the validity of asset information in digital systems that are constantly changing, where responses are required rapidly. Here, researchers might compare models, in which changes are made, and then corrected; with the more bureaucratic, pre-authorisation approach of configuration management. The broader visibility and interconnections between data-sets provided in an era of big data may alter the utility of different approaches.

Finally, there are theoretical connections to be made between the literatures. Our work has revealed particular disconnects between the literatures on configuration management and the strand of work on systems integration within the literature on complex projects. Further studies might explore their historical and contemporary interconnections between these, and situate concepts within broader literatures on modularity and product architectures that may be useful in understanding change. Such further research will continue to chart interconnections, described by Morris, between the evolution of project management and developments in systems engineering, modern management theory, and the evolution of the computer.

## CONFLICT OF INTEREST

The university and authors have a strong research collaboration with Crossrail, which is indirectly and directly involved in other research, has funded consultancy and has connections through advisory boards. We wish to confirm that there are no known conflicts of interest associated with this publication and there has been no significant financial support for this work that could have influenced its outcome.

## ACKNOWLEDGEMENTS

The authors acknowledge the strong contributions of the configuration managers involved in this research, Airbus, CERN and Crossrail, the centers of configuration management competence in these firms, and the EPSRC Centre for Innovative Manufacturing in Through-Life Engineering Services (EP/I033246/1) at Cranfield University, which funded this research as a feasibility study on "*Configuration Management in Through-Life Engineering*". The research was conducted by the team as part of the Design Innovation Research Centre (EP/H02204X/1) and Technologies for Sustainable Built Environments Centre (EP/G037787/1) at the University of Reading.

## REFERENCES

1. Alberts, D.S., Hayes, R.E., 2003. Power to the Edge: Command… Control… in the Information Age. CCRP Publishing.
2. Ali, U., Kidd, C., 2014. Barriers to effective configuration management application in a project context: An empirical investigation. Int. J. Proj. Manag. 32, 508–518.
3. Bachy, G., Hameri, A.-P., 1997. What to be implemented at the early stage of a large-scale project. Int. J. Proj. Manag. 15, 211–218.
4. Barton, D., Court, D., 2012. Making Advanced Analytics Work For You. Harv. Bus. Rev. 90, 78–83.
5. Bersoff, E.H., 1984. Elements of Software Configuration Management. IEEE Trans. Softw. Eng. 10, 79–87.
6. Billingham, V., 2008. Configuration management:Controlling your project assets. In: Billingham, V. (Ed.), Project management: How to plan and deliver a successful project. Studymates Ltd., Abergele.
7. BIM 2050 Group, 2014. Built Environment 2050: A Report on Our Digital Future. Construction Industry Council, London.
8. BIS/Industry Working Group, 2011. Building Information Modelling (BIM) Working Party Strategy Paper. Government Construction Client Group, London.
9. Boyd, D., Crawford, K., 2011. Six Provocation for Big Data, A Decade in Internet Time. Symposium on the Dynamics of the Internet and Society. Oxford Internet Institute.
10. Boyd, D., Crawford, K., 2012. Critical questions for big data: Provocations for a cultural, technological, and scholarly phenomenon. Inf Commun Soc 15, 662–679.
11. Braglia, M., Frosolini, M., 2014. An integrated approach to implement Project Management Information Systems within the Extended Enterprise. Int. J. Proj. Manag. 32, 18–29.
12. Brouse, P.S., 2008. Configuration management. In: Sage, A. (Ed.), Systems engineering and management for sustainable development. EOLSS, Oxford, pp. 214–242.
13. Brusoni, S., Prencipe, A., Pavitt, K., 2001. Knowledge Specialization, Organizational Coupling, and the Boundaries of the Firm: Why Do Firms Know More Than They Make? Adm. Sci. Q. 46, 597–621.
14. Burgess, T.F., Byrne, K., Kidd, C., 2003. Making project status visible in complex aerospace projects. Int. J. Proj. Manag. 21, 251–259.
15. Burgess, T., McKee, D., Kidd, C., 2005. Configuration management in the aerospace industry: a review of industry practice. Int. J. Oper. Prod. Manage. 25, 290–301.
16. Chen, H., Chiang, R.H.L., Storey, V.C., 2012. Business Intelligence and Analytics: From big data to big impact. MIS Q. 36, 1165–1188.
17. Constantiou, I.D., Kallinikos, J., 2015. New games, new rules: big data and the changing context of strategy. J. Inf. Technol. 30, 1–14.
18. Davenport, T.H., Barth, P., Bean, R., 2012. How 'Big Data' Is Different. Sloan Manag. Rev. 54, 22–24.
19. Davies, A., Hobday, M., 2006. The Business of Projects: Managing Innovation in Complex Products and Systems. Cambridge University Press, Cambridge.
20. Davies, A., Mackenzie, I., 2014. Project complexity and systems integration: Constructing the London 2012 Olympics and Paralympics Games. Int. J. Proj. Manag. 32, 773–790.
21. Davies, A., Gann, D., Douglas, T., 2009. Innovation in Megaprojects: Systems Integration at London Heathrow Terminal 5. Calif. Manag. Rev. 51, 101–125.
22. DOD, 1978. Configuration Control: Engineering Changes, Deviations and Waivers, DOD-STD-480A. DOD, 2013. Interim Standard Practice: Configuration management. Department of Defense (MIL-STD-3046(ARMY); AMSC 9275 AREA SESS).
23. Eisenhardt, K.M., Graebner, M.E., 2007. Theory building from cases: opportunities and challenges. Acad. Manag. J. 50, 25–32.
24. Estublier, J., 2000. Software configuration management: A roadmap Conference on the future of software engineering. The International Conference of Software Engineering, Limerick, Ireland, pp. 279–289.
25. Faucher, J.-B.P.L., Everett, A.M., Lawson, R., 2008. What do we know about knowledge? In: Koohang, A., Harman, K., Britz, J. (Eds.), Knowledge Management: Theoretical Foundations. Informing Science Press, Santa Rosa, CA, pp. 41–78
26. Floridi, L., 2012. Big Data and Their Epistemological Challenge. Philos. Technol. 25, 435–437. Galbraith, J.R., 1973. Designing Complex Organization. Addison-Wesley, Reading, MA.
27. Galbraith, J.R., 1977. Organization Design. Addison-Wesley, Reading, MA. Galbraith, J.R., 2014.

Organization Design Challenges resulting from Big Data. J. Organ. Des. 3, 2–13.

28. Gann, D.M., Salter, A.J., 2000. Innovation in project-based, service-enhanced firms: the construction of complex products and systems. Res. Policy 29, 955–972.
29. Gonzalez, P., 2002. A Guide to Configuration Management for Intelligent Transportation Systems. Department of Transport, USA.
30. Hameri, A.-P., 1997. Project management in a long-term and global one-of-akind project. Int. J. Proj. Manag. 15, 151–157.
31. Hameri, A.-P., Nitter, P., 2002. Engineering data management through different breakdown structures in a large-scale project. Int. J. Proj. Manag. 20, 375–384.
32. Hameri, A.-P., Puittinen, R., 2003. WWW-enabled knowledge management for distributed engineering projects. Comput. Ind. 50, 165–177.
33. Hobday, M., 1998. Product complexity, innovation and industrial organisation. Res. Policy 26, 689–710.
34. Hobday, M., Davies, A., Prencipe, A., 2005. Systems integration: a core capability of the modern corporation. Ind. Corp. Chang. 14, 1109–1143.
35. ISO, 2003. Quality management systems: Guidelines for configuration management, BS ISO 1007:2003. BSI, London.
36. Kidd, C., 2001. The case for configuration management. IEE (Institution of Electrical Engineers) (Review September). Kidd, C., Burgess, R.G., 2010. Managing configurations and data for effective project management. In: Morris, P., Pinto, J.K. (Eds.), Wiley Guide to Projects, Technology Supply-chain and Procurement Management, pp. 108–123.
37. Kitchin, R., 2014. The Data Revolution: Big Data, Open Data, Data Infrastructures and Their Consequences. SAGE Publications Ltd. Lagoze, C., 2014. Big data, data integrity, and the fracturing of the control zone. Big Data Soc. 1, 1–11.
38. Laney, 2001. Data Management: Controlling Data Volume, Velocity and Variety, Application Delivery Strategies.
39. LaValle, S., Lesser, E., Shockley, R., Hopkins, M.S., Kruschwitz, N., 2011. Big data, analytics and the path from insight to value. Sloan Manag. Rev. 52, 21–31.
40. Levitt, R., 2011. Towards project management 2.0. Eng. Proj. Organ. J. 1, 197–210. McAfee, A., Brynjolfsson, E., 2012. Big Data: The management of Revolution. Harv. Bus. Rev. 60–68.
41. Miles, M.B., Huberman, M.A., 1994. An expanded sourcebook: Qualitative data analysis. Second ed. Sage Publications, London. Military, 1988. Configuration Control: Engineering Changes, Deviations and Waivers, MIL-STD-480B.
42. Miller, R., Hobday, M., Leroux-Demers, T., Olleros, X., 1995. Innovation in complex systems industries: the case of flight simulation. Ind. Corp. Chang. 4, 363–400.
43. Moreira, M.E., 2010. Adapting configuration management for agile teams. Wiley, West Sussex.
44. Morris, P., 1997. The Management of Projects. Thomas Telford, London (book first published in 1994, preface 1997).
45. Morris, P., 2013. Reconstructing project management. Wiley, Chichester.
46. MPA, 2013. Are we any good at project controls - what are the cross-sector challenges for the future? Report of seminar 174 (1 Great George Street, London).
47. Pinto, J., 2013. Lies, damned lies, and project plans: Recurring human errors that can ruin the project planning process. Bus. Horiz. 56, 643–653.
48. PMBOK guide, 2013. A guide to the project management body of knowledge. 5th edition. Project Management Institute, Newton Square, PA.
49. Sapolski, H., 2003. Inventing systems integration. In: Prencipe, A., Davies, A., Hobday, M. (Eds.), The Business of Systems Integration. Oxford University Press, Oxford, pp. 15–34.
50. Shenhar, A.J., Dvir, D., 2007. Re-inventing project management. Harvard Business School, Cambridge, MA. Stake, R.E., 1995. The Art of Case Study Research.
51. Sage, Thousand Oaks, CA. UK Government, 2013. Construction 2025. HM Government, London. Viitanen, J., Kingston, R., 2013. Smart cities and green growth: Outsourcing democratic and environmental resilience to the global technology sector. Environ. Plann. A 45.
52. Whyte, J., Levitt, R., 2011. Information management and the management of projects. In: Morris, P.W.G., Pinto, J.K., Söderlund, J. (Eds.), The Oxford handbook of project management. Oxford University Press, UK, pp. 365–388.
53. Williams, T., 2009. Configuration management: Controlling change in complex projects. In: Williams, T. (Ed.), Construction Management: Emerging trends and technologies. Delmar Cengage Learning, New York, pp. 177–190.
54. Williams, N., Ferdinand, N.P., Croft, R., 2014. Project management maturity in the age of big data. Int. J. Manag. Proj. Bus. 7, 311–317.
55. Winch, G., 2010. Managing construction projects. 2nd edition. Blackwell Publishing, London. Windham, J., 2012. DoD Military Standard for Configuration Management. ACDM Conference, Destin, FL.
56. Wozny, R., Black, K., Guess, V., 2014. The CMII/IPE Model and PLM/PDM Tool: Functionality Needed to Support Implementation. White Paper, CMII-875A. CMII Research Institute.
57. Wu, X., Wu, G.-Q., 2014. Data mining with Big Data. IEEE Trans. Knowl. Data Eng. 26, 97–107.
58. Yin, R.K., 1994. Case Study Research: Design and methods. Sage, Thousand Oaks, CA.

CHAPTER 7

# PROGRAM MANAGEMENT APPROACH FOR LARGE-SCALE INFORMATION TECHNOLOGY DEVELOPMENT PROJECTS: A CASE STUDY

Vijay Somanchi[1] and Ravikiran Dwivedula[2]

[1] IBS Hyderabad, Hyderabad, India

[2] SKEMA Business School, Lille, France; IBS Hyderabad, Hyderabad, India

## ABSTRACT

**This case study presents the program management approach in managing large-scale information technology projects. Using the case of ACME Solutions Ltd., a large software development company, the authors first emphasize on the need to use program management over project management when managing related multiple information technology projects. Then, they explain the program lifecycle in this company and discuss the 'process' and 'people' related challenges across the program stages. Broadly, they observe that there is a lack of coordination between the stakeholders and processes of the program. Recommendations to overcome these limitations are discussed.**

## INTRODUCTION

Our view of project management has changed in the past two decades. Projects and Programs are now positioned as vehicles to put into operation the strategy and/or used to create conditions that shape newer strategies for an organization (see Morris & Jamieson 2005 for a detailed discussion on the relation between an organization's strategy, programs, and projects). This then has two implications. The first is that project management will function alongside the other business functions of the organization. Second, that the role of project program management is better understood in the implementation of such business strategy (see Cooke-Davies, Crawford & Lechler 2009). While at the strategic level, both project portfolios and project programs are focused on prioritizing the resources for optimal business performance (Partington 2000), programs offer a better methodology to deal with day-to-day coordination of projects so as to ensure their implementation success (Thiry 2004). While there is an extensive literature that discusses managing projects, multiple projects, and large-scale projects, research using program management as a theoretical lens to understand the dynamics of interrelated multiple projects is lacking. Also, most of the studies reported are from United States and Europe, and few from emergent economies such as India. This is significant considering that, for its Eleventh Five Year Plan for the period 2007-2012, the government of India has earmarked US$550 billion for infrastructure projects alone. Further, despite the economic meltdown and a cautious recovery, Indian software exports were valued to be around US$ 48-50 billion for the year 2009-10. Therefore, addressing these gaps in the project-program management research, our objective for this paper is to explain how a global information technology company is using Program Management as a framework to manage its suite of products in India.

**Citation:** Vijay Somanchi and Ravikiran Dwivedula, "Program management approach for large-scale information technology development projects: a case study," Journal of Project, Program & Portfolio Management Vol 1 No 1 (2010) 41-54. ISSN: 1838-7845.

We have organized our paper thus. In the 'Theory' section, we will first present the operational definition of Program Management for the purposes of this study. We will also highlight the need to use programs over projects. This will be followed by the 'Methodology' section, where we will explain our stance on the choice of research philosophy and for using a case study. In the following section, 'ACME's Program Management Approach for Product Development', we present the case study. Following a background note on the company, we will discuss the program organization structure, and the program lifecycle. Important challenges encountered across the program stages are presented with solutions to overcome them. This is followed by the Conclusion.

## THEORY

Program management is a method that ensures maximum gains for an organization by the integration of project management activities. While there are multiple perspectives (and definitions) to understand project program management, we will adopt the definition of program as:

- the means to implement an organization's strategy using optimal level of resources; and
- projects which are grouped purposefully to achieve business benefits.

Thus, we use Thiry's definition of a program (2004) – as being a collection of change actions (project and operational activities) purposefully grouped together to realize strategic and/or tactical benefits – as the operational definition of program management for this paper. A similar definition by United Kingdom's Office of Government of Commerce (OGC), in its widely accepted program management standard for managing successful programs (MSP), defines a program as "a temporary, flexible organization created to coordinate, direct, and oversee the implementation of a set of related projects and activities in order to deliver outcomes and benefits related to the organization's strategic objectives. (OGC 2007: 4; cited in Shao, Turner & Müller 2009). Program management itself is defined as the action of coordinating, directing, and implementing a dossier of projects and transformation activities to achieve outcomes and realize benefits that are of strategic importance to the business.

According to another influential project management body – The Project Management Institute (PMI® 2006; p.4), a program is a group of related projects managed in a coordinated way to obtain benefits and control not available from managing them individually. Program management is therefore defined as the centralized coordinated management of a program to achieve the program's strategic benefits and objectives.

The above definitions suggest that program management is essentially about building synergies across the projects (Blomquist & Müller, 2006), focusing on building networks across the program (Shao, Turner & Müller, 2009). It may not be as much about managing individual deliverables that contribute to the benefits of the program (PMI®, 2006, p.6).

### Need For Programs over Projects

Before we begin the discussion on program management, we first need to ask why do we need programs over projects? In other words, we ask why do 'projects' fail so that we need 'programs'. Research on project failures has been ongoing at least for two decades. Broadly, the authors have identified the causes to be both people and process related (Kappelman, McKeeman & Zhang 2006). Lawrence and Scanlan (2008), in their review of large-scale aerospace projects, have identified: poor initial planning, lack of clear objectives (and deliverables); improper resource allocations; poor risk management; poor change management; lack of buy-in from the stakeholders; and poor understanding of priorities as the major reasons for projects to fail. Specifically in case of Information Technology (IT) projects, Charette (2005) states that 5% to 15% of the IT projects are abandoned before delivery. In their review of IT project failures, Cerpa and Verner (2009) identified both process-related risks such as delivery date influencing the development process, improper risk management with risks not being re-assessed, and controlled; and delivery date decision being made without appropriate requirements information; and people-related risks such as lack of rewards, and unpleasant experience while working on the project. Similarly, Kappelman, McKeeman, and Zhang (2006) from their survey of 138 IT project managers report that lack of top management support, ineffective project manager, inadequate involvement of stakeholders, inadequately committed team, and lack of expertise as major people related problems leading to project failures. The critical process related problems were requirements and success criteria not being documented, improper change management process, ineffective scheduling, communication break—down between the stakeholders, prioritization of resources, and lack of business driver for the project.

These examples then support the view that 'project management' may be inadequate to manage the complexities associated with large-scale projects, where projects may have to be undertaken concurrently, and therefore a 'systemic' perspective is required. Previous studies seem to agree with this opinion. In a volatile business environment, program management is capable of providing a centralized view of all the projects in an organization. This leads to better prioritization, planning, and coordination of projects, which in turn ensures good governance of projects (Shehu & Egbu 2007; Shenu & Egbu 2010).

Williams and Parr (2006) suggested the following benefits of program management over project management:

- Effective execution of major business investment in projects
- Improved on time delivery by understanding key interdependencies between the projects and managing their interfaces
- Effective utilization of resources
- Identification and management of major project risks leading to efficient time and cost management
- Effective decision made through a business perspective, thus reducing the scope conflicts within the projects and the program
- Enhanced delivery capability by promoting shared practices among the program stakeholders
- Increased realization of benefits through integration of processes, system, people, and organizational change

The next question that is to be addressed is how should these projects be organized? Pellegrinelli (1997) and later Thiry (2004) suggest three Configurations – perspectives to manage projects and associated work (including programs) in groups:

- Portfolio or chunked configuration
- Strategic or Goal-Oriented configuration
- Incremental or Heartbeat configuration

When projects are grouped around a common 'theme', it is called a chunked or portfolio configuration. The primary objective is to achieve efficiency through prioritization of projects, identification of dependencies so that resources are better managed, and thus projects are better controlled.

When projects are grouped around a common 'purpose', it is called a strategic or goal-oriented configuration. The primary objective will be to increase the organizational effectiveness by translating business needs into actions, reduce uncertainty through iterative development, and develop a learning loop that fosters creativity.

When projects are grouped under a common 'platform', it is called as 'incremental' or a 'heartbeat configuration'. The platform may be a process, business system, or infrastructure. It would be possible for the organization to provide an integrative framework where the short-term requests can be mapped to the long-term strategy of the company, controlled changes are affected when necessary, and continuous reassessment (of the projects' performance) with a holistic perspective is possible.

Thus, such grouping of the projects seems to address the process- and people-related concerns that lead to failure of large-scale projects. In the following section, we will present the case study of a global information technology company, ACME Solutions Ltd. (referred to as ACME hereafter), where large-scale projects are managed as a program. The scope of this study is restricted to ACME's operations in their Development center in Hyderabad, India.

## METHODOLOGY

We have used a descriptive approach to study the problem. This approach describes the phenomena as they exist and goes beyond the exploratory research since it is undertaken to describe the characteristics of the issue. Thus, it is heuristic in nature and is grounded in Constructivist philosophy. This approach posits that knowledge does not reflect any transcendent reality but is contingent upon conventions, human perception, and social experience. This is to say that the authors' experience of working with the described program management approach has shaped their perceptions about these phenomena. From the epistemological perspective, the research instruments are the experiences (with Program management at ACME) of the authors themselves. Thus, it is a case of participatory action research.

The authors were engaged in a systematic process of self-reflection which involved – planning a change, acting & observing the process and consequences of change, reflecting on these processes and consequences, and re-planning when trying to understand a phenomena (Denzin & Lincoln 2005). This led to a descriptive case study. Although, case studies are useful for theory building in areas where existing theory is limited (Eisenhardt, 1989) and theories can be proposed using a single case study (Lee & Baskerville 2003; Yin 2003), this is not the purpose of this paper as the intention is only to provide a rich description of the case (Bogdan & Biklen, 1992).

### Background

ACME is a software product development company headquartered in the United States. It has evolved into a global corporation over a period of two decades, and employs more than 20,000 associates across the globe. It specializes in developing and marketing Enterprise Software Products for thousands of small, medium, and large companies, which are organized into different verticals such as Banking, Finance, Insurance, Manufacturing, Supply Chain Management, Process Manufacturing, and Human Capital Management. Each vertical develops its suite of products using Standard Development Kits (SDKs) that are highly customized to the client's needs. For example, ACME has specialized and well-developed software for Human Capital Management needs that comes with packaged functions such as Payroll, Benefits, Recruitment, Training and so on, so that customers can install and run the software as an 'out-of the-box solution' for their business. ACME also provides the facility of purchasing and using independent standalone components (independent functions such as Payroll or Recruitment) if required so that the customer need not buy the entire package and only purchase components that they require. In this way, ACME meets the customer requirements without relying on third-party solutions.

In such a project-organization, the key is to ensure coordination between the different types of project teams that are engaged in the development of either a complete enterprise solutions package or the standalone components of that enterprise solutions package. These project teams need to ensure that the product they develop is capable of working as a standalone but can also function with other modules. For example, while Payroll can work as an independent entity it should also work with other products such as Benefits Management, Training, or Career Management. In some cases, they also need to ensure that their software also works with third party software, if the customer so chooses. In order to meet this organizational requirement, each component has a different development team. This ensures that while each component is independent, they can also be integrated with another component or a product as required by the customer. This then means that at a given point of time, components or products may be in different stages of development. However, when releasing these components or products as a Suite, the different development teams need to ensure that the components and products are fully integrated such that the customer need not wait for a specific component to be released. In order to manage these complex 'streams' of work, ACME has adopted program management as a framework to control these related multiple projects.

### Program Organization Structure

As mentioned earlier, ACME's project management approach requires products/components to be developed independently, but to be released simultaneously. Therefore, ACME uses the 'Waterfall model'1 to develop these software. An apparent limitation of this approach is that a delay in the development of one or more components or products will necessitate revising the schedules for the rest of the components or products until all of them are in sync.

In order to overcome such risks, ACME has a program manager who manages all the threads (multiple tasks or processes) of the projects that are being undertaken as a part of that program. For example, for the 'Human Capital Management' program, the program manager is in charge of Payroll, Benefits, Recruitment, Career Management, Appraisal System, and Training; all of these components being managed as 'projects'. Under the program manager there is a senior project manager who is in charge of each (project) stream. The senior project manager is assisted by three leads or roles – project manager, quality assurance manager, and a product manager. While the project manager heads the project implementation, the product manager handles the requirements management. Figure 1 shows the program organization structure at ACME. A detailed description of the roles in this organization is discussed next.

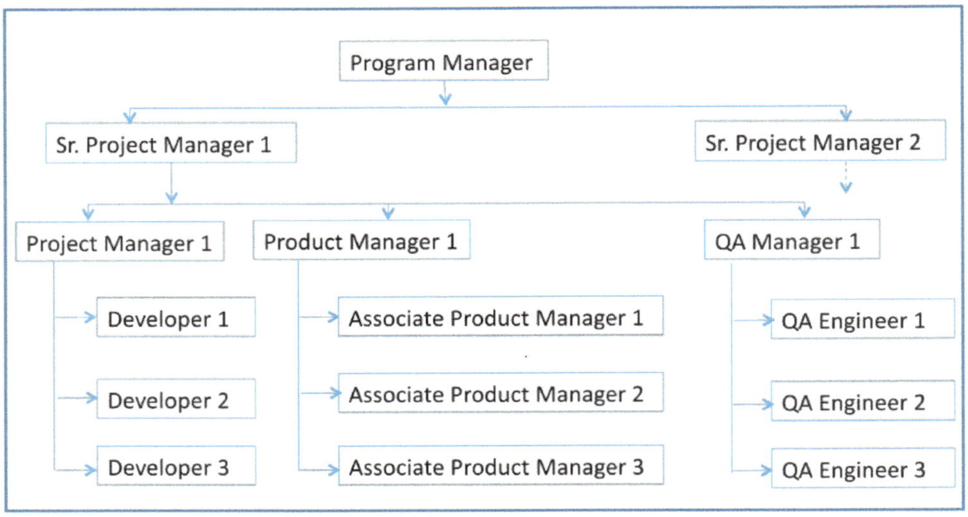


**Figure 1.** ACME program organization structure.

## *Program Manager*

The program manager is responsible for the overall planning, execution, and control of the program. The program manager coordinates the projects in their various stages of individual projects such that they meet the common release date (of the program).

## *Senior Project Manager*

The senior project manager oversees all the aspects of one project. The associated project manager, product manager, and Quality Assurance (QA) managers report to him. A senior project manager reports to the program manager. The senior project manager is the main person responsible for the delivery of the project related to his vertical on time.

## *Product Manager*

It is the job of the product manager and his team to interact, collect, assimilate, verify, and review the technical feasibility of the requirements of the customer and create the Functional Design Document and High Level Design Documents which are then passed on to the corresponding project manager. It is also the job of the product manager to determine what features will go into the current release and what can wait or need to be deferred.

## *Project Manager*

The project manager reviews the High Level Design Documents after doing the feasibility analysis. Each project manager has a team of developers reporting to them. These developers are entrusted with the responsibility of implementing the design using the SDKs.

## *Quality Assurance (QA) Manager*

The QA manager is responsible for the testing and validation of the software. The QA manager and their team of QA engineers are in-charge of the Unit testing, Integration testing, System Testing, Stress Testing and End-user testing to ensure that the software meets the industry standards or even surpasses it.

## *Developers*

Developers are programmers who are mainly responsible for the development of the code based on the design provided to them. It is their responsibility to ensure that they adhere to the functional design that has been provided to them by the design team. So developers have to have the right technical skills to convert the functional design into a working piece of code using the SDKs at their disposal.

## *Associate Product Managers*

They are responsible for the design and feasibility of the subcomponents of a product. They report to the product managers in charge of product design. Associate product managers determine the feasibility of a certain functionality being implemented in the current product. They do detailed analysis and submit their updates to the product managers.

### *Quality Assurance (QA) Engineers*

QA engineers do the quality assurance for the product. With various tools at their disposal, they take up unit testing, system testing, load testing and so on to minimize the bugs in the product. If any bug is found, QA testers reject the code and the developers responsible for the code will have to ensure that they fix the issues.

## Managing the Program Stages

The project-organization also discussed above poses certain inherent challenges. For example, since ACME tries to release the entire suit of products as a single package, a schedule overrun of one product can delay the release date of the entire program. Resource management is another critical issue. The scope of the different projects within the program will vary. Improper scope management will lead to underutilization of resources, which in turn will put pressure on the other projects that require these resources. Human factors such as unavailability of experienced personnel and employee attrition are also major problems. Issues such as these that occurred across the program's lifecycle at ACME are discussed below.

ACME's program lifecycle is composed of 4 stages – definition, planning, implementation, and appraisal. Conceptually, it corresponds to Thiry's program management lifecycle (Thiry, 2004) as shown in Figure 2.

### *Definition Stage*

In this stage, the purpose of the program is clarified. In the case of ACME, the fit between the various projects within the program and their scope is defined at this stage. Most importantly, the program manager identifies the various projects that are to be performed under one program and, if necessary, distributes the projects under various programs. Perhaps the most important activity of this stage is identification of the right people and resources to roll out the program. Allocation of resources was done using a 'bottom-up' approach where resources were allocated to a project, according to its size, and not for the entire program. Any ambiguities at this stage will lead to scope creep.

**Figure 2.** Program stages at ACME.

An important area of concern at this stage is to identify the key functionalities or activities for the entire program before organizing them into projects. Identifying the key people and resources required to take the program forward is also critical at this stage. If this exercise is not done properly, it will lead to problems in terms of determining project scope and consequently the scope of the program. The outcome of this exercise will largely influence the success and failure of the program.

### *Planning Stage*

Development of the 'Business Case', which justifies the business rationale of the program, is the key activity in this stage. At ACME, the business case is defined by capturing the market conditions and also the customer requirements. Every product (of the program) is determined such that it is aligned with the most generic business practices and processes. Identification of the right resources and technologies for the implementation of each project is done at this stage. For example, for the development of a self-service application (web-based application that any user can easily use) might require a developer who is comfortable with Java, JSP, and J2EE platforms.

An important concern at this stage is the differing perspectives of the technical and the nontechnical team members with respect to the objectives of the projects and the program. For example, if the technical architects are not familiar with the business objectives, and are not involved during the customer requirement analysis, the final software might prove to be unwieldy or difficult to use by the end-users. Another challenge is the availability of resources. So much so, that the design engineers may have to consider technology that is popular and easily available when required. As with the definition stage, scope creep is another major challenge in the planning stage. In our experience, scope creep led to several redesigns and necessitated revisiting the functionalities. This led to extra effort in terms of person-days and increased cost.

### *Implementation Stage*

The implementation stage includes the actual execution of the planned actions of the program. Thus, once the scope and functionality is determined, the implementation strategy is drawn out. Given the nature of the product suite, different functionalities require different technologies based on the kind of usage. For example, for an internal application that does not require a high number of users to access, a desktop client is sufficient; whereas, if multiple users will be accessing the application, then a web-based interface would be required. These two types of usage require different approaches to building the application.

Another important activity is the Product Review that is done from time to time to ensure that the product development teams are aligned to the initial framework of the design. Any design issues that were not considered are reviewed several times and a decision is taken based on the scope of the additional work involved.

Overlapping functionalities is another challenge that teams often face. In such scenarios, the functionalities have to be jointly developed so that each team gets to cooperate with the other team that partly owns the functionality.

It is very difficult to envisage a finished product in software without a model or concept. End-users have to be given a 'taste' of the new application, called the 'Conference Room Pilot' or CRP. Once the CRP is complete, it is quite possible that it would have to be revisited because the end-users want to add more functionality or richness to the interfaces. In addition, limitations of the new development tools or SDK might surface as these SDKs might not support certain functionalities.

Product and development reviews can bring out issues that could not be identified in the initial design phases, and these have to be managed. Such unforeseen issues can cause both major and minor interruptions in the progress and have to be resolved before moving forward. If not, workarounds have to be devised to ensure that the program gets back on track.

The other area of concern is the human factor. The SDKs need to be continuously upgraded to ensure ease of use by the end-users and also to be in sync with the latest technologies available. This is sometimes a steep learning curve for development teams and results in project slippages due to the extra time taken to get familiarized with the tool. Employee attrition is the other major human resource challenge. Employee turnaround at a critical stage of implementation can upset the schedule of the entire program. So employee management becomes critical for the program to stay on schedule.

Apart from retaining the employees, their engagement also is critical. Product redesigns lead to frequent changes in the schedule. Developers and design architects have to revisit the issues and re-estimate the effort. Sometimes they end up changing and discarding the earlier efforts. This leads to loss of morale and interest in the project. It is the role of the program manager to ensure that the employees are motivated throughout the program and the momentum is maintained. The team members have to be made aware of the exact scope of ownership of their area of expertise and if required need to be trained so that the program is not compromised.

### Appraisal Stage

Program appraisal is a continuous process that is performed at the end of every stage. Though the final appraisal is based on the released, well-working product, various milestones and performance standards would have been defined (in the planning stage) to continuously monitor and control the program.

In our experience, tracking the performance of a project in terms of the completion of certain scope at the end of a stage is not always accurate in software development projects. Even if the stage is complete, there is every possibility that the stage is revisited until the client's expectations are fully met. For example, in the implementation stage, software program coding is an important milestone. An accurate assessment of the project's (and program's) performance is only possible after a code freeze.

The other challenge at this program stage is that of measuring employee's performance. Given that software development is teamwork, identifying the individual's contribution to the team effort is difficult. So much so, that the team members perceive their performance ratings to be biased, which in turn leads to employee dissatisfaction.

### No Formal Closure

In the case of ACME, there is no formal program closure. This is because software development is an ongoing process. Even as a version (of the software) is released, the teams are engaged in the development of the next version of the software. No software is perfect in terms of defects and bugs. In addition, some of the functionalities may be too complex to be included in the earlier versions, and so have to be added as enhancements over a period of time. Apart from the technical factors, the teams also track the changing business requirements of their customers. New functionalities to be included in the software are reviewed and, if required, modified to meet customer expectations. Thus reviewing, fixing the bugs, re-evaluating, enhancing, optimizing and streamlining the software are ongoing processes that keep the teams working on the projects continuously. In short, it is a cyclical process that keeps the program always on. Hence there is no clear-cut termination or closure of the programs once the software is released into the market.

### Overcoming Challenges

As discussed above, there are several 'project management' and 'people' challenges with this program management approach. Over a period of time, ACME has developed well-defined processes to overcome these challenges. These processes are continuously perfected to meet the changing demands of the program. Some of the processes are described below:

### Continuous Review and Coordination within Projects and Program

Each team spends several person-hours each week reviewing progress. This is done both at team and project levels. There are several advantages that are associated with this process. Firstly, everyone in the team is aware of the current stage of the project or program at their own level. If not at a detailed level, at least at an overall level, each member is aware of the role and progress of their peers at the team level. This especially addresses the issue of employee attrition, where a team member is able to step into the role of a peer if needed.

This coordination between the team members is also extended to the program level, where each team is aware of their responsibilities, and dependencies on the other team. This interaction also helps teams discuss any overlapping issues that need the attention of both teams. Also, there is some degree of flexibility within the program stages to perform the project activities. For example, if the QA team has to test a certain functionality, say 'Func A', on a given date but is unable to develop the functionality, it can decide to work on another functionality, 'Func B' that is ready to be tested while work progresses on 'Func A'.

Also, work on the various projects is paced such that the critical activities, and the expected benefits to be realized from the program are distributed throughout the program cycle. This is done to spread the technical, people, and financial risks associated with program (through its cycle).

### *Resource Management – Training New Resources to Step In*

Even as the development teams are working on the projects, new hires and new members – even as they are being trained – are asked to assist the teams at various levels such as project and program documentation, writing technical manuals, code reviews, testing, etc. This helps in having a pool of resources who can step into the program with some level of awareness if required at any stage.

At some critical stages, stakeholders and customers are brought in to have a 'sneak-preview' as to how the product is shaping up. Their feedback is taken and used as inputs. This gives an outsiders' perspective on the product, which is very important for the program.

### *Partners' Inputs*

Just as customers are given previews, partners are also involved in the testing phase. This is because it is the partners who recommend ACME's products to their clients. Partners are likely to have an idea about what customers would like to have from ACME's solutions. So the partners' contribution at the testing stage is considered invaluable for the programs.

### *Motivating the Team Members to Keep Up the Momentum*

As with any program, it is important that the motivation levels of the teams are kept at high levels to ensure that the momentum is maintained on the projects. Hence, the program managers, project managers and senior project managers collaborate with human resources from time to time to conduct workshops, training and team-building activities. This ensures better cohesion among the team members.

### *Continuous Review of Processes – Refining the Process*

Though the processes are well established, each process is reviewed from time to time so as to fine tune them in case they are proving to be bottlenecks instead of being enablers. This helps in proactively managing and reengineering any redundant processes.

### *Continuous Review of Technology to Improve the Usability of the Software*

To ensure that technology acts as a tool for faster development, SDKs are updated by incorporating easy-to-use functionalities so that developers need not spend too much effort in learning to use the technology after each upgrade.

## CONCLUSIONS

In theory and practice, project management today is regarded as a strategic function. While the relation between the organization's strategy – programs and portfolios – and projects has been well documented through studies based in the developed countries, more research is warranted from the emerging economies. This article describes the program management approach of a global information technology company.

This case study brings to the fore challenges that are specific to coordination of: (i) processes, and (ii) people, when managing a program. We have observed the following patterns with respect to these challenges across the program's lifecycle:

- As the degree of uncertainty is higher in the initial stages of the program (design and planning), setting the objectives for the program by successfully managing the scope, and the coordination between the technical and non-technical project team members is critical.
- In the program implementation stage, managing unsystematic risks becomes a critical factor in the successful execution of the multiple projects and so the program. This problem is more evident if the program scope is not well defined in the planning stages. While this leads to rework (and hence schedule and budget overruns), it also affects the morale of the team members.
- In the program appraisal stage, recognizing the individual contribution of the team member vis-à-vis the team effort is a challenge.

Thus, the coordination between the stakeholders and processes of the program need be closely monitored across the program's lifecycle. This then necessitates continuous interaction between the various stakeholders of the program so that: (i) the program processes can be aligned to the changes in the internal or external environment in which the program operates, and (ii) all the program resources are optimally utilized.

## REFERENCES

1. Blomquist, R., Mueller, R. 2006, Middle Managers in Program and Portfolio Management Practices, Roles and Responsibilities, Project Management Institute, Newtown Square, PA.
2. Bogdan, R. & Biklen, S. 1992, Qualitative Research for Education, 2nd ed., Allyn & Bacon, Boston.
3. Cerpa, N. & Verner, J.M. 2009, Why did your project fail?, Communications of the ACM, vol. 52, no. 12, 132-134.
4. Charette, R. 2005, Why software fails, IEEE Spectrum, vol. 42, no. 3, 42-49.
5. Cooke-Davies, T.J., Crawford, L. & Lechler, T.G. 2009, Project management systems: moving project management from an operational to a strategic discipline, Project Management Journal, vol. 40, no.1, 110-123.
6. Denzin, N.K. & Lincoln, Y.S. 2005, The Sage Handbook of Qualitative Research, 3rd ed., Sage Publications, Thousand Oaks, CA.
7. Eisenhardt, K.M. 1989, Building theories from case study research, Academy of Management Review, vol. 14, no. 4, 532-550.
8. Kappelman, L.A., McKeeman, R. & Zhang, L. 2006, Early warning signs of IT project failure: the dominant dozen, Information Systems Management, vol. 23, no. 4, 31-36.
9. Lawrence, P. & Scanlan, J. 2008, 'Planning in the dark: why major engineering projects fail to achieve key goals,

Technology Analysis and Strategic Management, vol.19, no. 4, 509-525.

10. Lee, A. & Baskerville, R. 2003, Generalizing generalizability in information systems research, Information Systems Research, vol. 14, no. 3, 221-243.
11. Morris, P., & Jamieson, A. 2005, Moving from corporate strategy to project strategy, Project Management Journal, vol. 36, no. 4, 5-18.
12. OGC 2007, Managing Successful Programmes (MSP), The Office of Government Commerce, Norwich, UK.
13. Partington, D. 2000, Implementing strategy through programmes of projects, in R. Turner & S. Simister (eds), Gower Publishing, Aldershot, UK.
14. Pellegrinelli, S. 1997, Programme management: Organising project-based change, International Journal of Project Management, vol.15, no. 3, 141-149.
15. PMI 2006, The Standard for Program Management, Project Management Institute, Newtown Square, PA.
16. Shao, J., Turner, R. & Müller, R. 2009, The program manager's leadership style and program success: a literature review and research outline, Proceedings of IRNOP IX Research Conference, Berlin, 11-14th October.
17. Shehu, Z. & Egbu, C. 2007, The skills and competencies of programme managers, Proceedings of RICS-COBRA 2007 Annual Conference, 6-7 September 2007, Atlanta, Georgia.
18. Shehu, Z. & Egbu, C. 2010, The nature of programme management and how they differ from project management, http://zshehu.com/Papers/Programme%20Management%20-%20058%20-%20Revised.doc (Accessed 25 March 2010)
19. Thiry, M. 2004, Program management: a strategic decision management process, in P.W.G. Morris & J.K. Pinto (eds), The Wiley Project Management Resource Book, John Wiley & Sons, New York.
20. Williams, D. & Parr, T. 2006, Enterprise Program Management: Delivering Value, Palgrave Macmillan, New York, NY.
21. Yin, R.K. 2003, Case Study Research: Design and Methods, 3rd ed., Sage Publications, Thousand Oaks, CA

# SECTION III: AGILE METHODOLOGY

CHAPTER 8

# AGILE PROCESSES AND METHODOLOGIES: A CONCEPTUAL STUDY

Sheetal Sharma, Darothi Sarkar and Divya Gupta

Amity School of Engineering & Technology Amity University Noida

## ABSTRACT

**This paper deals with the comparative study of agile processes. The paper will serve as guide to other software development process models. Agile processes have important applications in the areas of software project management, software schedule management, etc. In particular the aim of agile processes is to satisfy the customer, faster development times with lower defects rate. This paper compares the agile processes with other software development life cycle models. Agile processes are not always advantageous, they have some drawbacks as well; the advantages and disadvantages of agile processes are also discussed in this paper.**

## INTRODUCTION

In software development life cycle, there are two main considerations, one is to emphasize on process and the other is the quality of the software and process itself. Agile software processes is an iterative and incremental based development, where requirements are changeable according to customer needs. It helps in adaptive planning, iterative development and time boxing. It is a theoretical framework that promotes foreseen interactions throughout the development cycle. There are several SDLC models like spiral, waterfall, RAD which has their own advantages. SDLC is a framework that describes the activities performed at each stage of a software development life cycle [1]. The software development activities such as planning, analysis, design, coding, testing and maintenance which need to be performed according to the demand of the customer. It depends on the various applications to choose the specific model. In this paper, however, we will study the agile processes and its methodologies. Agile process is itself a software development process [2]. Agile process is an iterative approach in which customer satisfaction is at highest priority as the customer has direct involvement in evaluating the software [3].

The agile process follows the software development life cycle which includes requirements gathering, analysis, design, coding, testing and delivers partially implemented software and waits for the customer feedback. In the whole process, customer satisfaction is at highest priority with faster development time. The following Figure. 1 , depicts the software development life cycle of Agile Process.

**Citation:** Sheetal Sharma, Darothi Sarkar and Divya Gupta, "Agile Processes and Methodologies: A Conceptual Study," ISSN : 0975-3397.

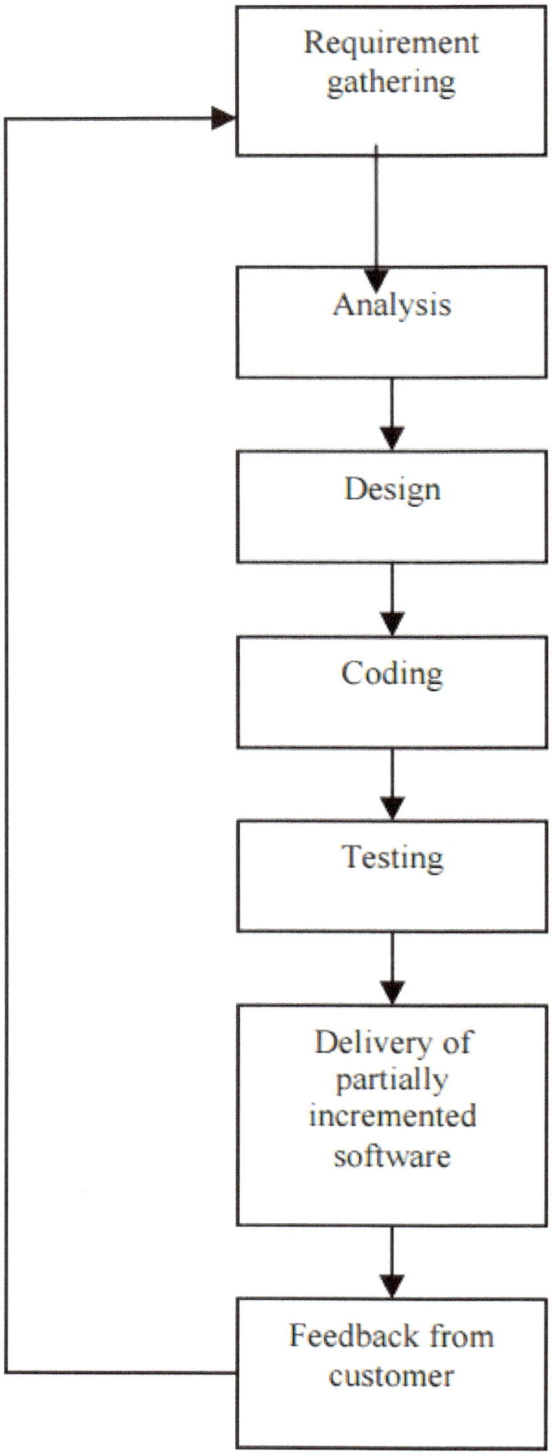


**Figure 1.** Phases of Agile Process.

This paper is organized as follows: Characteristics of Agile processes are presented in section II. Section III discusses the agile methodologies. Section IV discusses the advantages of Agile Process, Section V discusses the disadvantages of Agile Process, Section VI discusses the comparison of Agile with other SDLC models. Finally, conclusions are discussed in the section VII.

## CHARACTERISTICS OF AGILE PROJECTS

Agile process requires less planning and it divides the tasks into small increments. Agile process is meant for short term projects with an effort of team work that follows the software development life cycle. Software development life cycle includes the following phases

- Requirements gathering,
- Analysis,
- Design,
- Coding ,
- Testing,
- Maintenance.

The involvement of software team management with customers reduces the risks associated with the software. This agile process is an iterative process in which changes can be made according to the customer satisfaction. In agile process new features can be added easily by using multiple iterations.

### *Iterative*

The main objective of agile software processes is satisfaction of customers, so it focuses on single requirement with multiple iterations.

### *Modularity*

Agile process decomposes the complete system into manageable pieces called modules. Modularity plays a major role in software development processes.

***Time Boxing***

As agile process is iterative in nature, it requires the time limits on each module with respective cycle.

### *Parsimony*

In agile processes parsimony is required to mitigate risks and achieve the goals by minimal number of modules.

### *Incremental*

As the agile process is iterative in nature, it requires the system to be developed in increments, each increment is independent of others, and at last all increments are integrated into complete system.

### *Adaptive*

Due to the iterative nature of agile process new risks may occurs. The adaptive characteristic of agile process allows adapting the processes to attack the new risks and allows changes in the real time requirements.

### *Convergent*

All the risks associated with each increment are convergent in agile process by using iterative and incremental approach.

### *Collaborative*

As agile process is modular in nature, it needs a good communication among software development team. Different modules need to be integrated at the end of the software development process.

### *People Oriented*

In the agile processes customer satisfaction is the first priority over the technology and process. A good software development team increases the performance and productivity of the software.

## METHODOLOGIES

There are several methodologies through which we can implement Agile Projects. Here we have discussed three methodologies which are most widely used in Industry. The agile methods are focused on different aspects of the software development life cycle. Some focus on the practices (extreme programming, pair programming), while others focus on managing the software projects (the scrum approach).

### Extreme Programming (XP)

XP is the most successful method of developing agile software because of its focus on customer satisfaction. XP requires maximum customer interaction to develop the software. It divides the entire software development life cycle into several number of short development cycles. It welcomes and incorporates changes or requirements from the customers at any phase of the development life cycle.

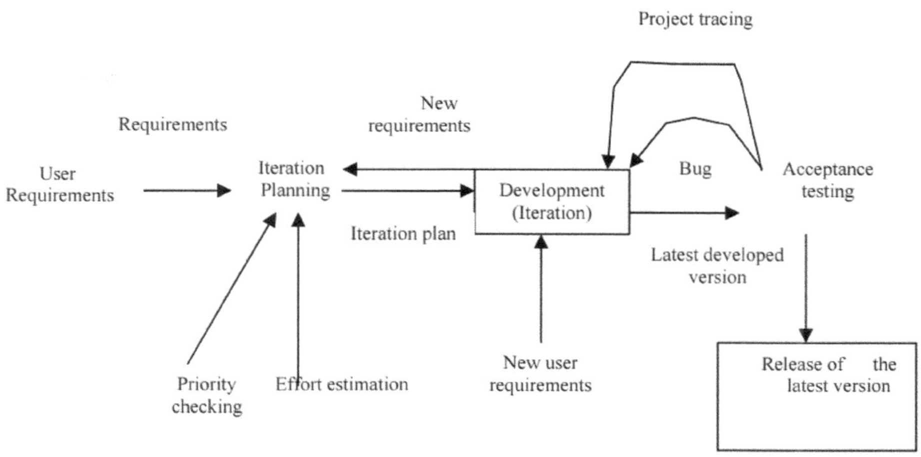


**Figure 2:** Method of developing agile processes using extreme programming.

The above diagram shows the complete method of developing agile process using XP method. Extreme programming starts with collecting user requirements. Depending upon these requirements the whole development process is divided into several small no of cycles. So the next phase is iteration planning i.e. deciding the no of cycles, prioritizing the requirements and estimating the amount of effort required to implement each cycle. Now each iteration is developed using pair programming. During the development phase new user requirements may come and the iteration plan should be adjusted according to that. Next step is to test the latest developed version for bugs, if detected; the bugs will be removed in the next iteration. After every acceptance testing project tracing should be done in which feedback is taken from the project that how much job has already been done.

XP has introduced many new things for developers like pair programming, extensive code review, code refactoring and open workspace [4].

### Scrum

Scrum is another popular method of agile development through which productivity becomes very high. It is basically based on incremental software development process. In scrum method the entire development cycle is divided into a series of iteration where each iteration is called as a sprint. Maximum duration of a sprint is 30 days.

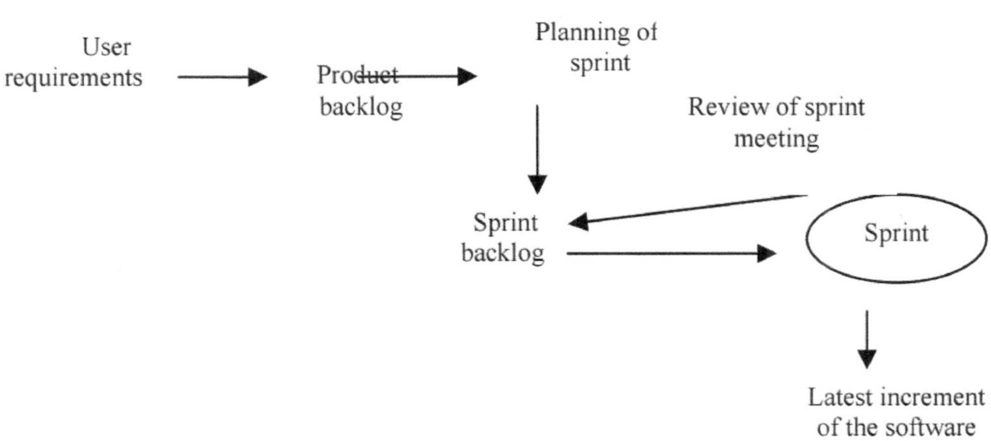


**Figure 3:** Method of developing agile processes using scrum.

The method starts with collecting user requirements but it is not expected that all the requirements should come out from the user at the beginning. User can change their mind at any time during development; they can add new features, remove or update some existing features. Next phase is to prioritize the requirements and the list is known as product backlog [5]. A proper planning for sprint should be done i.e. how many sprints are needed to develop the software, duration of the sprint, and what are the requirements from the product backlog should be implemented in each sprint. This particular list is known as sprint backlog. During each sprint one sprint meeting is held every day to take the feedback how much work has been done. After each sprint review is taken to determine whether all the requirements for that particular sprint have already been implemented or not and to decide the requirements should be implemented at the next sprint. After each sprint we get a working increment of the software

## Feature Driven Development (FDD)

FDD is one of the agile development methods. The key advantage of this method is to design the domain of the software to be produced before development.

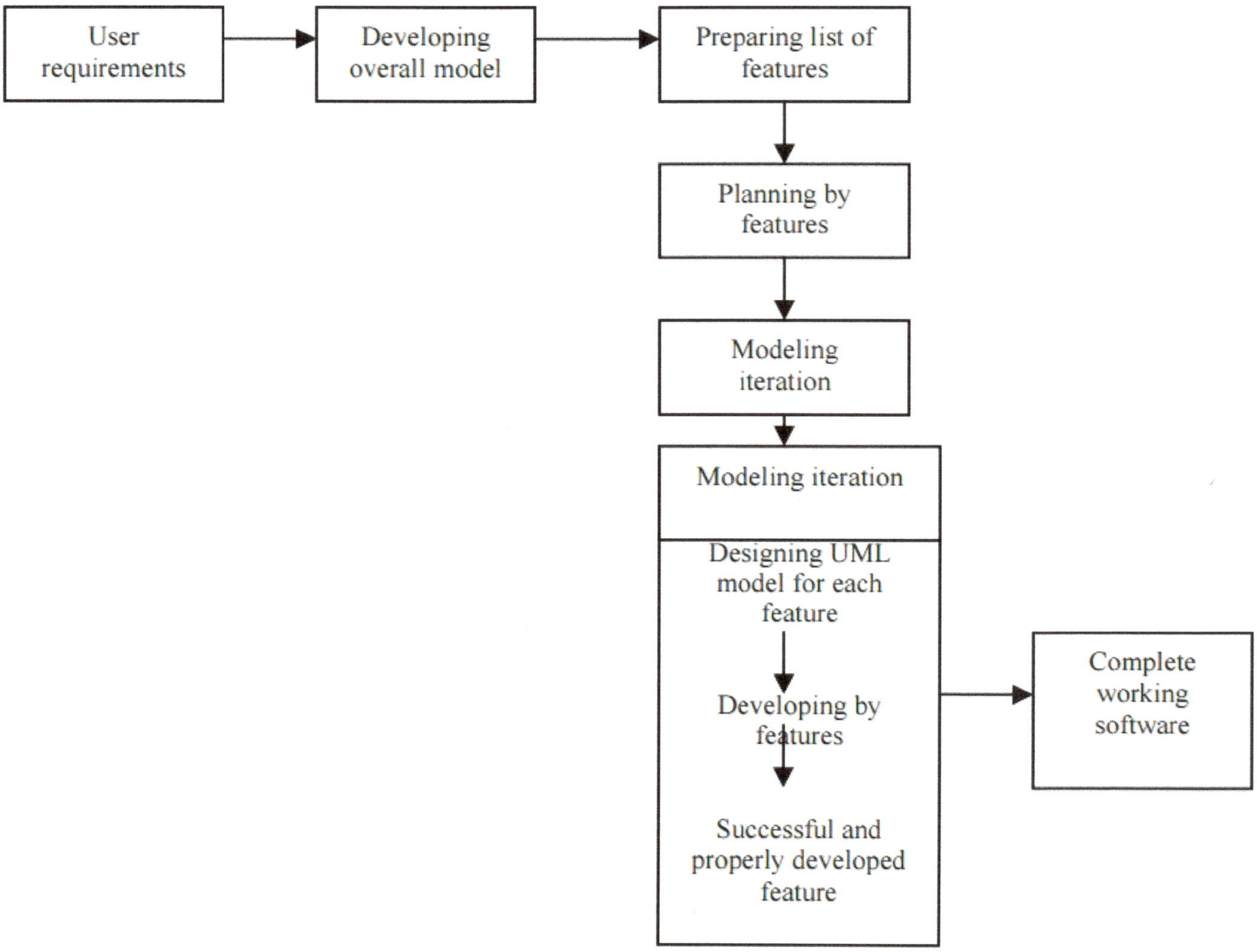


**Figure 4:** Method of Developing Agile Processes using FDD Graph.

The method starts with collecting the requirements from the users and building up the overall model of the project. The model gives the clear idea about the scope of the software. Next step is to make a list of features which are the client-valued functions [5]. For example 'authenticate the password', 'calculate the salary for each employee', 'calculate the income tax for each employee'. Now several groups of features are made based on their domains i.e. related features are combined into a single group. Next step is to make a plan for developing the features. Each group of features is assigned to a development team which is headed by one chief programmer. Last step is modeling iteration in which first UML modeling is done for each feature and then developing that particular feature. This step continues unless all the features get implemented successfully.

## Advantages

- Adaptive to the changing environment: In agile software development method, software is developed over several iterations. Each iteration is characterized by analysis, design, implementation and testing. After each iteration the mini project is delivered to the customer for their use and feedback. Any changes that upgrade the software are welcome from the customer at any stage of development and that changes are implemented.

- Ensures customer satisfaction: This methodology requires active customer involvement throughout the developmen[6]t. The deliverables developed after each iteration is given to the user for use and improvement is done based on the customer feedback only. So at the end what we get as the final product is of high quality and it ensures the customer satisfaction as the entire software is developed based on the requirements taken from customer.
- Least documentation: The documentation in agile methodology is short and to the point though it depends on the agile team. Generally they don't make documentation on internal design of the software. The main things which should be on the documentation are product features list, duration for each iteration and date. This brief documentation saves time of development and deliver the project in least possible time.
- Reduces risks of development: As the incremented mini software is delivered to the customers after every short development cycle and feedbacks are taken from the customers, it warns developers about the upcoming problems which may occur at the later stages of development. It also helps to discover errors quickly and they are fixed immediately.

## Disadvantages

- Customer interaction is the key factor of developing successful software: Agile methodology is based on customer involvement because the entire project is developed according to the requirements given by the customers. So if the customer representative is not clear about the product features, the development process will go out of the track.
- Lack of documentation: Though the least documentation saves development time as an advantage of agile method, on the other hand it is a big disadvantage for developer. Here the internal design is getting changed again and again depending on user requirements after every iteration, so it is not possible to maintain the detail documentation of design and implementation because of project deadline[7]. So because of less available information, it is very difficult for the new developers who join the development team at the later stage to understand the actual method followed to develop the software.
- Time consuming and wastage of resources because of constant change of requirements: If the customers are not satisfied by the partial software developed by certain iteration and they change their requirements then that incremented part is of no use. So it is the total wastage of time, effort and resources required to develop that increment.
- More helpful for management than developer: The agile methodology helps management to take decisions about the software development, set goals for developers and fix the deadline for them. But it is very difficult for the baseline developers to cope up with the ever changing environment and every time changing the design, code based on just in time requirements.

## COMPARISON OF AGILE PROCESS WITH OTHER SDLC MODELS

**Table 1.** Prcoess models

| Features | Different Process Models | | |
|---|---|---|---|
| | *Agile Process* | *Spiral Model* | *RAD Model* |
| Definition | Agile process is the ability to both create and respond to changing requirements of software. | Spiral model is the software development model which focuses on managing risks. | RAD model is "high speed adaptation of linear sequential model, in which component based construction is used. |
| Adaptability | ✓ | ✓ | X |
| Testing Phase | Unit, Integration , System testing | Unit, Integration and System testing | Unit |
| Quality Factors | ✓ | ✓ | X |
| Risk Analysis | X | ✓ | X |
| Off-the- Tools | X | X | ✓ |
| Failure normally due to | Code | Code | Architecture and design |
| Knowledge Required | Product and domain | Product and domain | Domain |
| Entry & exit Criteria | X | X | ✓ |
| Mock up | ✓ | ✓ | X |
| Extendability | ✓ | ✓ | X |
| Project management involvement | ✓ | X | ✓ |
| Higher Reliability | ✓ | ✓ | X |
| Time Boxing | ✓ | X | ✓ |

| Features | Different Process Models | | |
|---|---|---|---|
| | *Agile Process* | *Spiral Model* | *RAD Model* |
| Status of Development Team | Less experience required | Less experience required | More experience required |
| Use of reusable components | X | X | ✓ |
| Flexibility | ✓ | ✓ | X |
| Customer Involvement | ✓ | ✓ | X |

## CONCLUSION

In this paper we have discussed the software development life cycle models, the characteristics of agile process, and spiral model, methodologies of agile process, advantages and disadvantages. In the comparative study of agile software development with other software development models we conclude that agile project is much better than other software development process in terms of productivity, performance, faster time cycles, risk analysis. Agile processes are implemented in important applications such as web based, testing tools, etc.

## REFERENCES


1. Tobin J Lehman, Akhilesh Sharma , "Software Development as a service: Agile Experiences", in annual SRII Global Conference (2011).
2. Ahmed, S. Ahmad, Dr. N Ehsan, E. Mirza, S.Z. Sarwar,"Agile Software Development: Impact on Productivity and Qulaity", in the Proceedings of IEEE ICMIT.(2010).
3. B.Boehm and R.Turner, "Balancing Agility and Discipline: A Guide for the Perplexed, Addison, Wesley, 2003.
4. Jeffery A. Livermore, "Factors that Impact Implementing an Agile Software Development Methodology" in the Proceedings of IEEE (2007)
5. http://en.wikipedia.org/wiki/Scrum_(development)
6. B.Boehm, " Anchoring the Software Process," IEEE Software, July 1996.
7. B. Boehm and D.Port,"Balancing Discipline and Flexibility with the Spiral Model and MBASE". Crosstalk, Dec. 2001.

# CHAPTER 9 QUINTESSENCE OF TRADITIONAL AND AGILE REQUIREMENT ENGINEERING

Jalil Abbas

School of Computing and Information Sciences, Imperial College of Business Studies, Lahore, Pakistan

## ABSTRACT

**Requirement gathering for software development project is the most crucial stage and thus requirement engineering (RE) occupies the chief position in the software development. Countless techniques concerning the RE processes exist to make sure the requirements are coherent, compact and complete in all respects. In this way different aspects of RE are dissected and detailed upon. A comparison of RE in Agile and RE in Waterfall is expatiated and on the basis of the literature survey the overall Agile RE process is accumulated. Agile being a technique produces high quality software in relatively less time as compared to the conventional waterfall methodology. The paramount objective of this study is to take lessons from RE that Agile method may consider, if quality being the cardinal concern. The study is patterned on the survey of the previous research reported in the coexisting literature and the practices which are being pursued in the area.**

## INTRODUCTION

In software engineering, software development methodology known as software development life cycle (SDLC) is a sectionalisation of software development work. Common methodologies include Waterfall, Prototyping, Iterative and Incremental development, Spiral development, Rapid application development, Extreme Programming and other different kinds of Agile methodology. All these methods comprise of multiple phases and a variety of different activities. For instance design, re-factor, reuse, re-engineering and maintenance are some common activities, employed to complete software solutions. A wide variety of such frameworks have evolved over the years, each with its own recognized strengths and weaknesses. One software development methodology framework doesn't adequately suffice for all projects.

Over the years, most of the software development methods have been made immaculate and then referred to as traditional methods. One of the oldest of these traditional methods is waterfall which was firstly explained by Winston Royce in 1970 [1] . It is still very much in vogue widely practiced both in large and small projects [2] . The Waterfall model is a sequential design process which is used in software development processes where progress palpably is flowing downwards like a Waterfall through the phases of requirement gathering and analysis, design, coding, testing and maintenance. Every stage is to be treated separately at an opportune moment so you cannot jump stages. Documentation is done at every stage of a Waterfall model, providing an opportunity to the people to decipher as what has been done. Similarly testing is carried at every stage. Waterfall method is understood for its

**Citation:** Jalil Abbas (2016) Quintessence of Traditional and Agile Requirement Engineering. Journal of Software Engineering and Applications,09,63-70. doi: 10.4236/jsea.2016.93005

concrete and complete requirements and these features make this approach more viable and stable. It is often said about this method that spending more time early in the cycle can pave way to greater success at later stages.

The Agile development method came to limelight as the result of gathering of seventeen representatives from the software development industry in snowbird, Utah in 2001 [3] . Their intention was to develop innovative approaches to software development that would make organization react rapidly and adapt to volatile requirements and technologies.

In Agile Manifesto [3] they gave the identification of the following four priorities:

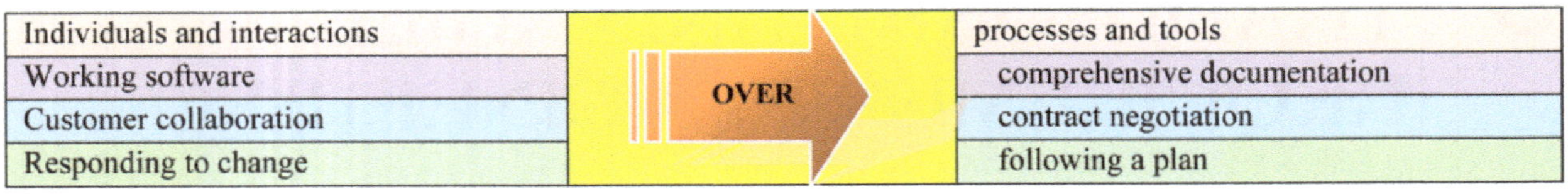


Priorities in Agile Manifesto

There exist multiple types of Agile methods as extreme programming, scrum, feature-driven development, dynamic system development method, adaptive software development, crystal and lean software development. What is common to all methods is the division of client's requirements into multiple release cycle which are available in smaller portions regarding to their business value [4] . These methods comprise of most recognizable quality factors such as cost effectiveness, efficiency, extendibility, maintainability, portability, reusability and robustness [5] .

The remainder of the paper is organized as follows: Section 2 gives a comparison between traditional and Agile software development methodologies. Section 3 explains the Requirement Engineering process. Section 4 describes the RE in waterfall and RE in Agile, also the challenges of traditional RE resolved by Agile RE are discussed. Conclusion is given at the end of paper.

## COMPARISON OF AGILE AND WATERFALL DEVELOPMENT METHODS

Agile and waterfall methods stand apart so far as their activities are concerned, as they are put to use within the development process [6] - [9] . To understand clearly the difference between Waterfall and Agile the comparison is made in a tabular form and is provided in Table 1.

## REQUIREMENT ENGINEERING

Software Requirements describe features and functionalities of the target system it also tells the expectations of the users from the software product .The requirements can be obvious or occult, either it is known or not known, expected or unexpected from client's point of view. The formidable single part of making a software system is deciding clearly as what to build. No other part of the conceptual work is as formidable as making the detailed technical requirements. The process to glean the software requirements from client, analyze and document them is named requirement engineering. It is sometime overlooked or assumed to be a straight and undistorted task [26] , requirements collecting for software development projects is the most difficult phase of any software development methodology. To determine software requirements is the fulcrum to any successful project. Requirements cannot be easily defined and estimated for managing any project [27] . Some studies have exposed that around 37% of the problems occurred during the development of system related to the requirement phases [28] and is graphically depicted in Figure 1.

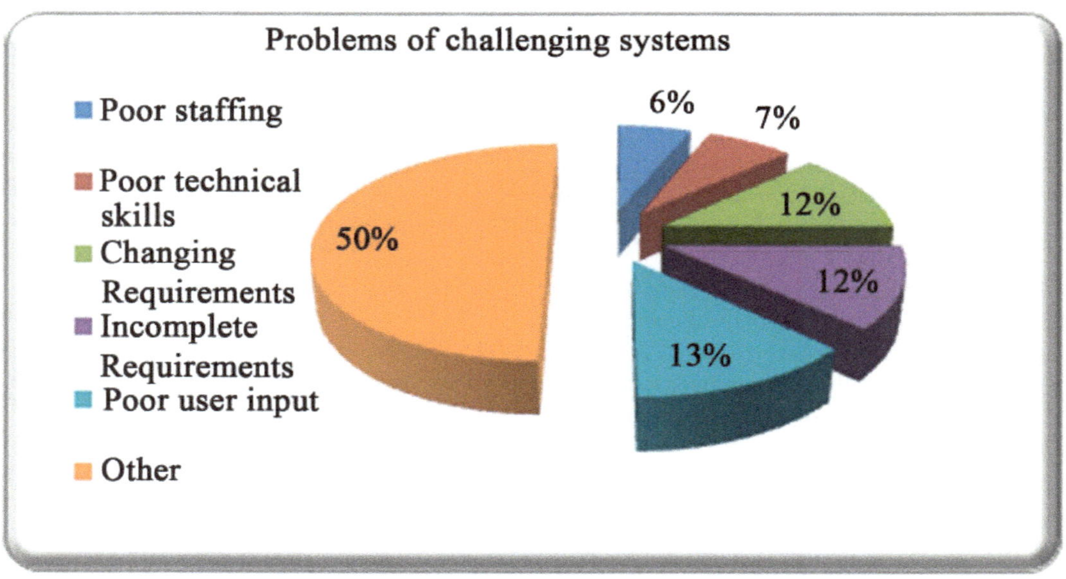


**Figure 1**. Problems of challenging system.

**Table 1**. Comparison of Waterfall and Agile development methods

| Metric | Traditional development process | Agile development process | Study that reported |
|---|---|---|---|
| SDLC | Linear | Iterative | [9] [10] |
| Development style | Traditional methods are predictive (plan?driven) | Agile methods are adaptive | [11] - [14] |
| Documentation | Enough documentation to be able to answer all questions that might be asked in the future. | Light (replaced by face to face communication) | [7] [15] |
| Customer involvement | in traditional approaches the customer is mainly engaged during the early phase of the project | Agile methods engage the customer throughout the whole development process. | [13] [16] - [18] |
| Change | Resistance to change | Welcoming to change, even changes are brought in late in the project. | [19] [20] |
| Size | traditional methods are able to manage effectively large project | Manage effectively requirements in small projects but not in large ones. | [13] |
| Planning scale | Long term | Short term | [13] |
| Management | process oriented, command and control | People oriented, leadership and conformity. | [11] [12] [15] [21] [22] |
| Team organization | Pre- structured teams | Self organizing teams | [23] |
| Ownership | Ownership belongs to only project manager | Shared ownership | [19] |
| Prioritization | Requirements are typically prioritized once. | Prioritize feature lists repeatedly during development | [24] |
| Customer feedback | At the termination of the project | At the completion of every sprint | [25] |
| Risk identification | No risk identification. | Early identification and mitigation in every sprint. | [25] |
| Time between specification & implementation | Long | Short | [13] |
| Delivery | Delivering artifacts phase wise and delivery of working software at the end of project. | Demonstration and delivering working software et the end of every sprint. | [25] |
| Measure of Success | Conformance to plan | Business value delivered | [3] |

Requirement engineering stresses the use of systematic and repeatable techniques that ensure the completeness, consistency and relevance of the system requirements. The process used for RE changes widely depending on the application domain, the people involved and organization developing the requirements. There exists a plethora of generic activities common to all processes. So RE process can be split up into 2-main assortments:

- Requirement Development
- Requirement Management

The goal of requirement development is to identify, capture and agree upon a set of functional requirements and product characteristics that will gain the stated business objectives. It contains four kinds of activities as shown in Figure 2 [29] .

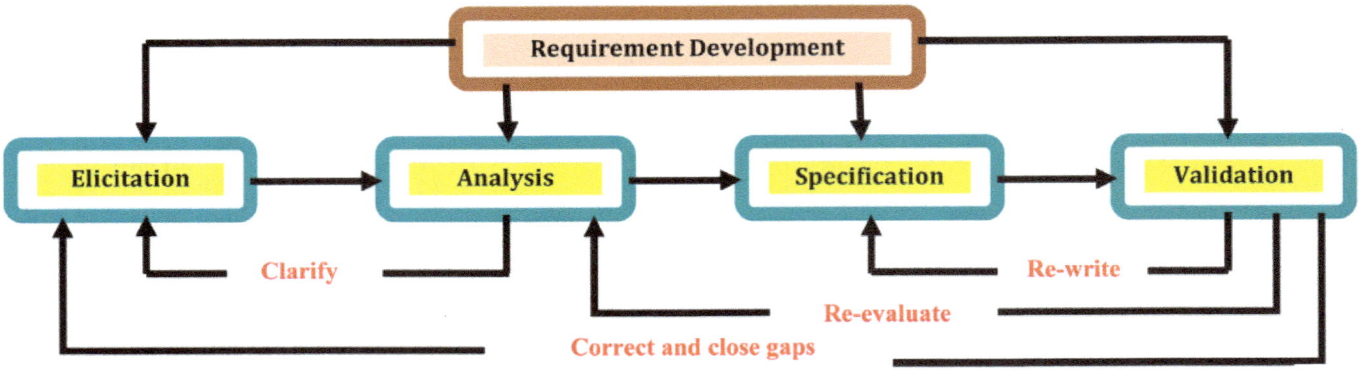


**Figure 2**. Requirement development activities.

- Elicitation: It is process discovering, reviewing, documenting, knowing user needs and constraints for the system.
- Analysis: It provides feedback loop to refine user's needs and restraints.
- Specification: It is process of documenting the user's needs and restraints.
- Validation: This ensures that the system requirements are complete, correct, consistent and clear.

However, the requirement management is the process of documenting, analyzing, tracing, prioritizing and agreeing on requirements and then controlling change and communicating to relevant stakeholders. It is a continuous process throughout a project. A requirement is a capability to which a project outcome (product or service) should conform.

## REQUIREMENT ENGINEERING IN AGILE AND WATERFALL

### RE in Waterfall

Requirement engineering involves a number of processes for gathering requirements in accordance with the needs and demands of users and stakeholders of the software product. Waterfall Requirement Engineering involves some important features that are elicitation, analysis, documentation and managing of the requirements [30] [31] as already mentioned in Section 3. In the waterfall model requirements engineering is presented as the first phase of the development process. This traditional approach to the RE process focuses on gathering all the requirements and preparing the requirements specification document up front before proceeding to the design phase [32] . In the waterfall method the project is separated into stages distinctly and commitments must be made at an early stage, which makes it hard to alter the requirements if customers change their minds. So waterfall is more suitable when the requirements will probably not be changed during the implementation time. In conclusion, the waterfall model takes a static viewpoint of Requirements Engineering by ignoring issues such as the volatility of requirements and its impact on earlier and later phases of development [33] .

### RE in Agile

According to various researchers Agile methodology and its family members are based on the following principles also known as Agile manifesto [34] - [37] :

| | | |
|---|---|---|
| Customer Satisfaction | Frequent Delivery | Motivated Team |
| Technical Excellence | Emergent Design | Incremental development |
| Embrace Change | Collaboration | High Bandwidth |
| Sustainable Pace | Simplicity | Continuous Improvement |

These principles are fairly simple in concept, but are profoundly deep in practice.

Agile assumes that requirements engineering continues through the lifetime of a system. In Agile, RE is achieved through continuous collaboration while requirement gathering, developing and testing may happen at the same time. This is achieved by applying the practice of evolutionary requirements which suggests that requirements should evolve over time. In Agile, the business requirements are elicited and documented in the form of user stories, which are from portrays user's perspective [38] . These user stories are used as a primary unit of work and continue to grow during the lifecycle of the project. Agile methods involve continuous planning, i.e. release planning, iteration planning and task level planning. Iteration planning is done for each iteration that spans from 1 to 3 weeks. It involves user story estimation, acknowledgement of the accomplishments of the previous iteration and determining overall progress and goals for the next iteration. Release plan is done for each release in which iteration length is decided, developers and customers unanimously decide what will be in a particular iteration; velocity points are determined per iteration. Task level planning involves the breaking down of user stories into subsequent tasks, allocation of tasks among team members and focus is put on implementation issues [39] - [42] . After the literature survey of RE in Agile the overall Agile RE process is accumulated and described in Figure 3.

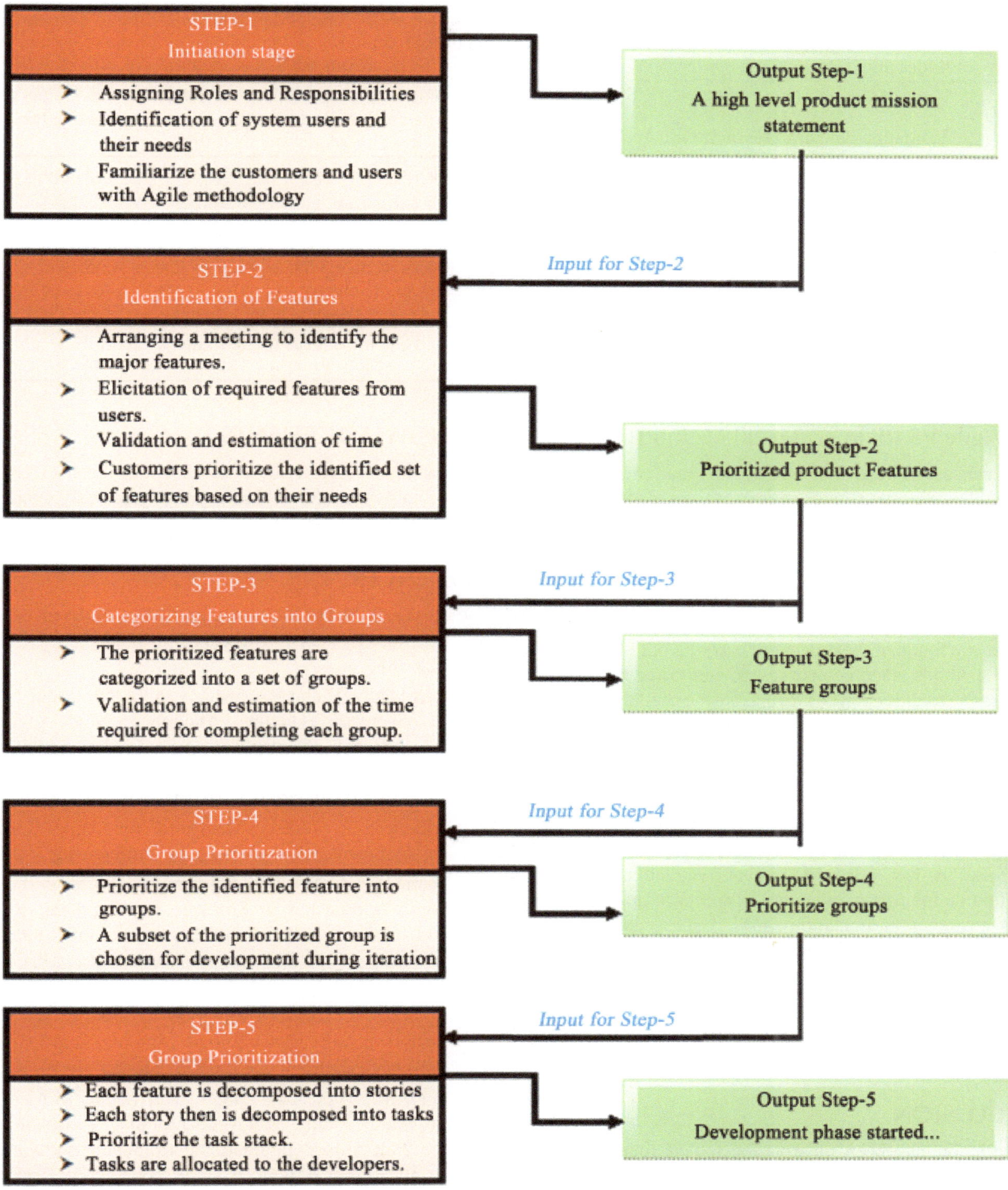


**Figure 3**. RE process in agile.

**Table 2**. Issues of RE in waterfall resolved by agile RE

| Issues of RE in Waterfall | Resolved by RE in Agile |
|---|---|
| Customer involvement: Customers are involved only during the beginning of requirement gathering and analysis [40] . | Customers are involved throughout the complete process. |
| Prioritization of requirements: Complete requirements for the full project are prioritized upfront and the prioritization is kept up through the project lifecycle, and reprioritization is arduous [47] . | Priorities are setup for all iterations that offer opportunities for getting desirable results and customer satisfaction [48] [49] . |

| | |
|---|---|
| Documentation: Totally emphasizes at properly gathering organizing and documenting all requirements and excludes any live meetings/conferences [14] . | User stories are concise and provide to-the-point explanation of user demands, obviate the need for maintaining long SRS documents. |
| Requirements validation: Validation happens late in the life cycle. | Prototyping helps in providing the customer with a blueprint of the product, and therefore helps in validating the requirements [50] . |
| Communication: It is a major factor in the delay and failure of software projects [40] . | It provides regular interaction with customer and among teams. |
| Over-scoping of requirements: It is the cause of rework, which in turn causes further investment. | Developers receive a list of features that are constantly prioritized so the chance of having to repeat allocation in projects is minimized. |
| Shall Argument: The worst thing of waterfall RE is "shall" argument i.e. system shall do it, etc. [46] . | Agile introduces the real time system. |

## RE in Agile VS RE in Waterfall Methods

It has been ascertained that traditional requirement process is a complex process where as real life development needs efficient requirement software which must have a flexible and speedy process. For a successful project an efficient RE process is needed. The objective of RE remains the same in all software methods, however RE in Agile and Waterfall methods is juxtaposed and opposite in nature [43] [44] . Remarkable variances are found in the process of carrying out RE activities in Agile methods when compared and contrasted to Waterfall methods. The traditional RE is facing many a challenges such as communication gaps, over scoping, requirement prioritization, validation and customer involvement [45] . These issues are resolved by Agile practices such as face to face communication for minimizing documentation and communication gaps, gradual detailing of requirements for reducing over scoping, requirement prioritization by customer based on the worth of business to deal with requirements validation and close interaction on the part of team and customer in order to avoid lack of customer participation [46] . Issues caused by the traditional RE and the solutions provided by the Agile RE are described in Table 2.

Therefore, we can summarize that several detrimental challenges posed by traditional RE can be eradicated or minimized by using Agile RE.

## CONCLUSION

Differentiation has been clearly drawn and found that the traditional RE and Agile RE are two different approaches so far as their rules and activities are concerned. Comparison between the two shows why people have gone from traditional RE to Agile RE. The underlying idea of this apparent shift was to shed light on the magnitude of Agile development for efficacious requirement engineering process. By doing so, resultantly Agile RE works better than the waterfall RE in disciplines like communication, customer collaboration, documentation, delivering outputs, requirement prioritization and validation, etc. Practitioners engaged will come to comprehend and evaluate the various impediments/obstacles encountered by them while using traditional RE.

## ACKNOWLEDGEMENTS

I, personally feel extremely beholden to Prof(R) Ghulam Qasim Shah who with self-abnegation graciously spared his time and reviewed this paper.

## REFERENCES

1. Royce, W.W. (1970) Managing the Development of Large Software Systems. Proceedings of IEEE WESCON, 26, 328-388.
2. Alsultanny, Y. and Wohaishi, A.M. (2009) Requirements of Software Quality Assurance Model. Second International Conference on Environmental and Computer Science, Dubai, 28-30 December 2009, 19-23. http://dx.doi.org/10.1109/icecs.2009.43
3. Alliance, A. (2001) Manifesto for Agile Software Development. http://www.Agilemanifesto.org/
4. Hamed, A.M.M. and Abushama, H. (2013) Popular Agile Approaches in Software Development: Review and Analysis. International Conference on Computing, Electrical and Electronics Engineering (ICCEEE), August 2013, 160-166.
5. Sirshar, M. (2012) Evaluation of Quality Assurance Factors in Agile Methodologies. International Journal of Advanced Computer Science, 2, 73-78.
6. Huo, M., Verner, J., Zhu, L. and Babar, M.A. (2004) Software Quality and Agile Methods. Proceedings of the 28th Annual International Computer Software and Applications Conference, Hong Kong, 28-30 September 2004, 520-525.
7. Boehm, B. (2002) Get Ready for Agile Methods, with Care. Computer, 35, 64-69. http://dx.doi.org/10.1109/2.976920
8. Dyba, T. and Dingsoyr, T. (2009) What Do We Know about Agile Software Development? IEEE Software, 26, 6-9. http://dx.doi.org/10.1109/MS.2009.145
9. Nerur, S., Mahapatra, R. and Mangalaraj, G. (2005) Challenges of Migrating to Agile Methodologies. Communications of the ACM, 48, 72-78. http://dx.doi.org/10.1145/1060710.1060712

10. Charvat, J. (2003) Project Management Methodologies: Selecting, Implementing, and Supporting Methodologies and Processes for Projects. John Wiley & Sons, Hoboken.

11. Fowler, M. (2001) The New Methodology. Wuhan University Journal of Natural Sciences, 6, 12-24. http://dx.doi.org/10.1007/BF03160222

12. Boehm, B. and Turner, R. (2004) Balancing Agility and Discipline: Evaluating and Integrating Agile and Plan-Driven Methods. In Proceedings of 26th International Conference on Software Engineering, 718-719.

13. Okoli, C. and Carillo, K. (2012) The Best of Adaptive and Predictive Methodologies: Open Source Software Development, a Balance between Agility and Discipline. International Journal of Information Technology and Management, 11, 153-166. http://dx.doi.org/10.1504/IJITM.2012.044071

14. Leffingwell, D. (2007) Scaling Software Agility: Best Practices for Large Enterprises. Pearson Education, New York.

15. Boehm, B. and Turner, R. (2005) Management Challenges to Implementing Agile Processes in Traditional Development Organizations. IEEE Software, 22, 30-39. http://dx.doi.org/10.1109/MS.2005.129

16. Paetsch, F., Eberlein, A. and Maurer, F. (2003) Requirements Engineering and Agile Software Development. In: Null, p. 308. IEEE.

17. Sillitti, A. and Succi, G. (2005) Requirements Engineering for Agile Methods. In: Engineering and Managing Software Requirements, Springer Berlin Heidelberg, 309-326. http://dx.doi.org/10.1007/3-540-28244-0_14

18. Cockburn, A. and Highsmith, J. (2001) Agile Software Development: The People Factor. Computer, 34, 131-133. http://dx.doi.org/10.1109/2.963450

19. Regev, G., Gause, D.C. and Wegmann, A. (2006) Creativity and the Age-Old Resistance to Change Problem in RE. 14th IEEE International Conference Requirements Engineering, Minneapolis/St. Paul, 11-15 September 2006, 291-296. http://dx.doi.org/10.1109/re.2006.13

20. Boehm, B. and Turner, R. (2003) Using Risk to Balance Agile and Plan-Driven Methods. Computer, 36, 57-66. http://dx.doi.org/10.1109/MC.2003.1204376

21. Vinekar, V., Slinkman, C.W. and Nerur, S. (2006) Can Agile and Traditional Systems Development Approaches Coexist? An Ambidextrous View. Information Systems Management, 23, 31-42. http://dx.doi.org/10.1201/1078.10580530/46108.23.3.20060601/93705.4

22. Highsmith, J.A. (2002) Agile Software Development Ecosystems. Addison-Wesley Professional, Boston, Vol. 13

23. Ashmore, S. and Runyan, K. (2014) Introduction to Agile Methods. Addison-Wesley Professional, Boston.

24. Racheva, Z., Daneva, M., Sikkel, K., Herrmann, A. and Wieringa, R. (2010) Do We Know Enough about Requirements Prioritization in Agile Projects: Insights from a Case Study. 18th IEEE International Requirements Engineering Conference (RE), 147-156.

25. Moniruzzaman, A.B.M. and Hossain, D.S.A. (2013) Comparative Study on Agile Software Development Methodologies. arXiv preprint arXiv:1307.3356.

26. Kitapci, H. and Boehm, B.W. (2007) Formalizing Informal Stakeholder Decisions—A Hybrid Method Approach. 40th Annual Hawaii International Conference on System Sciences, Waikoloa, 3-6 January 2007, 283c-283c. https://www.pwc.com/us/en/.../pwc-adopting-Agile-methodology.pdf

27. Polini, A. (2010) Software Requirements. http://www1.isti.cnr.it/~polini/lucidiSE/Requirements1.pdf

28. Sommerville, I. and Sawyer, P. (1997) Requirements Engineering: A Good Practice Guide. John Wiley & Sons, Inc., Hoboken

29. Pressman, R.S. (2005) Software Engineering: A Practitioner's Approach. Palgrave Macmillan.

30. Sommerville, I. and Kotonya, G. (1998) Requirements Engineering: Processes and Techniques. John Wiley & Sons, Inc., Hoboken.

31. Pandey, D., Suman, U. and Ramani, A.K. (2010) An Effective Requirement Engineering Process Model for Software Development and Requirements Management. International Conference on Advances in Recent Technologies in Communication and Computing (ARTCom), Kottayam, 16-17 October 2010, 287-291. http://dx.doi.org/10.1109/artcom.2010.24

32. Nuseibeh, B. and Easterbrook, S. (2000) Requirements Engineering: A Roadmap. Proceedings of the Conference on the Future of Software Engineering, 35-46. http://dx.doi.org/10.1145/336512.336523

33. Zhu, Y. (2009) Requirements Engineering in an Agile Environment. Uppsala University, Uppsala.

34. Kavitha, C.R. and Thomas, S.M. (2011) Requirement Gathering for Small Projects Using Agile Methods. IJCA Special Issue on Computational Science-New Dimensions & Perspectives, NCCSE.

35. Lucia, A.D. and Qusef, A. (2010) Requirements Engineering in Agile Software Development. Journal of Emerging Technologies in Web Intelligence, 2, 212-220. http://dx.doi.org/10.4304/jetwi.2.3.212-220

36. Paetsch, F. (2003) Requirements Engineering in Agile Software Development. Diploma Thesis, University of Calgary University of Calgary, Alberta.

37. Manifesto, C.H.A.O.S. (2013) Think Big, Act Small. The Standish Group International Inc. http://versionone.com/assets/img/files/ChaosManifesto2013.pdf

38. Inayat, I., Salim, S.S., Marczak, S., Daneva, M. and Shamshirband, S. (2014) A Systematic Literature Review on Agile Requirements Engineering Practices and Challenges. Computers in Human Behavior, 51, 915-929.

39. Cao, L. and Ramesh, B. (2008) Agile Requirements Engineering Practices: An Empirical Study. IEEE Software, 25, 60-67. http://dx.doi.org/10.1109/MS.2008.1

40. Helmy, W., Kamel, A. and Hegazy, O. (2012) Requirements Engineering Methodology in Agile Environment. International Journal of Computer Science Issues, 9, 293-300.

41. Jun, L., Qiuzhen, W. and Lin, G. (2010) Application of Agile Requirement Engineering in Modest-Sized Information Systems Development. Second World Congress on Software Engineering (WCSE), Wuhan, 19-20 December 2010, Vol. 2, 207-210.

42. Araujo, J. and Ribeiro, J.C. (2005) Towards an Aspect-Oriented Agile Requirements Approach. Eighth International Workshop on Principles of Software Evolution, 5-6 September 2005, 140-143. http://dx.doi.org/10.1109/iwpse.2005.31

43. Martakis, A. and Daneva, M. (2013) Handling Requirements Dependencies in Agile Projects: A Focus Group with Agile Software Development Practitioners. IEEE Seventh International Conference on Research Challenges in Information Science (RCIS), Paris, 29-31 May 2013, 1-11. http://dx.doi.org/10.1109/rcis.2013.6577679

44. Liu, L., Li, T. and Peng, F. (2010) Why Requirements Engineering Fails: A Survey Report from China. 18th IEEE International Requirements Engineering Conference (RE), Sydney, 27 September 2010-1 October 2010, 317-322. http://dx.doi.org/10.1109/re.2010.45

45. Inayat, I., Moraes, L., Daneva, M. and Salim, S.S. (2015) A Reflection on Agile Requirements Engineering: Solutions Brought and Challenges Posed. Scientific Workshop Proceedings of the XP2015, Trondheim, p. 6. http://dx.doi.org/10.1145/2764979.2764985

46. Soundararajan, S. and Arthur, J. D. (2009) A Soft-Structured Agile Framework for Larger Scale Systems Development. 16th Annual IEEE International Conference and Workshop on the Engineering of Computer Based Systems, San Francisco, 14-16 April 2009, 187-195. http://dx.doi.org/10.1109/ecbs.2009.21

47. Mulla, N. and Girase, S. (2012) Comparison of Various Elicitation Techniques and Requirement Prioritisation Techniques. International Journal of Engineering Research and Technology, 1, No. 3.

48. Wiegers, K. (1999) First Things First: Prioritizing Requirements. Software Development, 7, 48-53.

49. Papadopoulos, G. (2015) Moving from Traditional to Agile Software Development Methodologies Also on Large, Distributed Projects. Procedia—Social and Behavioral Sciences, 175, 455-463. http://dx.doi.org/10.1016/j.sbspro.2015.01.1223

CHAPTER 10

# AN EFFICIENT APPROACH FOR AGILE WEB BASED PROJECT ESTIMATION: AGILEMOW

Ratnesh Litoriya[1], Abhay Kothari[2]

[1]Department of Computer Engineering, JJT University, Rajasthan, India

[2]Department of CSE, SIMS, Indore, India.

## ABSTRACT

**There exist numerous sophisticated models and methods for estimating the size, cost and schedule of software projects. However, the ability to accurately predict the software cost of web based software for agile software projects is still dubious. The most appropriate web based software cost estimation in an agile software development environment is a big problem due to varying levels of customer requirement and different individual personnel capabilities. Also, the need to develop a separate model to estimate web based project is rising. In this research paper, we present AgileMOW, an approach to model a software cost estimation process which will evaluate effort and cost of software development for web based projects developed using Agile methodology with a number of constraints imposed by stakeholders and environmental characteristics, thereby satisfying multitudinous criteria by making use of COCOMO II model, a famous traditional algorithmic technique. Most importantly, the paper identifies the difference between conventional and web projects. The proposed estimation model enhances the level of visibility in the planning stages.**

## INTRODUCTION

Software projects generally follow the traditional development life cycle models [1]. Unfortunately these models do not result in successful product in terms of technology used and satisfaction of revised requirements at the time of product release. Software development effort estimation deals with the prediction of the probable amount of time and cost required to complete the specific development task. Predicting the estimates obtained at the early stages of development life cycle is inaccurate because of long duration between the signing of the project and its delivery, also not much details of the system is available at that time. The way we develop software is changing. Software is developed from requirements through Agile Web development; professionals join together for building blocks and reusable components using rapid application development process and continuous prototyping [2]. Things take place so quickly that it is tough to get a handle on their status and whether they are making suitable progress [3]. Web based projects are also hard to estimate, especially in agile environment with limited resources, software developers require to better predict the time and effort is essential to pull off such projects successfully. The result motivates industries and developers to adapt more iterative and incremental agile

**Citation:** R. Litoriya and A. Kothari, "An Efficient Approach for Agile Web Based Project Estimation: AgileMOW," Journal of Software Engineering and Applications, Vol. 6 No. 6, 2013, pp. 297-303. doi: 10.4236/jsea.2013.66037.

models. Software estimation is mandatory for software developers and their companies because it can provide cost control delivery accuracy and many other benefits. There are three elements under software Web cost estimation, i.e. software metric, web cost estimation model and software cost estimation tool [4]. Presently many quantitative models of software cost estimation have been developed. Most of the software estimation models available are based on some forms of regression technique, these models have a mathematical foundation and are constructed by collecting data on completed software project and developing regression equation relating them.

In this paper we introduce AgileMOW, an adaptation of a software estimation model to a particular context of agile methodology of software development. In the Second section, we briefly discuss about the software cost estimation models. Section 3 presents agile based web development projects and its characteristics, Section 4 highlights about challenges in web cost estimation, Sections 5 and 6 present the Agile software development and their manifestoes along with problem statement. The proposed model for agile web based software effort estimation is given and described in the following section.

## SOFTWARE COST ESTIMATION MODELS

Software industries and developers always interest to know the time estimation of software projects at the time of inception of software development. Cost models were only based on a single parameter such as program size. These models were not accurate and estimation done by comparing similar projects that have already been developed. Now a day in the light of software crisis all over the world, software estimation is a big challenge due to it allows for financial and strategic planning. Software cost estimation techniques can broadly be classified under algorithmic and non-algorithmic models [5] as shown in Figure 1.

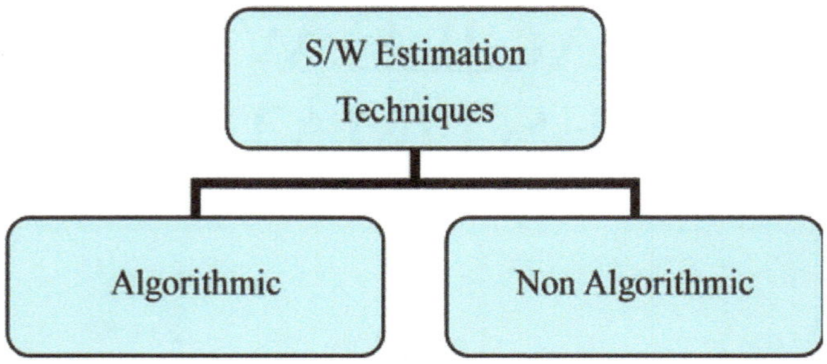


**Figure 1**. Software estimation classification.

Algorithmic models are based on the statistical analysis of historical data such as past projects. Non algorithmic techniques are based on new approach like expert judgment, price to win and machine learning.

### Algorithmic Models

Few very popular algorithmic models includes COCOMO II by Boehm's, function point by Albert's and SLIM by Putnam. All these models require inputs accurate estimate of specific attribute such as line of code (LOC), number of user screen, interface complexity etc. which are difficult to predict during the initial stage of software development.

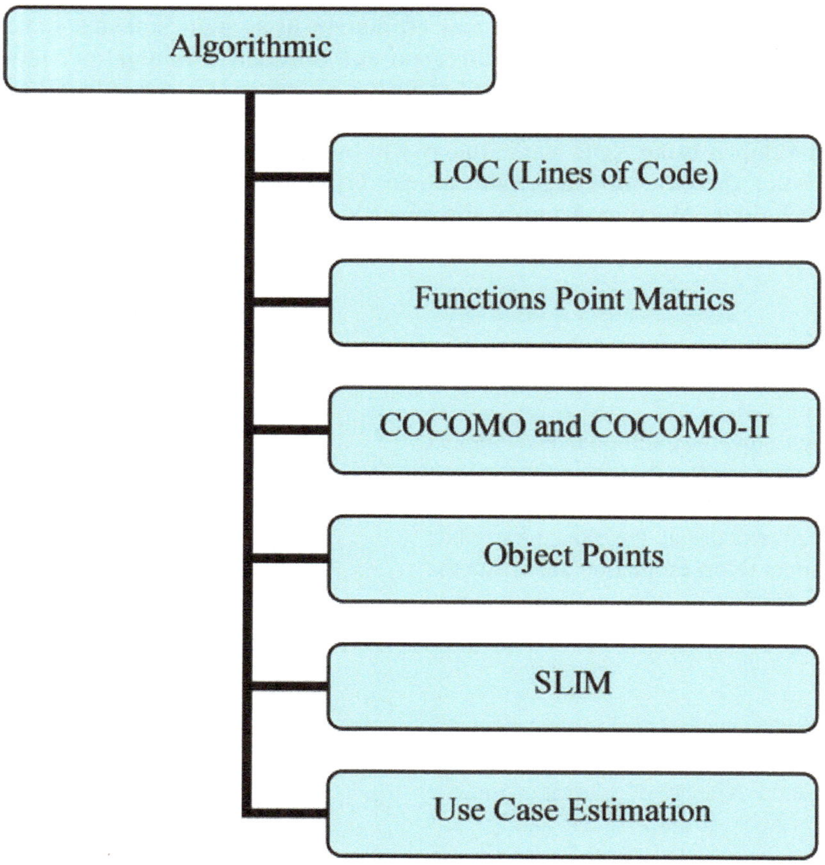


**Figure 2**. Algorithmic models.

Figure 2 illustrates some very popular algorithmic models. Calculating these models is hard due to inherent complex relationships between the related attributes. Despite attributes and relationships used to predict software development estimates could change over for different software development environment. The limitation of algorithmic models led to the introduction of non-algorithmic technique.

## Non Algorithmic Models

Non algorithmic models for software estimation came into the existence in early 90's. Researchers of their field found some new approaches supported by soft computing; they are artificial neural network, fuzzy logic and genetic algorithms.

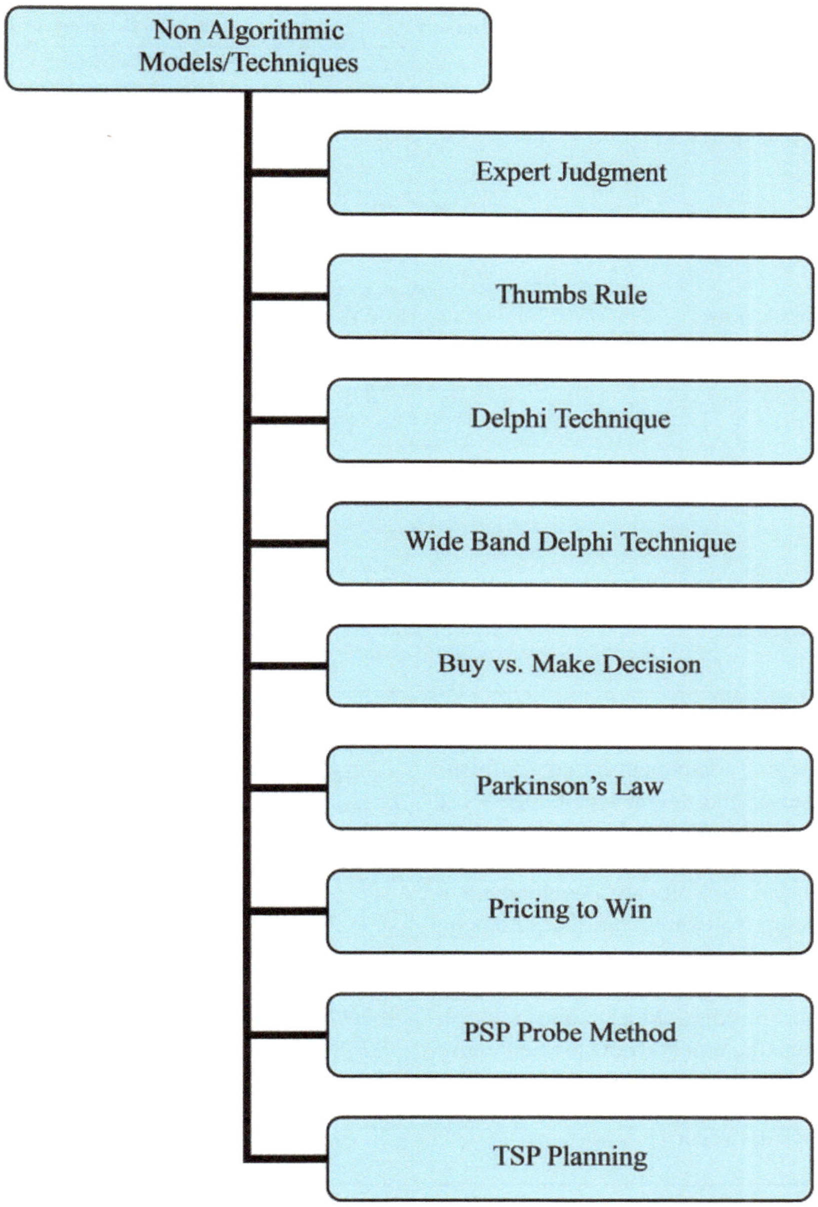


**Figure 3**. Non algorithmic mod.

Figure 3 summarize the non-algorithmic techniques. Expert Judgment is a non-algorithmic technique is carried out based on experience of project manager or a team of expert. Experience proves that model-based estimates do not perform considerably better than estimates exclusively based on expert judgment [6]. In Thumb Rule decision is taken based on personnel interest, it has certain drawbacks. In Delphi technique, no direct interaction is there among the experts, Coordinator look after the whole process. Wide Band Delphi technique introduced by Rand Corporation is a one to one interaction technique is carried out after mutual agreement among experts. Buy vs. Make decision is based on reusable Component based software development. In Parkinson's Law the project cost is calculated on the basis of resources available in an organization. In pricing to win estimation technique the project cost is determined from the customer's budget, however the approach is a businesslike but when detailed information is lacking it may be the appropriate strategy. PSP Probe Method introduced by Watt uses similar project and product work experiences when estimating future efforts. TSP Planning (Team software process) introduces team dynamics for planning, role definition and development phases over PSP trained and operating developers.

## AGILE BASED WEB DEVELOPMENT PROJECTS AND CHARACTERISTIC

During the past few years, estimators tried to estimate the cost and schedule for a Web based project. Apparently, developers use different high level technologies such as hypertext markup language, Java applets and script, and many more to generate software for the Web in the flash of an eye. But these special category projects beat estimation processes, defy models, and makes size metrics obsolete. With the advent of Agile process model of software project development generating numerous Web objects and making them functional in just a few months, this accelerated pace raises pressing questions.

**Table 1. Characteristics of conventional versus agile web development projects**

| Characteristics | Conventional Development | Agile Web Development |
|---|---|---|
| **Key objective** | Build quality software products at minimum cost | Bring worth products to market as rapidly as possible under varying requirements of clients |
| **Project size** | Medium to large (hundreds of team members) | Small (5 - 7 team members) |
| **Costing** | In millions | In thousands |
| **Development approach employed** | Classical, requirements-based, water fall or incremental delivery, uses cases, documentation-driven | Rapid application development, gluing building blocks less paper work, XP |
| **Major engineering technologies used** | Object oriented methods, generators, modern programming languages (C++), CASE tools, and so forth | Web object based methods, fourth- and fifth-generation technologies like JAVA. Net framework PHP etc. |
| **Processes employed** | Capability maturity model-based | *Ad hoc* |
| **Products developed** | Code-based systems, mostly new, some reuse, many external interfaces, often complex applications | Object-based systems, many reusable components (on line banking, web kiosk etc.), few external interfaces, moderately simple |
| **People involved** | Professional software engineers typically with 5+ years of experience in at least two application domains | Graphic designers, less experienced software engineers (2+ years), new appoints right out of school |
| **Estimating technologies used** | Algorithmic and non algorithmic techniques Analogy using historical data as its basis, SLOC or function point-based models, Work Breakdown Structure (WBS) approach for small projects | Analogy based upon current experience, "design-to-fit" based on available resources, WBS approach for small projects |

Table 1 emphasizes the move to Agile software development paradigm with component-based software development, systematic reuse, and visual technologies [7]. It discovers the move to quick-paced developments: Getting their software to market first is the top priority for firms doing business on the Web. The way of software development is shifting. Rather than develop software from requirements through the waterfall, Agile based Web development provides working software over comprehensive documentation professionals stick together building blocks and reusable components using iterative and incremental development, rapid application development methods and continuous prototyping. Agile Estimation Using Functional Metrics [8] is also a way of predicting web cost. Agile Web developments are also difficult to estimate particularly in firms with limited resources.

## CHALLENGES IN WEB COST ESTIMATION

Web projects are different and web development using agile methodologies are even different. To underscore the challenges involved in the area of Agile Web estimation, **Table 2** demonstrates the comparison of conventional estimation approach and agile web cost estimation challenges [7].

**Table 2**. Challenges of agile web development

| | Conventional Approach | Agile Web-based challenges |
|---|---|---|
| **Estimating process** | Use analogy supplemented by lessons gathered from past experience | Job costing done *ad hoc* based on inputs from the developers. |
| **Size estimation** | SLOC or function points are used. Separate models are used for COTS and reused software. | Applications are built using templates and a variety of web-based objects (html, applets, components, building blocks). |
| **Effort estimation** | Effort is estimated via regression formulas customized by cost drivers. | Effort is estimated by breaking the job down into tasks and identifying what is needed to do the work. |
| **Schedule estimation** | Schedule is estimated using a cube root relationship with effort. | Schedule is estimated based upon analogy. Models typically estimate schedules high because cube root relationship doesn't hold. |
| **Model calibration** | Measurements from past projects are used to calibrate models. | Measurements from past projects are used to identify myths. |

The key challenges are accurately estimating size and duration. New modified size metrics are desirable to handle with Web objects like shopping carts, Java scripts, and building blocks like Cookies, ActiveX controls, and Component Object Model components. New modified duration-estimating equations are required to address the fact that the cube root laws utilized by most estimating models just do not seem to work for the Web.

## AGILE SOFTWARE DEVELOPMENT

Agile software development is a collection of software development methods based on iterative and incremental development, where requirements and solutions evolve through collaboration between self-organizing, cross functional teams [9]. It promotes adaptive preparation, evolutionary development and delivery, a time-boxed iterative approach, and encourages rapid and flexible response to change.

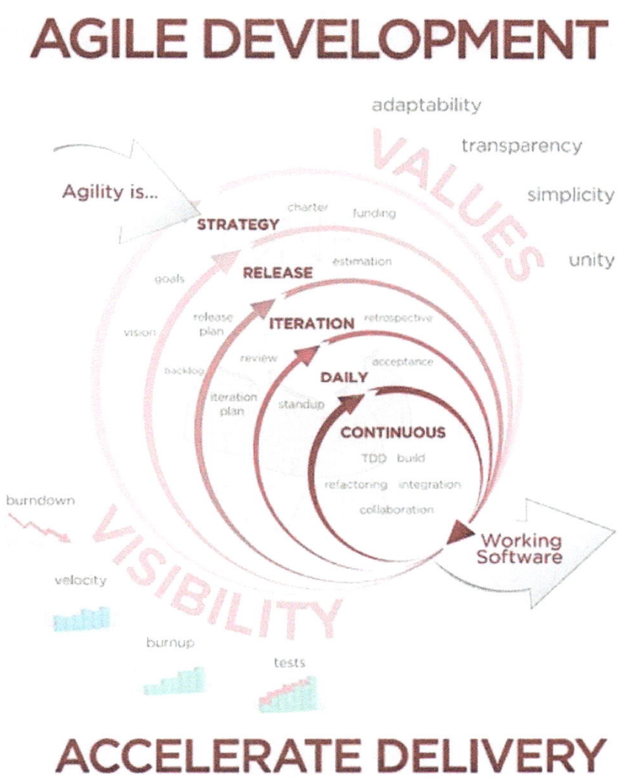


**Figure 4**. AGILE development poster [10].

Figure 4 shows the functioning of Agile development. It is a conceptual framework that promotes anticipated interactions throughout the development cycle.

### Manifestos for Agile Software Development

In 2001 Manifesto for Agile Software Development to define the approach published and came into the existence now known as agile software development. The four manifestoes are as follows:

- Individuals and interactions over processes and tools;
- Working software over comprehensive documentation;
- Customer collaboration over contract negotiation;
- Responding to change over following a plan.

### Agile Methods and Characteristics

There exist many specific agile development methods. Majority promote development, collaboration, teamwork, and process adaptability throughout the life-cycle of the project. Agile methods break tasks into small increments with least planning and do not directly engross long-term planning [11]. Iterations are short time frames that typically last from one to four weeks. Each iteration involves

a cross functional team working in all functions: planning, requirements analysis, design, coding, unit testing, and acceptance testing. At the end of the iteration a working product is demonstrated to stakeholders. This minimizes overall risk and allows the project to adapt to changes quickly. Agile Methods are in Wide-Spread Use, few popular methods involves:

- Extreme Programming (Kent Beck);
- Scrum (Ken Schwaber, Jeff Sutherland, Mike Beedle);
- Crystal (Alistair Cockburn);
- DSDM (Arie van Bennekum);
- Feature-Driven Development (Jeff De Luca);
- Lean Development (Bob Charette);
- Adaptive Software Development (Jim Highsmith).

## PROBLEM WITH EXISTING MODELS AND TECHNIQUES

The estimators presently have not agreed on how to develop estimates for Web-based projects developed by agile methodology. The difficulty is that the characteristics of the Web-based projects that are listed in Table 1 along with manifestoes of agile paradigm make it complicated for estimators to acclimatize and put already existing processes, metrics, and models to work functionally.

## PROPOSED MODEL FOR AGILE BASED WEB DEVELOPMENT

Predictive methods focus on configuration of a programmed plan to carry out the project. In contrast, adaptive methods focus on examining the current situation and finding the best solution in every step of performing the project [12]. The seed of web estimation for agile software projects (AgileMOW) is based on a multiple web object and multiple attribute approach. The architectural model illustrated in Figure 5 describes the idea of arriving at the influencing factors required to imitate the agile environment. The cost drivers and scale factors described in COCOMO II is an appropriate combination set of agile environmental and people attributes. The agile manifestoes impose certain constraints on the estimates. In order to identify the agile attributes, certain inbuilt issues in this environment are to be considered. Agile methods consider the human/people factor to be more significant than the process factor [13]. We propose the new model AgileMOW, the Web Model for agile software methods, because it is an adaptation and extension of the webMO [7] and Cocomo II early design model.

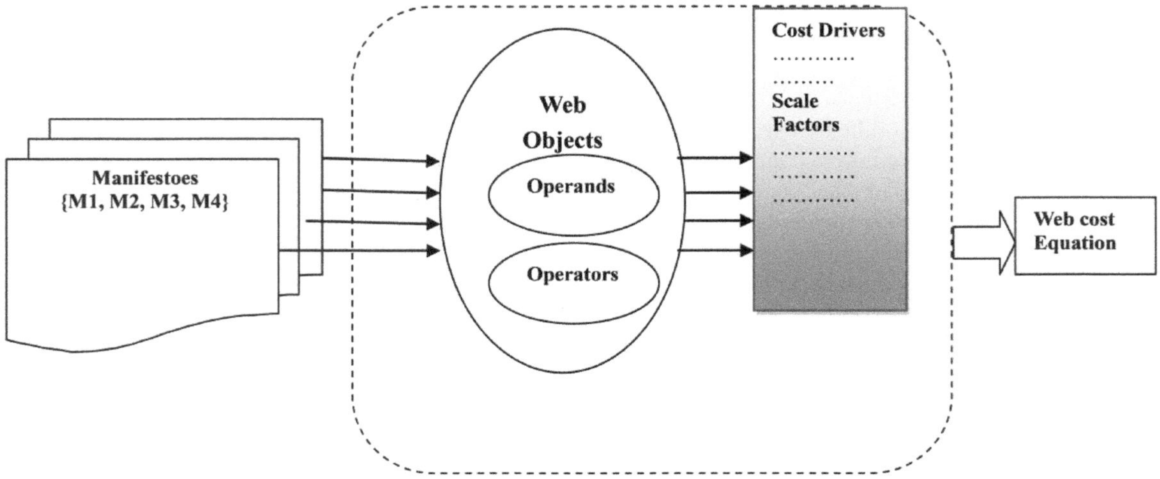


**Figure 5**. Proposed architecture of AgileMOW.

The formulation of any predictable processes essentially requires the various components to be predictable. Though people are not predictable components, therefore there exists a difficulty in forecasting and quantifying web based software developed using agile for cost estimation. In addition, uncertainty, risk factors, emerging requirements and complicated issues are presented in agile as in any other conventional software development process. The estimation of cost of web projects in an agile environment needs a mapping from the qualitative province to a set of quantitative values. To address this mapping, the key quality-attributes affecting the agile web based software development are tabulated in **Table 3** along with their rating levels. Rating levels refer to a statistical measure that comparatively signifies the effect of the attribute on the product quality and completion time respectively.

**Table 3**. Attributes and ratings relevant to agile manifestoes

| High priority attributes | Rating level | Low priority attributes | Rating level |
|---|---|---|---|
| Communication skills | | Process maturity | |
| Proximity of team | | Tool availability | |
| Feedback | | Tool familiarity | |
| Courage | | Conservativeness | |
| Managerial skills | | Following process mod | |
| Consistent working | | Training | |
| Technical ability | | Planning | |
| Debugging capability | | Pages of documents | |
| Reliability | | Project complexity | |
| Function points | | Other expenditure | |
| Ease of use | | Documentation resources | |
| Early delivery 5 | | Documentation period | |

## Size Estimation

Web-based projects are unsurprisingly small and intensive, so unavailability of an appropriate effort estimation model move forwards developers to make highly risky estimations. Moreover, the rapid evolution and growth of Web related technology, tools and methodologies makes historical information quickly old-fashioned. Size estimation of web development for agile methodology can be expressed in terms of, web objects [7]; size metrics computes size by considering every one of the various elements that make up the web application into account. We have used Halstead equation for Volume (i.e., a proposed measure of size that is language independent and is related to calculate the length of the program in terms of operands and operators) as follows:

$$S = (W_1 + W_2) \cdot \log_2 (w_1 + w_2)$$

where $W_1$ = total occurrence of Web Operand estimator;

$W_2$ = total occurrences of Web Operator estimator;

$w_1$ = number of unique Web Operands estimator;

$w_2$ = number of unique Web Operators estimator.

## Effort Estimation

Size estimation is just the primary step in developing a model that precisely estimates Web development costs in agile paradigm and schedule. The key issues revolve around the formation of the mathematical equations for effort. Though the traditional cube-root relationship between effort and duration in most estimation models does not seem to accurately predict Web development schedules for agile environment due to people centric approach. The proposed effort model AgileMOW is a mix of expert judgment and data from different academic projects using regression analysis. Its mathematical formulation rests upon parameters from both the Cocomo II and Soft Cost-OO software cost-estimating models along with manifesto attributes of agile methodologies. We have taken the value range of exponents from webMO model proposed by Donald J. Reifer. Equation 2 shows the AgileMOW model for estimating equations for effort (in person-months) as noted the resulting effort estimation model has 24 manifesto attributes and fixed power laws.

$$\text{Web Effort}\left[E\right] = A\prod \text{cfwa}_i \left(\text{size}\right)^{P_1}$$

where A is constant.

$P_1$ is power factor; cfwa is agile manifesto attributes for agile web development; size is the number of web objects.

Cost factor of this formula will be decided based on the effect of manifesto attributes on cfwa and which have been named as cfwa in this formula.

## CONCLUSIONS

The market fruition compels clients to adopt agile development paradigm for very short-term Web projects. Very often the results are deficient, unreliable and hard to maintain applications that fail to meet the software industry needs, generally, the agile web effort estimation is not able to predict and help to avoid these problems.

In this paper, we aim to address the numerous open issues in web development particularly in context to agile software development by analyzing data from completed agile Web development projects. Though agile is relatively a new and less mature scenario for developers, they spend time on trying to estimate the web development effort pragmatically and reliably, they usually have very little or almost none historical information. Agile characteristics tend to make web estimations less reliable regarding both time and cost. In order to get speedy and reliable effort estimations of Agile based Web development projects, this paper presented the AgileMOW model. It does not substitute the expert estimator, but it offers a tool for achieving a more accurate estimation, based on agile manifestoes and web characteristics.

## REFERENCES

1. L. Lazić, et al, "Two Novel Effort Estimation Models Based on Quality Metrics in Web Projects," WSEAS Transactions on Information Science and Applications, Vol. 7, No. 7, 2010, pp. 923-934.
2. Ziauddin, S. K. Tipu and S. Zia, "An Effort Estimation Model for Agile Software Development," Advances in Computer Science and Its Applications (ACSA), Vol. 2, No. 1, 2012, pp. 314-324.
3. S. F. Ochoa, et al., "Estimating the Development Effort of Web Projects in Chile," Proceedings of the First Latin American Web Congress (LA-WEB 2003), 10-12 November 2003, pp. 114-122.
4. T. C. Hooi, Y. Yusoff and Z. Hassan, "Comparative Study on Applicability of WEBMO in Web Application Cost Estimation within Klang Valley in Malaysia," IEEE 8th International Conference on Computer and Information Technology Workshops, Sydney, 8-11 July 2008, pp. 116-121.
5. S. Kumari and S. Pushkar, "Comparison and Analysis of Different Software Cost Estimation Methods," International Journal of Advanced Computer Science and Applications, Vol. 4, No. 1, 2013, pp. 153-157.
6. M. Ruhe, et al., "Cost Estimation for Web Applications," Proceedings of the 25th International Conference on Software Engineering, Portland, 3-10 May 2003, pp. 285-294.
7. D. J. Reifer "Web Development: Estimating Quick-toMarket Software," IEEE Software, Vol. 17, No. 6, 2000, pp. 57-64.
8. Vice President David Consulting Group, "Agile Estimation Using Functional Metrics," Thomas Cagley.
9. Mendes and Mosley, "Web Cost Estimation: An Introduction," pp. 182-190.
10. http://commons.wikimedia.org/wiki/File:Agile_Software_Development_methodology.jpg
11. "Agile Estimation: Characteristics, Techniques and Complexities," Tools Journal, pp. 1-4.
12. B. Nasr-Azadani and R. M. Doost, "Estimation of Agile Functionality in Software Development," Proceedings of the International Multi-Conference of Engineers and Computer Scientists, Hong Kong, 19-21 March 2008, pp. 1338-1341.
13. S. Chandrasekaran, R. Lavanya and V. Kanchana, "MultiCriteria Approach for Agile Software Cost Estimation Model".

CHAPTER 11

# THE SUCCESS FACTORS OF RUNNING SCRUM: A QUALITATIVE PERSPECTIVE

Rich C. Lee[1,2]

[1]System Technology Group, IBM, Chinese Taipei

[2]Department of Computer Science, National Taipei University of Technology, Chinese Taipei.

## ABSTRACT

**Scrum—Agile programming—is getting more attention in Software Engineering practices. Many software projects began with small and were not certain about the requirements until projects have completed; this makes Scrum more appropriate than other development methodologies. This paper reintroduced Scrum from qualitative perspective by applying ethnography and in-depth interview to two different types of project teams to articulate what the success factors are for running Scrum framework. It clearly demonstrated how qualitative research could help in disclosing the essence of facts during the Scrum adaptation in depth. It also articulated how these successful factors mutually affect to one another from System Dynamics perspective and to give further recommendations to Scrum teams and those who tend to apply Scrum development methodology.**

## INTRODUCTION

Software development is a process of communication [1]. There are many approaches [2] helping the development to produce qualified software to stakeholders. Many software projects began with small and were not certain about the requirements until projects have completed. The requirements are sensitive and volatile to environment changed. Stakeholders did not have a clear picture of what software features were in the early stage of development. Therefore Agile Programming approach was called since early-planned approaches cannot answer well to the nature of software development—the software changes and evolves all the time. Each software development project has its uniqueness and varies to others. The variance may root from the nature of the requirements, the capability of development team, the difference of development approaches, and other organizational culture wise factors.

Scrum is an innovative approach to getting work done. Scrum is an agile framework for completing complex projects. Scrum originally was formalized for software development projects, but works well for any complex, innovative scope of work. The possibilities are endless. The Scrum framework illustrated on Figure 1 is deceptively simple.

There are several key roles in Scrum framework:

- Stakeholders: the mission owners, possess the idea about why to build, what to build, and how processes should be;
- Product owner: the product development owner, closely working with stakeholders, creates a prioritized wish list-stories—called a Product Backlog;
- Scrum Master: the facilitator, closely working with product owner, makes sure the stories in the product backlog will successfully delivered as workable sub-products;
- Scrum Team: the developers, closely working with Scrum Master, deliver workable sub-products according to the product backlog.

**Citation:** R. C. Lee, "The Success Factors of Running Scrum: A Qualitative Perspective," Journal of Software Engineering and Applications, Vol. 5 No. 6, 2012, pp. 367-374. doi: 10.4236/jsea.2012.56043.

Scrum Master with the team invites the product owner to debrief the stories in product backlog. Scrum Master leads a Sprint Planning with the team to disassemble the story into tasks, a Sprint Backlog. It is a Scrum team effort to decide how to implement and who should do the tasks. Daily-Scrum is a group meeting to discuss the progress of task implementation and technical issues. Scrum Master keeps the team focused on its goal. At the end of the sprint, the process of development, the work should be potentially shippable, as in ready to hand to stakeholders. The sprint ends with a sprint review and retrospective. As the next sprint begins, the team chooses another chunk of the product backlog and begins working again. The cycle repeats until enough items in the product backlog have been completed, the budget is depleted, or a deadline arrives. Which of these milestones marks the end of the work is entirely specific to the project. No matter which impetus stops work, Scrum ensures that the most valuable work has been completed when the project ends.

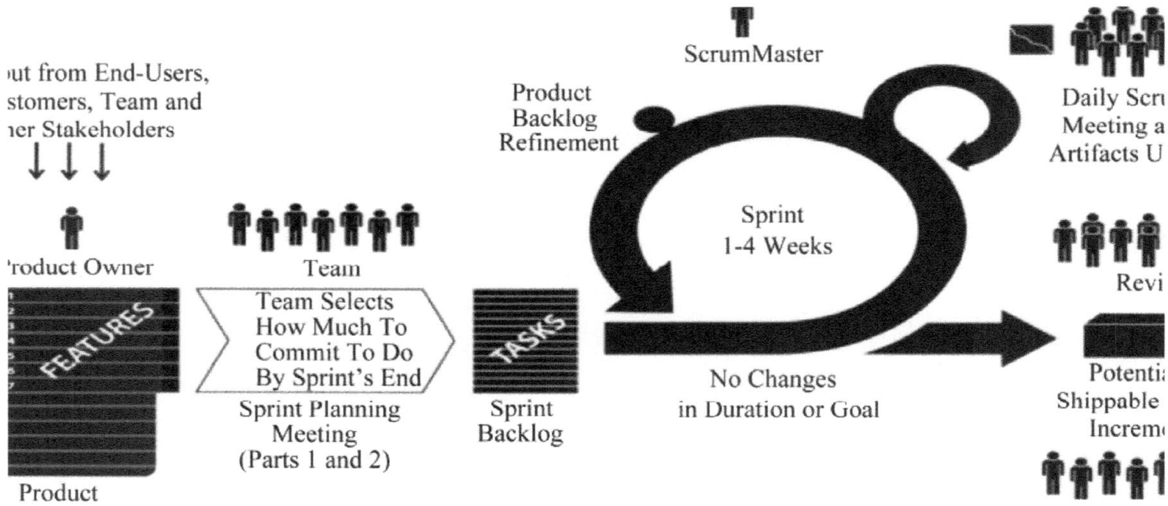


**Figure 1**. Scrum framework. Courtesy from "the Scrum primer" [3].

The success of Scrum framework requires mature capabilities such as technical and communication. Project teams are formed to achieve the strategic objectives of the organization, such as increasing market share, launching a next generation product, improving quality, enhancing customer relationships and for other purposes. Previous research on project management stressed the technical dimension of the project, such as project scheduling, resource leveling, risk mitigation and project control. However, the human side of the project, such as finding the optimal combination of team member's personality has been ignored. Unfortunately, project members play extremely important roles in achieving the project objectives and it is believed project members must be assigned based on the project needs not only technically, but also mentally. In other words, it is critical to discover if the structure of the project team can accomplish project objectives before the project begins. After adjusting the team members to meet the project requirements, project performance can be significantly improved; and if adjustment is made to the best possible balance condition, the team performance can even be upgraded to the highest level [4].

Software projects are different to one and another. It is not easy to generalize theories and to deliver tangible lesson-learn to the practitioners. The practitioners are looking for answers to improve their software development under similar culture and scenarios. To generate useful knowledge, it requires retrospection on what had not considered and what had done well from empirical cases in depth [5]. Qualitative research is a type of scientific research. In general terms, scientific research consists of an investigation that:

- seeks answers to a question;
- systematically uses a predefined set of procedures to answer the question;
- collects evidence;
- produces findings that were not determined in advance;
- produces findings that are applicable beyond the immediate boundaries of the study.

To understand the project performance applying Scrum framework in depth, particular in resource capability arbitration among multiple Scrum teams, qualitative research can disclose the complexity of project activities and interaction among team members. This research was designed and trying to answer the following questions:

- What are the critical factors of success team communication in running Scrum?
- How Scrum Master alleviates the challenge when team members lack of skills to complete the assigned task?
- Should Scrum Masters exchange resources for specific skill required tasks?
- What are the criterions of resource exchange among Scrum teams?

## Research Design

Qualitative research is especially effective in obtaining culturally specific information about the values, opinions, behaviors, and social contexts of particular populations. The strength of qualitative research is its ability to provide complex textual descriptions of how people experience a given research issue. It provides information about the "human" side of an issue—that is, the often contradictory behaviors, beliefs, opinions, emotions, and relationships of individuals. Qualitative methods are also effective in identifying intangible factors, such as social norms, socioeconomic status, gender roles, ethnicity, and religion, whose role in the research issue may not be readily apparent. When used along with quantitative methods, qualitative research can help us to interpret and better understand the complex reality of a given situation and the implications of quantitative data. Although findings from qualitative data can often be extended to people with characteristics similar to those in the study population, gaining a rich and complex understanding of a specific social context or phenomenon typically takes precedence over eliciting data that can be generalized to other geographical areas or populations [6].

Figure 2 illustrated the research process. This research process takes advantage of two powerful methods in deep disclosing phenomenon, qualitative research and system dynamics. In system dynamics, a causally-closed system is one in which the causes creating the behavior of interest lie within the system. A causally-closed system still is open in the sense that it can receive material, energy, random disturbances, and test inputs from outside the boundary [7]. This research relies on qualitative research to form the conceptual model—system dynamics model—for further phenomenon articulation. Most of all, by using the system dynamics tool, the researcher can give conditional parameters to see what the model behaves later to form the recommendations r policy to move the outcome towards more positive direction.

The research process begins with interesting phenomenon observed, reviewing the literature to see if previous studies could explain the phenomenon or not, a more clearer picture of research questions are formed, choosing appropriate research subjects and explain why and how the research will be conducted, undertaking a series of qualitative activities, confirming the theoretical foundation of observed artifacts via further literature review, forming theoretical models to answer the research questions, developing causal-loop analytical model, simulating various scenarios for research implication and recommendations to practitioners.

# DATA GATHERING

## Theoretical Background for Data Gathering

Scrum teams are self-organized, are facilitated by rich communication and a collaborative environment and are usually considered effective for colocated projects with a small team size [8]. Office layout often determines the effectiveness of team communications, it plays a powerful role in shaping a diverse range of psychological and behavioral outcomes, including individual work motivation, job satisfaction, and patterns of interactions [9]. The effective leadership of self-managing teams requires strong interpersonal and group process skills as well as external skills of information seeking and giving—plus advocacy and negotiation [10]—which is the cornerstone of makes Scrum process success. Agile Development Framework such as Scrum, requires a daily face to face communication with customers and co-workers to understand and fulfill their requirements [11]. Collaboration tools can play significant role in facilitating the team intensive communication, they are used to mitigate the communication cost. Individual leadership can help Scrum team making development decisions swiftly during the Scrum processes [12]. Although making decision swiftly does not imply the quality of outcome, but holding up issue certainly will be more devastated than need-tore adjusted decision, because Scrum process is all about embrace changes.

## Data Gathering Context

**Table 1** illustrated how and what information should be gathered from the informants to disclose the research questions. There were four categories of data, namely environment, communication, project, and retrospection. The major research tools were observation and interview. Collecting the data from multiple perspectives were to clarify whether these contexts having influences to the success of Scrum. The retrospection in Scrum is to create the "inspect and adapt" cycle for how a team works together and alters their practices to improve how they work by constantly asking three questions:

- what do we need to continue doing;
- what didn't work;
- what do we need to start doing [13].

It is not feasible to compare the software development performance across teams. The complexity of the projects was not identical, and the capabilities of development team were also varied. In Scrum, the burn-down chart—illustrated in Figure 3—is used to show, each day, a new estimate of how much work (measured in person hours) remains until all tasks are finished. Ideally, this is a downward sloping graph that is on a trajectory to reach "zero effort remaining" by the last day of the Sprint [3].

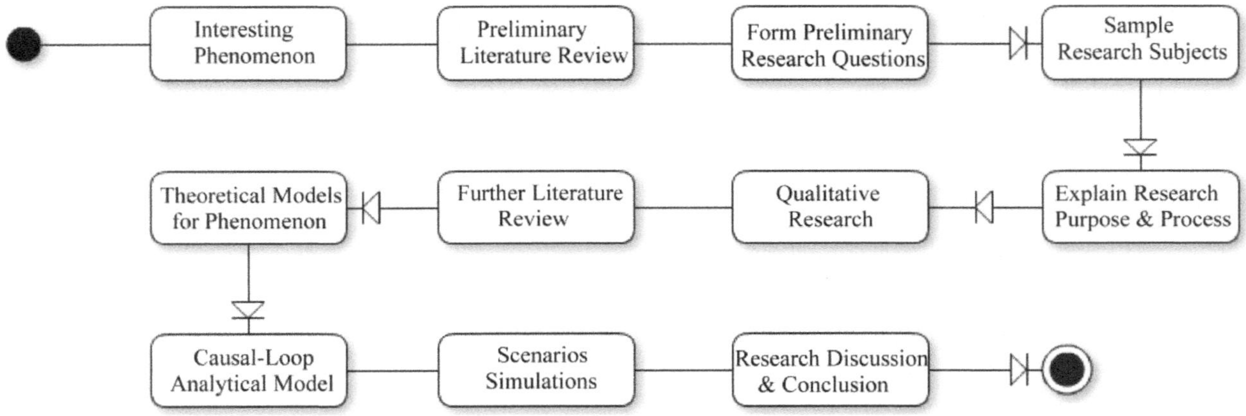


**Figure 2**. Qualitative research design.

**Table 1**. Data gathering context

| Source of Data | Research Tools | Context |
|---|---|---|
| Environment | Observation | Office Layout<br>Culture and Atmosphere |
| Communication | Observation and Interview | Individual Leadership<br>Interpersonal Skills<br>Tools Used<br>Vendors and External Experts |
| Project | Observation and Interview | Complexity<br>Sprint Performance |
| Retrospection | Observation and Interview | Framework Enhancement<br>Technological Barriers Overcome |

## Research Subjects and Working Environment

Two Scrum teams of different companies were sampled for Qualitative Research subjects. Both teams were newbies in running Scrum. Team A is a development team in maintaining in-house developed Manufacture Execution System (MES). Team B is a small software company delivering commercial applications to various line of business.

Team A: There were several slogans placed on the walls about performance and efficiency. Team members were scattered sitting in their cubicles. The office was very quiet, people kept their voice low in conversation. They are required to use system to reserve meeting rooms before team discussion. The meeting rooms are usually fully booked. They cannot post unauthorized wallpapers in the office. Managers usually hesitate in approving posters to keep the office clean in appearance. The company does not allow employees to use instant manager tools such as MSN and Gtalk. They use emails as their major communication channels.

Team B: The office was in an over thirty-year building. Books and magazines were scattered in different places. Cafeteria area was full of foods and drinks. Project milestone charts were posted on various walls. Team members communicated thoughts via voices and with eye-contacts. The office was full of multi-channel of communication about technical discussions and requirement clarification. The team members use Internet free tools as their communication carriers. Google Chrome is their major workbench. There was a rather large open space in the center of the office, members frequently sat on the floor and drew ideas on large size papers. They use Group Note software as a Kanban system [15] to facilitate the software development process; the system becomes a good alternative for managers who need an easy-to-follow set of guidelines for their project management without having to resort to weeks of training [16].

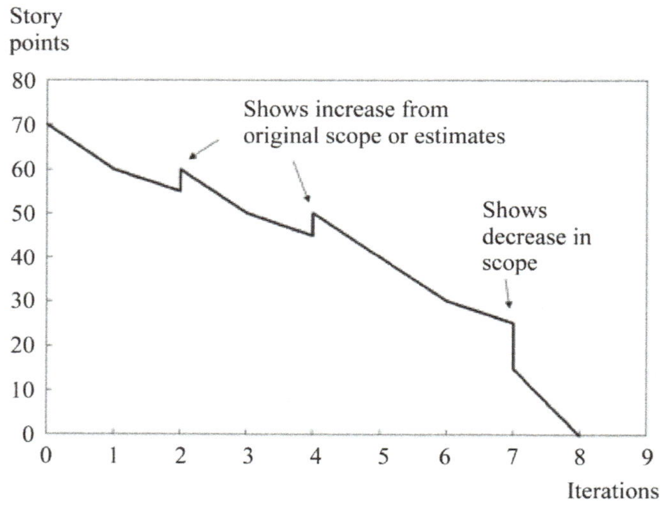


**Figure 3**. Burn-down chart sample. Courtesy from "crystal clear" [14].

## Requirements and Challenges

Successfully eliciting the software requirements from stakeholders is a challenge. Requirements are considered to be a set of knowledge that facilitates business processes or help organization achieving business goals, and they are about:

- Customer Perspective where the requirements regarding the quality of service desired are defined, also the knowledge concerning their perception of the service delivered;
- Business Perspective where the requirements regarding the structure of the business process are defined;
- Employee Perspective where the requirements concerning the skills and experiences are defined and also the knowledge used in the processing of activities

based on the knowledge gathered during the previous processing steps;

- Product Perspective where the requirements regarding the specification of the final product are defined [17].

Intensive communication among stakeholders, product owners, and team members are the effective approach in gathering such knowledge [18].

Team A: The software project was to migration their MES to new tentative use database. There were thousands programs in various types:

- web applications using J2EE platform;
- batch programs running on the database server using C++/C language;
- database native SQL scripts.

This was the first time of migrating applications from different brand of database as they used currently. They relied on external expert to guide them go through the migration process. The company wished the project could close within three months.

Team B: The software project was an inventory system running on a cloud computing environment—Google App Engine. The stakeholder wanted the system to help them managing visibility of inventory for their business partners. This was the first journey of developing applications on the platform; many required technical skillsets were not built among the team members. After serious evaluation, they chose Python as their programming language. The contract stated a penalty term if the project did not complete within six months.

## Field Notes in Summary

Field Notes refer to transcribed notes or the written account derived from data collected during observations and interviews. The field notes generally consist of two parts:

descriptive • in which the observer attempts to capture a word-picture of the setting, actions and conversations;

- reflective in which the observer records thoughts, ideas, questions and concerns based on the observations and interviews [19].
- This Participant Observation used a semi-structural field note covering important aspects of the critical successful factors of applying Scrum from literature review as follows:
- Personal attributes of Product Owner, Scrum Master, and Team Members may change their reactions and decisions when team skills do not meet the project requires [20];
- Characteristics of user stories—the requirements — are allocated to a sprint and then implemented and delivered to the stakeholders [21];
- Project required team competence—team might not possess all skills that the project requires;
- Team autonomy—the team had discretion, freedom, and independence in making project-related decisions, such as choosing tools/technologies, setting goals, and handling user requirement changes, and assigning personnel to the team [22];
- Team diversity—the diversity and heterogeneity of team members' expertise areas, skills, prior work experiences, and functional backgrounds [22];
- Team response extensiveness—how much a software team incorporates changing requirements in system scope, input data, output data, business rules/processes, data structure, and user interfaces [22];
- Team response efficiency—the relative level of time, cost, personnel, and resources needed by the software team to respond to and incorporate a given requirement change [22];
- Software development performance—on-time completion, on-budget completion, and software functionality are important dimensions of evaluating the software development performance [22].

Tables 2 and 3 were the field note summaries for both teams.

## RESEARCH PROPOSITIONS AND CONCLUSION

To evaluate software development performance is complex and full of tangled factors with the characteristics of:

- constantly changing—software requirements are volatile;
- tightly coupled—factors are mutually affected with one another;
- governed by feedback—the influenced factor often affects the source;
- nonlinear—the compound behavior of a factor may have nonlinearity due to feedback loop;
- history-dependent—factors are subject to change by their previous states [23].

StockFlow diagram is used to describe the complexity among these factors. The factor in box shape is called Stock which accumulates the outcome of its influenced factors. The arrow means where the influenced factor is pointed. The double-lined arrow means that the influencing factor has continuous impact on the target factor with a speed. The link means which factor is influenced. Positive sign on the link means reinforcing the impact, while negative sign means balancing the impact.

Based on the analysis from the research notes, **Figure 4** illustrated the Stock-Flow diagram of Scrum performance dynamics. The Stocks were labeled in box shapes with yellow color background. Software Development Performance was influenced by:

- On-Time Completion—fewer schedules delayed implied greater performance;
- On-Budget Completion—less budget consumed implied greater performance;
- Software Functionalities—more complex functionalities implied poor performance;
- Development Efficiency—more efficient in development implied greater performance.

Software Team Characteristics was influenced by:

- Personal Attributes—more willingness to collaborate with others implied positive attitude;

- Software Team Autonomy— more freedom to collaborate implied positive attitude;
- Software Team Diversity—more relevant skills to the project implied positive attitude.

Team Competence was influenced by:

- Prior Experiences—more relevant experiences from similar previous projects implied greater competence;
- External Experts—more external helpers implied greater competence;
- Learning Curve— more difficult in skillsets building implied less competence.

Software Development Agility was influenced by:

- Team Attitude—more positive in attitude implied better agility;
- Software Team Response Extensiveness— more communications among the team implied better agility;
- Software Team Response Efficiency—more effective communications implied better agility;
- Team Skills—better team capability implied better agility;
- Characteristics of Stories—more complicated User Stories implied less agility.

**Table 2.** Field note summary of team A

| Field Note Summary of Team A | | |
|---|---|---|
| Personal Attributes | Product Owner | He has been in the company for over ten years. He often looked into the details of works and asked sharp questions. He used to argue the purpose of the software to business objectives with stakeholders. |
| | Scrum Master | He often goes out with members for pleasures. He usually has lunch with members if no further meeting ahead. He stressed on the details of technologies used and broke down User Stories to small tasks for members to complete. |
| | Team Members | They spent much time in testing software before update version. Members were very skeptical about new technologies and always asked for proven references in their sector. |
| Characteristics of User Stories | The User Stories were much elaborated and well planned based on the MES they had been maintained for years. Stakeholders were the key users of operations. The bottom line was to keep MES as it was before the migration. Each story was broken down to small tasks that could be completed within a short period of time, usually a day. | |
| Team Competence | The migration project required deep understanding about the features of new database. It also required extensive experience in migrating software over the database change. Both competences were inadequate within the team. Team spent much time in finding the appropriate solutions during the migration. They invited external experts to participate their Daily Scrum whenever it was needed. | |
| Team Autonomy | Scrum Master played a technical lead role rather than a facilitator in Scrum process. When there was a dispute among team members, Scrum Master made the final decision. Sometimes, team members just followed what Scrum Master implied about how to do the tasks. In the Scrum Retrospection, most discussions were laid on technical issues; as to the process improvement recommendation was rarely brought out. They needed to schedule each discussion and reserving meeting room. Many issues had been accumulated in team members' unsolved pipeline before next meeting began. | |
| Team Diversity | Team members have been working together for at least three years. They were trained for mastering their MES with required competences. Each member had been assigned to maintain different modules of MES before Scrum initiated. | |
| Team Response Extensiveness | Team members did not use any holistic software tool to manage the Scrum processes, they used spreadsheets instead. Scrum Master kept complaining about the responsiveness of updating the spreadsheets. | |
| Team Response Efficiency | Scrum Master asked members to bring their issues to the next Daily Scrum meeting. The meeting rooms were competing resource of the company. If the meeting room could not be booked, Scrum Master had to postpone the Daily Scrum meeting until the meeting room was available again. Team member used emails and short chats to clarify development issues with others. Keeping office quiet was a part of the company's culture and a required discipline for every employee. | |
| Software Project Performance | The software functionalities were clear but the team members were not familiar with the core technologies and previous experiences in new database migration. The project was delayed and exhausted extra budget for hiring external experts. External experts had no experience in running Scrum framework. They took the lead of as soon as they joined the development. They often rejected the requests of explanation why from Team members due to limitation of remaining time of the project. The project had further delayed; more budgets were consumed, because team members were reluctant to report the complexity of the system to external experts. Product Owner had disputes with the external experts about the progress of the development especially during the final phase of testing. External experts complained about the team did not report the missing links of the suggested implementation. | |

**Table 3**. Field note summary of team B

| Field Note Summary of Team B | | |
|---|---|---|
| Personal Attributes | Product Owner | She played a System Analyst role to the project. She was busy in eliciting the application requirements from stakeholders. She called Scrum Master several times a day asking about the progress of the project. Some stakeholders complained to General Manager of the company about her persistence in maintaining the original requirements from changing. She frequently asked team to enhance the working software to meet her standard of acceptance. Team received less requests of modifying the software from the stakeholders after her acceptance of the software. |
| | Scrum Master | He was a certified Scrum Master and a believer of Agile programming. He often complained Product Owner did not have enough time of explaining what requirement was in detail to the team. He had coffee meetings with the team at least twice a week. Occasionally, he invited team members to Karaoke and drinking beers together. |
| | Team Members | Team often went out together for pleasure during the weekends. They shared thoughts and personal experience on Facebook from time to time. Team members used Planning Poker [24] to arbitrate the argued development approaches. |
| Characteristics of User Stories | | The project was the first time for both stakeholders and the Scrum Team taking advantage of cloud computing. Scrum Master changed the deliverables of tasks derived from stories frequently in the early phase of the project before external experts came in. Many tasks were dropped because the wrong approaches had been taken. |
| Team Competence | | Team members' former experiences were majorly on Microsoft technologies; few had developed application using open-source technologies before join the company. Python was chosen based on Google document suggestion. Team spent much time in learning Google Application Programming Interfaces (API). |
| Team Autonomy | | Scrum Master encouraged team members to have short chat whenever there was a doubt about how to proceed next. Team members posted their sample codes on the wall for technology exploration sharing. Planning Poker was not used as frequently as in their previous projects because too much uncertainty in the mastering Google APIs. Team meetings for technologic discussion were held twice a day in the early phase of development before external experts joined in the project. Scrum Master broke down the stories into tasks; some tasks were serving the same purpose because best-practice had not explored yet. |
| Team Diversity | | Team members were hired for their expertise on Microsoft technologies. They all were familiar with database, web, and object oriented programming in using Microsoft technologies. |
| Team Response Extensiveness | | Team members often delayed their tasks because spending too much time in discussions and answering questions from others. In order to make effective communication, they used software tools for knowledge sharing. They changed their previous behavior—ask-before-do—to check-before-ask after many best-practices had been explored. They posted important sample codes of using Google important APIs on the walls of the office. Some team members used ear sets to block the noises while working but remained alert for messages. |
| Team Response Efficiency | | Team used Group Note software for pending issues and short conclusions of discussions. Google's Instant Messenger, Gtalk, was extensively used in communication among team members. Scrum Master asked members to clean up pending requests before off as possible; members did their best in answering the requested issues. For those unsolved requests, team members would leave them to the next Daily Scrum meeting. |
| Software Project Performance | | The project was not severely delayed because the company had decided to hire external experts in the early phase of the development. The company allocated budget for external experts as a part of the quotation to stakeholders. The external experts had no experience in Scrum practice before. Scrum Master trained Scrum framework to external experts first before they devoted to the project. The software functionalities were delivered within budget. |

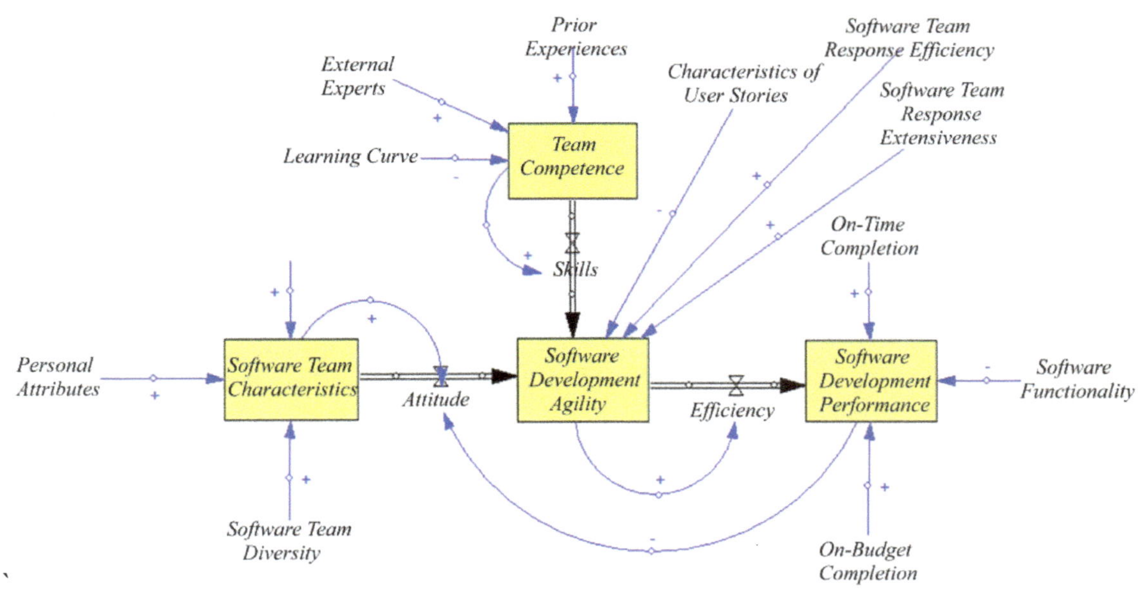


**Figure 4**. Scrum performance dynamics.

Case study is a suitable research methodology for software engineering research since it studies contemporary phenomena in its natural context. This paper followed a criteria about what a good qualified qualitative research on software engineering should contain [25]. These criteria ask for the research to have clear cases with research objectives, applying theories; it must be relevant to the research questions, and making implications to the practitioners.

## REFERENCES


1. A. Gopal, T. Mukhopadhyay and M. S. Krishnan, "The Role of Software Processes and Communication in Offshore Software Development," Communications of the ACM, Vol. 45, No. 4, 2002, pp. 193-200. doi:10.1145/505248.506008
2. M. Aoyama, "New Age of Software Development: How Component-Based Software Engineering Changes the Way of Software Development," 1998 International Workshop on CBSE, Kyoto, 25-26 April 1998, pp. 124-128.
3. http://assets.scrumtraininginstitute.com/downloads/1/scrumprimer121.pdf
4. J. Y. Yeh, C. C. Wei, C. S. Wei and D. F. Lei, "The Impact of Team Personality Balance on Project Performance," African Journal of Business Management, Vol. 6, No. 4, 2012, pp. 1674-1684.
5. G. Cugola and C. Ghezzi, "Software Processes: A Retrospective and a Path to the Future," Software Process: Improvement and Practice, Vol. 4, No. 3, 1998, pp. 101-123.doi:10.1002/(SICI)1099-1670(199809)4:3<101::AID-SPIP103>3.0.CO;2-K
6. http://www.fhi360.org/en/RH/Pubs/booksReports/QRM_datacoll.htm
7. J. W. Forrester, "System Dynamics, Systems Thinking, and Soft OR," System Dynamics Review, Vol. 10, No. 2-3, 1994, pp. 245-256. doi:10.1002/sdr.4260100211
8. P. Abrahamsson, O. Salo, J. Ronkainen and J. Warsta, "Agile Software Development Methods: Review and Analysis," VTT Publications, Espoo, 2002.
9. M. C. Davis, D. J. Leach and C. W. Clegg, "The Physical Environment of the Office: Contemporary and Emerging Issues," International Review of Industrial and Organizational Psychology, Vol. 26, 2011, pp. 193-237.
10. V. U. Druskat and J. V. Wheeler, "Managing from the Boundary: The Effective Leadership of Self-Managing Work Teams," Academy of Management Journal, Vol. 46, No. 4, 2003, p. 435. doi:10.2307/30040637
11. Y. L. Chen, "Analysis of the Agile Deployment," Master's Thesis, University of Gothenburg, Gothenburg, 2010.
12. N. B. Moe, T. Dingsoyr and T. Dyba, "Overcoming Barriers to Self-Management in Software Teams," Software, Vol. 26, No. 6, 2009, pp. 20-26. doi:10.1109/MS.2009.182
13. C. Keith, "An Agile Retrospective," Game Developer Con- ference, February 2008.
14. A. Cockburn, "Crystal Clear: A Human-Powered Methodology for Small Teams," Addison-Wesley, Boston, 2005.
15. M. Ikonen, P. Kettunen, N. Oza and P. Abrahamsson, "Exploring the Sources of Waste in Kanban Software Development Projects," 36th Euromicro Conference on Software Engineering and Advanced Applications, Lille, 1-3 September 2010, pp. 376-381.
16. L. D. Rola, "Kanban for Small Software Projects," Project Background Report, The University of Manchester, Manchester, 2011.
17. A. E. Roger, F. N. Marcel and A. C. Lopez, "Business Process Requirement Engineering," International Journal on Computer Science and Engineering, Vol. 2, No. 9, 2010, pp. 2890-2899.
18. M. R. Haas, "Knowledge Gathering, Team Capabilities, and Project Performance in Challenging Work Environments," Management Science, Vol. 52, No. 8, 2006, pp. 1170-1184. doi:10.1287/mnsc.1060.0530
19. E. Fossey, C. Harvey, F. McDermott and L. Davidson, "Understanding and Evaluating Qualitative Research," Australian & New Zealand Journal of Psychiatry, Vol. 36, No. 6, 2002, pp. 717-732. doi:10.1046/j.1440-1614.2002.01100.x
20. M. Luz, D. Gazineu and M. Teófilo, "Challenges on Adopting Scrum for Distributed Teams in Home Office Environments," World Academy of Science, Engineering and Technology, No. 59, 2009, pp. 308-311.
21. J. Highsmith and A. Cockburn, "Agile Software Development: The Business of Innovation," Computer, Vol. 34, No. 9, 2001, pp. 120-127. doi:10.1109/2.947100
22. G. Lee and W. Xia, "Toward Agile: An Integrated Analysis of Quantitative and Qualitative Field Data on Software Development Agility," MIS Quarterly, Vol. 34, No. 1, 2010, pp. 87-114.
23. J. D. Sterman, "System Dynamics Modeling," California Management Review, Vol. 43, No. 4, 2001, pp. 8-25.
24. J. Grenning, "Planning Poker or How to avoid Analysis Paralysis while Release Planning," Hawthorn Woods: Renaissance Software Consulting, Vol. 3, 2002.
25. P. Runeson and M. Höst, "Guidelines for Conducting and Reporting Case Study Research in Software Engineering," Empirical Software Engineering, Vol. 14, No. 2, 2009, pp. 131-164. doi:10.1007/s10664-008-9102-8

# SECTION IV: PROCESS MANAGEMENT AND TOOLS

CHAPTER 12

# ENHANCING SOFTWARE PROCESS MANAGEMENT THROUGH CONTROL CHARTS

Vipul Vashisht

Quality Department, Polaris Financial Technology Limited, Gurgaon, India.

## ABSTRACT

**In software development life cycle, Software Process Management (SPM) acts as a significant part throughout the execution of project. In this study, the application of control chart for analyzing the stability of software process and defects in the software product is discussed. This paper will discuss the analyzing impact or collision of rework effort, defect density, inspection performance and productivity by using control charts. This paper also explains the benefits and challenges of using control charts in software organization.**

## INTRODUCTION TO SOFTWARE PROCESS MANAGEMENT

With the increasing interest in predictability and effectiveness of software development practices, SPM (Software Process Management) has become a crucial aspect in the Software Engineering field. The effectiveness of software development process depends upon how well software process model is aligned. In order to carry out effective data based on decision making, it is highly essential that the software process model is managed and analyzed accurately. Developing concern in evolving efficient approaches to SPM has led to focusing on software process modeling such as formal analysis and fine grained modeling. Recently, different formal processes of software process modeling approaches to being introduced and entirely depend upon Petri net [1].

**Citation:** V. Vashisht, "Enhancing Software Process Management through Control Charts," Journal of Software Engineering and Applications, Vol. 7 No. 2, 2014, pp. 87-93. doi: 10.4236/jsea.2014.72010.

According to Khan [2] the software process management is used to make rational and reasonable decisions and some methods applied for systematic analysis of process execution and relative factors of environment are essential. Though, many formal approaches are primarily concentrated on the techniques of process modeling rather the techniques of software process management. These techniques of formal analysis are targeted mainly to configure proper model mathematically. The techniques of formal analysis offer major ways to develop software process management and their maturity with suitable software process model. But, simply setting up with better software process model does not essentially make sure the efficiency in the actual process actions.

In this paper, the author have tried to highlight the role of control charts in SPM, analysis of process parameters like rework, productivity, defect density using control charts. The paper also discusses the challenges faced by software organizations in using the control charts followed by the conclusion and future work.

## ROLE OF CONTROL CHARTS IN SOFTWARE PROCESS MANAGEMENT

The focus on SPC techniques in the field of software industry has been growing since the last decade. Several organizations have advanced maturity levels of software process improvement models including Capability Maturity Model (CMM) [3], Capability Maturity Model Integration (CMMI) [4] and SPICE ([5,6]). These models are used to develop direct software companies to implement SPC techniques as an important step for achieving the maturity levels of process at a higher extent. The software process improvement models suggest control charts are applied in the project level process control and organizational level process for the improvement purposes. It has also increased focus on sub process monitoring and probabilistic prediction models in CMMI certified organizations. As per CMMI processes, sub process monitoring and defect prediction model (DPM) implementation is mandatory under the areas of Quantitative Management process.

The sub process is a subset of process, but it represents as a significant and an independent set of activities that can be controlled. In a software development life cycle, if construction is the process the following are the sub processes

- Program Spec preparation
- Program Spec Review
- Unit Test Plan preparations
- Unit Test Plan review
- Coding
- Code review
- Unit testing
- Independent Unit Testing/Peer Testing

Throughout the project duration, execute various processes are executed. However, many sub processes that make or break the project success. These sub processes are directly connected to the organization business objectives/customer requirements.

The important common tools are mainly used in Control Charts. It operates on the statistical rules of Central Tendency and Dispersion. Central Tendency implies location of mid-point in a group of values. e.g. Average or Mean denoted by X.

- Dispersion implies spread around mean or distance between values. e.g. Range, Standard Deviation.
- Any process has variation. The control chart consists of two kinds of variation.
- Variation occurred by normal process operation is known as Common Cause.
- Variation occurred by sudden and abnormal changes are known as Special Cause.

Common cause variation is almost random but occurred between predictable bounds that denotes a stable process. Special cause variation indicates unstable process that is no longer predictable.

All classical control charts includes a centerline and control limits on both sides of the centerline. The centerline is usually the average of the set of values. The two control limits such as (Upper Control Limit (UCL) and Lower Control Limit (LCL)) are contained the value of +/− 3 sigma; where sigma denotes the standard deviation (denoting distance from the center point). 3-sigma limits result in very few false alarms and that point indicates outside the limits are highly possible in special causes.

Card [7] has mentioned that control charts are regarded as statistical data analysis refined tools that involve lower and upper restrictions to find variations. These charts are most commonly used in statistical process control analysis. A control chart is used to control and assess the variability of product or processes characteristics. Generally, preparing a control chart involves setting up the upper and lower control limits of data differences from the average value of a data set. If an examined data value lies outside the control limits then it would trigger the analysis. The usage of SPC and control charts may help to diminish and develop the differences in the implementation of a defined software process. Figure 1 shows the sample control chart:

The characteristic reasonable lower and upper bounds may be set up distinctly. Sometimes they may reflect the expectations of customers. On the other hand, the bounds may be based on the experiences of past software management process. From the average value the standard deviation may be used as these limits. For example, if one SD (Standard Deviation) is used as the lower and upper control limits then in an examination that falls outside of these limits can be produced for possible alarm and attention. In software project management, the idea of a control chart along with the use of SD as the lower and upper limit may be used to examine and track a particular characteristic of a methodology or a product. The usability characteristic may be examined through usability testing in case of a product [8].

Florac and Carleton [9] have described that to make use of control charts for the software processes, then the statistical process control must be identified first. The features that can be studied for the result of this process involves delivering defect density, productivity, performance review and rework effort among others. To control charts, the major focus is an advantageous statistical process control guidelines and tools are offered for the improvement of process, process management and measurement within the software field.

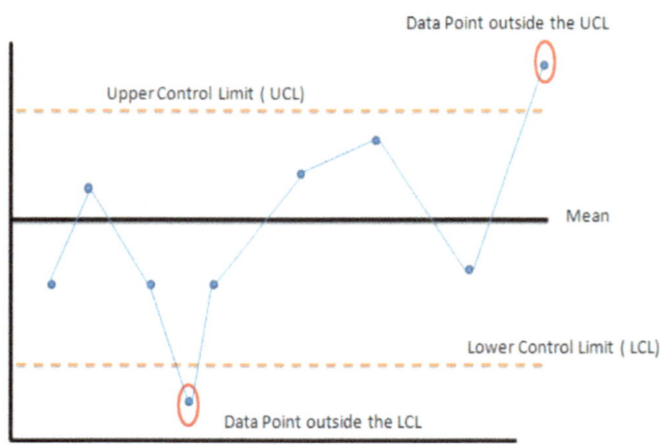


**Figure 1**. Sample control chart.

The most frequently used chart for separate data is the XmR chart. XmR charts are specially used if little is known about the underlying distribution or if the justification for assuming a binomial or poisson process is relatively questionable. XmR chart can be used to monitor turnaround time across production problems or coding effort across units examples include the u-chart for Poisson data and the p-chart for binomial data.

## ANALYZING REWORK EFFECT USING CONTROL CHART

Lantzy [10] has mentioned that rework is referred as the complete hours invested that was affected by unplanned mistakes or changes. Some of the modifications may be extra demands of customers, which are considered as developments. Classifying these rework as developments or not depends on the target of estimating the effort of rework. The rework effort is a good indicator for the quality of software process as it reveals an importance of effort the researcher invests suitable to former mistakes and doing things "First time Right". Rework enhances the costs of software project and does not add any value to the project. Any project that is completed successfully for the first time requires no rework. Rework effort therefore stands as one of the major factors behind cost incurred by an organization owing to poor quality of developed software. Cost of Poor Quality (COPQ) is a software quality metric used in determining the cost incurred on poorly delivered software. Rework effort is one of the factors of internal failures that result in the increase of COPQ [11] Houston [12] classifies the costs of software quality into two cost groups' of achieving quality and costs since lack of quality. Rework acts as leading role in the second group. Rework shows the influence of defects directly next to their amount or cost as its focus on the value of effort. As a result, defect counts and the effect of reworks considered as a supplementary evaluations for analyzing the products of software and process quality. An operational definition of the percentage of rework can be defined as:

$$\text{Percentage of rework} = (\text{Effort of rework})/(\text{Total effort})$$

Conradi et al. [13] has mentioned that the percentage of rework gives the understanding about an associating cost or amount of rework with regard to complete effort. Cost of rework in a software environment could be cost incurred in fixing defects under warranty or fixing user acceptance testing defects. A sample individual chart is shown in Figure 2.

In Figure 2 the points that lie above the UCL reveal examples in which several defects identified per unit effort overrun the process of performance limits. It might be owing to low quality of product or highly effectiveness on the inspection process. At the same time, the points that lie below the LCL represent small process of inspection in which numerous defects on products remain undetected or greater quality in product where the product has really negligible amount of defects. In both these cases, the defect density measures are used to gaining a proper understanding during interpretation of the results [14].

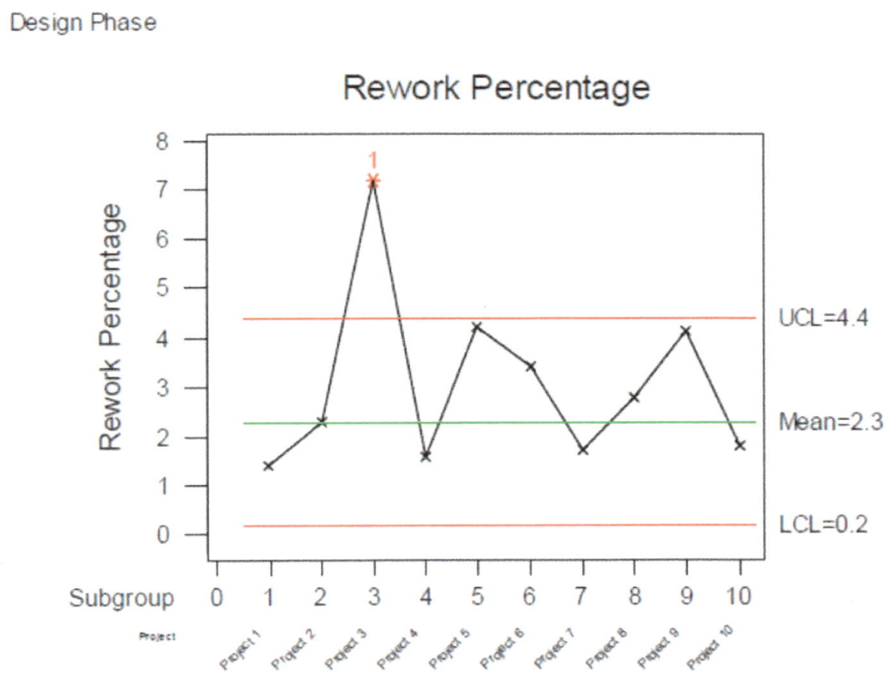


**Figure 2**. Sample individuals control chart for a percentage of rework.

## ANALYZING PRODUCTIVITY USING CONTROL CHART

Florac and Carleton [9] have described that productivity refers to the number of results generated/unit invested. For example, the number of results is the amount of painted coke bottles, refined burden of petroleum or the length of a pressed metal sheet. Measures of input contain different types such as used paint weight, for refinement number of catalyst joined or more electrical energy essential to organize pressing machines. The major results are the products of work in software development namely documents and code. And the size estimation is used to express the amount of product work generated. On the other side Jakolte and Saxena [15] have mentioned that the main input for the product work production is the HR (Human Resource). Effort is used to quantitatively measure the number of utilization of work force. The measure of productivity turns out to be the work product size generated per unit attempt. Productivity is a critical and important measure as it gives straight involvement regarding how effective the software processes are executed. The data on productivity is used to make achievable plans, to visualize the influences of development activities and also to predict deficiencies in software processes. The productivity element or factor consideration is the most important for high management since greater productivity gets lesser prices, develops chances for gains and develops rivalry forces in the market. Figure 3 shows the individual control chart for productivity.

In Figure 3, the data points that surpass upper control limit that represent an efficient study or a quick process of analysis. Similarly, less productivity measure may represent an ineffective analysis of need or a very brief, complex, or meticulous study. If the documents of software are ordered timely in graphs, a developing or reducing tendency can be identified on the other side. The researcher is capable to view the influence of any development studies. After predicting the outliers future analysis should be essential to invent the deviation effects and obtain appropriate significant measures [16].

## ANALYZING DEFECT DENSITY USING CONTROL CHART

According to Radice [17] Defect Density is referred as many defects as per size of the product. The defect density formula can be defined as:

$$\text{Defect density} = (\#\text{ of defects})/(\text{size of the product})$$

The metric data interpretation and analysis depends on consideration that on an average researchers have particular expectancy of defect count for each unit of software artifact that is being inspected. The measure of identifying most of the anticipated defects during the software inspection process stands as an indicator for exhibiting the effectiveness of the process of inspection. For these reason, it describe about these impacts is that statistical process control needs rational data sampling. If a sample of data has varied distributions, the difference will be increased and the control chart sensitivity will be reduced greatly. A study conducted by Kumuro [18], reveals an example of the impact of review speed on the quality of the review process. The below graph shows the XmR chart plotted with values of review speed of a specific document review. One review is detected and its values are encircled in Figure 4.

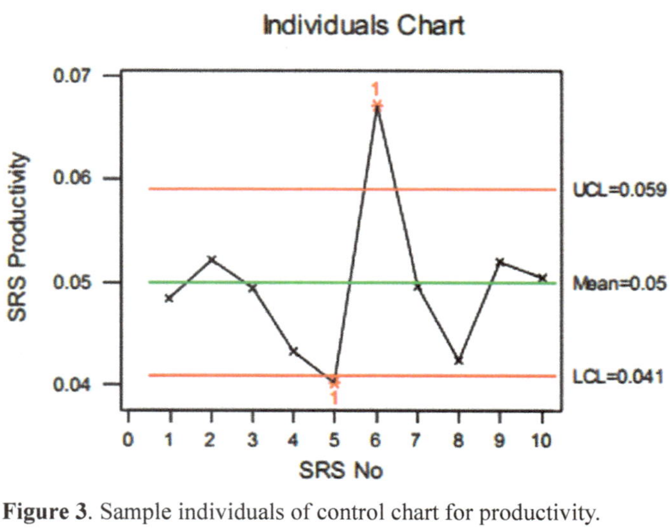


**Figure 3**. Sample individuals of control chart for productivity.

Figure 5 illustrates Z chart representing values of Defect density plotted for the above depicted review data:

This value is actually not a mistake but relatively small when compare to the values adjacent to it. Thus it can be inferred that this review was organized too rapidly and there may exist huge defects in documents to be reviewed. Viewing into the review record it turned out that critics attempted to inspect many documents about 3 times bigger than mean. Therefore, the suitable activities were to re-inspect document after categorize into more than 3 parts. Repeating again, this type of analysis can enhance stabilization of the process of peer review [19]. The above example makes it clear how control charts are useful in identifying defect density.

## BENEFITS TO SOFTWARE ORGANIZATIONS IN APPLYING CONTROL CHARTS FOR MANAGING SOFTWARE PROCESSES

According to Carleton [20] Statistical process control is a strong component to optimize the quantity of data required for utilization in making determinations of management. Statistical techniques offer a comprehension of baseline of business, insights of process improvements, visible and active involvement and value communication and process results. Likewise, Florac et al. [21] has pointed out that SPC offers real time identification to set up baselines of controllable method, set study and develop capabilities of dynamical process and concentrate on business fields requiring software development process. As per argument from Kim [22], SPC moves far away from decision making As a result, the software organizations cannot instantly realizes the advantages of these statistical process control techniques. Weller [23] has mentioned that statistical process control needs well formulated procedures. It requires a high level of commitment from management and an organizational climate where people are not offended when problems arise. Above all, SPC requires a discipline of strictly following the formulated procedures. Many software organizations that have implemented control charts for implementing software process control in the software life cycle development process have been greatly benefited from them. The client base of statistical process control ranges from startups of small technology, whose core business is software development to big IT firms that leverage development of software to develop operational performance and business systems. Control charts pave a way for continuous process improvement, reduce cost, minimize or reduce defects, improve productivity and finally improve the total quality of the end deliverable.

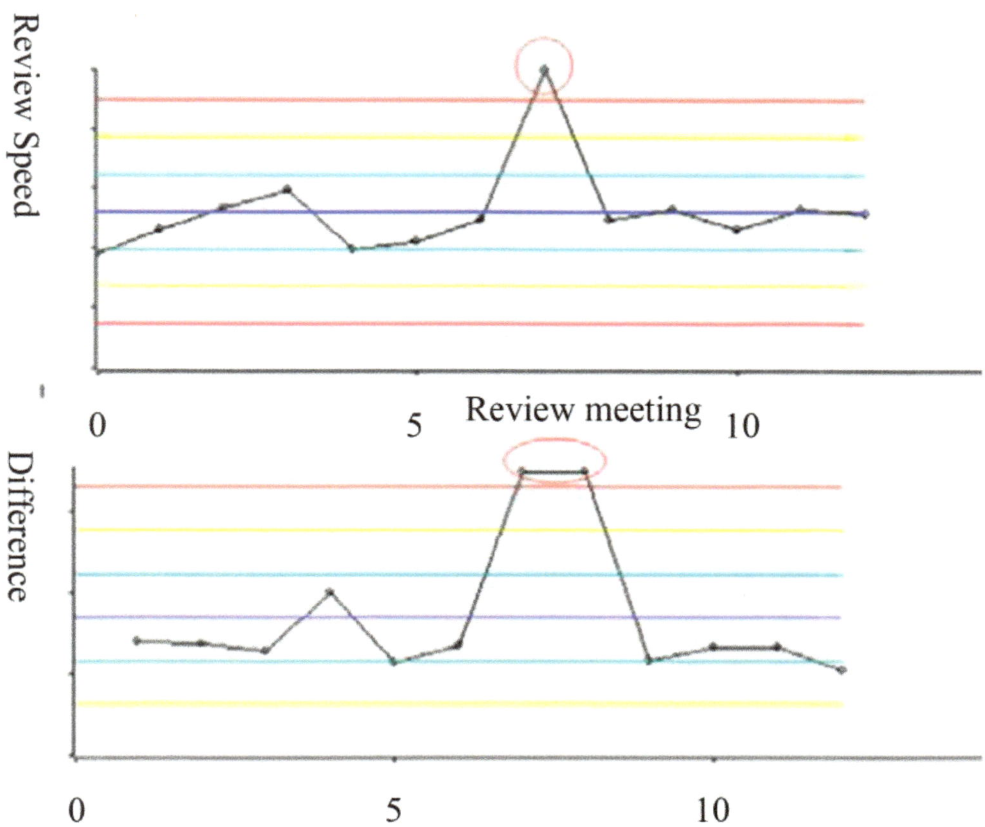


**Figure 4**. Review speed: XmR chart.

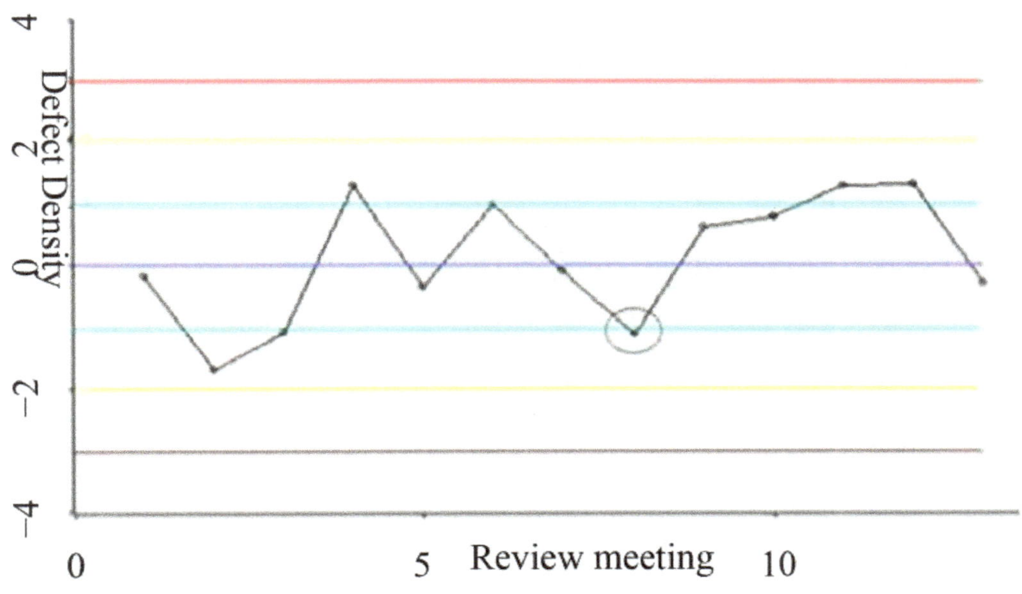


**Figure 5**. Defect density Z chart.

Usage of control charts can lead to reduction in the control limits causing process improvements. It has been observed that rigorous monitoring of control charts plotted for process parameters like defect density and taking timely corrective and preventive actions would lead to process improvements. For example—if there is a data point outside the control limits for higher defect count in a module showed as a spike in control chart, timely action taken to remove the root cause will eliminate the similar pattern in further data points. Such data points are known as special causes of variation. Figure 6 depicts a sample comparison where current control limits have come down from the historical limits showing process improvements. There are other cases which are inherent in process known as common causes of variation. Common causes are depicted as patterns of data points within LCL and UCL and are addressed through Normality rules.

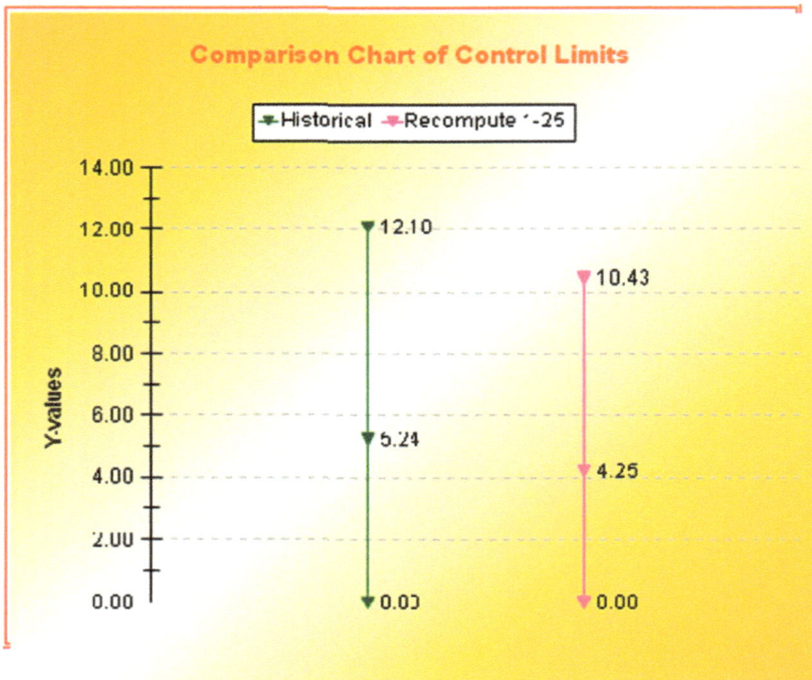


**Figure 6**. Sample comparison chart of control limits.

It can be thus clearly understood thus that statistical process control has found a prime position in the IT sector too, offering multiple benefits in improving the overall quality of the software process.

## CHALLENGES ENCOUNTERED BY SOFTWARE ORGANIZATIONS IN APPLYING CONTROL CHARTS FOR MANAGING SOFTWARE PROCESSES

Jones [24] has pointed out that monitoring the stability of software process in small organizations is a challenging problem for the software engineers. The software companies trust the quality of product merely as much as the production quantity. Cngussu et al. [25] has pointed that to make sure a higher quality level is maintained, software firms must be determined to formulate a quality policy that is dedicated to complete satisfaction of customers. The policy may include regular reliability and quality developments with every employee playing an essential role.

Caivano [26] has mentioned that to meet the challenge of data analysis, software companies should develop statistical process tools to monitor process capability using control charts and make them possible for all employees with a shared liability for analysis of data. A strategic team organizes continuous meetings to share successful statistical process control measures and take decisions based on the statistical analysis tools. According to Sargut and Demirors [27], some of the additional challenges of statistical process control for software organizations are:

- Statistical process control is considered to be a management tool;
- control charts are considered as an additional work for operator;
- statistical process control are not supported with software tool;
- statistical process control is not built into the process of manufacturing;
- experienced operators are endangered by new processes that may replace them;
- manufacturing and quality are not on similar page with SPC; and
- the success of SPC is not reported with transparency.

## CONCLUSIONS

Authors have implemented the control charts for monitoring multiple process parameters like defect density during unit testing, code review, system testing. The results of implementation in more than 40 projects were studied. C charts were used to monitor defect density during unit testing, code review, and system testing while XMR charts were used to monitor actual effort during the same phases. Just in time data analysis was performed by team where the defect density and effort were analyzed using the control limits set from the historical limits arrived from organization baseline of similar projects. The results were quite encouraging and there were lots of benefits achieved through the analysis. Control charts helped in performing the timely analysis for data points for special causes of variation and data points that follow a specific pattern. The team can take timely corrective and preventive actions to ensure that the similar defects/ issues are prevented from occurring in later phases of SDLC.

Application of statistical process control (SPC) in software industries, a decade ago had been a challenging task for researchers and software engineers. Every software metric had specific complexities and characteristics regarding its collection, definition and explanation. Despite these challenges, our interpretation suggests that researchers in the past and at present have proven that the application of SPC techniques via control charts has several positive effects that include reduction in cost, minimization of defects and error rates, improvement of the software quality end deliverable, thereby improving the overall profitability of the software organization. Alignment with goals of a business forms the key to a successful software process improvement. Statistical process control can help in indicating the direction to which a software process must be improved for better results.

However, it may be recommended that not all major software process should be using control charts for process measurements. Other useful statistical techniques, such as confidence intervals and prediction modeling could be better measurement tool in certain situations. Projects that are short duration, having small teams, and low business criticality may not be the best candidates for SPC monitoring using control charts. In such situations, this could result in process overhead for the project team and the overall morale of team could come down. SPC monitoring using control charts should be the best used in monitoring the most critical quality processes. These processes could vary from project to project depending upon scope and business goals. The decision to use control part for SPC should be taken into consideration the duration of project, the size of the team, availability of data and criticality of the process parameter that is to be measured. The training of the team on using the control charts and their analysis is the key to success of this initiative.

With the advent of several automated statistical process control software tools, applying SPC through control charts has become a much easier process to all software organizations of today. Therefore, it can be concluded that control charts are really helpful in software organizations by adding the value of quality at the end deliverables, and also deliver to their clients.

## FUTURE WORK

The analysis can be performed in startup or a small organization to understand whether the SPC can still produce beneficial outcomes. Also, domains such as ERP Implementation can be studied for possible usage and benefits of control charts.

## REFERENCES


1. W. Laurie, "Lecture Notes on Software Process Improvement," Software Engineering Institute, 1993, Paper 191.
2. A. K. Khan, "Amalgamation of Personal Software Process in Software Development Practice," Star Journal, 2012.
3. M. C. Paulk, B. Curtis, M. B. Chrissis and C. V. Weber, "Capability Maturity Model for Software," Version 1.1 (CMU/SEI-93-TR-024, ADA 263403), Software Engineering Institute, Carnegie Mellon University, Pittsburgh, 1993.
4. CMMI Product Team, "CMMISM for Systems Engineering, Software Engineering, and Integrated Product and Process Development (CMMISE/SW/IPPD, V1.1), Continuous Representation," Carnegie Mellon University, 2001.
5. Information Technology, Software Process Assessment, Part 4: Guide to Performing Assessments (ISO/IEC 15504-4:1998(E)).
6. "ISO/IEC TR 15504-5 Information Technology, Software Process Assessment," 1998.
7. D. Card, "Statistical Process Control for Software?" IEEE Software, Vol. 11, No. 3, 1994, pp. 95-97. http://dx.doi.org/10.1109/52.281722
8. C. Ho and K. E. Case, "Economic Design of Control Charts: A Literature Review for 1981-1991," Journal of Quality Technology, Vol. 26, No. 1, 1994, pp. 39-53.
9. J. W. A. Florac and A. D. Carleton, "Measuring the Software Process: Statistical Process Control for Software Process Improvement," Addison-Wesley, 1999.
10. M. A. Lantzy, "Application of Statistical Process Control to Software Processes," WADAS '92, Proceedings of the Ninth Washington Ada Symposium on Empowering Software Users and Developers, 1992, pp. 113-123. http://dx.doi.org/10.1145/257683.257717
11. EU, "Quantifying Quality Costs and the Cost of Poor Quality in Translation: Quality Efforts and the Consequences of Poor Quality in European Commission's Directorate," 2012.
12. D. Houston, "Cost of Software Quality: Justifying Software Process Improvement to Managers," Software Quality Professional, Vol. 1, No. 4, 1999, pp. 8-16.
13. R. Conradi, C. Fernström and A. Fuggetta, "A Conceptual Framework for Evolving Software Processes," ACM SIGSOFT Software Engineering Notes, Vol. 18, No. 4, 1993, pp. 26-35. http://dx.doi.org/10.1145/163626.163631
14. M. Komuro, K. Otokozawa and Y. Kimura, "Improvement of Peer Review Process based on Quantitative Effect Analysis of Actual Performance of Projects," SEC Journal, Vol. 1, No. 4, 2005, pp. 6-15.
15. P. Jakolte and A. Saxena, "Optimum Control Limits for Employing Statistical Process Control in Software Process," IEEE Transactions on Software Engineering, Vol. 28, No. 12, 2002, pp. 1126-1134.
16. J. Romine, "Using Statistical Techniques to Manage Software Projects with Data," SEPG 2002 Conference, 18-21 February 2002.
17. R. Radice, "Statistical Process Control for Software Projects," 10th Software Engineering Process Group Conference, Chicago, 1998.
18. M. Kumuro, "Experiences of Applying SPC Techniques to Software Development Processes," Shanghai, 20-28 May 2006, pp. 574-584.
19. P. Jalote, "Software Project Management in Practice," Addison-Wesley, 2002.
20. A. Carleton, "Statistical Process Control for Software (Software Technology Review)," Carnegie Mellon University, 2001.
21. A. W. Florac, A. D. Carleton and J. R. Barnard, "Statistical Process Control: Analyzing a Space Shuttle Onboard Software Process," IEEE Software, Vol. 17, No. 4, 2000, pp. 7-106.

22. E. Weller, "Practical Applications of Statistical Process Control," IEEE Software, Vol. 17, No. 3, 2000, pp. 48-55. http://dx.doi.org/10.1109/52.896249

23. S. B. Kim, "Integration of Data Mining Algorithms and Statistical Process Control," Seoul National University, Seoul, 2009.

24. C. Jones, "Software Assessments, Benchmarks, and Best Practices," Addison Wesley Longman Inc., 2000.

25. J. W. Cngussu, R. A. DeCarlo and A. P. Mathur, "Monitoring the Software Test Process Using Statistical Process Control: A Logarithmic Approach," Proceedings of the 9th European Software Engineering Conference, 2003, pp. 253-265.

26. D. Caivano, "Continuous Software Improvement through Statistical Process Control," Proceedings of the 9th European Conference on Maintenance and Reengineering, 2005, pp. 288-293.

27. K. U. Sargut and O. Demirors, "Utilization of Statistical Process Control (SPC) in Emergent Software Organizations: Pitfalls and Suggestions," Software Quality Journal, Vol. 14, No. 2, 2006, pp. 135-157.

CHAPTER 13

# EVALUATING PROJECT MANAGEMENT SOFTWARE PACKAGES USING A SCORING MODEL—A COMPARISON BETWEEN MS PROJECT AND PRIMAVERA

Hani Gharaibeh

PMPC Consulting Inc., Amman, Jordan

## ABSTRACT

**Since the Mid 1980's, an increasing number of project management software packages (PMSP) has appeared in the market to support project management organizations. Despite the wide spread of PMSP, projects based organizations are left unguided as to how they should select the most appropriate software tool for their intended business use. The aim of this research was to apply a scoring model developed using ISO/IEC 14,000 software evaluation criteria to evaluate the effectiveness of two software packages in terms of functionality and price, and produce a summary of the evaluation records. To achieve research objective, a questionnaire survey method was used to investigate the two different project management software packages. One questionnaire was circulated among software users in various locations and another was targeting the software vendors. The findings of this study revealed differences between the two packages under investigation and highlighted the strength and weakness of each package. The author was able to assess the efficiency of each software package and provided a score for each attribute which helps the user to understand how the software package performs. This investigation revealed that the software user is not concerned with the most sophisticated package, or the package that has more advanced tools and features. What is more important for the user is their need to produce simple time charts, simple resource and cost analysis and basic reports.**

## INTRODUCTION

Computer systems are known to have a role in all aspects of the engineering business. The revolution in the field of computer software in the last decade has been enormous. Now, engineers and managers working in the engineering industry can no longer ignore the facilities and tools in computer technology if they wish to become successful.

In the engineering industry, several software packages have been developed to enhance the various project stages. Starting with the design stage, the marketing of architectural, engineering, and construction software is very impressive, as it is exemplified by colors, 3-D drawings animation, audio video effects, and much more. Now there are even other software systems that help in cost estimation, construction documents preparation, quantity surveying, and of course, project scheduling and management [1] .

In the world of project management, computer applications play an increasing role in the delivery of projects. Software programs are involved in just about every aspect of project work from the discovery of a problem or an opportunity, to the

**Citation:** Gharaibeh, H. (2014) Evaluating Project Management Software Packages Using a Scoring Model—A Comparison between MS Project and Primavera. Journal of Software Engineering and Applications, 7, 541-554. doi:10.4236/jsea.2014.77050.

commissioning and start-up of the new facility. Computer tools are now involved with every aspect in the project, providing solutions that will help in faster project completion, lower costs as well as improving the productivity and accuracy of work. Projects require participation and support from all levels within an organization, and so teams are the foundation of a successful project. Modern software packages provide comprehensive information on all the projects in the business, from executive-level summaries to detailed work assignments, so each team member can confidently contribute to the project's success.

Growth for most businesses is a result of successfully developing a project that generates new products and services. This day-to-day explosion of new products and services is driving the challenges that face most companies. Limited skilled resources, constantly changing project priorities and shortened development cycles magnify these challenges. Thus, it is no longer business as usual. The ability to make decisions, choose the right projects, will determine how effectively projects are deployed and how quickly the company's products and services get to market.

To create strategic business advantages and get the products to market fast, leading companies are effectively using project management. They need the most advanced and modem project management software. Process and resource management software that offers the combined benefits of' managing projects and building and using standard methodologies to help companies minimize project lifecycles, and deliver uncompromising project results [2] .

In the world of engineering and construction, a long time concern has been the concept of project scheduling by CPM. For many in the industry, CPM was seen as a system that somebody else should use. Of all modern engineering and construction tools, CPM was one of the very first to be computerized. CPM was initially aimed to improve construction labor productivity. Eventually other aspects such as, procurement and management decisions were included in the CPM planning networks and schedules. Today there are many CPM-based computer tools for scheduling and project management.

Where at one time most schedules showed only construction activities, current usage includes a full range of project phases and tasks, including producing, services, site analysis activities, schematic design services, design development services, and so on. PRIMAVERA offers to manage not only the project time, but also the costs and the use of resources. This is done by estimating activities in terms of their time, their resource requirements and their cost.

The initial concept of CPM was to plan activities using networks of logical relationships and then to create Gantt or bar charts to communicate the information. The current marketing approach, however, is to plan the work on screen using bar charts, connecting the bars for logic if needed, and then automatically converting the plan to a CPM/PERT network in a precedence diagram format [1] .

A widely used package, created for the engineering and construction industry, is Primavera software. PRIMAVERA is now written for Windows as GUI packages (Graphical User Interface). This means that the package depends on graphics and charts to illustrate the different tools and functions it provides. PRIMAVERA offers to organize, analyze, communicate and accelerate projects. The main planning graphic in PRIMAVERA, as in most other GUI packages is the Gantt charts.

PMSP although not specially written for the engineering and construction industry, includes: Microsoft Project and Computer Associates Super. Microsoft Project is seen by some as a lower cost, individual scheduling tool suitable as a feeder to more comprehensive PMSP for large projects, such as Open Plan and Primavera. Some lower price applications are Timeline Track from Primavera and Open Plan Desktop. Sure Track and TimeLine are simple, computerized bar chart drawing tools [1] .

According to Levine, PMSP can be classified according to three levels/types follows:

- The Bare Bones Level: The software containing very basic functions operating within limitations.
- The Mass-Market Level: This project management software attempts to provide the basic tools and features for a variety of project management activities.
- The Advanced-Moderate Level: These highly sophisticated programs have a resultant increase in complexity and speed of operation [3] .

Although, this classification of PMSP was proposed by Levine in 1986, the available PMSP tools in the market today still fit neatly into this categorization. The Mass-Market level of PMSP includes packages such as CA Superproject, Micro planner, on Target, Project Scheduler, Timeline and MS-Project for Windows. These soft- ware packages range in price from US $200 to US $1000 and provide the general project management techniques of PERT/CPM, Gantt chart, resource leveling, WBS and cost tracking. The downfall of this range of PMSP is that they do not provide the ability to schedule and track multiple projects, and therefore are only useful for single project.

The advanced-moderate level of PMSP are highly sophisticated programs that provide a great number of functions ranging in price from approximately US $1500 to US $16,000, depending on the functionality and de- sired hardware platform. These packages include: Cresta PMS, Kemal PMS, Micrplanner X-pert, Primavera, X-pert for Windows, and the majority of the PMSP that require Unix as the hardware platform. These packages are recommended for multiprojects with several thousand activities or many subcontractors.

As software packages are generic, they apply to large segments of the market, ensuring sales and profits for the software vendor. However, the generalized nature of software packages guarantees that they are not designed to suit all of the functionality requirements of every organization.

The purpose of software packages is to provide a relatively cheap product that meets the basic needs of organizations, attempting to solve a problem experienced by many. The other major advantages of software pack- ages are that they can be acquired, installed and operated within weeks, while the level of user support is high [4] .

In 1994, a survey was conducted with 1500 software professional in North America. The survey analyzed software product installations and purchase plans for the feature/ function requirements. The objective of the re- search was to aid software vendors to better understand user requirements and the decision process buyers undergo when selecting software products. Respondent to the survey cited purchasing off-the-shelf applications as the most suitable and most popular choice. The survey has also found that product features and functions and ease of use have been rated respectively as the number one and two buying criteria for the past eleven years. However, in 1994 user support, that is service and training, overtook the number one and two positions.

Different methods are used by different people to select project management software. One approach is studying the experience of others, validating their experience and relating that to your situation. Another approach is to conduct trials on small problems, which will help to understand and use the software. Some project management experts prefer to apply the package or tool on real projects. This has one disadvantage that it is a lengthy process and this is only practical as a means of evaluating few products [5] .

In general, it is advisable to follow recommendations of national bodies, expert group (for example the Project Management institute) or consultants in the project management area. These groups are familiar with soft- ware packages and their potential uses for various activities and industry needs.

## THE PURPOSE OF SOFTWARE EVALUATION

Today the use of information technology is growing; the number of critical computer systems is also growing. The quality of software in these systems is important because software faults may lead to serious consequences. Thus, it is important before starting the evaluation process to define, what is meant by the evaluation of project management software? It is the process of quantifying the different tools and features provided by a software package in a way that will help to compare it with different software packages.

Software products are extremely varied. They are written and produced to fulfill very diverse requirements. Their context for use can also be very varied, such as in the case of application software in a management in- formation system. The primary purpose of software product evaluation is to provide quantitative results concerning software product quality that is comprehensive and acceptable.

The evaluation process is described as a procedure that allows expression of evaluation requirements in terms of quality characteristics, as defined in ISO/IEC 9126. The evaluation takes into account various documents that can be considered as part of the software product. Design documentation, test or validation reports, and source code or user documentation. It is recommended by the ISO standards that the evaluator use a library of evaluation modules that define evaluation methods. These evaluation modules could be standardized, although no provision for that is proposed in the standard. The evaluation leads to the production by the evaluator, of an Evaluation report [6] .

There are different types of evaluation. The evaluation process can he classified by the party concerned with the evaluation, and the evaluation could be classified based on the stage at which the software is being evaluated [6] .

## OBJECTIVE & METHODOLOGY

To investigate the effectiveness of PMSP, the author has to collect an enormous amount of data for both soft- ware users and software vendors. The data collected can be applied using the scoring model developed by the author. The best method to achieve this objective is to use a survey/questionnaire method as this method will enable the collection of large amount of data from variety of software users in several locations and from different industries.

Surveys are statistical research method used to collect data from a large group of participant. Surveys are very useful research instrument to collect data on phenomena that cannot be observed. Surveys could be of different types including: structured, semi-structured and unstructured questionnaire surveys. In a survey, researchers use a random sample to represent the entire population. Basha and Harter in 1980 define population as “any set of persons or objects that possesses at least one common characteristic” [7] .

The best method to achieve this objective was the use of questionnaire survey forms. Surveys are statistical research method used to collect data from a large group of participant. Surveys are very useful research instrument to collect data on phenomena that cannot be observed. Surveys could be of different types including: structured, semi-structured and unstructured questionnaire surveys. In a survey, researchers use a random sample to represent the entire population.

Surveys may have advantages as a research method.

- they are not expensive,
- participants can respond quickly and can be widely spread geographically,
- participants can respond after gathering information or taking time to think about their responses,
- it participants privacy while they respond,
- allow respondents to read questions rather than hear them loud,
- those who participate can do so according to what is most convenient for their schedule,
- participants can look at the entire survey, giving context to questions and
- participants are also unaware of the feelings or wishes of the researcher [8] .

The objective of this research paper was to apply a scoring model developed previously by the author based on ISO/IEC 14598-1 software evaluation criteria to help evaluate two different software packages. The scoring model uses a score card which assigns scores for each software attribute in order to assess the effectiveness of the software package.

## DATA COLLECTION

### Overview

The data collected in this particular research, originates from questionnaires sent to the software user, representing any individual or organization that is likely to use project management software to perform its activities; and the software vendor, being the project management software company that delivers this product to the user.

In order to test the validity of this scoring model, the author chooses to assess two different software packages by applying the model to it. The software packages chosen were: Microsoft Project and Primavera due to their common and wide application among engineering and construction firms.

## Software User Survey Form

The software user questionnaire would be used to support the vendor questionnaire, by targeting organizations that use project management software to monitor and coordinate their projects. In this particular study, a soft- ware user survey form was distributed among 110 companies across Australia. The survey form was distributed in five cities: Sydney, Melbourne, Brisbane, Adelaide and Perth. Almost 35 companies responded to the survey which helped to gather data about the assessment of various software characteristic and attributes both from a technical perspective (so called operational characteristics) and system requirements (so called general information system characteristics).

The survey form consisted of the following sections:

- Section A: which would include general information on the software used by the company, and the size of project management activities conducted by them? It would also contain company details. It was hoped that this section would reveal the popularity of project management software to those organizations and the degree of importance of the software itself.
- Section B: which would help weighting the evaluation criteria? It will focus on obtaining a numerical assessment for the different attributes listed in the software evaluation criteria. This assessment represents the degree of importance of each attribute expressed as a percentage as seen by the software user. This will be referred to as the weight of the attribute. Each characteristic set itself will have a relative weight and the sub characteristics included in each criterion will have a different weight as well. The section will be organized in the form of tables that list the main characteristics used and the sub characteristic sets associated with it, as well as, the different attributes associated with each sub characteristic set in separate tables. Each table consists of two columns. Column one that lists the characteristics/attributes and column two contains the degree of importance given to the particular attribute in terms of the overall characteristics examined.
- Section C: This would involve the attributes. This section was part of the questionnaire sent to software users who are using either MS-Project or Primavera in planning to help in scoring the attributes listed in Section B, and give their personal judgment of how the tested software achieves each attribute. The score will be assigned based on a point scale (0 - 3). It will reflect the performance of the software package in respect to each attribute. Where zero represents a poor performance and 3 represents an excellent performance.

Finally the user was allowed to comment on the contents of the questionnaire and the investigation itself.

To be assigned a score, the software package must achieve the condition stated for each performance category. Since this is a subjective assessment that might differ from one person to another, the four point's scale as illustrated in Table 1 was selected to minimize the personal error in each assessment. Once the scores are obtained for all the attributes, it will be installed into the scoring module. For each of these attributes listed in the model the following were calculated: a score that represents the assessment of the software user to how each software package covers this attribute, a relative weight (X) of each sub-characteristic set defined within the operational or general information system characteristics, and a weighted score was calculated by multiplying the score of each attribute with the relative weight of that sub-characteristic set. Finally a relative weighted score (Y) for each sub-characteristic set was calculated to be the sum of all the weighted scores of the attributes that belongs to it.

## Software Vendor Survey Form

Two software vendors in the investigation were Primavera Systems Inc., and Microsoft Corporation, which produce the software Microsoft Project. Both vendors have an outstanding reputation in Australia and world- wide. Their products are widely used at both the individual and organizational level.

The data collected using this questionnaire was necessary to the evaluation process to be used in the scoring module. The structure of the questionnaire consists of three sections: Section A, the general information, Section B, the general system requirements and Section C, the life cycle cost information.

Section A covered general information including the software company details and the respondent's name. This section meant to help estimate the size of the software company both in Australia and worldwide and to help establish a general background on the experience of the software company in the field of project management.

Section B will cover the data required in evaluating the general system characteristic, including information on technical support, compatibility, training, security and hardware requirements.

Section C presents the collected data necessary to work out all the different cost items associated with the software package. Such information will help in evaluating the third characteristic set, which is the cost of the software package. These cost items are listed in Table 2.

**Table 1**. Scoring criteria for each software attribute

| Score | Performance | Condition |
|---|---|---|
| 0 | Poor | If the attribute does not exist at all in the software package |
| 1 | Bad | If the attribute exist, but presented badly (there are minor problems, weak points in the use of attribute) |
| 2 | Good | If the attribute is achieved within minimum requirements or average performance |
| 3 | Excellent | If the attribute is expressed very well with powerful tools provided in this attribute |

**Table 2**. Software cost elements

| Cost Item | Unit |
|---|---|
| Purchase cost of software | $/licence |
| Installation fee | $/licence |
| Maintenance cost | $/year |
| Upgrading cost | $/year |
| Hardware equipment cost | $ |
| Learning cost of the software | $ |
| Expected operating life | years |
| Total cost of the software | $ |

The cost is a significant part of the evaluation process, since a decision to purchase a software package will very much depend on the cost of the package as well as other considerations. It was for this reason that, the user was given the choice in the questionnaire form to rate the degree of importance of the cost from amongst the other criteria items. Two questionnaire forms were sent out one for Primavera Systems Inc. (Brisbane) and the other one to Microsoft Australia Corporation (Sydney). Results of the data collected in these questionnaires will be discussed later in this paper.

## DATA ANALYSIS

Since software is considered the main topic of this investigation, it was extremely important to collect information regarding both the software packages under investigation. Indeed this information was most useful in the evaluation process. Both companies: Microsoft Australia Corporation and Primavera Systems Inc. responded to the questionnaire.

As indicated in the second part of the survey forms, both software providers satisfy the documentation requirements identified in the evaluation criteria. They provide the user with user and technical manuals when purchasing the software. In addition to that, they provide auxiliary materials such as demo CDs, brochures, booklets, etc. This approach is important as the software user ranked the documentation of the software as the second most important item in the general system requirements of the software, with a relative weight of 20%. In the documentation characteristics, PRIMAVERA achieved superiority over MS-Project by scoring higher in terms of the area of support for user and technical manuals (2 and 2 for PRIMAVERA, 1.73 and 1.8 for MS- Project respectively). In contrast, MS-Project scored higher in terms of supporting auxiliary materials with the software (1.6 for PRIMAVERA, 1.7 for MS-Project respectively).

With a relative weight of 16% the compatibility of the software came third in terms of the general systems characteristic. Both MS-Project and PRIMAVERA satisfy this requirement. However, PRIMAVERA was found to be compatible with several project management systems. MS-Project was found to be better only in terms of compatibility with MS-Office applications, which was expected from a Microsoft product scoring 1.91. PRI- MAVERA only scored 1.20 on this attribute. In terms of compatibility with other project management software and information management systems, however PRIMAVERA achieved better results scoring 1.5 and 1.8 while MS-Project scored only 1.3 and 1.7 respectively. In terms of compatibility with programming languages and database management systems, MS-Project is compatible with C+, Visual Basic and C sharp. PRIMAVERA is al- so compatible with C+, as well as SAP and the Oracle database.

The technical support sub characteristics came forth in the degree of importance with a relative weight of 15%. This sub characteristic was achieved well in both software packages. Both software suppliers indicated that they provide technical services such as: implementation, consultation and training courses on the use and application of the software package. Additionally both vendors conduct seminars and workshops to introduce the new user to the last updated versions of their products. The attributes in the technical support were another success for PRIMAVERA over MS-Project. MS-Project was only better in the process of installing and operating the software, scoring 2.27, while PRIMAVERA scored only 1.83 on this attribute. Meanwhile, PRIMAVERA scored better in terms of support for technical services and training courses, (2 and 2 for PRIMAVERA, 1.38 and 1.9 for MS-Project respectively) on these attributes.

With a 40% relative weight, the user friendliness characteristics proved to be the most important item for the software user. In examining the different attributes of this group, MS-Project achieved better results than PRIMAVERA in terms of a shorter time period to learn the software package, clearer screen messages and dialog boxes, and the undo redo option. PRIMAVERA was better than MS-Project only in terms of the organization of the menu structures and commands.

The security sub characteristics of the software came last in terms of the degree of importance for the soft- ware user with a relative weight of only 9%. This was because the user was more interested in characteristics like user friendliness and documentation. However PRIMAVERA achieved a higher success level than MS- Project in terms of both security on accessing project files and security on target plans.

## THE SCORING MODEL

In a previous research phase, the author developed a scoring model based on the ISO/IEC criteria illustrated in Figure 1 and data gathered from variety of software users in the engineering and construction industry. The scoring model included two type of characteristics to be evaluated in a software package: the operational characteristics which refers to the technical features and tools available within the package which affects the functionality of the software, and the general information system characteristics which refers to the non-technical software features that are essential to have not only in a project management software package but in any soft- ware product. Each level was further broken down into sub-characteristics that define the key aspects that should be present in a PMSP and finally each sub-characteristic was broken down into the smallest measurable units in the software (the so called attributes). Each attribute was given a weight (0% - 100%) to represent the degree of importance of this attribute in terms of the overall assessment criterion.

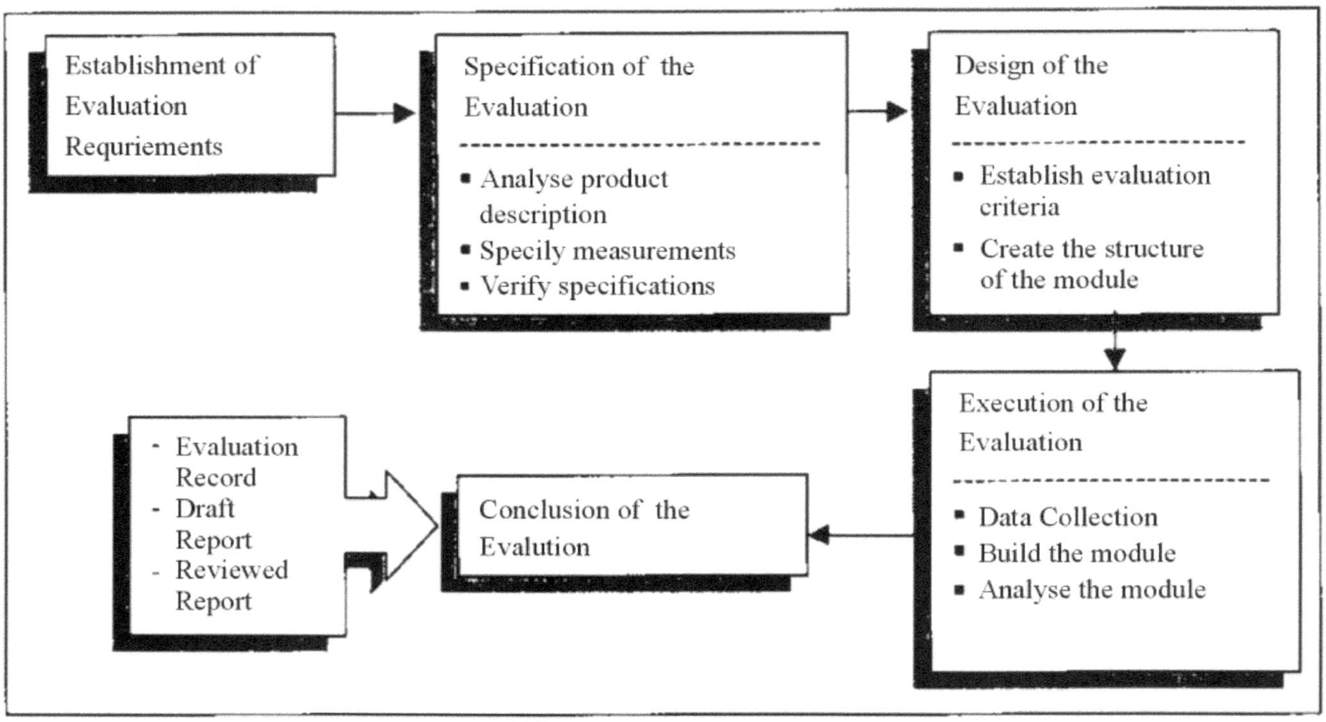


**Figure 1**. Evaluation process as identified by ISO/IEC: 14598-1.

The first step in building the scoring module was to calculate the average score assigned by each software user for each attribute, the average score is called the "aggregated value" and is calculated using the below formula:

$$\text{Aggregated value} = f\frac{(A^*0)+(B^*1)+(C^*2)+(D^*3)}{A+B+C+D} \quad (1)$$

where:

A: number of users assigning a score of ZERO for a specific attributes.

B: number of users assigning a score of ONE for a specific attributes.

C: number of users assigning a score of TWO for a specific attributes.

D: number of users assigning a score of THREE for a specific attributes.

After calculating the aggregated value for each attribute and for both software packages under investigation, the score is then installed into the scoring module.

The second step is to determine the weight assigned for each attribute which is a percentage assigned by each software user to represent the degree of importance of each software attribute in terms of the sub-characteristic set for which this attribute belongs. The average weight is then calculated by summing all the weights assigned divided by the number of software users responding to the questionnaire. This represents the average weight for each software attribute. This percentage is inserted in the scoring model.

The third step is to calculate the weighted score for each software attribute which is calculated according to the formula below:

$$\text{Weighted Score} = \text{Aggregated Score Value} * \text{Average Weight} \quad (2)$$

The weighted score is then inserted into the scoring model against each software attribute.

The fourth step in building the scoring model was to calculate the relative weight (X) for each sub characteristic set which represents the degree of importance of each sub characteristics set in terms of overall software evaluation criteria. The relative weight is calculated as an average number resulted by adding all relative weight percentages assigned by software users and divide this by the number of software users. This number is then inserted in the scoring model

The values of X as obtained from software users as follows:

X1 = 33 X6 = 40

X2 = 15 X7 = 20

X3 = 14 X8 = 16

X4 = 19 X9 = 15

X5 = 19 X10 = 9

The fifth step is to calculate the relative weighted score which represents the aggregate of all weighted scores for each sub characteristic set and is calculated using the formula below:

$$\text{The Relative weighted Score } (Y) = \sum \text{ Weighted scores for each sub characteristic set.} \quad (3)$$

## EVALUATION RESULTS: MS PROJECT AND PRIMAVERA SOFTWARE

Now that we have built the structure of the scoring model which will be used to evaluate and compare the two different project management software package, we can start applying the above equations of the scoring model to the data obtained which will give the following values for Y (See the scoring module Table 3 for each soft- ware package)

- For Microsoft Project:

Y1 = 1.99 Y2 = 1.75 Y3 =1.59

Y4 = 1.56 Y5 = 1.82 Y6 = 1.74

Y7 = 1.67 Y8 = 1.35 Y9 = 1.78 Y10 = 1.97

- For Primavera

Y1 = 2.26 Y2 = 2.26 Y3 = 2.12

Y4 = 1.63 Y5 = 2.11 Y6 = 1.91

Y7 = 1.43 Y8 = 1.91 Y9 = 1.96 Y10 = 1.84

Now that we have the values of X, Y for each sub characteristic set, we can work out the values of A which represents the total score of the software package in terms of the operational characteristic as follows:

$$A = \sum_{i=1}^{5} Xi \cdot Yi = X1 \cdot Y1 + X2 \cdot Y2 + X3 \cdot Y3 + X4 \cdot Y4 + X5 \cdot Y5 \quad (4)$$

Applying this equation to each software package under investigation will result in:

A (for MS-Project) =178 points

A (for Primavera) = 209 points

Similarly the value of B representing the performance of the software package in terms of GIS characteristics can be calculated as follows:

$$B = \sum_{i=6}^{10} Xi \cdot Yi = X6 \cdot Y6 + X7 \cdot Y7 + X8 \cdot Y8 + X9 \cdot Y9 + X10 \cdot Y10 \quad (5)$$

Applying this equation to each software package under investigation will result in:

B (for MS-Project) =179 points

B (for Primavera) = 181 points

Using the values of (m, n), which represents the relative weight of the operational characteristics and the gen- eral system information characteristics of the software as assigned by software users to be 60% and 40% respec- tively. Applying this to the equation below will yield the value of C which represents the total weighted score for each software package

$$C = A*m + B*n \quad (6)$$

Therefore,

C for MS-Project = 178 × 0.60 + 179 × 0.40 = 178 points

C for Primavera = 209 × 0.60 + 181 × 0.40= 198 points

The scoring model discussed above is indicated in Table 3.

In order for the value of C to be a true measure of the performance of the software, it has to be compared to the worst and best outcome that could be achieved by the software tested using this module. Therefore, the minimum and maximum value of C should be calculated and will be called C.min and C.max respectively. This will give the user or the evaluator a range for the minimum and maximum level of quality of the software ac- cording to this scoring module. A better sense of the efficiency of the software package can therefore be achieved.

In calculating C.min and C.max the same weights (m, n) and the same relative weights (X values) are used. However, the scores will be totally different and hence, the values of Y will be different.

The best PMSP, according to this module will score the maximum value on all attributes, assuming the soft- ware satisfies all the attributes fully and achieves excellent performance. In this case, a score of three was as- signed to each attribute. It must he remembered that the worst PMSP will not score zero for all the attributes, because zero means that the attribute does not exist at all. A package that represents the minimum acceptable level of quality will score one point on all attributes.

To achieve the minimum level of quality in the software, the value of A and B should be 100 and to achieve the maximum level of quality, the value of A, B should be 300.

Using m = 60%, n = 40%, the value of C is calculated as follows:

$$\text{C.min} = A*m + B*n \ (\text{for Min level of quality})$$
$$= 100 \times 0.6 + 100 \times 0.4 = 60 + 40 = 100 \text{ points} \quad (7)$$

$$\text{C.max} = A*m + B*n \ (\text{for Max. level of quality})$$
$$= 300 \times 0.6 + 300 \times 0.4 = 180 + 120 = 300 \text{ points} \quad (8)$$

According to the scoring module, the value of C for MS-Project is178 and the value of C for Primavera are 198. Comparing this with the value of C.min and C.max, it can be seen that both software packages fully satisfy the minimum quality level according to this scoring module. However, both are still far from reaching the highest quality level able to be achieved by this scoring module. In comparing the value of C each package achieved to C.max will give the efficiency of the software in terms of the technical aspects examined.

$$\text{Efficiency of the Package } E = C/\text{C.max} * 100\% \quad (9)$$

Therefore,

Efficiency of MS-Project = 178/300 = 59%

Efficiency of PRIMAVERA = 198/300 = 66%

**Table 3**. The scoring model used in the evaluation process

(a)

| | Software Evaluation Criteria | Weight | MS Project | | Primavera | |
|---|---|---|---|---|---|---|
| | Operational Characteristics<br>Relative Weight m = 60 | 0% - 100% | Score | Weighted Score | Score | Weighted Score |
| | Software Attributes: | | | | | |
| | Time Management<br>Relative weight X1 = 33 | | 2.18 | 0.59 | 1.83 | 0.49 |
| 1 | Setting up your project plan | 27 | 2.09 | 0.54 | 2.67 | 0.69 |
| 2 | Defining activities and relations | 26 | 1.9 | 0.32 | 2.33 | 0.40 |
| 3 | Calendars | 17 | 1.91 | 0.32 | 2.33 | 0.40 |
| 4 | Network calculations | 17 | 1.64 | 0.21 | 2.17 | 0.28 |
| 5 | Network graphics | 13 | | | | |
| | Relative weighted score Y1 = | | | 1.99 | | 2.26 |
| | Resource Management<br>Relative weight X2 = 15 | | | | | |

| | | | | | | |
|---|---|---|---|---|---|---|
| 6 | Resource identification | 23 | 1.90 | 0.44 | 2.50 | 0.58 |
| 7 | Resource allocation | 22 | 1.55 | 0.34 | 2.33 | 0.51 |
| 8 | Resource levelling | 19 | 1.60 | 0.30 | 2.17 | 0.41 |
| 9 | Ability to handle resource over allocation | 17 | 1.78 | 0.30 | 1.80 | 0.31 |
| 10 | Type of resource graphics available | 19 | 1.91 | 0.36 | 1.83 | 0.35 |
| | Relative weighted score Y2 = | | | 1.75 | | 2.15 |
| | Cost Management<br>Relative weight X3 = 14 | | | | | |
| 11 | Assigning cost information on activities | 26 | 1.73 | 0.45 | 2.33 | 0.61 |
| 12 | Cost Breakdown Structure | 24 | 1.70 | 0.41 | 2.17 | 0.52 |
| 13 | Cost Calculations | 18 | 1.63 | 0.29 | 2.20 | 0.40 |
| 14 | Support of uncertainty analysis | 15 | 0.90 | 0.14 | 1.50 | 0.23 |
| 15 | Cost graphics | 17 | 1.78 | 0.30 | 2.17 | 0.37 |
| | Relative weighted Score Y3 = | | | 1.59 | | 2.12 |
| | Reporting<br>Relative weight X4 = 19 | | | | | |
| 16 | Type of standard reports | 29 | 1.60 | 0.46 | 1.83 | 0.53 |
| 17 | Report generation | 34 | 1.40 | 0.48 | 1.60 | 0.54 |
| 18 | Integration with word processor | 19 | 1.64 | 0.31 | 1.40 | 0.27 |
| 19 | Report presentation | 18 | 1.73 | 0.31 | 1.60 | 0.29 |
| | Relative weighted score Y4 = | | | 1.56 | | 1.63 |
| | Control and Monitoring<br>Relative weight X5 = 19 | | | | | |
| 20 | Saving project baseline plans | 26 | 1.86 | 0.48 | 2.00 | 0.52 |
| 21 | Outlining and data banding | 20 | 1.57 | 0.31 | 2.50 | 0.50 |
| 22 | Support of WBS | 25 | 1.89 | 0.47 | 2.00 | 0.50 |
| 23 | Multi project management | 19 | 1.90 | 0.36 | 2.17 | 0.41 |
| 24 | Web publishing and internet capabilities | 10 | 1.86 | 0.19 | 1.75 | 0.14 |
| | Relative weighted score Y5 | | | 1.82 | | 2.11 |

(b)

| | Software Evaluation Criteria | Weight | MS Project | | Primavera | |
|---|---|---|---|---|---|---|
| | General Information System Characteristics<br>Relative Weight m = 40 | 0% - 100% | Score | Weighted Score | Score | Weighted Score |
| | Documentation<br>Relative weight X6 = 40 | | | | | |
| 25 | User manuals | 48 | 1.73 | 0.83 | 2.00 | 0.96 |
| 26 | Technical manuals | 29 | 1.80 | 0.52 | 2.00 | 0.58 |
| 27 | Auxiliary Material | 23 | 1.70 | 0.39 | 1.60 | 0.37 |
| | Relative weighted score Y6 | | | 1.74 | | 1.91 |
| | Compatibility<br>Relative weight X7 = 20 | | | | | |
| 28 | MS Office Applications | 47 | 1.91 | 0.90 | 1.20 | 0.56 |
| 29 | Other PMSP | 30 | 1.30 | 0.39 | 1.50 | 0.45 |
| 30 | Operation Systems | 23 | 1.67 | 0.38 | 1.80 | 0.41 |
| | Relative weighted score Y7 | | | 1.67 | | 1.43 |
| | Security<br>Relative weight X8 = 16 | | | | | |
| 31 | Security to access project files | 49 | 1.3 | 0.64 | 2.00 | 0.98 |
| 32 | Security of baseline plans | 51 | 1.4 | 0.71 | 1.83 | 0.93 |
| | Relative weighted score Y8 | | | 1.35 | | 1.91 |
| | Technical Support<br>Relative weight X9 = 15 | | | | | |
| 33 | Installation and maintenance | 26 | 2.27 | 0.59 | 1.83 | 0.48 |
| 34 | Customer service/help | 41 | 1.38 | 0.57 | 2.00 | 0.82 |
| 35 | Training courses | 33 | 1.90 | 0.63 | 2.00 | 0.66 |
| | Relative weighted score Y9 | | | 1.78 | | 1.96 |
| | User Friendliness<br>Relative weight X10 = 9 | | | | | |
| 36 | Time to learn the software | 29 | 2.36 | 0.68 | 2.00 | 0.58 |
| 37 | Help wizards | 14 | 2.00 | 0.28 | 2.00 | 0.28 |
| 38 | Menu structure and commands | 23 | 1.73 | 0.40 | 2.20 | 0.51 |
| 39 | System messages and dialogue boxes | 17 | 1.90 | 0.32 | 1.60 | 0.27 |
| 40 | Multi undo-redo | 17 | 1.70 | 0.29 | 1.20 | 0.20 |
| | Relative weighted score Y10 = | | | 1.97 | | 1.84 |
| | Total Weighted Score (C) | | | 178 | | 198 |

These results show that PRIMAVERA is better than MS-Project by 20, points or 7% in terms of efficiency. Moreover, by looking at the values of A and B for each package, it can be seen that PRIMAVERA achieved this superiority over MS-Project through the operational characteristics of the software (measured by the value of A). PRIMAVERA scored 209 points while MS-Project only scored 178 points. Thus the functions of the software and the technical features provided in PRIMAVERA are better than in MS-Project. For the general system characteristics, measured by the value of B, both softwares achieved almost the same results with PRIMAVERA scoring 181 points and MS-Project scoring 179 points. This means that the general characteristics examined are almost the same for the two packages. However, comparing the different values of Y achieved by each software in these characteristics, it appears that MS-Project achieved slightly better results in compatibility. This is something to be expected from software produced by the biggest computer software corporation in the world Microsoft. However, PRIMAVERA provides better security tools for accessing project files and baseline plans.

So far this analysis has only examined the software in terms of the operational and general systems characteristics. As mentioned earlier, cost is a significant part of the evaluation criteria; therefore, a cost effectiveness analysis has to be performed.

The third part of the software supplier survey form was concerned with collecting information on all cost items associated with the software package. The following cost items were assessed:

- Price of the software package
- Installation cost
- Maintenance and upgrading cost
- Hardware equipment cost
- Learning cost

Using the data obtained from the survey forms, the cost of the software was calculated as follows:

- Cost for Primavera (Operation life of the software 2 years)
  - Price of the software license = AUS S 8000/ license
  - Installation fee AUS $800/license
  - Maintenance and upgrading cost 1600 S/year × 2 years:= AUS $3200
  - Learning cost = 58 Si hour × 24 hour AUS $1400 (3 day course, 24 hours)
  - Hardware equipment required to operate the software as indicated by the supplier arc: RAM 16 MB, CPU 486 at least, HDD 200 MB
  - Hardware parts cost = AUS $85

Total Cost of Primavera Software = AUS $13485/one license

- Cost for Microsoft Project (Operation life of the software 2 year)
  - Price of the software license AUS $11001 license
  - Maintenance and installation cost = 105 S/year × 2 years = AUS $210
  - Upgrading cost = 600 $/year × 2 years = AUS $1200
  - Learning cost = AUS $390 (2 day course, 16 hours)
  - Hardware equipment required to operate the software as indicated by the supplier arc: RAM 32 MB, CPU Pentium 100 MHZ at least, HDD 1.0 GB
  - Hardware parts cost = AUS $200

Total Cost of MS Project AUS $3100/one license

Finally to include the cost as part of the evaluation criteria, a cost effective ratio were calculated as follows:

$$\text{Cost Effectiveness Ratio } (\text{C.E.R}) = \frac{\text{Total weighted score}}{\text{Total cost \$}} \quad (10)$$

In general, this equation assumes the total cost to be as important as the operational and general information characteristics of the software. According to this equation 50% weight is assigned to the cost and 50% to the other criteria items. However, in this study the software user indicated in the survey form that the cost (on average) is only worth 24% as compared to other criteria items and not 50%. The operational and general system characteristics in the software were given 76%. Thus, a correction factor of 76/24 should be installed in this equation. Having said that, the cost effectiveness ratio calculated for MS-Project and Primavera Project Planner is as follows:

- CER (MS-Project) = 178/3100 × (76/24) = 0.182
- CER (PRIMAVERA) = 197/13485 × (76/24) = 0.046

After performing the cost effectiveness analysis, it can be seen that the results dramatically changed. Taking the cost into consideration, PRIMAVERA no longer is the preferred option. With a cost effectiveness ratio of 0.182, Microsoft project seems to be a better option to select, despite the success of PRIMAVERA in the other technical aspects of the software.

Again examining the detailed information on the cost of each software package, it can be seen that the cause for this huge difference in cost comes mainly from two items. Firstly, the cost of the software licenses itself. One license of PRIMAVERA costs AUS $8000 while MS-Project costs only AUS $1100/license. Secondly, the learning cost. At the time where Primavera provides the course of PRIMAVERA at a cost of AUS $1400/person, Microsoft can give a very reasonable price of AUS $390/person for the learning course in Microsoft project.

The final analysis of the scoring module recommends selecting Microsoft Project since it satisfies all the evaluation criteria items at a higher CER. However, if the cost was not a significant factor in the selection process, Primavera is recommended as it offers better tools and features from a technical point of view. Table 4 below summarizes the results of the evaluation process conducted on both software packages.

**Table 4**. Summary of the evaluation results

| | Software Evaluation criteria | | MS-Project | Primavera P3 |
|---|---|---|---|---|
| | Operational characteristics<br>M = 60% | Range of Y (0 - 3) | Value of Y | Value of Y |
| 1 | Time management | | 2.01 | 2.28 |
| 2 | Resource management | | 1.75 | 2.15 |
| 3 | Cost management | | 1.59 | 2.12 |
| 4 | Reporting | | 1.56 | 1.63 |
| 5 | Control and monitoring | | 1.82 | 1.63 |
| | Value of A (operational) | Range (100 - 300) | 178 points | 209 points |
| | General system characteristics<br>n ? 40% | | | |
| 1 | Documentation | | 1.74 | 1.91 |
| 2 | Compatibility | | 1.67 | 1.43 |
| 3 | Security | | 1.35 | 1.91 |
| 4 | Technical support | | 1.78 | 1.96 |
| 5 | User friendliness | | 1.97 | 1.84 |
| | Value of B (general system) | Range (100 - 300) | 179 points | 181 points |
| | Value of C (total weighted score) | Range (100 - 300) | 178 points | 198 points |
| | Efficiency E % | | 59 | 66 |
| | Total cost AUS $/license | | 3100 | 13485 |
| | Cost effectiveness ratio CER | | 0.182 | 0.046 |

## CONCLUSIONS

On the evaluation of Microsoft Project, the application of an evaluation module on this software was successful. The evaluation results of Microsoft Project, according to the scoring module, indicate the following:

- The software achieves an acceptable level of quality in terms of the operational and general system characteristics, the best performance of the software in the operational characteristics was found to be in the time management attributes, particularly in relation to setting up the project plan and identifying activities and relationships. This was totally consistent with the user requirements in time management attributes, giving the soft- ware package a big advantage. The software also performed well in relation to control and monitoring, which was also important to the software user.
- The worst results for Microsoft Project in the operational characteristics were in reporting attributes. Microsoft Project scored under two points in all these attributes. This result is not totally unexpected, since a practical examination of the reporting tools in the software will reveal that MS-Project has a very limited reporting capability. Indeed the reports available are very few, and there is a very limited ability for report customization and generation.
- Microsoft Project achieved prominent success with the user friendliness characteristics. The user needs were a relatively short time in which to learn the basic functions of the software. In addition to that, the software has a very well organized menu structure and commands.
- In terms of general systems characteristics, the weak point in the software was the security tool. The soft-

ware performance was only average in providing security for project files and baseline plans.

- The software user survey indicates that Microsoft Project remains the most popular and commonly used PMSP among the software packages in the market. Around 80% of the selected sample indicated that they use MS-Project in project planning and management.
- Although MS-Project does not provide sophisticated tools and advanced control features like PRIMAVERA, the results of the scoring module recommend the selection of this package. It satisfies the user's requirements in terms of operational and general system characteristics combined with very low cost.

On the evaluation of Primavera Software, the evaluation results of Primavera according to the scoring module indicate the following:

- With an overall efficiency of 66%, the software achieved an acceptable level of quality. Moreover, in terms of operational and general system characteristics, PRIMAVERA was found to be much better than Microsoft Project. In the attributes of time management, only setting up the project plan was better in Microsoft Project, while PRIMAVERA scored higher points in defining activities and relationships, network calculations and net- work graphics.
- PRIMAVERA's other advantage over MS-Project was in resource management. In all the attributes of this group, PRIMAVERA performed much better than MS-Project, especially in relation to resource allocation and leveling,
- In the general system characteristics of the software, PRIMAVERA achieved acceptable results in all the attributes of this group. The best performance for PRIMAVERA was found in the technical support attributes, especially in terms of technical services and training courses on the software use and applications.
- Only in terms of compatibility did PRIMAVERA score less than MS-Project This was because the latter being a Microsoft product, is more compatible with other Microsoft applications (Word, Excel, Access, etc.).
- Despite the fact that PRIMAVERA is better than MS-Project in terms of both the operational and general system characteristics. It is not the most suitable PMSP to be selected according to the scoring module. The cost of the software package influences this outcome. While MS-Project is offered in a reasonable price of AUS $3100/license, PRIMAVERA is much more expensive (cost AUS SI3485/license). This places PRIMAVERA with a CER of 0.046 in a weak position against other PMSP available in the marketplace.

Generally speaking, this investigation revealed that the software user most of the time is not concerned with the most sophisticated PMSP, or the package that has more advanced tools and features. What is more important for the user is their need to produce simple time charts, simple resource and cost analysis and basic reports. However, it was found that large project management organizations are conducting professional project management that require the use of sophisticated project management software packages, which offers a variety of tools and capabilities, and thus, the cost were irrelevant to them. On the other hand, a small organization is only concerned with the basic tools and capabilities of the software and thus, the cost of the software package is highly significant to them.

In addition to the technical aspects of the software package, it has to be user friendly and compatible with other Microsoft Office applications. If this was achieved, then the software is considered highly efficient. How- ever, this is only one part of the equation; the other part of the equation will be the cost, which is not less important than the other aspects. A reasonable price, in addition to the needs mentioned would make the chosen soft- ware the best alternative.

Hani Gharaibeh Finally, the results of the scoring module revealed that PRIMAVERA is ahead of MS-Project by 20 points in terms of operational and general system characteristics. However, a comparison between the two packages, incorporating the cost, will make MS-Project a better alternative. The question remaining then is whether an additional 20 points, or an increase of 7% in efficiency of the software, is equivalent to the huge difference in cost.

## REFERENCES


1. Suhanic, G. (2001) Computer-Aided Project Management. Oxford University Press, New York.
2. Gido, J. and Clements, J.P. (1999) Successful Project Management. South Western Hill, Berkeley.
3. Levine, H. (1986) Project Management Using Microcomputers. Osborne McGraw, New York City.
4. Connell, J. and Shafer, L. (1987) The Professional User's Guide to Software Evaluation. Wiley Publishing, Inc., Indianapolis.
5. Law, D. (1993) Evaluating Methods and Tools in Software Quality Management, 17. American Elsevier Publishing Company, Inc., New York.
6. ISO/IEC DIS 14589-1 (1996) Information Technology-Software Product Evaluation. NY, USA.
7. Busha, C.H. and Harter, S.P. (1980) Research Methods in Librarianship: Techniques and Interpretations. Academic Press Inc., Orlando.
8. Mangonie, T.W. (1995) Mail Surveys: Improving the Quality. Sage Publication, Nostrard Reintold Company, New York, 129.
9. Shtub, A. and Brand, J.F. (1994) Project Management, Engineering Technology and Implementation. Prentice Hall Inc., Upper Saddle River.

CHAPTER 14

# ONTOLOGIES FOR SOFTWARE PROJECT MANAGEMENT: A REVIEW

Panos Fitsilis, Vassilis Gerogiannis, Leonidas Anthopoulos

Business Administration Department, Technological Educational Institute of Thessaly, Larissa, Greece

## ABSTRACT

**Software Project Management is a knowledge intensive process that can benefit substantially from ontology development and ontology engineering. Ontology development could facilitate or improve substantially the software development process through the improvement of knowledge management, the increase of software and artefacts reusability, and the establishment of internal consistency within project management processes of various phases of software life cycle. A large number of ontologies have been developed attempting to address various software engineering aspects, such as requirements engineering, components reuse, domain modelling, etc. In this paper, we present a systematic literature review focusing on software project management ontologies. The literature review, among other, has identified lack of standardization in terminology and concepts, lack of systematic domain modelling and use of ontologies mainly in prototype ontology systems that address rather limited aspects of software project management processes.**

## INTRODUCTION

Project Management (PM) is widely accepted today as an important management tool in business development and business success. In this context, a large number of PM frameworks, methodologies and approaches have been developed over the past few decades. Among the most popular are the "Project Management Body of Knowledge" (PMBOK) from Project Management Institute [1] , the "IPMA Competence Baseline" (ICB) from International Project Management Association [2] and the "Projects IN a Controlled Environment" (PRINCE2) from the Office of Government Commerce in UK [3] .

Similarly in the area of software engineering, the goal is to find repeatable processes that improve both productivity and quality. For this reason, a large number of software process models have been developed, namely Waterfall, Prototyping, RAD (Rapid Application Development), Incremental, Spiral, UP (Unified Process) XP (Extreme Programming), Scrum, etc. [4] attempting to address the optimal way to develop software based on the specialties of each problem domain and the characteristics of each software development paradigm. Even though software project management attracted significant attention from both industry and academia, a great number of projects still fail to meet their requirements in terms of time delays, cost overrun and quality restrictions. These failures are attributed to the facts that software projects are complex

**Citation:** Fitsilis, P. , Gerogiannis, V. and Anthopoulos, L. (2014) Ontologies for Software Project Management: A Review.Journal of Software Engineering and Applications, 7, 1096-1110. doi: 10.4236/jsea.2014.713097.

undertakings, relying heavily on human knowledge and human interaction. Many studies on various types of software projects have proven that their outcomes are far from the complete fulfilment of the initial requirements [5] [6] .

Srikantaiah et al. [7] argued on the need of convergence of project management and knowledge management subject areas since knowledge management is becoming a very important element for project success and organizational performance. In order to achieve project knowledge management and knowledge reuse, several enabling activities and alternative approaches should be considered. One of these approaches is considered to be ontological engineering.

Gruber [8] defined ontology as the formal specification of a shared conceptualization. Ontologies allow the specification of concepts with attributes of a specific type. Concepts can be organized in a hierarchy (using the specialization relationship between two concepts). A general review regarding ontological engineering foundations and a survey of most well-known ontologies can be found in [9] . An illustration of the relationship between ontological engineering and other disciplines (software engineering and object oriented software development, in particular) is given in [10] . The most prominent and standardized ontology languages is OWL 2 [11] and among the development tools, Protégé ontology development tool has been widely used in many cases.

Ontology development in the field of project management and software engineering could benefit substantially the software development process through the improvement of knowledge management process, the increase of software and artefacts reusability, and the establishment of internal consistency within project management processes, to be used for specialized purposes in various phases of the software life cycle.

Considering the large number of ontologies developed, ranging from generic ontologies to domain and application specific ontologies and the lack of taxonomy and standardization, it is quite difficult for the researchers and the practitioners to evaluate and use these ontologies in a successful way and to develop further the concepts, the methodologies and the tools needed for applying the ontological paradigm to real life projects.

This is the problem that this survey is attempting to address: to present in a systematic way the available in the literature ontologies addressing project management, as well as ontologies modelling specific software development lifecycles or addressing specific problem areas of software projects from the software project management perspective.

The remainder of the paper is structured as follows. Section 2 provides an overview of project management methodologies and of ontological engineering and defines the context of this survey. Section 3 presents the research methodology and Section 4 introduces the ontologies and offers a classification of them based on various criteria. The final section presents the conclusions and possible future research directions.

## PROJECT MANAGEMENT AND ONTOLOGICAL ENGINEERING

Traditional software development methodologies grew out of a need to control large development projects, and from the difficulties of estimating and managing these efforts to reliably deliver results. These difficulties are inherited in the nature of software and they were identified from the early years of software system development and unfortunately most of them still remain. Most of the scepticism expressed in the legendary book of Frederic Brooks, "the mythical man-month" thirty years ago is still a reality [12] .

Agile methodologies attempt to overcome these obstacles by changing the approach used to develop software and manage projects. Agile software development attempts to put the software being developed first and to acknowledge that the user requirements change, responding quickly to the users' needs, producing frequent and regular, software releases, etc.

The Manifesto for Agile Software Development was released in February 2001 by a group of 17 software process methodologists, who attended a summit meeting to promote a better way of developing software and then formed the Agile Alliance. The Manifesto for Agile Software Development can be found on the Agile Alliance website.

Since then, a number of software development methods subscribed to this approach. The list varies depending on different viewpoints and interpretations, but in general the list in the literature includes Extreme Programming (XP), Scrum, Feature-Driven Development (FDD), Adaptive Software Development (ASD), Crystal Clear Methodology, etc.

Most agile development methods were created within corporations by software process experts as an attempt to improve existing processes. For example, XP was created by Kent Beck during his work on the Chrysler Comprehensive Compensation System payroll project. Kent Beck refined the development method used and the result was published in his book "Extreme Programming Explained" [13] . Similarly, FDD was initially introduced by Jeff De Luca to meet the specific needs of a 15 month, 50 person software development projects at a large Singapore bank in 1997. FDD was influenced by ideas of Peter Coad on object modelling. The description of FDD was first introduced in the book "Java Modelling in Color with UML" by Peter Coad, Eric Lefebvre and Jeff De Luca in 1999 [14] . A more generic description of FDD decoupled from Java can be found in the book "A Practical Guide to Feature-Driven Development" [15] .

On the other end, more conventional methodologies rely heavier on processes, linear development cycles and waterfall like software development life cycles. Along with predictability, they inherited a deterministic, reductionist approach that relied on task breakdown, and was predicated on stability—stable requirements, analysis and stable design. This rigidity was also marked by a tendency towards slavish process "compliance" as a means of project control [16] .

Project Management Body of Knowledge (PMBOK) developed by Project Management Institute is the best representative of this approach [1] . PMBOK formally defines a large set of project processes that describe activities throughout a project's life cycle. These processes are organized into two axes: into five process groups and into nine knowledge areas that will be described briefly in the following section. Within PMBOK each process is described in terms of inputs (documents, plans, design, other data, etc.), outputs (documents, products), tools and techniques (mechanisms that are applied to inputs for producing outputs) and without being too specific provides guidance to someone that wishes to apply the processes [1] .

Similar approaches have been introduced by other international bodies or associations such as International Project Management Association (IPMA) and the Association for Project Management in UK (APM). IPMA defined a Competence Baseline (ICB), which describes the necessary competences for project management. According to IPMA ICB three are the basic capabilities areas:

- contextual (project orientation, objective, portfolio; implementation of plans and portfolio; permanent organization; business; system, product and technology; personnel management; health, safety, security and environment; finance and legality);
- behavioral (leadership, liability and motivation; self-control; self-confidence; relaxation; openness; creativity; outcome orientation; efficiency; consultation; negotiation; conflicts and crisis; reliability, appreciation values, etiquette);
- technical (successful project management; interested parties; project requirements and objectives; risk and opportunity; quality; project organization; teamwork, problem resolution; project structure; scope, area and capability of fulfilment; time and project phases; resources; costs and finance; delivery and contract; changes of management and administration; information and documentation; communication; initialization; termination) [2] .

Software engineering community has recognized quite early, ontologies as a promising way to address current software engineering problems [17] [18] . For example, ontologies are proposed to be used in requirement engineering, software design, software maintenance, software reuse and knowledge management etc. Moreover, software engineering technologies have been proposed and developed for modelling and reasoning with the use of ontologies. These synergies between ontologies and software engineering have also attracted attention of standardization bodies and have some on-going activities.

In order to facilitate the work of researchers and practitioners Happel and Seedorf [18] defined a simple classification scheme that allows a better differentiation among the various software engineering ontologies. They use two dimensions for ordering ontologies. Firstly, according to their position in the Software Engineering life cycle (analysis, design, development, testing, etc.) and, secondly, according to their usage.

Ruiz and Jilera [19] in their survey presented the state of the art with regard to use of ontologies in software engineering and software technology. They offered a taxonomy for software engineering ontologies and they presented representative cases of such ontologies.

On the same topic Zhao et al. [20] classified available ontologies for semantic web based software engineering, and presented the overall picture in this area. According to Zhao, each ontology is characterized by:

- The software process model used (e.g. Waterfall, Incremental, Spiral, Agile, etc.);
- The software development phase (e.g. Requirements Engineering, Design, Implementation, Testing, Maintenance, All);
- The artefact type (e.g. Software Architecture, Code and Document).

In this paper, and according to the taxonomies presented, we utilize Zhao [20] classification to review various software development ontologies presented in the relevant literature, according to the project management approach used, the software process employed, and the software development phase used.

## RESEARCH METHODOLOGY

The aim of this paper is to study software project management ontologies in order to reuse/develop an upper software project management ontology that will be used for automated knowledge extraction from social networks. Having this as the main objective it becomes obvious that existing literature had to be reviewed in order to:

- To better understand the fundamental concepts and the knowledge that constitute the software project management knowledge area;
- To examine and if possible to evaluate software project management ontologies;
- To determine the main application areas of the existing software project management ontologies.

The examined area is quite wide since it refers to the intersection of project management, software engineering, software life cycle processes and knowledge management

In order to achieve these objectives, a systematic literature review, was conducted by the authors. This survey relied on surveying and using secondary sources [21] .

The study consisted of two steps. The first step involved literature search, while the second step was focused on the taxonomy of the works and their critical analysis.

At the first step of the literature search, the authors attempted to locate and retrieve articles focused on ontologies that are related to:

- Project management in general;
- Project management knowledge areas based in PMBOK;
- Project management methodologies (e.g. ICB IPMA, PRINCE);
- Software process models;
- Software life cycle phases.

The study was mainly conducted with the use of Google Scholar, since this tool is indexing texts from all major on-line repositories (e.g. Science direct, IEEE, and ACM). The study examined only books, articles in academic journals/ conferences and grey literature while we excluded industrial white papers and articles on IT professional websites.

Table 1 presents all the terms that were used for this research along with the number of works that satisfied the research queries.

Subsequently, the retrieved articles and materials were systematically and critically analyzed. The inclusion criteria were:

The study should be focused mainly on project management topics;

The presented ontology or system should have a project management perspective;

The study should be focused on software development or software maintenance processes (other studies were excluded).

The set of remaining works is presented in the next sections.

**Table 1**. Search terms

| Search Query in Google Scholar | No. of Results |
|---|---|
| "Project Management Ontology" AND PMBOK | 41 |
| "Project Management Ontology" AND ICB | 11 |
| "Project Management Ontology" AND PRINCE | 8 |
| "Project Management Ontology" AND Agile | 17 |
| "Project Management Ontology" AND Scrum | 3 |
| "Project Management Ontology" AND XP | 4 |
| "Project Management Ontology" AND FDD | 0 |
| "Project Management Ontology" AND CMM | 14 |
| "Project Management Ontology" AND SPEM | 4 |
| "Project Management Ontology" AND (UP OR RUP) | 79 |
| "Project Management Ontology" AND SWEBOK | 7 |
| "Project Management Ontology" excluding the words (-PMBOK -ICB -PRINCE -Agile -Scrum -XP -FDD -CMM -SPEM -UP -RUP -SWEBOK) | 12 |
| "Project Scope Management" AND Ontology | 49 |
| "Project Time Management" AND Ontology | 67 |
| "Project Cost Management" AND Ontology | 60 |
| "Project Quality Management" AND Ontology | 63 |
| "Project Communication Management" AND Ontology | 24 |
| "Project Human Resource Management" AND Ontology | 36 |
| "Project Risk Management" AND Ontology | 367 |
| "Project Procurement Management" AND Ontology | 44 |

## ONTOLOGIES FOCUSING ON PROJECT MANAGEMENT PROCESS

The ontologies presented in this section are focusing on project management models without focusing software projects. A short introduction to the main concepts of each ontology along with possible applications is presented.

PROMONT [22] is a project management ontology developed to model project management specifications. It provides the basis of common vocabulary of terms and methods and thus enables better project management. PROMONT formalizes the typical elements used for project structuring (such as task, milestone, resource or checklist). Further PROMONT defines a set of relationships. The categorization builds on the fact that, just like concepts, relations can be arranged into a "is derived from" hierarchy.

Hughes [23] developed an ontology based on the PRINCE2 project management method [3] . The prototype ontology has been developed in OWL as a collection of axioms and using the Protégé 4 ontology editor. The produced ontology is used in checking the compliance of suppliers stated methods with standards. However, it presents difficulties for domain experts as its reasoning rules can be counter-intuitive.

Sheeba et al. [24] presented an ontology to be used for the automatic classification of learning materials according to PMBOK structure of knowledge. This facilitates the search for learning materials within the given domain. The Rational Unified Process (RUP) was used to define axioms describing the relationships between the main concepts.

Bodea et al. [25] developed SinPers system which is a web based personalized e-learning system focused on project management. The learning material that was used was structured with the development of an ontology that modelled International Project Management Association Competence Baseline (ICB) [2] . The ontology developed in SinPers contained 200 concepts, 406 competences, 366 learning objects, and various relationships.

Ruiz-Bertol et al. [26] used OWL and SWRL languages for defining the PM ontologies and rules, respectively. They presented an example of different types of rules that can be applied on this specific ontology. In this way, they demonstrate how further knowledge can be derived and, thus, decision-making for managing projects can be improved.

Aramo-Immonen [27] explored project management by providing a PM ontology for managers. This ontology is a classification of management disciplines for project managers. The objective of this study is to help system integrators to manage the evolution of projects during their life-cycles in terms of this ontology. The disciplines defined in this ontology are project integration management, project scope management, project time management.

Dong et al. [28] proposed an ontology for a real-time project monitoring system (ORPSM). Their objective was to resolve the ambiguity issue in project monitoring processes produced by a number of factors. This ontology is part of a framework that incorporates a series of ontologies for knowledge management and term disambiguation by focusing on project monitoring processes, and a number of metrics for assisting management of project organizations to monitor projects.

Wong et al. [29] presented in their paper "Developing PMIS for Business Projects Based on Social Science Research Findings and Ontology Modelling" a model, to be used as a reference, to guide the business project management practice in order to increase chances of project success. Its representation as the Business Project Management (BProjM) ontology and expedites the injection of this new domain knowledge into a software solution. The ontology has been defined in Unified Modelling Language (UML); and provides an example of how the resulting model can be used as the foundation to support the development of an integrated Project Management Information System (PMIS) for business projects.

Further, a number of PM ontologies have been developed focusing on specialized PM subject areas.

For example, Project Metrics Ontology (PMO) was an ontology originally developed by BBN Technologies/Verizon in 2002 and is not meant to cover all typical project management issues. Instead of this, it focuses on providing an ontology that represents metrics for a specific project. This allows for example to perform performance measurements of specific projects or sub-projects.

IT-CODE is an ontology that was defined to describe the project team of a building project within the IC- CODE project itself. This ontology focuses on providing typical project management classes such as "Task", "Actor", "Project" or "Activity". It contains 32 different classes and an additional set of 26 properties [30] .

The OZONE ontology [31] is an ontology that focuses on task scheduling. It provides a generic perspective for building scheduling systems and was used for configuring constraint-based scheduling systems. In OZONE, scheduling is defined as a process for feasibly synchronizing the use of RESOURCES by ACTIVITIES to satisfy DEMANDS over time.

Similarly, Rajpathak et al. [32] developed a generic task ontology again focusing on scheduling. It is referred as a "task ontology" for emphasizing that it describes the class of scheduling tasks, independently of the various ways by which these tasks can be solved. Further, it takes into account cost related issues.

On the subject area of human resource management, personnel selection, competence management, etc. are common issues addressed by Human Resource Ontologies. Mochol, Oldakowski and Heese [33] have developed a Human Resource Ontology to support the Recruitment Process. This HR-ontology is mainly based on the German version of the HR-XML standard developed by the HR-XML Consortium. HR-XML is a library of more than 75 interdependent XML schemes which define data components for various HR transactions, as well as options and constraints governing the use of these components. The ontology was adapted so the Industry sub-ontology to use both the German Classification of the Industry Sector (WZ2003) and the North American Industry Classification System (NAICS). For the occupational classification the German Occupation Codes (BKZ) are used along the Standard Occupational Classification (SOC) System.

Dorn et al. [34] developed an ontology containing concepts of HRM for two different projects: a meta-search engine for job searching in job portals and for a university competence management system. In their paper, they presented the requirements derived from these two projects and they describe the design of the ontology. This ontology is characterized by its integration of job descriptions, concepts for evaluating competencies on different levels and evidences for competencies. The definition is also aligned to HR-XML for the definition of competence profiles.

Schmidt and Kunzmann [35] [36] describe an ontology that integrates concepts from skill management and learning. Their approach is similar to Dorn et al. [34] , however, they do not consider job descriptions composed of required competencies. In the same paper a holistic view of the organization and of the HR problem area is presented showing how the ontology is covering different organizational aspects.

Gómez-Pérez et al. developed an ontology for HR based on standards [37] . More specifically, they developed SEEMP ontology as a common "language" as a controlled vocabulary in order to describe the details of a job posting and the CV of a job seeker. SEEMP Ontology is composed of thirteen sub-ontologies: Competence, Compensation, Driving License, Economic Activity, Education, Geography, Job Offer, Job Seeker, Labor Regulatory, Language, Occupation, Skill and Time.

Peng and Nunes [38] systematically analyzed research works and proposed a total of 40 ERP post-implementation risks related to diverse operational, analytical, organization-wide and technical aspects. A risk ontology was subsequently established to highlight these ERP risks, as well as to present their potential causal relationships. An overview of the project management ontologies, their focus and their application is presented in Table 2.

**Table 2**. Project management related ontologies

| Authors/Ontology Name | Main Focus | Applications |
|---|---|---|
| Abels et al. [22] /PRO-MONT | Project Management | Knowledge management in virtual organizations. Promote common understanding between virtual teams. |
| Hughes [23] /Prinny | Prince Project Management Methodology | Used for checking the compliance of suppliers stated methods with standards and supporting process model tailoring. |
| Sheeba et al. [24] | PMBOK | Used for automatic classification of learning materials to the Project Management knowledge area domain. |
| Bodea et al. [25] /SinPers system | IPMA ICB | Used within a web based personalized e-learning system focused on project management for the classification of the learning material. |
| Ruiz-Bertol et al. [26] | General approach of Project management | Demonstrated how knowledge can be derived in order to support project management decision process. |
| Aramo-Immonen [27] | Mainly on PMBOK | Offers a classification of project management concepts. |
| Dong et al. [28] | General approach of Project management | To be used for knowledge capture, storage, sharing and term disambiguation in project monitoring processes. |
| Wong et al. [29] /Business Project Management (BProjM) ontology | General approach of Project management | Reference for development of an integrated Project Management Information System (PMIS). |
| BBN Technologies-Verizon/ Project Metrics Ontology (PMO) | General approach of Project management | The ontology represents project metrics in order to perform project performance measurements. |
| Smith and Becker/OZONE [31] | Scheduling problem domain | The OZONE ontology is focusing on scheduling problems and can be apply from manufacturing production scheduling, project planning and it mainly concerned in modelling scheduling problem domain. |
| Rajpathak et al. [32] | Scheduling problem domain | The task ontology can now be used as a knowledge capturing tool in various domains for increasing reusability. The given ontological framework provides a fairly fine-grained structure that is needed to build the scheduling systems. |
| Mochol and Oldakowski [33] | Human Resource Management/ Recruitment process | To be used for the development of a recruitment platform. |
| Dorn et al. [24] | Human Resource Management | To be used for a meta-search engine for searching for jobs in job portals and for a university competence management system. |
| Schmidt and Kunzmann [35] [36] | Human Resource Management/ Skill management | The ontology is used for competency management and knowledge management. |
| Gómez-Pérez et al. [37] / SEEMP | Human Resource Management/ Recruitment | SEEMP is a reference ontology to be used for modelling job offers and curriculum data. |
| Peng and Nunes [38] /Repo | Risk Management for post implementation of ERP Systems | The risk ontology can be used as a systematic tool and checklist for risk identification, assessment and management, as well as for strategic planning and decision-making. |

## ONTOLOGIES FOCUSING ON SOFTWARE PROCESS MODELS

A software process ontology [20] defines software activities, phases, and process models. Each phase is specified by a sequence of activities, each process model is described by process phases and each activity is associated with the artefacts it produces. Generally, a software project regardless its size and type, follows a Software Development Life Cycle (SDLC). In this section, we will discuss ontologies that are coupled with specific SDLC, such as Scrum, RUP, etc. In the next paragraphs ontologies based on SDLCs are presented.

Lin et al. [39] developed an ontology, named K-CRIO that allows the description of a specific kind of business processes: those that are dedicated to the design of a product. K-CRIO ontology describes the key concepts and relationships of software development process and it illustrates the use of the ontology by taking the example of the Scrum development process.

Santana [40] attempted to model Scrum [41] software methodology in OntoSCRUM ontology. The main purpose according to the author for this ontology was to reuse project artefacts and to share tacit knowledge within organizations and project teams.

Zualkernan [42] presented an ontology for Generating Assessments for the Scrum Process. The motive is to create assessments for a correct understanding of a process that can be used in a software development company.

Similarly Valaski et al. in [43] developed an ontology so called OntoRUP having as purpose to classify the learning material in software engineering. For this purpose they combined Software Engineering Body of Knowledge (SWEBOK) [44] and the Rational Unified Process (RUP) [45] . SWEBOK was used to define the structure of the software engineering knowledge area, while RUP was used for defining the axioms that represent relationships between concepts and to enable the reasoning to SWEBOK knowledge areas.

An alternative proposal for software process ontologies was made by Parson [46] , who designed an ontology based on an analysis of a number of commonly used agile methods like Scrum [41] , XP [13] , FDD [14] , etc. Parson took seven agile methods and attempted to summarize their terminology, and built an initial ontology of agile methods that attempts to encompass the various characteristics of commonly used methods. On this sense, his work can be considered as a generic ontology for agile process. Advancing on his research, Parsons [47] deals with Aspect Oriented Software development and agile methods integration. The author proposed an ontology enabled development based on an analysis of existing ontologies of aspect oriented programming, a proposed ontology of agile methods, and a derived ontology of agile aspect oriented development.

Ceravolo et al. [48] defined Extreme Programming Ontology (XPO), a formal model that describes the concepts of Extreme Programming (XP) methodology [13]. XPO is based on a set of core components modelling three main concepts: Organizational Role, Product and Phase. XPO can be used for indexing relevant documents, XP artefacts and Wiki pages, in order to mine and analyze agile processes, programmers' activity and repositories content.

Siddiqui and Alam [49] developed an ontology for Feature Driven Development (FDD) life cycle that can be used for application model development to feature design and implementation. Features are precisely defined in the OWL-based domain model. Transition from OWL based domain model to feature list is directly defined in transformation rules.

Capability Maturity Model Integration (CMMI) is a process reference model that was developed by the Software Engineering Institute (SEI) of Carnegie Mellon University. CMMI addresses the development and maintenance activities applied to both products and services. This model could be used for improving processes, and measuring the capability of a process or the maturity of an organization. CMMI components (including a model, its training materials, and appraisal related documents) are designed to meet the needs of some specific areas of interest, which is called constellation. There are three constellations as supported by the framework: CMMI for Development [50] , CMMI for Services, and CMMI for Acquisition.

There are only a few studies on CMMI ontology in the literature. Soydan and Kokar [51] developed an ontology of the capability maturity model, the staged representation CMMI-SW (focusing on Software Engineering). The ontology has been developed in OWL-DL. The ontology includes 309 classes and 4 kinds of properties (consistsOf, satisfiedBy, achievedBy and subClassOf).

Similarly, Sharifloo et al. [52] introduced an ontology for CMMI for Acquisition based on SUMO [53] upper ontology.

Gazel et al. [54] presented an ontology-based software process assessment tool which was developed to support data collection phase of process assessment and to track conformance of software processes to CMMI as the process reference model.

Using on the work of Soydan et al. [51] , Rungratri and Usanavasin [55] developed Project Assets Ontology (PAO), an ontology which merges CMMI process areas and project assets. PAO was developed in the context of a framework called "CMMI v.1.2 based Gap Analysis Assistant Framework (CMMI-GAAF)" that has a primary objective the automatic gap analysis with respect to CMMI.

Lee et al. [56] [57] developed an ontology-based intelligent decision support agent (OIDSA) for project monitoring and control of capability maturity model integration (CMMI). Liao et al. [58] aimed to create generic Software Process Ontology (SPO) and strived to ensure that it covered the requirements of both CMMI and ISO/IEC 15504 [59] . A process was represented by atomic practices and to that end; an organization's process model could be represented by using SPO.

Líška and Navrat [60] presented an approach that uses Software Process Meta-Model (SPEM) [61] for improvements that are rooted in knowledge engineering approaches. They show how SPEM can be used in the Semantic Web technical space by developing a SPEM ontology. Consequently, they use this SPEM ontology for project plan generation and verification

Falbo and Bertollo [62] based on the idea of standard software processes, created the Software Process Ontology -SPO. This ontology evolved over the last years, with help of a Foundational ontology (UFO, unified foundational ontology).

In addition, Falbo et al. [63] evolved all these artefacts and created what he called Ontology Language Patterns for Software Process (OLP-SP). The idea lying behind was to define pieces of software process ontologies that can be reused by other ontologies. This ontology is shown to be expressive enough to be used as a common ground for mapping the software process fragments of standards such as ISO/ IEC 12207-ISO 9001:2000-ISO/IEC 15504, CMMI, RUP and SPEM.

In [64] an ontology model of software engineering to represent the knowledge needed in software development is presented. They have analyzed the characteristics of software engineering ontology and defined graphical notations of modelling software engineering ontology as an alternative formalism.

Klieber et al. [65] introduced an ontology to automatically support the software documentation process. Therefore, they introduced a software documentation ontology that is populated automatically through analyzing source code, documentation and code executions and made accessible to developers via a wiki.

Guizzardi et al. [66] presented the latest developments in the UFO foundational ontology. In particular, they presented new versions of two fragments of UFO, namely UFO-B (concerned with events) and UFO-C (dealing with social and intentional concepts).

Sarantis and Askounis [67] developed a project management ontology as a reference for e-Government projects. Their model enables knowledge reuse, collaboration and interoperability between all stakeholders related with the implementation of such type of projects. On the same topic, Magoulas et al. [68] developed a quality ontology that formalizes all the needed knowledge for the realization of a multi-perspective and adaptive evaluation of e-government services.

ICONS project [69] , even though it was a research project, developed a Structural Fund Project Knowledge Portal for managing projects of European Commission Structural Funds that included a domain ontology. This Domain Ontology provides the conceptual foundation for all knowledge management applications, mainly PM related, and included the Concept Glossary, which defined the Structural Fund domain ontology. Moreover, this ontology provided support for both expert and non-expert use of the underlying knowledge representations and knowledge management services, as well as support for the automatic inference engine helping users find and merge information.

Mendes and Abran [70] presented a prototype of an ontology, which is able to represent the domain of Software Engineering, based on the SWEBOK guide. A literal extraction from the guide results in approximately 4000 concepts.

Sicilia et al. [71] also proposes a SWEBOK based ontology with a descriptive part in order to identify artefacts and activities and prescriptive part, with approaches and concrete activities' rules for "commonly accepted" practical activities.

Hilera et al. [72] proposed an ontology called OntoGLOSE based on the Software Engineering Terminology Glossary, published by IEEE. OntoGLOSE includes about 1500 concepts, corresponding to 1300 glossary terms with their different meanings.

**Table 3**. Ontologies focusing on software process models

| Authors/Ontology Name | Focus | Main Application |
|---|---|---|
| Santana [40] /Onto-SCRUM | SCRUM | To reuse project artifacts and to share tacit knowledge within organizations and project teams. |
| Zualkernan [42] | SCRUM | To create assessments for a correct understanding of a process that can be used in a software development company. |
| Valaski et al. [43] | RUP, SWEBOK | To classify the learning material in software engineering. |
| Parson [46] [47] | SCRUM, XP, FDD, etc. | To summarize the terminology of agile software development methodologies terminology, and built an initial ontology of agile methods that attempts to encompass the various characteristics of commonly used methods. |
| Ceravolo et al. [48] defined Extreme Programming Ontology (XPO) | XP | For analysis and mining of agile processes in order to identify critical factors in agile software development. |
| Siddiqui and Alam [49] | FDD | The ontology will be used for semantic web application, for feature design and implementation. |
| Soydan and Kokar [51] | CMMI-SW | Modelling CMMI-SW. |
| Gazel et al. [54] | CMMI | The ontology was used to support the data collection phase of process assessment and to track conformance of software processes to CMMI as the process reference model. |

| | | |
|---|---|---|
| Rungratri and Us-anavasin [55] /Project Assets Ontology (PAO) | CMMI | To develop a framework called "CMMI v.1.2 based Gap Analysis Assistant Framework (CMMI-GAAF)" that has a primary objective the automatic gap analysis with respect to CMMI. |
| Lee and Chen [56] / OIDSA | CMMI | To be used for intelligent decision support for project monitoring and control of capability maturity model integration. |
| Liao et al. [58] | CMMI, ISO/IEC 15504 | To represent a process model. |
| Sharifloo et al. [52] | CMMI for Acquisition | To be used for an application that evaluates the maturity level of an organization and offers recommendations. |
| Lin et al. [75] | CMMI, IEEE/EAI 12207 | To develop a model that integrates concepts from both standards. |
| Líška and Navrat [60] | SPEM | Demonstration on how SPEM can be used for project planning. |
| Falbo and Bertollo [62] | Standard software processes | A model for helping software development organizations to use standards in their software process improvement efforts. |
| Falbo et al. [63] /OLP-SP | Standard software processes | An ontology that can be reused from other ontologies. |
| Mendes and Abran [70] | SWBOK | For modelling software engineering discipline. |
| Sicilia et al. [71] /Onto-SWEBOK | SWBOK | To be used as review tool for SWBOK itself. |
| Klieber et al. [65] | Expert Location | To be used for knowledge discovery within "KnowMiner" framework with the primary goal to ease usage for non-knowledge discovery experts. |
| Sarantis and Askounis [67] | E-Government | To be used for e-Government projects to enable knowledge reuse, collaboration and interoperability between stakeholders. |
| Magoulas et al. [68] | Quality Management | A quality ontology to be used for the evaluation of e-government services. |
| ICONS Project [69] | Project Knowledge | To be used in a Structural Fund Project Knowledge Portal for managing projects of European Commission Structural Funds. |
| Hilera et al. [72] /Onto-GLOSE | Document Annotation | OntoGloss ontology is used for a document annotation tool that uses pre-defined concepts in ontology to mark?up a document with software engineering terms. |
| Ruiz et al. [74] | Software maintenance projects | The ontology is part of MANTIS software engineering environment having as objective to reuse information, knowledge and expertise generated during the maintenance of software projects. |
| García et al. [76] | Software measurement | For standardizing the software measurement terminology. |
| Girardi and Faria [77] / GRAMO | Requirements management, domain modelling | Used from ONTODUM for domain engineering. |
| Settas and Stamelos [73] /PROMAISE | Software antipatterns | Used for software project managers to select antipatterns. |
| González-Pérez and Henderson-Sellers [78] | Software Development | An ontology for software development methodology that include a metamodel and an architecture. |
| Lin et al. [39] /K-CRIO | Process management | K-CRIO is an ontology of organizations for their understanding, analysis and also enables reasoning. The K-CRIO ontology is illustrated by an example of a software development organization that follows the waterfall process. |
| Fable et al. [79] /ODE | Software Development | To be used in an ontology based software development. |

Settas and Stamelos [73] developed a Software Project Management Antipattern Intelligent System (PROMAISE) that uses antipattern ontologies in order to provide intelligent and up to date advice to software project managers regarding the selection appropriate antipatterns in a software project.

Beyond the above, the literature contains a large number of ontologies can be found for various engineering aspects such as metrics, software maintenance, software quality, various software processes, specialized subjects or sectors, etc. [74] -[78] . However, these ontologies are not focused on project management and as such they are not included in this paper. An overview of the ontologies focusing on software process models is presented in Table 3.

## CONCLUSIONS

This paper confirmed that a large number of ontologies in the areas of software project management and of software engineering have been developed. The authors performed a systematic literature review and they focused on ontologies that address the project management process or on ontologies that enable Ontology-Enabled Development (ontologies are used as a support tool for developers). Further, even though in the case software project management lower level processes have been examined (e.g. project time management and project cost management), we have selected to examine only generic software engineering ontologies addressing well established and well known software engineering processes (e.g. RUP and CMMI) or practices (e.g. XP and Scrum). This choice was made since a very large number of ontologies have been developed to address software engineering specific subdomain (e.g. requirements management, analysis and design). In many cases, there are overlaps making it extremely difficult for the research to categorize ontologies in disjoint categories.

This systematic research has illustrated that the most important issue in ontology usage in the area of software project management is standardization. The large number of project management methodologies and of software process models creates an extremely difficult environment to comprehend and to use. The reasons that contribute to this complexity are the existence of various overlapping standards both in the areas of project management and in the areas of software engineering. Quite commonly ontologies based on SWEBOK or PMI include hundreds of concepts and terms. Further, the large number of available software process models makes knowledge sharing difficult. Secondly, in many cases studied ontologies are experimental which implies that they have not been used in real cases or they do not cover all subject areas of PM or all phases of software process.

From this study, it was made clear that a reference ontology in the subject area of software project management is missing. This ontology should be developed from an international and well established organization in order to increase the likelihood of increased adoption and of usage in real life cases.

## ACKNOWLEDGEMENTS

Panos Fitsilis, Vassilis Gerogiannis, Leonidas Anthopoulos (European Social Fund) and Greek national funds through the Operational Program "Education and Lifelong Learning" of the National Strategic Reference Framework. In particular, the research work has been financed by the R & D project "ONSOCIAL" which take place in the context of the "ARCHIMEDES III" National Research Programme.

## REFERENCES

1. Rose, K.H. (2013) A Guide to the Project Management Body of Knowledge (PMBOK® Guide)—Fifth Edition. Project Management Journal, 44, e1.http://dx.doi.org/10.1002/pmj.21345
2. International Project Management Association (2006) ICB-IPMA Competence Baseline Version 3.0. International Project Management Association, Nijkerk.
3. Office of Government Commerce (2009) Directing Successful Projects with PRINCE2. The Stationery Office, Norwich.
4. Sommerville, I. (2004) Software Engineering. International Computer Science Series.
5. Standish Group (2009) Chaos Summary 2009: The 10 Laws of CHAOS.http://www.portal.state.pa.us/portal/server.pt/document/690719/chaos_summary_2009_pdf
6. Charette, R.N. (2005) Why Software Fails [Software Failure]. IEEE Spectrum, 42, 42-49.http://dx.doi.org/10.1109/MSPEC.2005.1502528
7. Srikantaiah, T., Srikantaiah, T.K., Koenig, M.E. and Al-Hawamdeh, S., Eds. (2010) Convergence of Project Management and Knowledge Management. Scarecrow Press, Plymouth.
8. Gruber, T.R. (1995) Toward Principles for the Design of Ontologies Used for Knowledge Sharing? International Journal of Human-Computer Studies, 43, 907-928.http://dx.doi.org/10.1006/ijhc.1995.1081
9. Suárez-Figueroa, M.C., García-Castro, R., Villazón-Terrazas, B. and Gómez-Pérez, A. (2011) Essentials in Ontology Engineering: Methodologies, Languages, and Tools. CIB Conference W078-W012—2nd Workshop on EEB Data Models, Sophia Antipolis, 26-28 October 2011, 9-21.
10. Devedzić, V. (2002) Understanding Ontological Engineering. Communications of the ACM, 45, 136-144. http://dx.doi.org/10.1145/505248.506002
11. Motik, B., Patel-Schneider, P. and Parsia, B. (2009) OWL 2 Web Ontology Language: Structural Specification and Functional-Style Syntax. World Wide Web Consortium. W3C Candidate Recommendation. http://www.w3.org/TR/2009/CR-owl2-syntax-20090611
12. Brooks Jr., F.P. (1995) The Mythical Man-Month, Anniversary Edition: Essays on Software Engineering. Pearson Education, Upper Saddle River.
13. Beck, K. (2001) Planning Extreme Programming. Addison-Wesley Professional, Boston.
14. Coad, P., Luca, J.D. and Lefebvre, E. (1999) Java Modeling Color with Uml: Enterprise Components and Process with Cdrom. Prentice Hall PTR, Upper Saddle River.
15. Carmichael, A. and Haywood, D. (2002) Better Software Faster. Prentice Hall Professional Technical Reference.

16. Augustine, S., Payne, B., Sencindiver, F. and Woodcock, S. (2005) Agile Project Management: Steering from the Edges. Communications of the ACM, 48, 85-89.http://dx.doi.org/10.1145/1101779.1101781

17. Gašević, D., Kaviani, N. and Milanović, M. (2009) Ontologies and Software Engineering. In: Staab, S. and Studer, R., Eds., Handbook on Ontologies, Springer, Berlin, 593-615.http://dx.doi.org/10.1007/978-3-540-92673-3_27

18. Happel, H.J. and Seedorf, S. (2006) Applications of Ontologies in Software Engineering. Proceedings of Workshop on Sematic Web Enabled Software Engineering (SWESE) on the ISWC, Athens, 6 November 2006, 5-9.

19. Ruiz, F. and Hilera, J.R. (2006) Using Ontologies in Software Engineering and Technology. In: Calero, C., Ruiz, F. and Piattini, M., Eds., Ontologies for Software Engineering and Software Technology, Springer, Berlin, 49-102. http://dx.doi.org/10.1007/3-540-34518-3_2

20. Zhao, Y., Dong, J. and Peng, T. (2009) Ontology Classification for Semantic-Web-Based Software Engineering. IEEE Transactions on Services Computing, 2, 303-317.http://dx.doi.org/10.1109/TSC.2009.20

21. Saunders, M.N., Saunders, M., Lewis, P. and Thornhill, A. (2011) Research Methods for Business Students. 5th Edition, Pearson Education, Essex.

22. Abels, S., Ahlemann, F., Hahn, A., Hausmann, K. and Strickmann, J. (2006) PROMONT—A Project Management Ontology as a Reference for Virtual Project Organizations. In: On the Move to Meaningful Internet Systems 2006: OTM 2006 Workshops, Springer, Berlin, 813-823.

23. Hughes, R.T. (2010) Project Management Process Ontologies: A Proof of Concept. Proceedings of the 15th Annual Conference of UK Academy for Information Systems, Oxford, 23-24 March 2010.

24. Sheeba, T., Krishnan, R. and Justin Bernard, M. (2012) An Ontology in Project Management Knowledge Domain. International Journal of Computer Applications, 56, 1-7. http://dx.doi.org/10.5120/8884-2881

25. Bodea, C., Trandafir, I. and Borozan, A.M. (2008) Assessment of Project Management Knowledge Using Semantic Networks in the SinPers System. Proceedings of the 22nd IPMA World Congress on Project Management, Rome, 9-11 November 2008, 1314-1319.

26. Ruiz-Bertol, F.J., Rodríguez, D. and Dolado, J. (2011) Applying Rules to an Ontology for Project Management. Proceedings of the 16th Spanish Conference on Software Engineering and Databases, Coruña, 5-7 September 2011, 5-7.

27. Aramo-Immonen, H. (2009) Project Management Ontology—The Organizational Learning Perspective. Tampereen teknillinen yliopisto, Julkaisu-Tampere University of Technology, Tampere, 836.

28. Dong, H., Hussain, F.K. and Chang, E. (2011) ORPMS: An Ontology-Based Real-Time Project Monitoring System in the Cloud. Journal of Universal Computer Science, 17, 1161-1182.

29. Wong, S.M., Lafaye, J.Y. and Boursier, P. (2010) Developing PMIS for Business Projects Based on Social Science Research Findings and Ontology Modelling. Proceedings of the International Conference on Information Systems (IADIS'10), Porto, 18-20 March 2010, 283-291.

30. Lai, Y.C., Christiansson, P. and Svidt, K. (2002) IT in Collaborative Building Design (IT-CODE). Proceedings of the European Conference on Information and Communication Technology Advances and Innovation in the Knowledge Society, Salford, 18-21 November 2002, 323-331.

31. Smith S.F. and Becker, M.A. (1997) An Ontology for Constructing Scheduling Systems. In: Working Notes of 1997 AAAI Symposium on Ontological Engineering, AAAI Press, Palo Alto, 120-127.

32. Rajpathak, D., Motta, E. and Roy, R. (2001) A Generic Task Ontology for Scheduling Applications. Proceedings of the International Conference on Artificial Intelligence, Las Vegas, 25-28 June 2001.

33. Mochol, M., Oldakowski, R. and Heese, R. (2004) Ontology Based Recruitment Process. In: Dadam, W.P. and Reichert, M., Eds., GI Jahrestagung 2, Springer, Heidelberg, 198-202.

34. Dorn, J., Naz, T. and Pichlmair, M. (2007) Ontology Development for Human Resource Management. Proceedings of the 4th International Conference on Knowledge Management, Vienna, 27-28 August 2007, 109-120.

35. Schmidt, A. and Kunzmann, C. (2006) Towards Human Resource Development Ontology for Combining Competence Management and Technology-Enhanced Workplace Learning. Lecture Notes in Computer Science, 4278, 1078-1087.http://dx.doi.org/10.1007/11915072_10

36. Schmidt, A. and Kunzmann, C. (2007) Human Resource Development with Ontology-Based Competency Catalogs. In: Cunningham and Cunningham, Eds., eChallenges 07, Den Haag.

37. Gómez-Pérez, A., Ramírez, J. and Villazón-Terrazas, B. (2007) An Ontology for Modelling Human Resources Management Based on Standards. In: Apolloni, B., Howlett, R.J. and Jain, L., Eds., Knowledge-Based Intelligent Information and Engineering Systems, Springer, Berlin, 534-541. http://dx.doi.org/10.1007/978-3-540-74819-9_66

38. Peng, G.C. and Nunes, M. (2009) Surfacing ERP Exploitation Risks through a Risk Ontology. Industrial Management and Data Systems, 109, 926-942.http://dx.doi.org/10.1108/02635570910982283

39. Lin, Y., Hilaire, V., Gaud, N. and Koukam, A. (2012) Scrum Conceptualization Using K-CRIO Ontology. In: Data- Driven Process Discovery and Analysis, Springer Berlin Heidelberg, Berlin, 189-211. http://dx.doi.org/10.1007/978-3-642-34044-4_11

40. Santana, A., Lóscio, B.F. and Freitas, F. (2013) A Scrum Application Ontology for Support Historical Data Management of Projects. Centro de Informática—Universidade Federal de Pernambuco, Recife.

41. Schwaber, K. (2004) Agile Project Management with Scrum. Microsoft Press, Redmond.

42. Zualkernan, I.A. (2008) An Ontology-Driven Approach for Generating Assessments for the SCRUM Process. In: Fujita, H. and Zualkernan, I.A., Eds., New Trends in Software Methodologies, Tools and Techniques. IOS Press, The Netherlands.

43. Valaski, J., Malucelli, A., Reinehr, S.S. and Santos, R. (2011) Ontology to Classify Learning Material in Software Engineering Knowledge Domain. In: ONTOBRAS-MOST, UFPE, Recife, 37-47.

44. Bourque, P. and Fairley, R., Eds. (2014) SWEBOK 3.0: Guide to the Software Engineering Body of Knowledge. IEEE Computer Society Press.http://www.computer.org/portal/web/swebok

45. Rational Software (2011) Rational Unified Process Best Practices for Software Development Teams, Rational Software. White Paper TP026B, Rev 11/01, Rational Software, Cupertino.https://www.ibm.com/developerworks/rational/library/content/03July/1000/1251/1251_bestpractices_TP026B.pdf

46. Parson, D. (2011) Agile Software Development Methodology, an Ontological Analysis.http://www.academia.edu/1020810/Agile_software_development_methodology_an_ontological_analysis

47. Parsons, D. (2011) An Ontology of Agile Aspect Oriented Software Development. Research Letters in the Information and Mathematical Sciences, 15, 1-11.

48. Ceravolo, P., Damiani, E., Marchesi, M., Pinna, S. and Zavetarelli, F. (2003) A Ontology-Based Process Modelling for XP. Proceedings of the Tenth Asia-Pacific Software Engineering Conference, Chiang Mai, 10-12 December 2003, 236- 242.http://dx.doi.org/10.1109/APSEC.2003.1254376

49. Siddiqui, F. and Alam, M.A. (2012) Ontology Based Feature Driven Development Life Cycle. International Journal of Computer Science Issues, 9, 207-212.

50. CMMI Product Team (2010) CMMI for Development, Version 1.3.

51. Soydan, G.H. and Kokar, M. (2006) An OWL Ontology for Representing the CMMI-SW Model. Proceedings of ISWC 2006 Workshop on Semantic Web Enabled Software Engineering, Athens, 6 November 2006.

52. Sharifloo, A.A., Motazedi, Y., Shamsfard, M. and Dehkharghani, R. (2008) An Ontology for CMMI-ACQ Model. Proceedings of the 3rd International Conference on Information and Communication Technologies: From Theory to Applications (ICTTA), Damascus, 7-11 April 2008, 1-6.

53. Suggested Upper Merged Ontology (SUMO) http://www.ontologyportal.org

54. Gazel, S., Akçapinar Sezer, E. and Tarhan, A. (2012) An Ontology Based Infrastructure to Support CMMI Based Software Process Assessment. Gazi University Journal of Science, 25, 155-164.

55. Rungratri, S. and Usanavasin, S. (2008) Project Assets Ontology (PAO) to Support Gap Analysis for Organization Process Improvement Based on CMMI. In: Making Globally Distributed Software Development a Success Story, Springer, Berlin, 76-87.

56. Lee, C.S., Wang, M.H. and Chen, J.J. (2008) Ontology-Based Intelligent Decision Support Agent for CMMI Project Monitoring and Control. International Journal of Approximate Reasoning, 48, 62-76. http://dx.doi.org/10.1016/j.ijar.2007.06.007

57. Lee, C.S. and Wang, M.H. (2009) Ontology-Based Computational Intelligent Multi-Agent and Its Application to CMMI Assessment. Applied Intelligence, 30, 203-219.http://dx.doi.org/10.1007/s10489-007-0071-1

58. Liao, L., Qu, Y. and Leung, H. (2005) A Software Process Ontology and Its Application. Proceedings of ISWC 2005 Workshop on Semantic Web Enabled Software Engineering, Galway, 6 November 2005, 6-10.

59. ISO (2004) ISO/IEC 15504?2:2003/Cor.1:2004(E). Information Technology—Process Assessment—Part 2: Performing an Assessment. International Organization for Standardization, Geneva.

60. Líška, M. and Navrat, P. (2010) An Approach to Project Planning Employing Software and Systems Engineering Meta-Model Represented by an Ontology. Computer Science and Information Systems, 7, 721-736. http://dx.doi.org/10.2298/CSIS091110030L

61. OMG (2008) Software & Systems Process Engineering Meta-Model Specification, Version 2.0. Object Management Group, Needham. http://doc.omg.org/formal/08-04-01.pdf

62. Falbo, R.A. and Bertollo, G. (2010) A Software Process Ontology as a Common Vocabulary about Software Processes. International Journal of Business Process Integration and Management, 4, 239-250.

63. Falbo, R.A., Barcellos, M.P., Nardi, J.C. and Guizzardi, G. (2013) Organizing Ontology Design Patterns as Ontology Pattern Languages. ESWC'2013.

64. Wongthongtham, P., Chang, E., Dillon, T. and Sommerville, I. (2009) Development of a Software Engineering Ontology for Multisite Software Development. IEEE Transactions on Knowledge and Data Engineering, 21, 1205-1217.

65. Klieber, W., Sabol, V., Muhr, M., Kern, R., Öttl, G. and Granitzer, M. (2009) Knowledge Discovery Using the KnowMiner Framework. Proceedings of the IADIS International Conference Information Systems, Barcelona, 25-27 February 2009, 9.

66. Guizzardi, G., de Almeida Falbo, R. and Guizzardi, R.S. (2008) Grounding Software Domain Ontologies in the Unified Foundational Ontology (UFO): The Case of the ODE Software Process Ontology. Proceedings of CIbSE, Recife, 13-17 February 2008, 127-140.

67. Sarantis, D. and Askounis, D. (2009) A Project Management Ontology as a Reference for E-Government Projects. Proceedings of International Conference for Internet Technology and Secured Transactions, London, 9-12 November 2009, 1-8.

68. Magoutas, B., Halaris, C. and Mentzas, G. (2007) An Ontology for the Multi-Perspective Evaluation of Quality in E-Government Services. Electronic Government, 4656, 318-329.

69. Staniszkis, E. and Nowicki, B. (2004) ICONS Based Knowledge Management in the Process of Structural Funds Projects Preparation. Proceedings of e-Challenges e-2004 Conference, Vienna, 27-29 October 2004.

70. Mendes, O. and Abran, A. (2005) Issues in the Development of an Ontology for an Emerging Engineering Discipline. Proceedings of the First Workshop on Ontology, Conceptualizations and Epistemology for Software and Systems Engineering (ONTOSE), Alcalá de Henares, 9-10 June 2005, 139-144.

71. Sicilia, M., Cuadrado, J.J., Garcia, E., Rodriguez, D. and Hilera, J.R. (2005) The Evaluation of Ontological Representation of the SWEBOK as a Revision Tool. Proceedings of the 29th Annual International Computer Software and Application Conference (COMPSAC), Edinburgh, 26-28 July 2005, 26-28.

72. Hilera, J.R., Sánchez-Alonso, S., García, E.A. and Del Molino, C.J. (2005) OntoGLOSE: A Lightweight Software Engineering Ontology. Proceedings of the 1st Workshop on Ontology, Conceptualizations and Epistemology for Software and Systems Engineering (ONTOSE), Alcalá de Henares, 9-10 June 2005, 9-10.

73. Settas, D. and Stamelos, I. (2007) Towards a Dynamic Ontology Based Software Project Management Antipattern Intelligent System. Proceedings of the 19th IEEE International Conference on Tools with Artificial Intelligence, Patras, 29-31 October 2007, 186-193.

74. Ruiz, F., Vizcaíno, A., Piattini, M. and García, F. (2004) An Ontology for the Management of Software Maintenance Projects. International Journal of Software Engineering and Knowledge Engineering, 14, 323-349. http://dx.doi.org/10.1142/S0218194004001646

75. Lin, S., Liu, F. and Loe, S. (2003) Building a Knowledge Base of IEEE/EAI 12207 and CMMI with Ontology. Proceedings of the Sixth International Protégé Workshop, Manchester, 7-9 July 2003. http://protege.stanford.edu/conference/2003/abstract.html

76. García, F., Bertoa, M.F., Calero, C., Vallecillo, A., Ruíz, F., Piattini, M. and Genero, M. (2006) Towards a Consistent Terminology for Software Measurement. Information and Software Technology, 48, 631-644. http://dx.doi.org/10.1016/j.infsof.2005.07.001

77. Girardi, R. and Faria, C. (2003) A Generic Ontology for the Specification of Domain Models. Proceedings of the 1st International Workshop on Component Engineering Methodology (WCEM'03) at Second International Conference on Generative Programming and Component Engineering, Erfurt, 22-23 September 2003, 41-50.

78. González-Pérez, C. and Henderson-Sellers, B. (2006) An Ontology for Software Development Methodologies and Endeavours. In: Calero, C., Ruiz, F. and Piattini, M., Eds., Ontologies for Software Engineering and Software Technology, Springer-Verlag, Berlin, 123-151.

79. Falbo, R.D.A., Natali, A.C.C., Mian, P.G., Bertollo, G. and Ruy, F.B. (2003) ODE: Ontology-Based Software Deve- lopment Environment. IX Congreso Argentino de Ciencias de la Computación, La Plata, 6-7 October 2003, 1124- 1135.

CHAPTER 15

# MULTIPERSPECTIVE REPRESENTATION OF INTERNAL CONTROLS IN BUSINESS PROCESSES

Iheb Abdellatif, Alain April

Department of Software Engineering and Information Technologies, Ecole de Technologie Supérieure, Montreal, Canada.

## ABSTRACT

**The internal control process, which is designed to help an organization accomplish specific control objectives, is one of the most important processes, as it can determine whether or not the organization is in compliance with its internal or external requirements. Internal controls emerge from different perspectives. Currently, experts view and act on one control perspective at a time, which creates inefficiencies and duplication. This software engineering research is aimed at proposing a multiperspective framework for representing internal controls, in order to obtain a centralized and comprehensive view of all internal control mechanisms. To carry out this research, we also needed to represent the many different stakeholder perspectives of internal controls. Based on a literature review of mathematical and psychological analysis, we searched for the most suitable multiperspective representation of internal controls, and assessed the many representation options using the AHP (analytical hierarchical process) sensitivity analysis approach. This approach has been applied to a study group which has been called to answer to a questionnaire.**

## INTRODUCTION

The global economic environment continues to evolve and generate obligations and constraints for organizations, especially those that are publicly listed. At the organizational level, internal control objectives are related to the reliability of financial reporting, timely feedback on the achievement of operational and strategic goals, and compliance with laws and regulations. The establishment of internal controls is a process involving the stakeholders in the organization, each with their own particular perspective (i.e. general manager, accountant, information technology expert, internal auditor, security manager, etc.). That perspective determines the way in which the stakeholder will influence the selection of the internal controls for the organization's business processes. In a typical organization, we can distinguish a number of perspectives, the most recognized of which are:

- management,
- security,
- IT auditing,
- compliance,
- quality assurance.

For each of these perspectives, internal control experts have proposed numerous national and international standards, as well as operating practice manuals, also known as best practice frameworks (for example, ISO 27000 for IT

**Citation:** I. Abdellatif and A. April, "Multiperspective Representation of Internal Controls in Business Processes," Journal of Software Engineering and Applications, Vol. 5 No. 12, 2012, pp. 971-982. doi: 10.4236/jsea.2012.512112.

security, COSO for organizational governance, COBIT for IT governance, and SOX for accounting compliance) to help with their implementation. One of the many challenges in adopting internal controls in documented organizational processes is to meet the requirements of these many different perspectives in a structured way.

Despite awareness of the importance of internal controls and recent research proposals in the field of multiperspective business process analysis [1], there is currently no methodology that helps with the implementation of internal controls that consider more than one perspective in a business process representation. Today, internal control representation is often too specific and only oriented toward one perspective (e.g. IT, finance, or auditing). This often results in internal controls being duplicated within an organization, which gives rise to many different, often unrelated or conflicting, process representations and separately maintained business.

This may be exacerbated in large organizations that suffer from a lack of communication between departments or branches, or both.

This research proposes to develop a multiperspective framework (see research question 3 in **Figure 1**) for representing business process controls to be used by a corporate business process repository.

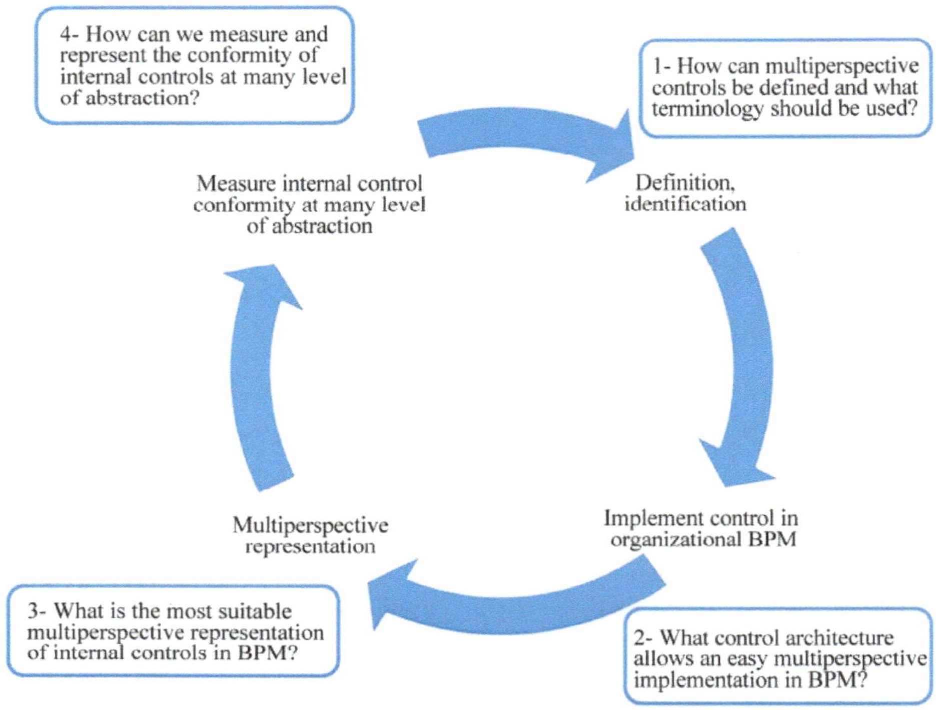


**Figure 1**. The four research questions addressed here.

This paper is organized as follows: We first present a summary of the various internal control representation approaches published in the literature, followed by a list of the framework alternatives and our choice of the proposal that best suits our requirements. We next describe a possible implementation of this representation with an initial prototype. Finally, and then we present the research activities we have planned, as well as future prospects to improve this initial proposal.

## INTERNAL CONTROLS AND EXISTING APPROACHES

Several approaches are presented in the literature to address the issue of representing internal controls in a business process [2-15]. These approaches currently consider only one stakeholder. Before summarizing these approaches, we introduce the concept of internal control and its related concepts.

### Definition of Internal Control

In general, a control can be defined as a set of activities to ensure that a process is predictable, stable, and operating in a consistent manner, and is more or less acceptable to the stakeholders [16]. This definition presents a general notion of control which draws heavily on the production and engineering domains, where processes are, in most cases, measurable (with physical indicators such as temperature, pressure, load, etc.). Typically, these controls operate in real time [17].

In the business domain, internal controls are based on the same concept and are as important as they are in the production and engineering domains, except that they do not often measure in real time. This is mainly because, in the production and engineering domains, processes are of short duration and more strictly controlled in terms of time than processes in the business field. For example, in an assembly line (a manufacturing process in which parts are added to a product in a sequential manner to create a finished product), the controls must respond quickly and report any malfunction to the supervisor in real time. Otherwise, the organization can suffer huge losses. In contrast, the objective of an internal control in the business domain is to ensure that the business processes [15]:

- Align with the objectives and strategic visions of the organization
- Comply with internal policies, legislation, or other external constraints
- Are efficient and effective (ensuring a certain level of quality), and
- Are run in a secure manner, protecting corporate assets.

In the literature, internal controls are classified into three categories [3], depending on the business process level (strategic, organizational, or operational):

- Strategic controls ensure the application of the organization's policies.
- Organizational controls operate within the framework of the strategic controls put in place; however, they are specific to a particular entity (project, product, function, responsibility center, etc.).
- Operational controls are derived from organizational controls, and ensure that the organization operates continuously (on a daily basis).

Strategic, organizational, and operational controls focus on two questions: 1) Is the strategy being implemented as planned? and 2) Are the results produced by the strategy those that were intended? [3].

Several control methodologies (COSO, COBIT, CMMI, etc.) apply the concept of internal control, especially after the financial scandals and frauds that occurred during 2000 (Enron, etc.) and the introduction of the SarbanesOxley law (SOX) [18]. These methodologies are all based on the realization that there is need for internal controls within an organization, as well as on the structure of these controls. In fact, these methodologies suggest that an internal control must specify:

- The objective to be achieved by implementing the internal control in question. This allows the link to be made between the internal controls and the organization's business goals.
- The risk, in cases where the internal control is not established or respected. This makes it possible to gauge the importance of the internal control to be put in place and to justify its implementation cost.
- All the practices to follow to establish the internal control.
- If the internal control is specific to a given process, or generic for a set of processes.
- Who is responsible for ensuring that the internal control performs optimally?
- The business level at which the internal control is applied (strategic, organizational, or operational).

Control methodologies guide organizations in the process of establishing internal controls. However, they do not describe, technically, how to establish or adapt the internal controls to specific situations. They often provide guidelines that can be used as general directions for the process of implementing specific internal controls. It is up to each organization to select the internal controls that are appropriate for their needs, and to put them in place in their processes.

## Existing Internal Control Approaches

In this section, we present the internal control perspectives that exist in the literature, and show how these perspectives are consolidated in the organization. We also show how the control's objectives can differ from one perspective to another, and the characteristics that are common to the internal control approaches that exist in the literature.

As explained earlier, choosing a specific internal control is the responsibility of many different stakeholders. During the process of internal control definition, each of them (i.e. general manager, auditor, financial manager, security manager, etc.) tries to define, from his perspective, the specific controls that are necessary, and the manner in which they should be implemented in the organizational processes. This allows the organization to choose among the many control methodologies proposed, depending on their individual stakeholder perspective:

- management,
- security,
- IT auditing,
- compliance,
- quality assurance.

In general, organizations should try to consolidate all the available perspectives to better serve their customers and compete in their market. For each individual perspective, a list of internal controls is proposed, and these controls can overlap. As illustrated graphically by Radovanovic et al. [19] (see **Figure 2**), several perspectives are represented: COBIT for internal IT auditing, ITIL for IT services, ISO 9001 for quality assurance, and ISO 17799 for security.

However, the internal controls that co-exist in an organization have different objectives, which may differ from one perspective to another. For example, the main objective of the internal controls from the IT security perspective is to protect assets from fraud and inappropriate use. From the internal auditing perspective, the control's main objective is to measure the degree of conformity through qualitative measures based on the results of scaled checklists [20], or even by associating scores with audit evidence and adjusting these scores according to the conformity of each element [21]. This arises from the nature of the audit activity itself, which is defined as a control and counseling activity conducted by a domain expert to improve the quality and conformity of the business process. For this purpose, an auditor needs to know what controls are implemented in a business process and the degree of compliance (or conformity). From a quality assurance perspective, organizations have other concerns related to the performance and quality of their processes. Given the increasing competition between organizations and the growing complexity of processes and procedures, organizations are constantly looking to improve the quality of their products by adopting quality standards, such as ISO 9001 [22], best practice frameworks, such as CMMI [23], or quality approaches, such as Six Sigma (6σ) and Lean [24].

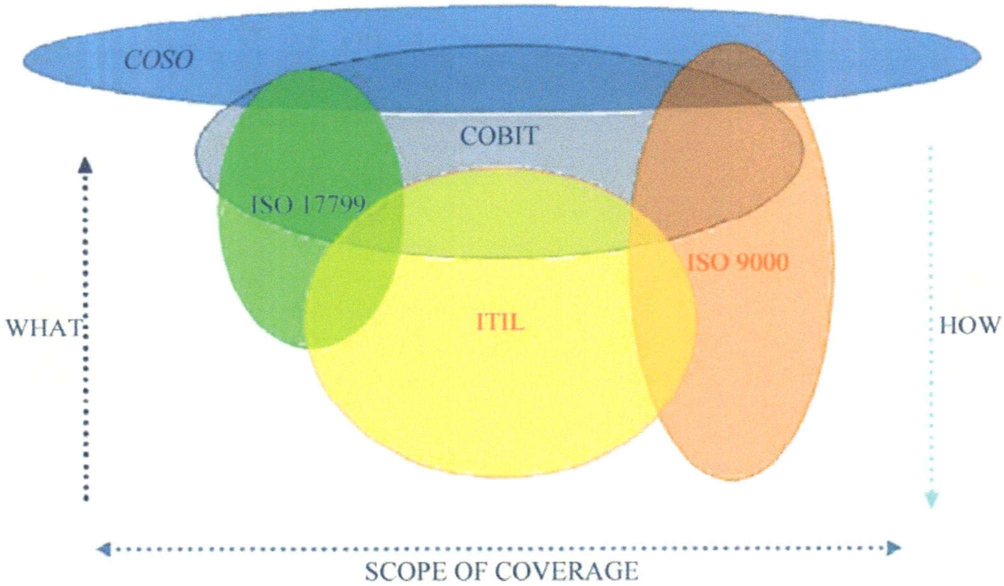


**Figure 2**. COBIT as a consolidated framework [19].

Looking at all these perspectives, we see that the majority of the process control approaches published in the literature are model-driven [2,6,14,15,25], i.e. process controls are defined when modeling the organization's business process using graphical representation. Karimi, Wolter et al. [6,25] propose model-driven approaches aimed at the establishment of policies and security controls. These approaches propose modeling the security controls on the business process graphically, with annotations, in order to allow business and security experts to define the security controls collaboratively and at the same level of abstraction. Wolter et al. [25] reflect these controls by means of physical security constraints written in XACML (Extensible Access Control Markup Language) that define a declarative access control policy language implemented in XML and a processing model describing how to measure authorization requests according to the rules defined in policies.

**Figure 3** gives an example of two different model driven approaches in which authors annotate the process activities depicted in business processes [2,11] (**Figure 3**(a)) or create special shapes [12] (**Figure 3**(b)) to graphically represent internal controls. These graphical representations are then later translated into an executable script that is ready to deploy on an application server (like Apache, JBoss, etc.). Once deployed, the script is verified using a model checking technique.

Regardless of the type of representation used, the internal control approaches found in the literature do not take into consideration the control's perspectives. Every control is represented using the same annotation or shape. In a world where there are many competing perspectives, this makes it difficult to distinguish individual perspectives, and could lead to confusion among the stakeholders when they participate in the process of implementing internal controls in the organizational processes.

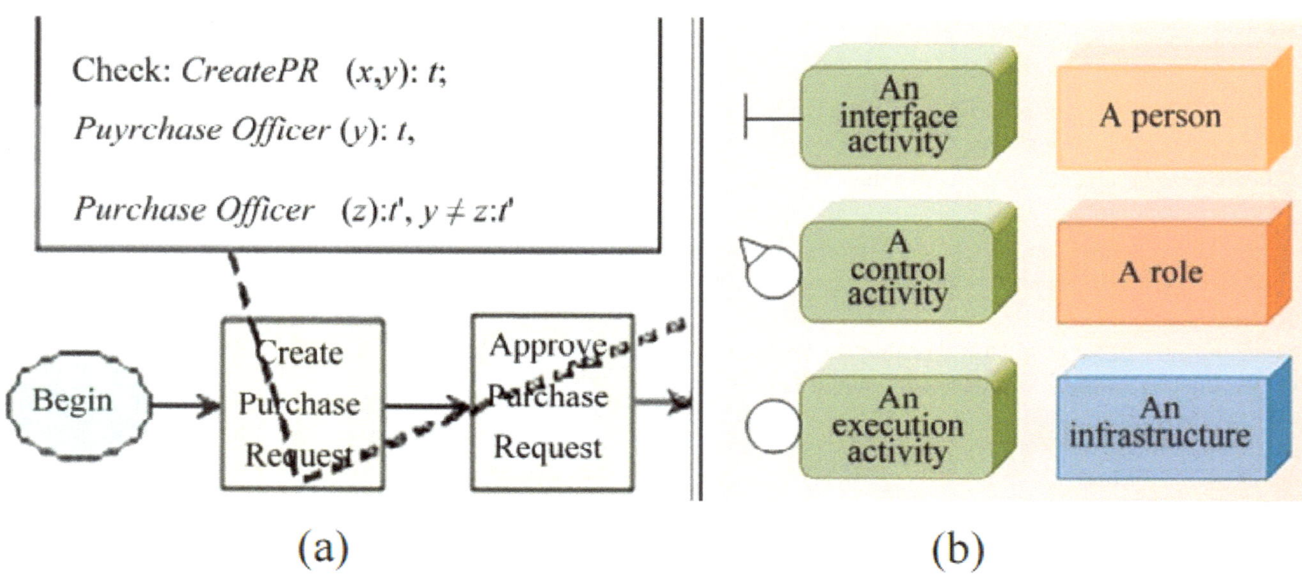


**Figure 3**. Examples of internal control representations [2, 12].

In the next part of this paper, we propose a solution to this problem in the form of a multiperspective graphical representation that combines as many different control perspectives as possible. The proposed approach builds on the concepts published by Monsalve, April, and Abran [1], who proposed a multiperspective BPM notation that identifies the specific BPM constructs preferred by stakeholders. Before describing the proposed multiperspective framework in more detail, a synthesis is required of the many different approaches currently used to graphically represent hierarchical information (such as internal controls).

## HIERARCHICAL INFORMATION REPRESENTATION APPROACHES

Information visualization is a research domain that has been growing in popularity in recent years. It is defined as the study of interactive visual representations of abstract data to reinforce human cognition. The visualization of hierarchical information constitutes a specific research area, in which data are represented using tree structures. In this section, we present a synthesis of popular hierarchical frameworks, and compare the proposals in an attempt to answer the following question: Which hierarchical framework is best suited for visualizing a multiperspective representation of internal controls?

### Tree Layout

In the literature, flowcharts are the form of hierarchical data representation most often used. In fact, the flowchart representation is a special case of the representational structure known as a "tree". In the literature, we find several types of trees, the most popular being [26] the following:

- Vertical tree (flowchart) (Figure 4(A)): This is a typical tree layout in which the root node is at the top and the leaves are at the bottom.
- Horizontal tree (orientation from right to left, or left to right) (Figure 4(B)): This tree is identical to a conventional vertical tree, except that its root is on the left and its leaves are on the right.
- Icicle tree (Figure 4(C)): This is a tree in which nodes are represented by rectangles. Nodes of the same level are on the same line, beside one another. The root of the tree is represented by the biggest rectangle. Each leaf rectangle is placed below the rectangle of its parent. The size of the rectangle is proportional to the size of the node.
- Radial tree (Figure 4(D)): This is a tree in which the nodes are placed in concentric circles, and the center is the root of the tree.
- Concentric circles (Figure 4(E)): These are defined as the circular form of an icicle layout, in which the size of the nodes is proportional to the angle swept by each one.

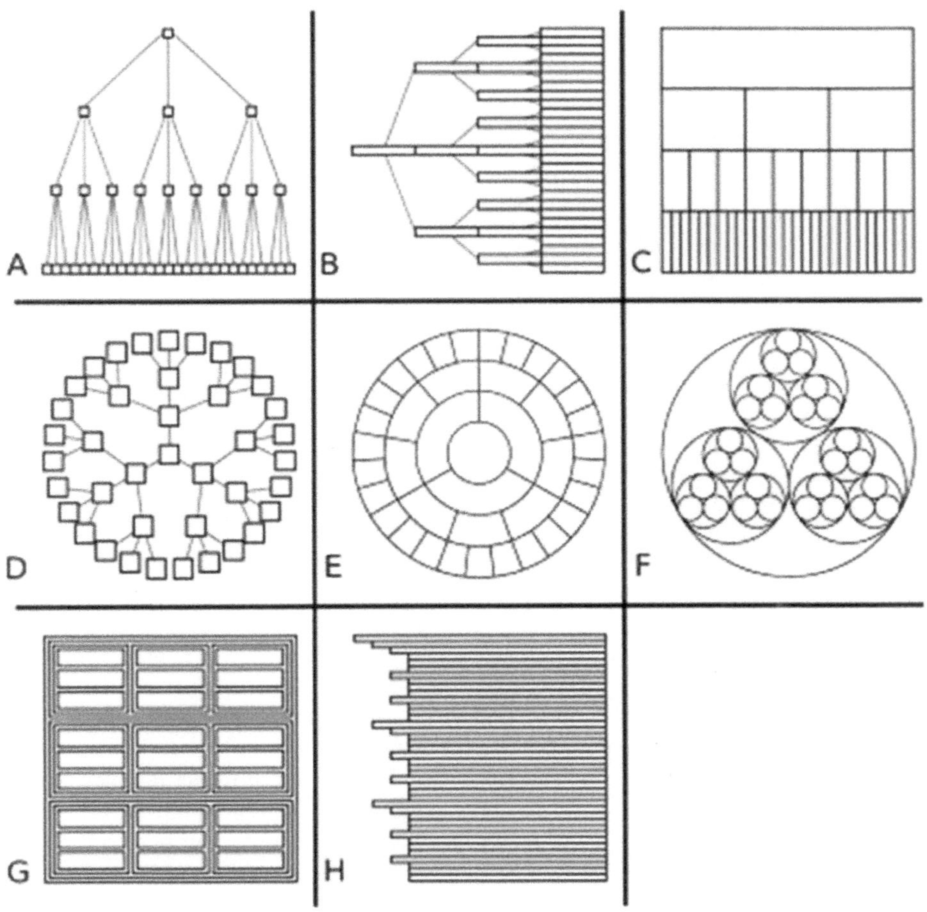


**Figure 4**. Tree layouts [26].

- Nested circles (Figure 4(F)): These forma tree lay out in which each node is represented by a circle. In each parent circle, we find the circles illustrating the descendant nodes.
- Treemap (Figure 4(G)): This layout is similar to the nested circles layout, except that in a Treemap, nodes are represented by rectangles rather than circles. In the Treemap, the display space is divided into rectangles (one for each node). Each parent rectangle includes the rectangles of its descendant nodes, and so on.
- Indented tree (Figure 4(H)): This tree is similar to the Windows Explorer tree, in which the nodes are listed one under the other. The parent node is at the top of this list.

All the tree layouts presented above are considered as two-dimensional representations. However, there are also three-dimensional representations. An example is the conical tree.

Plaisant, Grosjean, and Bederson [27] maintain that the three-dimensional representation approaches are more attractive than their two-dimensional counterparts; however, they do not currently manage space effectively, and they also increase the complexity of the representation for the user, in terms of both understanding and interaction. For these reasons, we have opted to restrict our research to the potential of two-dimensional tree layout techniques to solve our problem.

At this stage of our research, several questions can be asked: Of all these tree layouts, is there one that is better for visualizing multiperspective internal controls? If so, which criteria should be used to choose the tree layout?

In order to answer these two questions, we have conducted a literature review of the research conducted on this topic.

## Comparison of Tree Layouts

Several publications compare tree layouts and attempt to determine which layout is the most suitable for representing structured data. In comparing tree layouts, these publications focus primarily on two criteria: 1) space management, and 2) usability.

McGuffin and Jean-Marc [26] compare the different representations of two dimensional trees mathematically, using the space management criterion. Their assumption is that the size of the node labels tends towards 0 when the tree size tends towards infinity. That study is aimed at comparing the performances of trees by studying the speed of the tendency of their labels to move towards 0. Their findings reveal that the Treemap is the layout that can ensure more efficient management of the representation space. This can be explained by the fact that the Treemap uses all the display space to represent its contents. However, the continual division of the triangles in the Treemap can cause thin and elongated triangles that become difficult for the user to select or compare. In order to remedy this problem, Bruls, Huizing, and Van Wijk [28] proposed an algorithm to approximate the ratio of the Treemap rectangles to 1. The resulting rectangles will be "squarified", and therefore easier to select and compare.

Another limitation of the Treemap presented in the literature is that the structure of the tree is not clearly visualized, especially in the case of large or balanced trees (i.e. each parent has the same number of descendants, and all the descendants are the same size). In the case of balanced trees, Treemaps will be similar to regular grids, and so it will be difficult to determine their structures (differentiating the parents from the descendants).

The limitations of the Treemap are related more to the usability criterion than to the space management criterion. In effect, allow a clear perception of the tree structure and facilitate the selection of the rectangles are considered as to be usability criteria that ensure better use of the Treemap. Usability is defined by ISO 9241-11 [29] as "the degree to which a product can be used by specified users to achieve specified goals effectively, efficiently, and ensuring a certain level of user satisfaction." So, in addition to the effectiveness and efficiency of an interface, user preference (or user satisfaction)is a major criterion in determining the degree of usability of an interface. Applying this definition in the context of trees, Barlow and Neville [30] attempt to decompose the usability criterion into 3 subcriteria:

- ease of interpretation;
- node magnitude; and
- user preference.

In the literature, usability is measured mainly by conducting experiments with the help of users, asking them to execute a specific task (such as "select the deepest leaf in the tree" or "select the immediate ancestor of two nodes", etc.) and measuring their performance (time, success rate, eye-tracking, etc.) [30-32]. Other approaches to measure the usability of tree layouts are based on mathematical models, such as the Hickman model (used to estimate the reaction time of the user), and the Fitts model (used to estimate the movement time of the user). Finally, experimental approaches are considered the most effective way to measure the usability of tree layouts [26]. However, these approaches do not lead to the same findings in terms of which tree layout is the most suitable for visualizing structured information. In fact, the tasks on which the user performance measures are based differ from one approach to another, and depend mainly on the application domain (i.e. datamining, business, IT, etc.) and on what researchers expect from these layouts. For these reasons, we have found contradictions between the approaches and their findings. For example, in [33], the horizontal tree layout is recommended, with the nodes displayed on multiple columns (see **Figure 5**). According to [32], the horizontal tree, even when it is oriented from left to right (normal reading direction in Latin languages), is not as efficient as, for example, the vertical layout (with the root at the top and the leaves at the bottom). This is explained by the fact that, in the case of the horizontal tree, the distance would be greater than for the vertical tree, as the nodes travel horizontally, and it would be much worse if the nodes with the same parent were displayed in multiple columns, one beside the other, as they are in [33]. By contrast, in the case of vertical trees, the nodes travel vertically, and so the travel distance would be shorter. Some researchers [32] are aware of this difference in the findings, and claim that their results and conclusions are valid only for the tasks and the domain they are evaluating. For this reason, it is difficult to determine which tree layout is better in terms of usability. Nevertheless, it is possible to determine which layout is better for a set of tasks, or for a particular domain (bounded by these tasks).

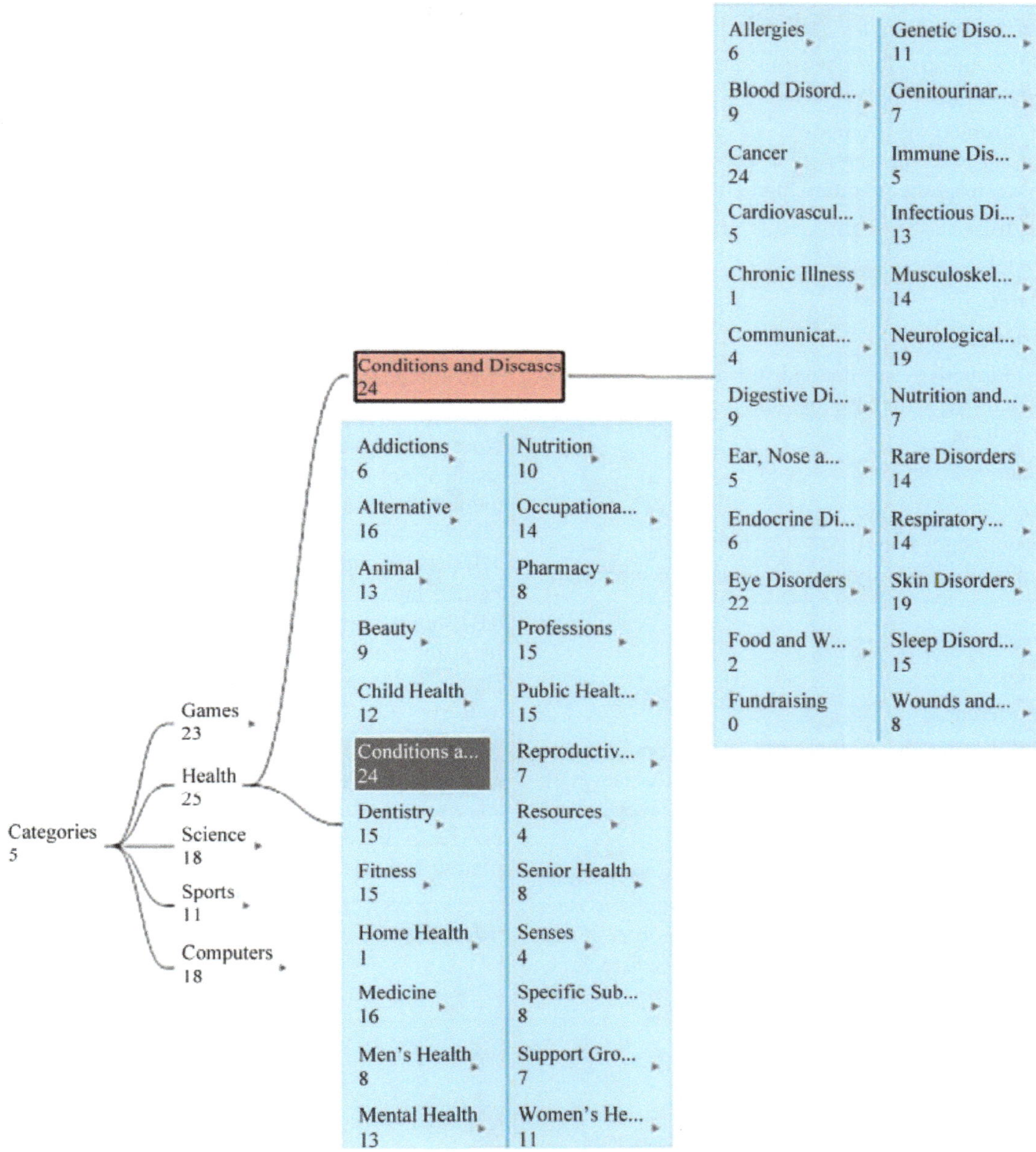


**Figure 5**. Multi-column tree [33].

Developing an exhaustive task list is not the only difficulty in measuring the usability criterion. In the approach proposed by Barlow and Neville [30], for example, despite the fact that they have compiled an extensive list of tasks to evaluate several types of trees (i.e. organizational chart, nested circles, Icicle, and Treemap), the authors could not definitively identify the most usable layout. This could be explained by the fact that there are better interface layouts for some tasks, but not for all of them).

After conducting this literature review, we can say that the Treemap is the preferred option in terms of space management, and that there is no clear consensus on usability. In fact, usability is difficult to measure. In the next section, we propose ways to address these issues, in order to select the most appropriate tree layout for the visualization of multiperspective internal control.

## ILLUSTRATION OF THE PROPOSED SOLUTION

In this section, we use the analytical hierarchy process (AHP) to identify the most appropriate tree layout for the multiperspective representation of internal controls. Based on the AHP results, we developed a prototype using the representation we selected for multiperspective internal control.

### Modeling the Decision Problem with AHP

The problem of selecting the most appropriate tree layout to represent a multiperspective internal control can be summarized as a multicriteria analysis problem. Such problems can be resolved using approaches like AHP, which is a structured technique for organizing and analyzing complex decisions, based on mathematical and psychological analysis. The decision to use the AHP technique is based on its ability to:

- decompose a complex problem into simpler modules,
- define a priority order for each criterion,
- provide a means for checking the consistency of judgments made on the criteria.

An AHP problem is composed of criteria and their alternatives. In our case, the alternatives consist of the various tree layouts taken from the literature, namely:

- Vertical trees,
- Horizontal trees,
- Radial trees,
- Indented trees.

Once the alternatives are defined, we need to define the criteria on which we will base our choice. The first level criteria are as follows:

- space management,
- usability.
- As recommended by ISO 9241-11 [29], we will decompose the usability criterion into three subcriteria, namely:
- effectiveness,
- efficiency,
- users preference.

**Figure 6** illustrates the multicriteria problem modeled in AHP. This model consist of four levels: The objective (level 0), the first criterion (level 1), the second criterion (level 2), and the various possible alternatives (level 3).

Once we've formalized the problem in AHP (as represented in **Figure 6**), we need to assign a weight to the criteria at each level. Then, for each of these criteria, we define the order of tree layouts according to their performance with respect to these criteria. In this step, the ideal approach is to define a list of tasks to measure the performance of the tree layouts with respect to this criterion. However, this would require the development of an interface for each type of tree, and consequently a great deal of effort. For this reason, and to limit the number of interfaces to be developed, we perform one iteration to identify weights for the alternatives, based on: 1) the opinion of 15 experts in the internal control analysis field, and 2) the results of similar experiments published in the literature; and a second iteration (which will be the subject of a future paper), based on our results from the first iteration. We then develop an interface for the two preferred alternatives, and conduct experimental case studies in which we invite users to execute some predefined tasks and measure their performances.

The first experimental case study has been completed. The experts were asked, by email, to fill out an online questionnaire (using a tool named Expert Choice [34]) in which they had to compare criteria at the same level, two by two (**Figure** 7(A)), as well as the tree layouts for each criterion (Figures 7(A) and (B)) shows a completed questionnaire in which an expert found the tree layout to be more usable than space efficient. **Figure** 7(B) shows the weighting of the various tree alternatives for the space management criterion. The judgments illustrated in **Figure** 7(B) are specified based on the work of McGuffin and Jean-Marc (2010).

**Figure 8** illustrates the results once the weights had been set. Based on these results (28.23% for the vertical tree), we can conclude that vertical trees were preferred by the experts and seem to be best suited to represent multiperspective internal controls.

However, the results for the radial tree are only slightly different, at 26.99%.

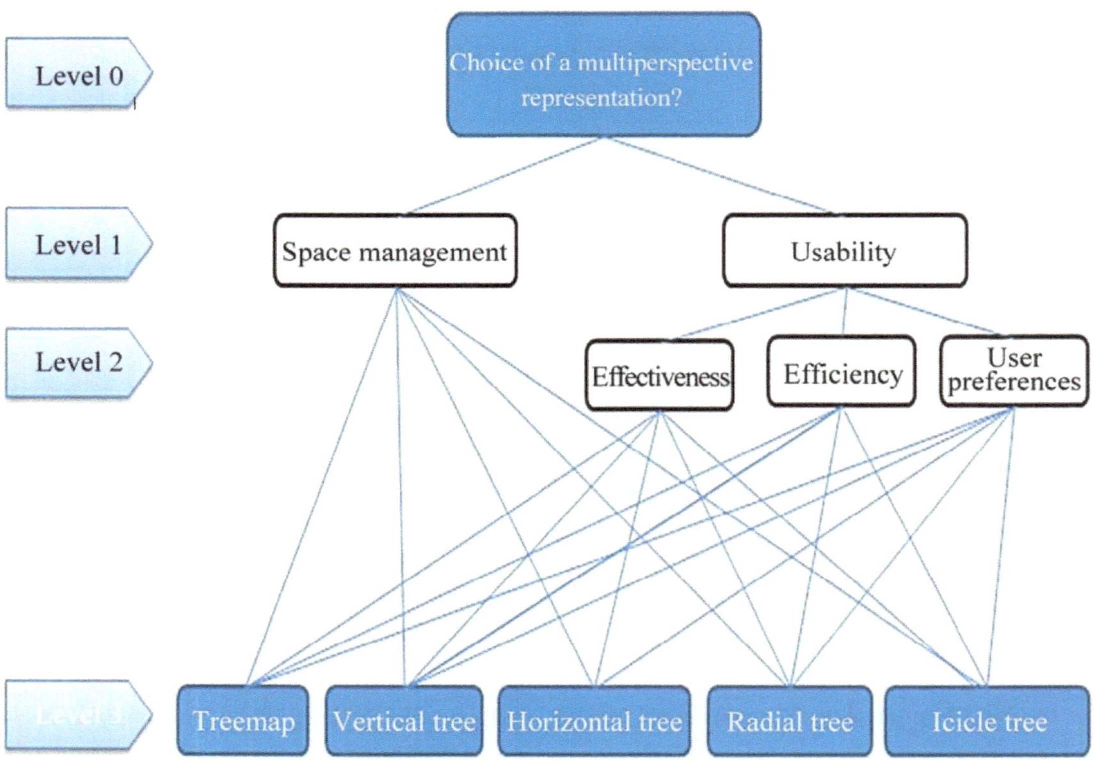


**Figure 6**. Modeling the decision problem using AHP.

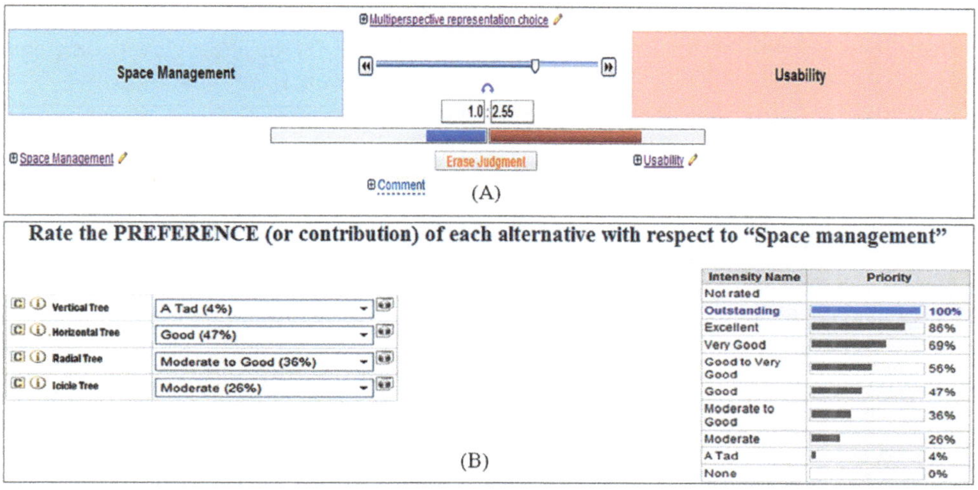


**Figure 7**. Example of the first case study questionnaire.

| Alternative Name | All Participants |
|---|---|
| Vertical Tree | 28.23% |
| Horizontal Tree | 24.48% |
| Radial Tree | 26.99% |
| Icicle Tree | 7.83% |

**Figure 8**. Weighted alternatives vector.

The AHP technique suggests that a sensitivity analysis be performed to validate these results, by varying the weights of the various criteria and assessing the impact of this variation on the order of the alternatives (**Figure 9**).

The findings of the sensitivity analysis confirm that the results obtained are fairly robust and reliable. The vertical tree layout is considered the best alternative, with a variation of 15% for the usability criterion relative to the space management criterion. In other words, the order of the alternatives remains the same, on condition that the experts do not change their mind and favor the space management criterion over the usability criterion. Even if this variation occurs, it must not exceed the 15% margin of the current weighting. If it does, the radial tree becomes the most appropriate framework for representing the internal controls, according to the experts.

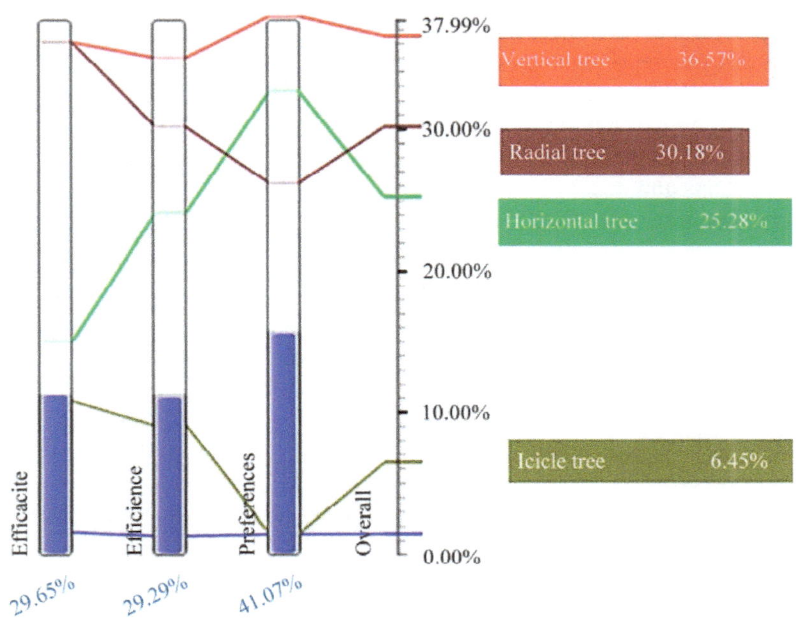


**Figure 9**. AHP sensitivity analysis.

Although 15% is a fairly reassuring margin, we have chosen to provide the user with two additional opportunities to represent the multiperspective internal controls: vertical trees and radial trees. The prototypes of these two representations are presented below.

## Proposed Multiperspective Representation of Internal Controls

In this section, we present a prototype interface of the proposed multipespective representation of internal controls using the vertical and radial tree layouts. The actual prototypes will be developed and tested by users in a future case study.

The proposed prototype will offer four hierarchical representation levels, namely:

- Level 1: objectives of the controls,
- Level 2: business level (strategic, organizational, operational),
- Level 3: internal controls,
- Level 4: business processes.

The proposed interface will present these levels by highlighting the internal controls, along with their multiperspective aspects. The interface has been designed to offer vertical and radial trees to represent structured internal controls. The user interface invites the user to select one of the internal control objectives that the organization aims to achieve (an example of the user interface is provided in **Figure 10**).

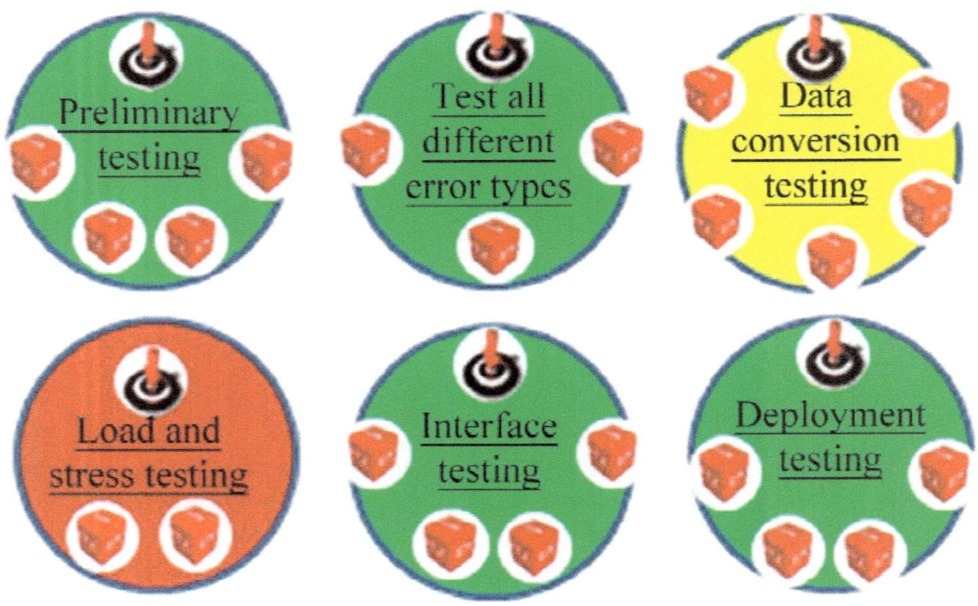


**Figure 10**. Internal control objectives of the organization.

Once a control objective has been selected, the interface changes the display to a multiperspective view of that internal control. Based on the user preference, the internal control will be presented in either a radial tree representation (**Figure 11**) or a vertical tree representation. Due to space limitations, we present only the radial tree representation here. Our proposed vertical tree representation is similar to the classic flowchart, and we use the same icons and data as in the radial representation (only the layout changes).

In **Figure 11** below:

- The business levels are illustrated by the icons , , and to indicate levels 1, 2, and 3 respectively.
- The perspectives are represented by the icons COBIT, CMMI, and COSO to indicate(in this case) COBIT, CMMI, and COSO respectively.
- The internal controls are represented by circles labeled with unique identifiers. Note that the label orientation remains the same (left to right), regardless of the location of the internal control node in the circle (right or left semicircle). The circle colors change from green to yellow to red, according to the conformity of the internal control (Green = Conforming, Yellow = Partially conforming, red = Non-conforming). The control color is determined as in [21], and is explained in another publication.
- The business processes are represented by blue circles, with an identifier for each of them, as for the internal controls.

In a radial representation, the user can choose to focus on just one of the displayed nodes, in this case selecting the node in question and clicking on it. The selected node is then displayed on the whole screen, including the details of the branches for which it is a parent. For example, when a user selects one of the business level nodes (i.e. strategic, tactical, or operational), the interface will interactively adapt to the desired view, and the selected level will appear in the center of the screen with all the control perspectives (**Figure 12**(a)). The user can also select one of the perspectives, for example COBIT, to see which COBIT controls have been implemented, in which of the organization's business processes, their level of conformity, etc. (**Figure 12**(b)).

By double clicking one of process nodes, the selected process is displayed, showing the location of the parent control (**Figure 13**).

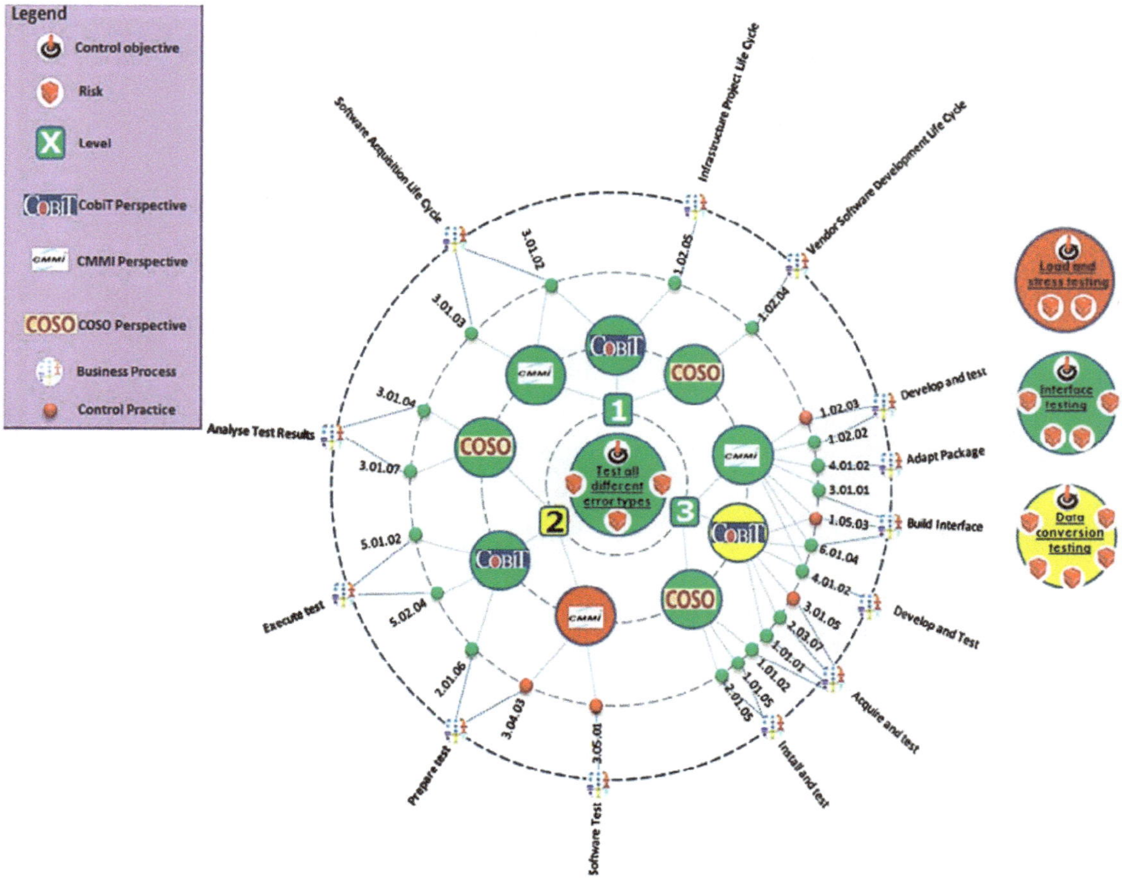


Figure 11. Multiperspective representation of internal controls.

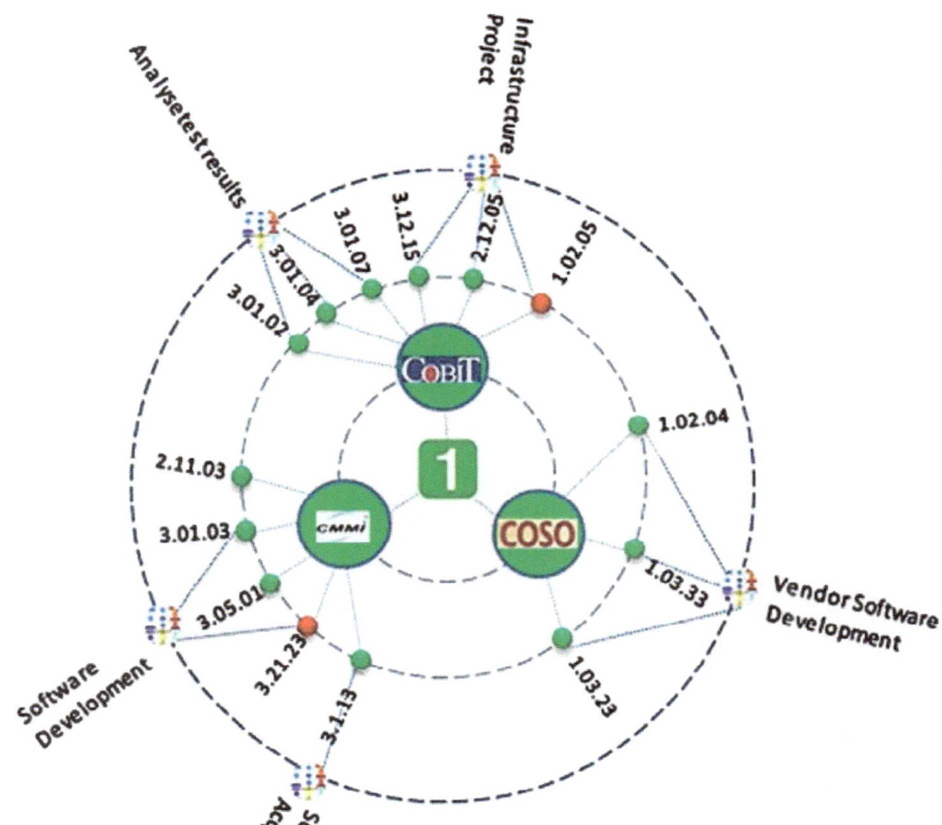


(a)

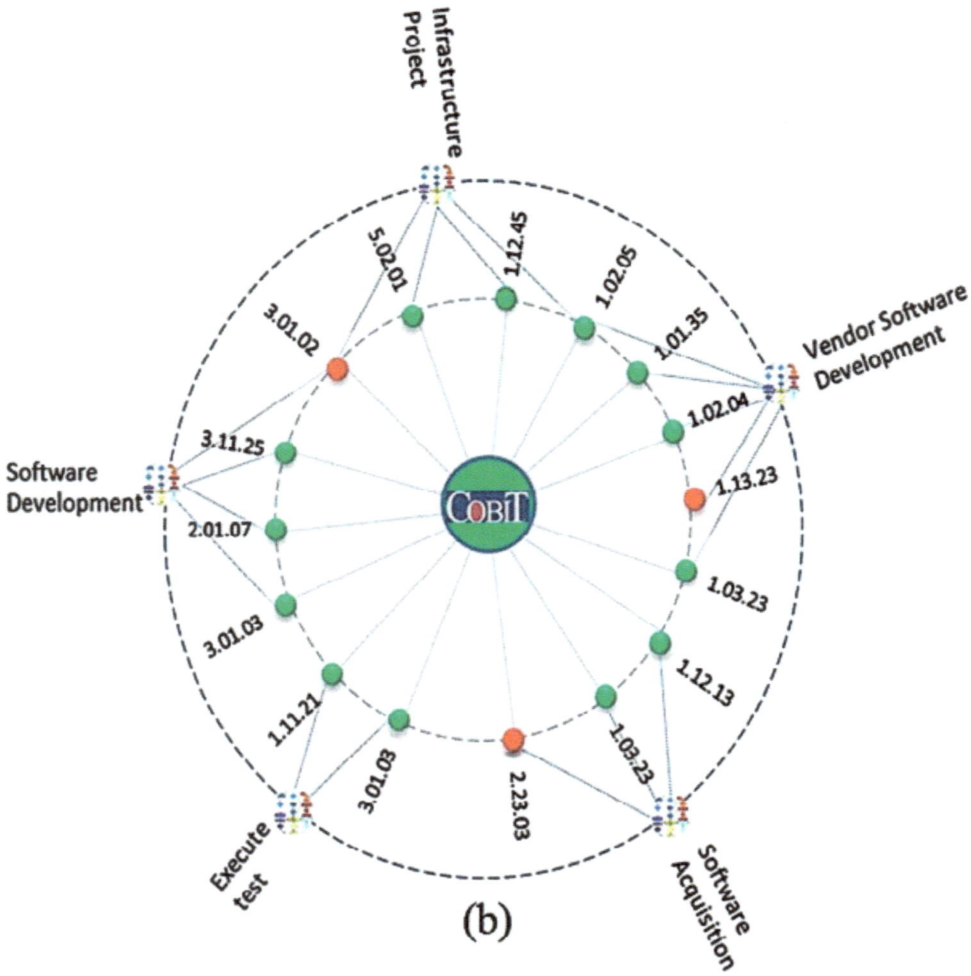


**Figure 12**. Multiperspective views of internal controls.

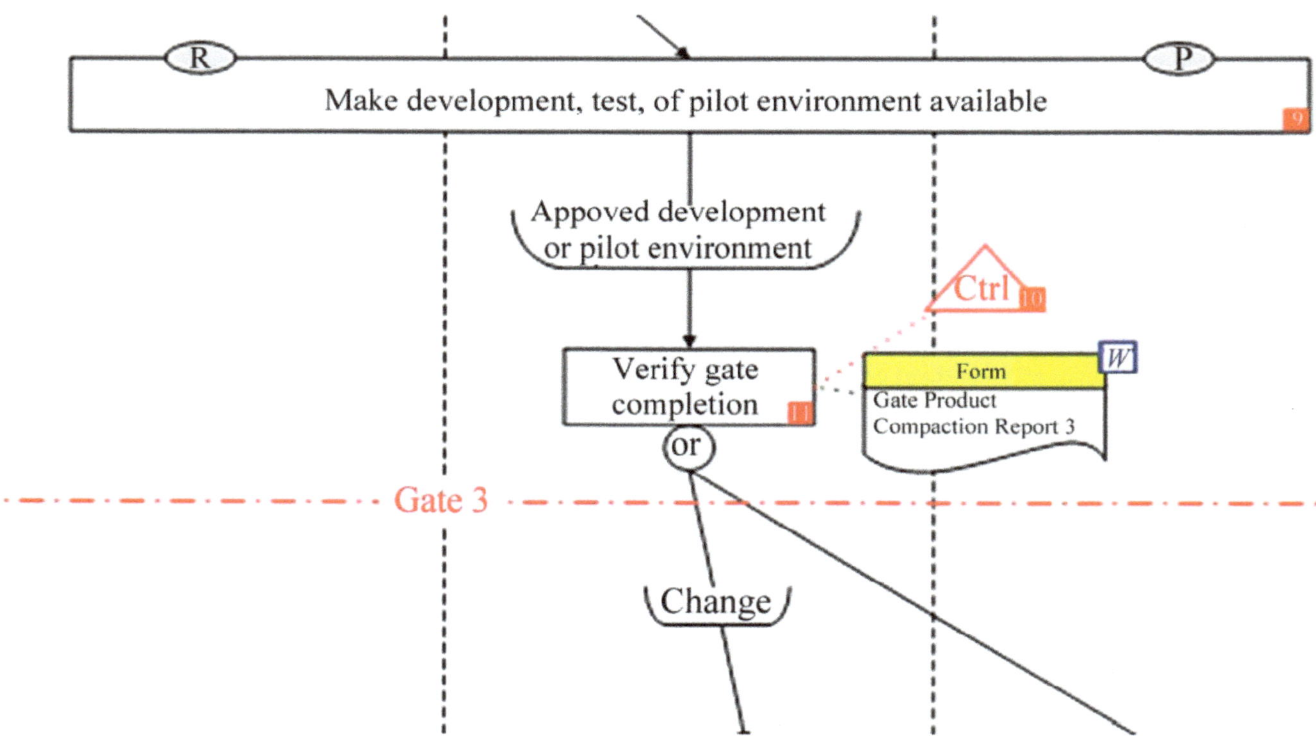


**Figure 13**. Example of the internal controls in a business process.

## DISCUSSION, CONCLUSION, AND RESEARCH OUTLOOK

Internal control is one of the most important processes in the business process management lifecycle. The business process must conform to internal controls issued from a number of perspectives. However, not only are current representation approaches monoperspective, current BPM notations do not consider the many control perspectives involved in modeling business processes (the internal controls are modeled using simple annotations, and the same annotation is used for all the controls).

The proposed approach is promising, because of its ability to enable the user to move from a global view of the internal controls (**Figure 11**) to a very detailed view, which enables the user to see when the internal control was implemented, and where (**Figure 13**). The move from the global view to the detailed view is achieved by providing the user with a multiperspective view of the control objectives. This means that stakeholders with different perspectives (management, IT, security, internal auditing, compliance, quality assurance, etc.) can share the same BPM organizational repository, and the same vision and understanding of the controls implemented.

Our continuing research will involve the further development of the prototype and more case studies, using industrial settings. In this case study, we invited users to execute specific tasks and measure their performance to determine which representation layout (vertical or radial) to select as the most appropriate for representing a multiperspective view of the internal controls in BPM. We also began working on the three research questions presented in **Figure 1**.

## REFERENCES


1. C. Monsalve, A. April and A. Abran, "Representing Unique Stakeholder Perspectives in BPM Notations," Proceedings 8th ACIS International Conference on Software Engineering Research, Management and Applications (SERA), Montreal, 24-26 May 2010, pp. 42-49.doi:10.1109/SERA.2010.16
2. S. Sadiq, G. Governatori and K. Niamiri, "Modeling Control Objectives for Business Process Compliance," 5th International Conference on Business Process Management, Vol. 4714, 2007, pp. 149-164. doi:10.1007/978-3-540-75183-0_12
3. J. E. Gamble and A. A. Thompson Jr., "Essentials of Strategic Management: The Quest for Competitive Advantage," 3rd Edition, McGraw-Hill Inc., New York, 2012.
4. C. Stefansen and S. E. Borch, "Using Soft Constraints to Guide Users in Flexible Business Process Management Systems," International Journal of Business Process Integration and Management, Vol. 3, No. 1, 2008, pp. 26-35. doi:10.1504/IJBPIM.2008.019345
5. L. Turner and A. Weickgenannt, "Accounting Information Systems: Controls and Processes," 2nd Edition, Wiley, San Francisco, 2012.
6. V. R. Karimi, "Formal Analysis of Access Control Policies for Pattern-Based Business Processes," 2009 World Congress on Privacy, Security, Trust and the Management of E-Business, Saint John, 25-27 August 2009, pp. 239-242.doi:10.1109/CONGRESS.2009.18
7. R. K. Vahid, "Verification of Access Control Policies for REA Business Processes," Computer Software and Applications Conference, Vol. 2, 2009, pp. 422-427. doi:10.1109/COMPSAC.2009.170
8. C. Ramaswamy, "Business Process Driven Framework for Defining an Access Control Service Based on Roles and Rules," 23rd National Information Systems Security Conference, Baltimore, 16-19 October 2000.
9. S. Huang, H. M. Cai and B. Y. Xu, "A Resource StateBased Business Process Control Mechanism for BPM," International Conference on Progress in Informatics and Computing (PIC), Piscataway, 10-12 December 2010, pp. 1157-1161.doi:10.1109/PIC.2010.5687985
10. Y. C. Ren, T. Xing, D. Y. Jiang and P. Zhu, "Research on Software Quality Control Method Based on Control Chart," IEEE 2nd International Conference on Computing, Control and Industrial Engineering (CCIE), Jinzhou, 20-21 August 2011, pp. 274-277.
11. B. B. Anderson, J. V. Hansen, P. B. Lowry and S. L. Summers, "Model Checking for E-Business Control and Assurance," IEEE Transactions on Systems, Man, and Cybernetics, Part C: Applications and Reviews, Vol. 35, No. 3, 2005, pp. 445-450.doi:10.1109/TSMCC.2004.843181
12. G. Succi, L. Benedicenti, S. de Panfilis and T. Vernazza, "Activity-Based OO Business Modeling and Control," IT Professional, Vol. 2, No. 3, 2000, pp. 45-50. doi:10.1109/6294.846211
13. I. Oditis and J. Bicevski, "The Concept of Automated Process Control," Computer Science and Information Technologies, Vol. 756, 2010, pp. 193-203. http://www.lu.lv/materiali/apgads/raksti/756_pp_193-203.pdf
14. M. Kehlenbeck, T. Sandner and M. H. Breitner, "Managing Internal Control in Changing Organizations through Business Process Intelligence—A Service Oriented Architecture for the XACML Based Monitoring of Supporting Systems," 43rd Hawaii International Conference on System Sciences (HICSS), Honolulu, 5-8 January 2010, pp. 1-10.doi:10.1109/HICSS.2010.262
15. I. Bider and A. Striy, "Controlling Business Process Instance Flexibility via Rules of Planning," International Journal of Business Process Integration and Management, Vol. 3, No. 1, 2008, pp. 15-25. doi:10.1504/IJBPIM.2008.019344
16. Business Dictionary, "Process Control," 2011. http://www.businessdictionary.com/definition/businessprocess.html
17. A. Zakarian, P. Wickett and Y. Siradeghyan, "Quantitative Model for Evaluating the Quality of an Automotive Business Process," International Journal of Production Research, Vol. 44, No. 6, 2006, pp. 1055-1074. doi:10.1080/00207540500371949
18. Addison-Hewitt, "Sarbanes-Oxley Act," 2012. http://www.soxlaw.com/
19. D. Radovanovic, T. Radojevic, D. Lucic and M. Sarac, "IT Audit in Accordance with COBIT Standard," MIPRO,

Proceedings of the 33rd International Convention, Opatija, 24-28 May 2010, pp. 1137-1141.

20. A. April, A. Abran and E. Merlo, "Process Assurance Audits: Lessons learned," Proceedings of the International Conference on Software Engineering, Kyoto, 19- 25 April 1998, pp. 482-485. doi:10.1109/ICSE.1998.671611

21. R. Ouanouki and A. April, "IT Process Conformance Measurement: A Sarbanes-Oxley Requirement," Proceedings of the IWSM, Mensura, Palma de Mallorca, 5-8 November 2007, pp. 26-37.

22. D. Hoyle, "ISO 9000 Quality Systems Handbook," 5th Edition, Butterworth-Heinemann, Amsterdam, 2006.

23. T. Kasse, "Practical Insight into CMMI," 2nd Edition, Artech House, Boston, 2008.

24. T. T. Allen, "Introduction to Engineering Statistics and Six Sigma: Statistical Quality Control and Design of Experiments and Systems," Springer, London, 2006.

25. C. Wolter, M. Menzel, A. Schaad, P. Miseldine and C. Meinel, "Model-Driven Business Process Security Requirement Specification," Journal of System Architecture, Vol. 55, No. 4, 2009, pp. 211-223. doi:10.1016/j.sysarc.2008.10.002

26. M. McGuffin and R. Jean-Marc, "Quantifying the SpaceEfficiency of 2D Graphical Representations of Trees," Information Visualization Journal, Vol. 9, No. 2, 2010, pp. 115-140.

27. C. Plaisant, J. Grosjean and B. B. Bederson, "Space Tree: Supporting Exploration in Large Node Link Tree, Design Evolution and Empirical Evaluation," IEEE Symposium on Information Visualization (INFOVIS), 29 January 2003, pp. 57-64.doi:10.1109/INFVIS.2002.1173148

28. M. Bruls, K. Huizing and J. J. Van Wijk, "Squarified Treemaps," Proceedings of the Joint EUROGRAPHICS and IEEE TCVG Symposium on Data Visualization, Vienna, 29-31 May 2000, pp. 33-42.

29. International Organization for Standardization, "ISO 9241-11 Ergonomic Requirements for Office Work with Visual Display Terminals (VDTS)—Part 11: Guidance on Usability," International Organization for Standardization, Genova, 1998. http://www.iso.org/iso/catalogue_detail.htm?csnumber=16883

30. T. Barlow and P. Neville, "A Comparison of 2-D Visualizations of Hierarchies," IEEE Symposium on Information Visualization INFOVIS, 2001, pp. 131-138.

31. J. Stasko, R. Catrambone, M. Guzdial and K. McDonald, "An Evaluation of Space-Filling Information Visualizations for Depicting Hierarchical Structures," International Journal of Human-Computer Studies, Vol. 53, 2000, pp. 663-694. doi:10.1006/ijhc.2000.0420

32. M. Burch, N. Konevtsova, J. Heinrich, M. Hoeferlin and D. Weiskopf, "Evaluation of Traditional, Orthogonal, and Radial Tree Diagrams by an Eye Tracking Study," IEEE Transactions on Visualization and Computer Graphics, Vol. 17, No. 12, 2011, pp. 2440-2448. doi:10.1109/TVCG.2011.193

33. S. Hyunjoo, K. Bohyoung, L. Bongshin and S. Jinwook, "A Comparative Evaluation on Tree Visualization Methods for Hierarchical Structures with Large Fan-Outs," 28th International Conference on Human Factors in Computing Systems, Atlanta, 2010. doi:10.1145/1753326.1753359

34. Expert Choice, "Expert Choice Software," 2012. http://www.expertchoice.com/

# SECTION V: PROJECT RISK MANAGEMENT

CHAPTER 16

# SOFTWARE DEVELOPMENT PROJECT RISK MANAGEMENT: A NEW CONCEPTUAL FRAMEWORK

Lazaros Sarigiannidis, Prodromos D. Chatzoglou

Production & Management Engineering Department, Democritus University of Thrace, Xanthi, Greece.

## ABSTRACT

**The frequently observed positive impact of adopting risk management strategies on projects' overall outcome has led many software development organizations to appreciate its significant role in the pursuit of cost reduction, schedule overruns decrease and, generally, improved performance. In line with this issue, this study investigates a wide range of relevant literature, proposes a new conceptual framework for managing risk in software development projects, introduces new conceptual factors, brings out their interrelation, and suggests new prospects and managerial implications for both practitioners and academics. The conceptual framework has two basic axes. Firstly, the determination of the impact of constructs such as Project Characteristics, Project Risk Management Team, Risk Identification Approaches, and Project Quality on the level of Project Risk. The majority of the items used to measure these constructs are proposed for the first time in the literature. Additionally, the assessment of the impact of Project Risk (and all of the dimensions that compose it), simultaneously with the estimation of the impact of the Residual Performance Risk on the final subjective and objective Project Performance could provide project managers with a better picture of the effectiveness and adequacy of their risk management practices.**

## INTRODUCTION

Risk management has been applied to various fields like the national security, exploration of space, nuclear reactors, security, construction industry and financial investments [1]. This research will focus on the study of various approaches of risk management applied to software development projects. Although they have been applied with success in the last decades, dealing with problems in the development of various systems, the fact that a large percentage of the systems is never completed, or fails to operate effectively and efficiently [2-11], renders the study of these approaches even more imperative.

The fact that the majority of the software development organizations perceive risk in a different and not systematic way contributes to the increase of project development instability and ineffectiveness. Kwak and Ibbs [12] identified risk management as the least applied scientific field among the various knowledge areas of project management. In line with Kwak and Ibbs study, Adams and Pinto [13] research states that risk management has not received sufficient attention and does not appear to be widely accepted within the software engineering community. Dedolph [14] implies that the reason for the software risk management neglection is primarily the organizational inertia and their native resistance to change, due

**Citation:** L. Sarigiannidis and P. Chatzoglou, "Software Development Project Risk Management: A New Conceptual Framework," Journal of Software Engineering and Applications, Vol. 4 No. 5, 2011, pp. 293-305. doi:10.4236/jsea.2011.45032.

to the difficulty of risk management value assessment, the lack of resources, the need for structural changes and other.

Given the complexity of most software projects and the several risk types emerged during the development/implementation stages, the abandonment of risk management to human intuition and initiative [15] can sometimes be proven effective, yet remains an insufficient substitute of the constant professional and stable approach of risk management.

Risk management of software development projects was recognized as an independent field of research in 1989, when Barry W. Boehm lead the way with his pioneering book "Software Risk Management". Since then, this particular issue has been discussed and studied quite thoroughly, especially in the beginning of '90s. The work of Boehm [16,17] and Charette [18,19] laid the foundations for the extensive contribution of the Software Engineering Institute (SEI) in the middle of '90s [20-25], that even today acts as an archetype in several references in risk management literature.

The goal of the current study is the creation of a new research model, which emerged from a thorough examination of the literature, and will be used to measure various conceptual factors and their relationships in order to achieve a better and more complete understanding of risk management as an organizational process. In doing so, the effect of several organizational strategies and characteristics on the determination of the risk level of software projects, as well as its consequential influence on the total project performance, will be assessed. In Sections 2 and 3 the conceptual framework and the research questions are presented, respectively, while some concluding remarks are provided in Section 4.

## LITERATURE REVIEW

### Risk Identification Approaches

As Schoenthaler [26] mentioned, based on his practical experience, it is undeniable that the systematic use of risk management into the project development process will have a considerable negative impact on project risks level. In an attempt to promptly, effectively and easily identify risk, managers of software projects have been using various methods. Four of them are going to be discussed below, in a similar way as they were classified by Kulik and Weber [27].

The first one is the Ad-hoc Approach, which provides an assessment of risks when the initial symptoms appear on the project, as well as their mitigation with unofficial way. The second approach is called Informal Approach [28] and includes a discussion with people, who are directly or indirectly involved with the project, concerning the several risk issues that appear (or will possibly appear) and the recording and documentation of the risks for future use. The third is named Periodic Approach and, as it can be understood from its title, involves the use of repetitive procedures for the identification and specification (quantitatively and qualitatively) of the risks. Finally, the fourth approach is the Formal Approach for the identification of the various risks [29]. According to this approach, a thorough and in-depth assessment of each risk by independent individuals is performed.

An international research on software development risk management, carried out in 2001 by the Research Corporation KLCI, indicated that the most common risk identification approach is the informal, used by 37% of the respondents, while Ropponen's [30] study enforces the impression of the absence of a framing thinking about software risk concept and managerial implications by project managers.

### Project Characteristics

The factors that characterize and, in many occasions, shape the development process of a project, affect to a great extend the determination of its risk level. In the present research, five main characteristics of the software development projects will be studied.

The first of these is Project Scope, which in this case is going to be studied through an indicator, Project Duration [31,32]. This indicator is selected as the measure for project scope because, as Wallace et al. [32] propose, the collection of duration information is easy for most projects and it is suitable to survey-based data collection procedures.

The second characteristic has to do with whether a project is carried out totally In-house or in collaboration with external providers (Outsourcing) [33]. It has been stressed that outsourcing, as a strategy of gaining competitive advantage for a company, is particularly effective yet equally risky (due to the complexity and sometimes the vagueness that characterize its procedures) compared with the in-house method [32,34,35]. Still, despite the rapid increase of outsourcing in developing software projects in the past few years (in 2005, 75% of the USA organizations outsource to some extent), its effect on the projects' risk level, and especially on those taking place in countries with less developed infrastructures, have been studied poorly by literature [36].

The third characteristic of a software project that will be examined by this study is its Strategic Orientation [32,37]. The strategic nature of a system can be measured by the classification of the projects as 1) strategic, 2) organizational and 3) informational.

Moreover, Project Diversity constitutes a structural form that is expressed in work specialization terms [38]. In this research, the project diversity will refer to the differentiation level that appears in the knowledge background, capabilities and experience among the project development participants [39].

The fifth and final characteristic is the Type of System being developed [5,40,41]. The failure to identify, understand and confront the risks that are connected to different project types is an important and defining factor for the problems during the realization of the project, concealing the real project risks from their developers (that is, by differentiating the perceptions that they have formed for them) [42]. Six main types of software development projects can be distinguished [5], in spite of Glass [3] statement for curious biases and omissions in Jones' list:

- Management Information Systems, which are the most common software applications,
- System Software, like for example the operating systems involving software that facilitates software applications (Application Software),
- Commercially-marketed Software,

- Military Systems, which are created for securing rules and models in military data,
- Contract or Outsourced Software projects in the civilian domain, and
- End-user Software projects (software developed by users, not programmers).

## Risk Dimensions

Barki et al. [43] suggest that the software project risks consist of interrelated dimensions and their assessment should not be made with the use of a one-dimension scale, but, on the contrary, every dimension should be defined separately, theoretically as well as empirically. The multidimensional assessment of risk can supply a clear specification for research and practical purposes [44].

Despite the significance of studying risk through its dimensions, very few researches have been carried out on this issue. McFarlan [45] found three major dimensions of risk in the software development process: project size, technology experience and project structure. He suggested, also, that project administrators should develop a complete and aggregated software risk profile for every software project. Boehm [17] proposed a software risk management framework that included the evaluation and control of risk and conducted a list with the top ten risks based on his personal professional experience. In spite of all these, Boehm's list was lacking some theoretical substantiation [46] and, moreover, due to its complexity and other factors that characterize software projects (e.g. invisibility, flexibility and conformity) [47], it ceased having any diachronic value. Barki et al. [43] conducted a comprehensive review of studies related to software development risk and then they proposed 35 measures for its estimation. These measures were categorized in five dimensions: technological newness, application size, expertise, complexity of the application and organizational environment. Although this research delivered a quite useful and understandable instrument for measuring risk, it was noticed that the risk evaluation scale was extremely complicated [46,48]. Heemstra and Kusters [49], based on previous studies and their professional experience, composed a list of 36 risk variables that were later grouped into 9 categories. Moynihan [50], in co-operation with 14 experienced Irish application developers, evolved a total of 21 points that are risk related. Ropponen and Lyytinen's [51] questionnaire was relied on Boehm's [17] checklist, and distinguish 6 risk components based on a survey of project managers including almost 1100 projects. Furthermore, the Hierarchically Holographic Modeling framework, introduced by Longstaff et al. [52], brings out 32 risks in seven dimensions of systems integration. Houston [53] also proposed a list of 29 software development risk factors, considering them as the most important and frequently cited in the existent literature. Cule et al. [54] categorize risks into four dimensions according to their source (task, client, environment, self), which includes 55 software risks, and they proposed a risk management strategy for each dimension. Sumner [55], through structured interviews, compared the differences of software risks between MIS and ERP projects and proposed nine risks that are unique in ERP projects. Kliem [56] developed a list of 38 risks in BPR (Business Process Reengineering) projects, which were categorized in 4 main dimensions: people, management, business and technique. Schmidt et al. [57] identified 53 risk variables that were categorized in 14 factors and suggested that the difference in the culture of the three countries (Finland, China and USA) where their research was carried out, could affect considerably the list of risks. They finally concluded that only 11 of them have cross-cultural application. Addison [58] has used the Delphi technique to collect the opinions of 32 specialists and then presented a list of 28 risks for e-commerce projects.

This research will mainly be based on the dimensional distinction of a quite recent approach, the one proposed by Wallace et al. [48]. They proposed 27 software development risks that could be grouped into six dimensions, those referring to: Users [57,59-61], System Requirements [18,59,62,63], Project Complexity [43,64,65], Planning and Control [57,59,66,], Team [63,67-69] and Organizational Environment [5,43,70].

However, in contrast to the Wallace et al. [48] study, that evaluates only the extent to which each risk statement characterized the projects, and in line with Han and Huang [59] research, this study will attempt to assess both the probability of occurrence and the impact for each risk by the respondents, determining the risk level of each dimension. In order to calculate the risk exposure (RE) for each risk item, the formula of Cooper et al. [71] will be adopted. They propose that the traditional measurement of RE, as the product of possibility and consequence ($RE = P*C$) [17,28,49,59,72-74,] has significant disadvantages due to the fact that elements with high consequence, yet low possibility, can return low risk exposure factors and as so they can be falsely considered as insignificant. More specifically, they measure the RE with the following formula: $RE = P + C - (P*C)$ (the equation works only if the possibility of a risk to occur and the severity of its impact are in a scale from 0 to 1) [71]. The adoption of this formula in this study will hopefully give more stabilized, objective and realistic data about the significance, and hence the impact, of each risk dimension on the project.

## Project Risk Management Team

Many critical decisions are made by teams rather than by individuals, because group decisions are more consistent with rationality than individual ones [75]. In this study, the concept of the project risk management team will be also examined. This concept incorporates many diverse roles, such as the compilation and evaluation of the required project risk information and its sharing with the project risk manager, and also requires a detailed understanding of the current project risk management methodology being used [76]. However, nowadays, most risk analysis projects are unsuccessful since the internal experts and subject matter experts are excluded from the process [77], or there is not sufficient information about their personal characteristics, abilities and attitude towards risk. Ward [78] underlined this insufficiency and attempted to trace and theoretically analyze the most significant characteristics of the project participants who have taken on the difficult task of risk management. These characteristics include the Capability and Experience of the participants, their Motivation for accepting to undertake initiatives, which importance has been stressed by Boehm [79], and the Perceived Responsibilities in risk management. Despite the thorough and analytical theoretic foundation of the project risk management team concept, Ward [78] did not provide a research instrument for the measurement of this construct. In order to operationalize this construct, a deductive scale development approach will be utilized, while the development of the items will be based on the theoretical definition of the construct [80].

## Residual Performance Risk

The primary performance influence mechanism of a software project is a risk called Performance Risk which represents the difficulty in evaluating the final performance in terms of cost and schedule overruns [81]. According to Nidumolu [65,81], the estimated performance risk that is detected in the final development stages of a project is called Residual Performance Risk. This definition is used to clearly distinct it from the risk that is found during other phases in the project's development life cycle. Therefore, this risk refers to the difficulty in assessing the consequences of executing the project, during the final phase of its development.

Meyer et al. [82] introduced a more "forward thinking" approach that emphasizes on the uncertainty frame of a project. These researchers have agreed that, apart from the predictable uncertainty that can be controlled by the traditional methods of risk management, an unexpected uncertainty and a general chaos appears in many innovative projects. As a consequence of this notion of the project risk profile, the residual performance risk can be decomposed in two parts, based on the following equation [36,83]:

Residual Performance Risk = Residual Controllable Risk + Unforeseeable Risk

The Residual Controllable Risk is expressed by the uncertainty that continues to exist during the final stages of the software development projects that can be controlled, and even limited, with various ways. The Unforeseeable Risk is the uncertainty that cannot be identified or controlled while planning the project. However, despite the intention of previous studies [83] to examine these two dimensions of residual performance risk separately, no effort of this kind is recorded until today in the international literature. In the present study, a first attempt of disintegrating the factor of residual performance risk will be made, on the basis of the variables defined by Na et al. [83, 36] and their classification according to their notional coherence to the theory.

## Project Performance

The present research will concentrate on the project performance related results since performance is the dependable variable of most vital importance [81].

The performance of a software development project can be divided, for reasons of better, deeper and more circumstantial studying, into two main categories: the subjective and the objective performance [36]. These two categories used for measuring the performance are quite important for software developers, and users as well, since both of them affect directly or indirectly the execution and implementation of every project [84].

The factor of subjective project performance refers to the efficiency and efficacy by which a software development project is completed (according to the people involved in the project) [85] and bears in mind two basic dimensions [72,83,86]: the process performance and the product performance.

Process Performance is an efficiency measure for the software development process and can be described by three dimensions [81]: 1) the increase in the gained knowledge during the implementation of the project which is called Learning, 2) the management level in the development process that is named Control and 3) the quality of the relationship among the various participants (managers, technicians, analysts, programmers, external specialists, users etc.) through the duration of the software development process, that is called Quality of Interactions [87].

Product Performance is a measure for registering and illustrating the performance of the final product and is described by the following three dimensions [65,81]: 1) the technical performance of the software, that is called Operational Efficiency, 2) the respond quality to the needs of the software users, that is noted by the term Responsiveness and 3) the ability of the software to provide perceptible support to new products and functions and its Flexibility to the interchangeable organizational needs.

These two dimensions of project performance need to be estimated separately since there is not necessarily a high relationship between them [72]. For example, it is quite possible that a project with cost or schedule overruns problems will deliver a high quality product and vice versa.

Although the measurement of subjective performance has the plain advantage of the easy collection of necessary data [36], it deals intensely with the problem of standardization, since the evaluation of a project depend on personal judgment or moreover the mood of a certain manager [84].

Contrary to the subjective performance of a project, the objective performance includes some more quantified metrics like, for example, excess in terms of cost, effort and schedule. According to literature [36,88,89], it is suggested to measure both subjective and objective project performance, due to the special nature that characterizes software development projects.

## Project Quality

Another factor that can significantly define risks, as well as the level of their presence during the process of a project's software development, is project quality [90,91]. In the present study, the total quality of a project will be defined through the measurement of two main factors and the variables that define them according to literature [92,93]. These two fundamental factors are: process quality [94] and people quality. To begin with, people quality is divided into two main sub-factors, so that it can be measured with the utmost detail. These two sub-factors that compose it are management quality and staff quality.

Management quality includes variables like communications management adequacy, subcontract management adequacy, interaction management adequacy and internal management quality [95]. On the other hand, people quality involves the quality of non-administrative staff that is occupied with a project. For its measurement, variables like staff turnover, staff experience, staff motivation, staff training and programming language experience are used [92].

Process quality is a complex factor for defining project quality; it associates the project specification clarity with the development and testing process quality. Specification clarity is defined by the variables of specification process quality and requirements difficulty. Development and testing process quality consists of variables measuring the regularity of reviews, the quality of documentation and the level of independent testing. In the AgenaRisk manual of software risk modelling [95] for measuring the development and testing process quality, one more indicator is used—a model of the maturity of the capabilities that an organization has in executing specific organizational procedures, the Capability Maturity Model (CMM) [96]. In the present research CMM was omitted, mainly due to the non-categorization of many companies worldwide (especially in underdeveloped or developing countries) to its five levels [47,97].

A summary of the research constructs that compose the general risk management model is presented in Table 1, along with the number of items that measure them. What's more, Figure 1 illustrates the relationships that exist between them, which will be examined thoroughly in the following section.

**Table 1.** Summary of research constructs

| Factors | Sub-factors | Items | References |
|---|---|---|---|
| ***Project Characteristics*** | *Strategic Orientation* | 3 | [5,31-33, 37-39,98] |
| | *Project Scope* | 1 | |
| | *Outsourcing* | 1 | |
| | *Project Type* | 3 | |
| | *Project Diversity* | 3 | |
| ***Risk Identification Approaches*** | - | 4 | [27] |
| ***Risk Dimensions*** | *User* | 5 | [5,17,31,40, 43,45, 48-50,52, 54-68,70] |
| | *System Requirements* | 4 | |
| | *Project Complexity* | 4 | |
| | *Planning and Control* | 7 | |
| | *Team* | 3 | |
| | *Organizational Environment* | 4 | |
| ***Project Risk Management Team*** | – | 3 | [62,78] |
| ***Residual Performance Risk*** | *Residual Controllable Risk* | 2 | [36,45,65, 81-83,99] |
| | *Unforeseeable Risk* | 4 | |
| ***Project Quality*** | *People Quality* | 10 | [47,90-96] |
| | *Process Quality* | 6 | |
| ***Project Performance*** | *Subjective Performance* | 24 | [36,48,59, 65,72,81, 83,86,88, 89,97,100] |
| | *Objective Performance* | 3 | |

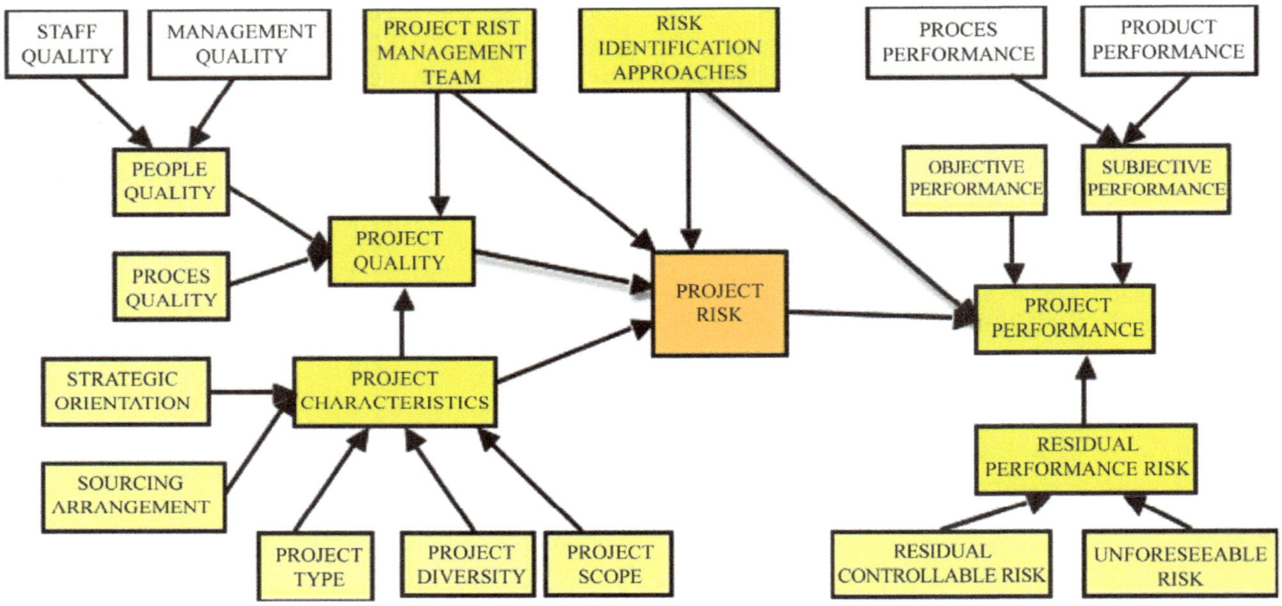


**Figure 1**. Conceptual framework.

## CONCEPTUAL FRAMEWORK

### The Relationship between Project Characteristics and Project Risk

In literature, there is a lack of studies that attempt to examine the various characteristics of software projects and the way different risk dimensions, especially, and the total level of risk, in general, are affected by them. This research will examine, five project characteristics, emerged from the literature, which have been discussed above [5,32,38].

First, the development of an application with strategic orientation has fundamental differences from the development of an application for automating various transactions or decision-making. For example, the survey of Wallace et al. [32] showed that strategic applications involve more complexity risk than information or transaction oriented applications. Yet, though it seems quite possible that projects of strategic nature differ from non-strategic projects in terms of risk, far too few empirical researches have been carried out examining the role various project characteristics play in the appearance and magnitude of these risks.

Moreover, although the relationship between project scope and software project risk is known from unpublished experiences, it has not been empirically tested in depth. However, a research by Huang and Han [46] elevated the fact that a parameter of the project scope, its duration, affects to a great extent some of the dimensions of risk, like those of planning and control, team, user and requirements as well. In total agreement with the survey of Huang and Han [46], two earlier surveys, those of Wallace et al. [32] and Zmud [101], verified this parallel relationship of project scope with risk. Wallace et al. [32] detected a clear influence of project scope on all risk dimensions, while Zmud [101] suggested that the higher level of uncertainty that is observed on projects with long duration is an outcome of the co-dependence between the various project procedures and the high level of co-operation that should be accomplished for the harmonic and effective management of people, of requirements and complexity.

Wallace et al. [32] revealed the insufficiency of surveys about the relationship between the use of outsourcing and project risk, and they verified that the use of outsourcing would bring a different risk profile compared to the complete use of intra-organizational resources for the development of a project. The use of one indicator for the two different strategies (in-house and outsourcing), in conjunction with the risk dimensions metrics, can lead to the exploration and projection of the main sections of a project that become more or less risky, according to the selection or not of an outsourcing strategy for their development. Through the empirical results of their survey, Wallace et al. projected the highest levels of risk on the dimensions of team and planning and control, in those cases that an organization decides to make use of the outsourcing strategy. In order to explain this limited relationship of outsourcing with the total level of risk (as it is defined by its 6 aforementioned dimensions), they stated that projects that are liable to outsourcing practices, justifiably tend to encounter greater challenges and difficulties, in terms of team communication and co-operation, provided that at least two organizations are engaged.

The issue of project diversity - although it has been a matter of examination in the field of software development many times in the past [38,39,98], concerning its relation and effect on the degree of success and performance of a project- is obviously absent from the international literature, as regards the examination of its relationship with the risk level of software projects.

Last but not least, Jones [5] defined six basic categories of software projects and correlated them with the most risky factors of the project, recognizing that different risks affect different software systems with different weight. Though, the Application Taxonomy catalogue that Jones presented constitutes an interesting contribution in the field of risk management, his research suffers many paradoxical tendencies and omissions that should be improved through future research. The present study is going to proceed towards this direction.

The main research question that emerges from the above discussion, illustrated in Figure 1, is the following:

*Research Question 1:* How the characteristics of a project affect the level of risk during the development process?

## The Project Risk Management Team Relationship with Project Risk

The importance of selecting the appropriate team that will carry out the risk management process, so as to enhance the effectiveness and performance of a project, was recognized by Ward [78]. Ward expressed the view that an effective risk management requires from project development team members to have the necessary motivation, capability and experience, as well as a deep understanding of their responsibilities both for the process and the outcome. He also stated that, if one of these requirements (motivation, capability and experience, perceived responsibilities) is missing, or cannot be elevated, then it will be desired to find a more adequate party for managing risk. Recognizing the importance of project participants' characteristics for the risk management process, as well as their effect on the total project performance, an attempt will be made to connect these characteristics with the software development risk. The examination of this link is another goal of the present study.

*Research Question 2:* How the characteristics of the risk management team affect the level of project development risk?

## The Relationship between Project Characteristics, Project Risk Management Team and Project Quality

After the analysis of those variables that define some of the elements that characterize a software project as well as its stakeholders, and their connection to the project risk, an attempt will be made to examine their interaction with project quality. The specific conceptual connection among these volatile factors, despite its obvious theoretical and practical value, has not been studied in depth in the past, at least not in the restricted framework of software development. For this reason, the examination and interpretation of these relationships were considered essential, despite their indirect reference to the main issue of the emergence, impact, mitigation and overall management of project risks. No matter what results-conclusions will be derived, a wider research framework in the field of risk management in the international literature will be hopefully triggered.

*Research Question 3:* How Project Characteristics affect Project Quality?

*Research Question 4:* How Project Risk Management Team Characteristics affect Project Quality?

## The Relationship of the Risk Identification Approaches with Project Risk and Project Performance

Kulik and Weber [27] classified the risk identification approaches for software projects in four main groups: ad-hoc, formal, informal and periodic. In the present research a step forward is going to be made, attempting to connect directly the risk identification approaches with the level of risk in the software development project and with the project performance. These relations will be studied in order to estimate the importance, uniqueness and effectiveness of every approach on the overall project risk assessment (as well as with each risk dimension) and on project performance, respectively.

*Research Question 5:* How does the use of different risk identification approaches on software projects affect the level of project risk involved?

*Research Question 6:* How does the use of different risk identification approaches on software projects affect project performance?

## The Relationship between Project Quality and Project Risk

Despite the fact that the quality issue in software development project has been taken into consideration in many research papers in the past (see Section 2.7), none of these studies investigated its importance and relationship with the conceptual factor of software development risk. In this study, a first attempt will be made to conceptualize this framework using the items suggested by Fenton's et al. [92] research for measuring project quality.

*Research Question 7*: How does the level of project quality affect its risk?

## The Relationship of Residual Performance Risk with Project Performance

Nidumolu [81] was the first to examine the relationship between project's residual performance risk and its actual performance. Data from 64 software development projects in the USA provided substantial foundation for his model. Nidumolu used residual performance risk as an intermediate factor among those of standardization, uncertainty of requirements and project performance. After the statistic analysis and the examination of the hypotheses, Nidumolu enunciated the existence of a negative consequence of residual performance risk on the process and product performance of the project.

Na et al. [83] attempted to examine the original model of Nidumolu's survey in the software development industry of Korea. By using identical structural models and by gathering data from Korean software projects that were developed from 1999 to 2000, they compared the findings of Nidumolu from the USA with those of their research. The analysis indicated that the mean of residual performance risk and its effect on the subjective performance of a project differs significantly between the two studies and the two countries, since the correlation coefficients between both residual performance risk and the two aspects of project performance are not statistically important for the data of the Korean research. According to Na et al. [83], a possible explanation for this observed difference is that in technologically developing countries like Korea, where the systematic use of risk management is still in early stages, the residual performance risk is less important and substantial for software development companies.

Extending the previous research, Na et al. [36] carried out a survey in three of the largest software development companies in Korea (companies that occupied at least 25.000 employees). In this survey, Na and his colleagues attempted to measure (in 123 software development projects), among others and the relationship between the residual performance risk and the objective performance of projects. They reported the existence of a positive and statistically important relationship between these factors.

A recent study by Jiang et al. [99] measured and evaluated the effect of the residual performance risk on the subjective performance of 151 organizations in the USA This research verified the negative relationship between these two factors.

Furthermore, since the Korean research [83] was designed to copy the previous American research [81], Na et al. did not try to collect data that would allow them to analyze the two elements of residual performance risk. As a result, they could not define the proportion of the unforeseeable risk and the residual controllable risk (through the aforementioned control techniques, at the final stage, though, of the development of a project), in the total residual performance risk. For this reason, another contribution of the present study would be the selection of appropriate data that will allow us to study and analyze thoroughly these two elements of a project's residual performance risk. Na et al. [83] stated that since managers of software projects continue to improve risk management practices, the mean residual controllable risk would gradually decrease. However, as the software development becomes more and more innovative and the development technology continues to improve rapidly, the risk of unexpected uncertainty and chaotic situations could emerge and quickly take gigantic dimensions.

*Research Question 8:* How does residual performance risk affect the performance (subjective and objective) of a project?

*Research Question 9*: How does unforeseeable risk and residual controllable risk affect the residual performance risk of a project?

## The Relationship of the Project Risk with the Project Performance

The relationship between the risk level of a project and its performance has been examined by several researches in the past [32,48,59,100]. In particular, Jiang and Klein [100] agreed that the various risks in software development consist a great problem that affects project performance. Wallace et al. [32] composed a model – that was established in the literature of project management and the sociotechnical theory, along with the special risk metrics – that is based on six risk dimensions and explains to a great extent the variability that occurs on the project performance. Wallace et al. [48] designed a model measuring project's performance and risk level, and they underlined the reverse relationship between the two concepts (especially the process instead of the product). Recently, Han and Huang [59] examined the relationship of software risks and their effect on project performance. In their article, they displayed the findings of an empirical research that was based on 115 software projects, about the possibility of appearance and the consequence of the six different dimensions of risks on project performance.

Considering the above surveys, and since the empirical data that describe the relationship between risk and project performance are rare and often fail to take into consideration the several risk factors that prevent their successful outcome, this study may emerge as a general framework for future research, so as to investigate the impact of project risk on both dimensions (subjective and objective) of performance, and to further examine those risk factors that are less projected in literature and have an important effect on project performance.

*Research Question 10*: How does the level of project risk affect the performance (subjective and objective) of a project?

## CONCLUDING REMARKS

In spite of the indisputable fact that in the past 20 years there have been noticed remarkable efforts internationally (found in literature), it is true that quite enough issues concerning risk management in software development projects remain unexamined and lack theoretical and practical support. The expected goal of this research is to bridge the gap between the existing literature and the appropriate practices in the management of software development projects by evaluating practitioners' needs for the successful management of software risks.

Through a brief literature review and the construction of a new research framework, an explicit conceptual framework has been formed. In this framework, a group of factors has been added for the determination of the total risk level and, moreover, its effect (and all of the dimensions that compose it) on the final subjective and objective project performance. The ineffective performance of many software projects and the consequential costs and time overruns, missed business prospects, and the rise of social distrust in the information technologies, give cause for reflection in the software project management field; this study will hopefully help in the evaluation and estimation of several project performance related aspects.

Part of the value of this framework lies in the conceptual representation of factors and the examination of the possible relationships between them, which have not received the appropriate attention when thinking about managing software development projects. While the value of the risk management has already been underlined in the past, and the fact that its theory has made a lot of advancements, there is no complete model yet describing and analyzing the relationships between all these organizational concepts in detail. More specifically, within the field of software development project risk management, there is not an extensive, well-grounded, distinct and applicable system, which will be able to guide project managers to follow reliable and successful management mechanisms. The proposed framework is considered to be an original and complete model that intends to contribute to literature by exploring the linkages among software project risk, risk identification approaches, project characteristics, project risk management team, residual performance risk, project quality and project performance.

In addition, it must be stressed that another significant goal of this paper is the recording and examination of these parameters of risk management in software development projects that can induce and motivate managers or project team members, to a more energetic role in the risk management practices. This study has provided many visions of software project risk that project managers should utilize in order to manage the potential risks related with a particular project and to evaluate effectively the possible alternatives. The multi-dimensional theoretical background of these practitioners is almost certain that will provide the necessary spark for the use of a thorough and systematic approach of risk management in the whole project lifecycle (in which risk is assessed in each phase of the project), and to develop the appropriate risk mitigation strategy in more timely and scientific way.

Finally, the project risk management issues are not usually in the agenda of the software development organizations (and especially at the small ones), because of the sensitive information that includes and the adherence to the "shoot the messenger" syndrome, which frequently discourages the members of the development team from bringing forthcoming or pending problems to the attention of management. So, this study may help to get over this lack of communication between project team members (who will find some helpful and practical insights in the theoretical framework of this research) and, mainly, by changing and integrating a new effectual culture considering the risks that their projects face.

The research model suggested here has to be validated using real life data. Authors have already constructed a structured questionnaire which has been refined in several pre-test stages and interviews with academics and practitioners (project managers and programmers) experts in software project development. The data collection process will commence by the end of January, 2011, while the first results are expected by the end of March, 2011.

## REFERENCES


1. J. H. Iversen, L. Mathiassen and P. A. Nielsen, "Managing Risk in Software Process Improvement: An Action Research Approach," MIS Quarterly, Vol. 28, No. 3, 2004, pp. 395-433.
2. W. W. Gibbs, "Softwares Chronic Crisis," Scientific American, Vol. 271, No. 3, 1994, pp. 86-95. doi:10.1038/scientificamerican0994-86
3. R. Glass, "Software Runaways—Some Surprising Find ings," The DATABASE for Advances in Information Systems, Vol. 28, No. 3, 1997, pp. 16-19.
4. J. Johnson, "My Life is Failure: 100 Things You Should Know to Be a Successful Project Leader," Standish Group International, West Yarmouth, 2006.
5. C. Jones, "Assessment and Control of Software Risks," Yourdon Press, Englewood Cliffs, 1994.
6. C. Jones, "Risks of Software System Failure or Disaster," American Programmer, Vol. 8, No. 3, 1995, pp. 2-9.
7. G. Klein and J. J. Jiang, "Seeking Consonance in Information Systems," Journal of Systems and Software, Vol. 56, No. 2, 2001, pp. 195-202. doi:10.1016/S0164-1212(00)00097-2
8. K. Lyytinen and R. Hirschheim, "Information Systems Failures—A Survey and Classification of the Empirical Literature," Oxford Surveys in Information Technology, Vol. 4, No. 1, 1987, pp. 257-309.
9. J. McManus, "Risk Management in Software Development Projects," Elsevier Butterworth-Heinemann, Amsterdam, 2004.
10. J. Ropponen and K. Lyytinen, "Can Software Risk Management Improve System Development: An Exploratory Study," European Journal of Information Systems, Vol. 6, No. 1, 1997, pp. 41-50. doi:10.1057/palgrave.ejis.3000253
11. D. Shafer, "Software Risk: Why Must We Keep Learning from Experience?" Dynamic Positioning Conference, Houston, 28- 30 September 2004, pp. 1-19.
12. Y. H. Kwak and C. W. Ibbs, "Calculating Project Managements Return on Investment," Project Management Journal, Vol. 31, No. 2, 2000, pp. 38-47.
13. K. M. Adams and C. A. Pinto, "Software Development Project Risk Management: A Literature Review," Proceedings of the 26th National Conference, Organizational Transformation: Opportunities and Challenges, American Society for Engineering Management, Rolla, October 2005, pp. 635-641.
14. F. M. Dedolph, "The Neglected Management Activity: Software Risk Management," Bell Labs Technical Journal, Vol. 8, No. 3, 2003, pp. 91-95. doi:10.1002/bltj.10077
15. J. Kontio, G. Getto and D. Landes, "Experiences in Improving Risk Management Processes Using the Concepts of the Riskit Method," Proceedings of the ACM SIGSOFT 6th International Symposium on Foundations of Software Engineering, ACM Press, New York, November 1998, pp. 163-174.
16. B. W. Boehm, "Software Risk Management," IEEE Press, Piscataway, 1989.
17. B. W. Boehm, "Software Risk Management: Principles and Practices," IEEE Software, Vol. 8, No. 1, 1991, pp. 32-41. doi:10.1109/52.62930
18. R. N. Charette, "Software Engineering Risk Analysis and Management," Intertext Publications, New York, 1989.
19. R. N. Charette, "Applications Strategies for Risk Analysis," McGraw-Hill, New York, 1990.
20. M. J. Carr, S. L. Konda, I. Monarch, F. C. Ulrich and C. F. Walker, "Taxonomy-Based Risk Identification," SEI Report CMU/SEI-93-TR-6, Carnegie Mellon University, Pittsburgh PA, 1993.
21. A. J. Dorofee, J. A. Walker, C. J. Alberts, R. P. Higuera, R. L. Murphy and R. C. Williams, "Continuous Risk Management Guidebook," Carnegie Mellon University, Pittsburgh, 1996.
22. R. P. Higuera, D. P. Gluch, A. J. Dorofee, R. L. Murphy, J. A. Walker and R. C. Williams, "An Introduction to Team Risk Management," SEI Report CMU/SEI-94-SR-01, Carnegie Mellon University, Pittsburgh, 1994.
23. R. P. Higuera and Y. Y. Haimes, "Software Risk Management," SEI Report CMU/SEI-96-TR-012, Carnegie Mellon University, Pittsburgh PA, 1996.
24. F. J. Sisti and S. Joseph, "Software Risk Evaluation Method," SEI Report CMU/SEI-94-TR-19, Carnegie Mellon University, Pittsburgh PA, 1994.
25. R. L. van Scoy, "Software Development Risk: Opportunity, Not Problem," SEI Report CMU/SEI-92-TR-30, Carnegie Mellon University, Pittsburgh PA, 1992.

26. F. Schoenthaler, "Risk Management in Challenging Business Software Projects," Proceedings of the 10th Anniversary IEEE Joint International Conference on Requirements Engineering, Essen, Germany, 9-13 September 2002, pp. 1-3.

27. P. Kulik and K. Weber, "Software Risk Management Practices—2001," KLCI Research Group, Dayton, 2001.

28. S. Ward, "Assessing and Managing Important Risks," International Journal of Project Management, Vol. 17, No. 6, 1999, pp. 331-336. doi:10.1016/S0263-7863(98)00051-9

29. K. Wiegers, "Know Your Enemy: Software Risk Management," Software Development, Vol. 6, No. 10, 1998, pp. 38-42.

30. J. Ropponen, "Software Risk Management—Foundations, Principles and Empirical Findings," Jyvaskyla University Printing House, Jyvaskyla, 1999.

31. S. Murthi, "Preventive Risk Management for Software Projects," IT Professional, Vol. 4, No. 5, 2002, pp. 9-15. doi:10.1109/MITP.2002.1041172

32. L. Wallace, M. Keil and A. Rai, "Understanding Software Project Risk: A Cluster Analysis," Journal of Information and Management, Vol. 42, No. 1, 2004, pp. 115-125.

33. R. Hirschheim and M. Lacity, "The Myths and Realities of Information Technology Insourcing," Communications of the ACM, Vol. 43, No. 2, 2000, pp. 99-107. doi:10.1145/328236.328112

34. P. D. Chatzoglou and L. Sarigiannidis, "Business Outsourcing and Organisational Performance: The Case of the Greek Hotel Industry," International Journal of Services Technology and Management, Vol. 11, No. 2, 2009, pp. 105-127. doi:10.1504/IJSTM.2009.022520

35. R. T. Nakatsu and C. L. Iacovou, "A Comparative Study of Important Risk Factors Involved in Offshore and Domestic Outsourcing of Software Development Projects: A Two-Panel Delphi Study," Information and Management, Vol. 46, No. 12, 2009, pp. 57-68. doi:10.1016/j.im.2008.11.005

36. K. S. Na, J. T. Simpson, X. Li, T. Singh and K. Y. Kim, "Software Development Risk and Project Performance Measurement: Evidence in Korea," The Journal of Systems and Software, Vol. 80, No. 1, 2007, pp. 596-605. doi:10.1016/j.jss.2006.06.018

37. E. Clemons, "Evaluation of Strategic Investments in Information Technology," Communications of the ACM, Vol. 34, No. 1, 1991, pp. 22-36. doi:10.1145/99977.99985

38. A. M. Aladwani, "IT Project Uncertainty, Planning and Success: An Empirical Investigation from Kuwait," Information Technology and People, Vol. 15, No. 3, 2002, pp. 210-226.

39. M. A. Campion, G. J. Medsker and A. C. Higgs, "Relations between Work Group Characteristics and Effectiveness: Implications for Designing Effective Work Groups," Personnel Psychology, Vol. 46, No. 4, 1993, pp. 823-850. doi:10.1111/j.1744-6570.1993.tb01571.x

40. D. Houston, G. Mackulak and J. Collofello, "Stochastic Simulation of Risk Factor Potential Effects for Software Development Risk Management," Journal of Systems and Software, Vol. 59, No. 3, 2001, pp. 247-257. doi:10.1016/S0164-1212(01)00066-8

41. C. Jones, "Software Assessments, Benchmarks, and Best Practices," Addison-Wesley, Boston MA, 2000.

42. D. Gotterbarn and S. Rogerson, "Responsible Risk Analysis for Software Development: Creating the Software Development Impact Statement," Communications of the Association for Information Systems, Vol. 15, 2005, pp. 730-750.

43. H. Barki, S. Rivard and J. Talbot, "Toward an Assessment of Software Development Risk," Journal of Management Information Systems, Vol. 10, No. 2, 1993, pp. 203-225.

44. M. Boban, Z. Pozgaj and H. Seric, "Strategies for Successful Software Development Risk Management," Management, Vol. 8, 2003, pp. 77-91.

45. F. W. McFarlan, "Portfolio Approach to Information Systems," Harvard Business Review, Vol. 59, No. 5, 1981, pp. 142-150.

46. S. J. Huang and W. M. Han, "Exploring the Relationship between Software Project Duration and Risk Exposure: A Cluster Analysis," Journal of Information and Management, Vol. 45, No. 3, 2008, pp. 175-182.

47. B. Hughes and M. Cotterell, "Software Project Management," 4th Edition, McGraw-Hill, New York, 2006.

48. L. Wallace, M. Keil and A. Rai, "How Software Project Risk Affects Project Performance: An Investigation of the Dimensions of Risk and an Exploratory Model," Decision Sciences, Vol. 35, No. 2, 2004, pp. 289-321. doi:10.1111/j.00117315.2004.02059.x

49. F. J. Heemstra and R. J. Kusters, "Dealing with Risk: A Practical Approach," Journal of Information Technology, Vol. 11, No. 4, 1996, pp. 333-346. doi:10.1057/jit.1996.7

50. T. Moynihan, "How Experienced Project Managers Assess Risk," IEEE Software, Vol. 14, No. 3, 1997, pp. 35-41. doi:10.1109/52.589229

51. J. Ropponen and K. Lyytinen, "Components of Software Development Risk: How to Address Them? A Project Manager Survey," IEEE Transactions on Software Engineering, Vol. 26, No. 2, 2000, pp. 98-112. doi:10.1109/32.841112

52. T. A. Longstaff, C. Chittister, R. Pethia and Y. Y. Haimes, "Are We Forgetting the Risks of Information Technology?" IEEE Computer, Vol. 33, No. 12, 2000, pp. 43-51.

53. D. Houston, "A Software Project Simulation Model for Risk Management," Ph.D. Thesis, Arizona State University, Tempe AZ, 2000.

54. P. Cule, R. Schmidt, K. Lyytinen and M. Keil, "Strategies for Heading off Project Failure," Information Systems Management, Vol. 17, No. 2, 2000, pp. 65-73. doi:10.1201/1078/43191.17.2.20000301/31229.8

55. M. Sumner, "Risk Factors in Enterprise Wide/ERP Projects," Journal of Information Technology, Vol. 15, No. 4, 2000, pp. 317-327. doi:10.1080/02683960010009079

56. R. Kliem, "Risk Management for Business Process ReenGineering Projects," Information Systems

Management, Vol. 17, No. 4, 2001, pp. 71-73.

57. R. Schmidt, K. Lyytinen, M. Keil and P. Cule, "Identifying Software Project Risks: An International Delphi Study," Journal of Management Information Systems, Vol. 17, No. 4, 2001, pp. 5-36.

58. T. Addison, "E-Commerce Project Development Risks: Evidence from a Delphi Survey," International Journal of Information Management, Vol. 23, No. 1, 2003, pp. 25-40. doi:10.1016/S0268-4012(02)00066-X

59. W. M. Han and S. J. Huang, "An Empirical Analysis of Risk Components and Performance on Software Projects," The Journal of Systems and Software, Vol. 80, No. 1, 2007, pp. 42-50. doi:10.1016/j.jss.2006.04.030

60. J. Jiang and G. Klein, "Risks to Different Aspects of SysTem Success," Information and Management, Vol. 36, No. 5, 1999, pp. 264-272. doi:10.1016/S0378-7206(99)00024-5

61. S. Sakhtevil, "Managing Risks in Offshore Systems Development," Communications, Vol. 50, No. 4, 2007, pp. 69-75.

62. B. Curtis, S. Ward and C. Chapman, "Roles, Responsibilities and Risks in Management Contracting," Construction Industry Research and Information Association (CIRIA) Special Publication 81, 1991.

63. O. Mizuno, T. Kikuno, Y. Takagi and K. Sakamoto, "Characterization of Risky Projects Based on Project Managers Evaluation," Proceedings of the 22nd InterNational Conference on Software Engineering, Limerick, 4-11 June 2000, pp. 387-395.

64. C. F. Kemerer and G. L. Sosa, "Systems Development Risks in Strategic Information Systems," Information and Software Technology, Vol. 33, No. 3, 1991, pp. 212-223. doi:10.1016/0950-5849(91)90136-Y

65. S. R. Nidumolu, "The Effect of Coordination and Uncertainty on Software Project Performance: Residual Performance Risk as an Intervening Variable," Information Systems Research, Vol. 6, No. 3, 1995, pp. 191-219. doi:10.1287/isre.6.3.191

66. S. P. Keider, "Why Systems Development Projects Fail," Journal of Information Systems Management, Vol. 1, No. 3, 1984, pp. 33-38. doi:10.1080/07399019408963043

67. T. K. Abdel-Hamid, "A Study of Staff Turnover, Acquisition, and Assimilation and Their Impact on Software Development Cost and Schedule," Journal of Management Information Systems, Vol. 6, No. 1, 1989, pp. 21-39.

68. F. P. Brooks, "No Silver Bullet: Essence and Accidents of Software Engineering," Computer, Vol. 22, No. 4, 1987, pp. 10-19. doi:10.1109/MC.1987.1663532

69. J. J. Jiang, G. Klein and T. Means, "Project Risk Impact on Software Development Team Performance," Project Management Journal, Vol. 31, No. 4, 2000, pp. 19-26.

70. S. L. Jarvenpaa and B. Ives, "Executive Involvement and Participation in the Management of Information Technology," MIS Quarterly, Vol. 15, No. 2, 1991, pp. 205-277. doi:10.2307/249382

71. D. F. Cooper, S. Grey, G. Raymond and P. Walker, "Project Risk Management Guidelines: Managing Risk in Large Projects and Complex Procurements," John Wiley and Sons Ltd., Chichester, 2005.

72. H. Barki, S. Rivard and J. Talbot, "An Integrative Contingency Model of Software Project Risk Management," Journal of Management Information Systems, Vol. 17, No. 4, 2001, pp. 37-69.

73. K. Padayachee, "An Interpretive Study of Software Risk Management Perspectives," Proceedings of the 2002 Annual Research Conference of the South African Institute of Computer Scientists and Information Technologists on Enablement Through Technology, Bela Bela, 2002, pp. 118-127.

74. S. L. Pfleeger, "Risky Business: What We Have Yet to Learn about Software Risk Management," Journal of Systems and Software, Vol. 53, No. 3, 2000, pp. 265-273. doi:10.1016/S0164-1212(00)00017-0

75. B. Rockenbach, A. Sadrieh and B. Mathauschek, "Teams Take the Better Risks," Journal of Economic Behavior and Organization, Vol. 63, No. 3, 2007, pp. 412-422. doi:10.1016/j.jebo.2005.04.023

76. L. Labuschagne, "Project Risk Management Roles and Responsibilities," 2010. http://www.zulanas.lt/images/adm_source/docs/2_full%20 paperENG.pdf

77. T. R. Peltier, "Risk Analysis and Risk Management," Information Systems Security, Vol. 13, No. 4, 2004, pp. 44-56. doi:10.1201/1086/44640.13.4.20040901/83732.7

78. S. Ward, "Requirements for an Effective Project Risk Management Process," Project Management Journal, Vol. 30, No. 3, 1999, pp. 37-43.

79. B. W. Boehm and R. Ross, "Theory-W Software Project Management: Principles and Examples," IEEE Transactions on Software Engineering, Vol. 15, No. 7, 1989, pp. 902-916. doi:10.1109/32.29489

80. T. R. Hinkin, "A Review of Scale Development Practices in the Study of Organization", Journal of Management, Vol. 21, No. 5, 1995, pp. 967-988. doi:10.1177/014920639502100509

81. S. R. Nidumolu, "Standardization, Requirements Uncertainty and Software Project Performance," Information and Management, Vol. 31, No. 3, 1996, pp. 135-150. doi:10.1016/S0378-7206(96)01073-7

82. A. Meyer, C. Loch and M. Pich, "Managing Project Uncertainty: From Variation to Chaos," Sloan Management Review, Vol. 43, No. 2, 2002, pp. 60-67.

83. K. S. Na, X. Li, J. T. Simpson and K. Y. Kim, "Uncertainty Profile and Software Project Performance: A Cross-National Comparison," The Journal of Systems and Software, Vol. 70, No. 1-2, 2004, pp. 155-163. doi:10.1016/S0164-1212(03)00014-1

84. T. Singh, "Software Development Risk Management in Information Technology Developing Countries: An Assessment on Subjective and Objective Performance," Thesis, University of Alabama in Huntsville, Huntsville, 2005.

85. C. Wohlin, A. V. Mayrhauser, M. Host and B. Regnell, "Subjective Evaluation as a Tool for Learning from Software Project Success," Information and Software

Technology, Vol. 42, No. 1, 2000, pp. 983-992. doi:10.1016/S0950-5849(00)00150-6

86. A. Rai and H. Al-Hindi, "The Effects of Development Process Modelling and Task Uncertainty on Development Quality Performance," Information and Management, Vol. 37, No. 6, 2000, pp. 335-346. doi:10.1016/S0378-7206(00)00047-1

87. J. Miller and B. A. Doyle, "Measuring the Effectiveness of Computer-Based Information Systems in the Financial Services Sector," MIS Quarterly, Vol. 11, No. 1, 1987, pp. 107-124. doi:10.2307/248832

88. L. C. Briand, K. E. Emam and F. Bomarius, "COBRA: A Hybrid Method for Software Cost Estimation, BenchMarking, and Risk Assessment," Proceedings IEEE International Conference on Software Engineering, Kyoto, 19-25 April, 1998, pp. 390-399.

89. A. R. Gray, S. G. MacDonell and M. J. Shepperd, "Factors Systematically Associated with Errors in Subjective Estimates of Software Development Effort: The Stability of Expert Judgement," 6th IEEE International Symposium on Software Metrics, Boca Raton, 4-6 November, 1999, pp. 216-227.

90. J. Herbsleb, D. Zubrow, D. Goldenson, W. Hayes and M. Paulk, "Software Quality and the Capability Maturity Model," Communications of the ACM, Vol. 40, No. 6, 1997, pp. 30-40. doi:10.1145/255656.255692

91. M. Ould, "Managing Software Quality and Business Risk," Wiley, Chichester, 1999.

92. N. Fenton, W. Marsh, M. Neil, P. Cates, S. Forey and M. Tailor, "Making Resource Decisions for Software Projects," Proceedings of the 26th International Conference on Software Engineering, Edinburgh, 23-28 May 2004, pp. 397-406. doi:10.1109/ICSE.2004.1317462

93. N. Fenton, M. Neil, W. Marsh, P. Hearty, L. Radliński and P. Krause, "On the Effectiveness of Early Life Cycle Defect Prediction with Bayesian Nets," Empirical Software Engineering, Vol. 13, No. 5, 2008, pp. 499-537. doi:10.1007/s10664-008-9072-x

94. G. Hoffman, "Integrating PSP and CMMI Level 5," STC Proceedings, 2003. http://www.stc-online.org/stc2003proceedings/PDFFiles/ pres1001.pdf

95. AgenaRisk, "Software Project Risk Model Manual. Bayesian Network and Simulation Software for Risk Analysis and Decision Support-AgenaRisk (Version 2.00)," 2005. http://www.agenarisk.com/

96. G. H. Subramanian, J. J. Jiang and G. Klein, "Software Quality and IS Project Performance Improvements from Software Development Process Maturity and IS Implementation Strategies," Journal of Systems and Software, Vol. 80, No. 4, 2007, pp. 616-627. doi:10.1016/j.jss.2006.06.014

97. M. Keil, L. Wallace, D. Turk, G. Dixon-Randall and U. Nulden, "An Investigation of Risk Perception and Risk Propensity on the Decision to Continue a Software Development Project," The Journal of Systems and Software, Vol. 53, No. 2, 2000, pp. 145-157. doi:10.1016/S0164-1212(00)00010-8

98. P. J. Guinan, J. G. Cooprider and S. Faraj, "Enabling Software Development Team Performance during Requirements Definition: A Behavioral Versus Technical Approach," Information Systems Research, Vol. 9, No. 2, 1998, pp. 101-125. doi:10.1287/isre.9.2.101

99. J. J. Jiang, G. Klein, S. P. J. Wu and T. P. Liang, "The Relation of Requirements Uncertainty and Stakeholder Perception Gaps to Project Management Performance," The Journal of Systems and Software, Vol. 82, No. 5, 2009, pp. 801-808. doi:10.1016/j.jss.2008.11.833

100. 100.J. J. Jiang and G. Klein, "Software Development Risks to Project Effectiveness," The Journal of Systems and Software, Vol. 52, No. 1, 2000, pp. 3-10. doi:10.1016/S0164-1212(99)00128-4

101. 101.R. W. Zmud, "Management of Large Software Development Efforts," MIS Quarterly, Vol. 4, No. 2, 1980, pp. 45-55. doi:10.2307/249336.

CHAPTER 17

# CATEGORIZATION OF SOFTWARE RELEASE RISKS AND ITS ABATEMENT STRATEGY

Arti Rana[1], S. P. Singh[2], Rachna Soni[3], Ashish Jolly[4]

[1]Amity Institute of Information Technology, Amity University, Noida (UP), India

[2]Birla Institute of Technology, Extension Centre, Noida, India

[3]Department of Computer Science, DAV College for Girls, Yamuna Nagar, India

[4]Department of Computer Science, Govt. College, Bherian (Pehowa), Haryana, India

## ABSTRACT

**Growing competition in the software industry with the persistently changing needs and the usual problems associated with software release, which have made acceptance of a new software in market, are extremely important for the success. Volatility in the software developmental processes is generally difficult to handle. The change request at any arbitrary point of time leads to the inevitable change and rework request. The software release process which broadly includes all the process that starts after the completion of development till the final deployment. This complete phase is exposed to various risks which may hamper the final result. This paper presents threat associated with software release activities and their possible mitigation and exploring the role played by the change management in controlling or reducing those risks. For the effective survival in ever changing software industry needs, Software Release Management takes a holistic view of the change and configuration relationship and work on the improvement strategies for the effective release with zero defect potential.**

## INTRODUCTION

The release management is a link between software development and its final deployment. The software release management handles the continuous pressure to have the release plan ready as early as possible and release processes including proceeds with progressions all through the release cycle as indicated by the unpredictability of accessibility of human asset and sudden changes in the technology or requirements because of moving business necessities. If not overseen prudently and timely, these repeating progressions can prompt a challenging relationship between release management and software development process prompting to sub-ideal choice making [1] .

The major objectives of the release management may include:

- To plan deployment of software on time;
- To give due thought to the standpoint of the customer throughout the planning and rollout of new release;
- To ensure that software changes are traceable;
- To make an effective utilization of available resources to optimize the cost;
- To ensure that proper measures are taken to acquaint the customer with usage of new software;
- To design a proper rollout plan for the effective software release;

**Citation:** Rana, A. , Singh, S. , Soni, R. and Jolly, A. (2014) Categorization of Software Release Risks and Its Abatement Strategy. Journal of Software Engineering and Applications, 7, 1039-1044. doi: 10.4236/jsea.2014.712091.

- To ensure the availability of back out plan in case of failure of new release for the smooth running and ensure stability;
- To be aligned with the change management and configuration management [2] .

## SOFTWARE RELEASE PROCESS GUIDELINES

Release planning is an extremely unpredictable issue as it incorporates the alternate points of view of diverse stakeholders, contending goals and having distinctive types of constraints [3] [4] . In the software having numerous of volatile features which are associated to each other with the precedence and/or coupling constraints between them. Moreover, resources, effort and budget constraints must be fulfilled for each one release. The general objective is to discover a "most guaranteeing" release plans such that the general worth and the level of fulfilment of distinctive stakeholders is to be augmented and produce feasible and valuable release plans according to the current business necessities inside time, plan and budget:

- Identify the requirements;
- Prioritize the multifaceted requirements and stakeholders;
- Clustering of similar requirements;
- Identification of constraints;
- Extent of stakeholders' involvement;
- Time and cost;
- Identification and abatement planning of Risks: Consideration of risk should be part of the planning process. Although hard to quantify, risk consideration helps to generate plans that are more likely to be feasible and operational;
- Planning of back out plan.

## ACTIVITIES OF RELEASE MANAGEMENT

### Release Planning

Planning a release includes designing release schedule for the entire project life cycle taking into consideration all the constraints and dependencies and once the plan is designed then gaining the consent on release content. Release planning outputs include the plan for a particular release and acceptance criteria for the release. Software release management should work in association with the change management to meet the changing needs of the stakeholders from the new release.

### Design, Build and Configuration of New Release

All the design procedures should be planned and properly documented for building release, the proper documentation helps in reusing defined procedures where possible. A configuration of a particular release of software may be some of which may be developed in-house and others bought in or the combined approach. All software constraints, parameters, test data and all the required software needed for the release should be under the control of Configuration Management Control. To ensure quality, various quality control checks should be performed on every phase of release of software. A complete record of the build results should be stored in the CMDB. Master details of the software installation and related instructions, documentation must be maintained in the DSL.

### Release Acceptance

The testing of the release before deployment ought to be performed completely. The back out methodology ought to additionally be tried as a piece of the testing action to guarantee the preparation of the reinforcement arranges if there should be an occurrence of disappointment. There ought to be a documentation of each one close down phase of testing. The deciding after-effects of the acknowledgement action should be an improvement on the overall software release. The end result of the acceptance activity should be a sign-off on the completeness and accuracy of the whole release.

### Rollout Plan

Rollout plan provides the details of complete release plan produced so far for exact installation process developed and the agreed implementation plan. Rollout planning deal with detailed schedule of release mentioning who will do, how to do and when to do.

### Communication, Preparation and Training

The clients support staff & connection building staff, need to recognize what is arranged and how it is to completed for guaranteeing its acceptability by the clients, which is trailed by the preparation session for the client and hand on experience to them by demonstrating learning period to them. The outputs of this phase should comprise of the final versions of the software for the user and supporting documentation and training material.

### Distribution and Release Deployment

Distribution of the software release from the build environment to the controlled test environment and then into the live. After deploying software, it is essential to check that the release ensures the acceptance of the stakeholders and considering the post release defects [4] [5] .

Table 1 summarizes all the software release phases with their sub activities based on the study of past release literature.

## SOFTWARE RISK MANAGEMENT

A software releases could be influenced by the substantial assortment of risks. With a specific end goal to comprehend risks and arrangement for its reduction it is essential to recognize the critical risks which may influence the software releases and sorted risks into distinctive classes. The release manager can then inspect the risks and recognize the danger connected with distinctive periods of release procedure [6] .

The risk might be extensively arranged in two primary classes which can influence a software project.

### Project Risks

Project risk concern is risk danger of calendar slippage. Since software is a non-physical, conceptual created by a gathering of individuals located at different places. As it is produced by engineers placed at different places dealing with distinctive modules, emulated by testing lastly release by the different teams. So it is extremely hard to control something which can't be seen through and through. The imperceptibility of the product being produced is an important reason behind why numerous software projects experience the ill effects of the risk of timetable slippage.

## Technical Risks

Technical risks are identified with software outline, execution, interfacing, testing, release and post release maintenance issues. Technical risks likewise incorporate vague particular, partial determination, fluctuating specifications and technical obsolescence. Most Technical risks happen because of the absence of endeavors by project teams on different aspects of advancement and release and eventually simply focus on one aspect and leaving different aspects totally [7] .

**Table 1**. Summary of Software Release activates at various phases

| Major Steps of Software Release | Sub Steps |
|---|---|
| Release planning | Determine objectives and constraints |
| | Determine stakeholders |
| | Determine schedules & baselines |
| | Determine available resources human & technology |
| Design, build and configuration | Redefine model and process design |
| | Improve user interface design |
| | Formally specifications of design |
| User acceptance testing | Independent release testing |
| | Guarantee the working of back out arrangement in the event that crisis |
| | Guarantee accuracy of the release |
| Rollout, communication, preparation and training: | Creating detailed timetable of events and who will do what |
| | User and support training |
| | Manuals |
| Release deployment | Final release product |
| | Track defects |
| | Characterize enhancements |
| | Iterate back to repair and enhance |
| Validate release | Determine the product is same as craved |

## Risk Assessment

The risks are assessed on the premise of their probability of event and harm it causes. The probability of a risk working out as expected (signified as RS). The result of the issues connected with that risk (meant as CS).

In light of these two elements, the necessity of each one risk might be registered:

$R = RS * CS$

This gives the R priority with which the risk is to be taken care of associated with the probability of event and level of outcomes brought on by the risk. In the event that all recognized risks are prioritized, then the no doubt and harming risks might be taken care of first and more extensive risk reduction systems could be intended for these risks [8] .

## Risk Abatement

After all the recognized risks of a task are evaluated, plans must be made to hold the most harming and the undoubtedly risks. Distinctive risks require diverse abatement techniques. Actually, most risks oblige creativity from the project manager in handling the risk.

There are three fundamental systems to anticipate risk restraint:

Evade the risk: The risk can be avoided by considering the customer as a prime; all the changes proposed by the user must be implemented as desired. The proper incentive schemes should be provided to the engineers to avoid end time manpower shortages at time of completion. There should be good employee retention policies.

Transfer the risk: This can be done by hiring specialized skilled people to avoid any kind of discrepancy between requirement and implementation, the critical components where possible should be outsourced to transfer the risk to third part, buying insurance cover, etc.

Risk reduction: The risk reduction should be ensured by maintaining all the check at every sing off, maintain the effective backup plans to meet up the worse situations in case of emergency [9] -[15] .

## RISK ABATEMENT STRATEGY

Following is a table considering all the software release activities along with the risks involved and its mitigation strategy. The investigation of the past papers and dialog infers that the significant likelihood of the fall in Release Planning, as this phase is the base of the entire process of release and has an impact over the complete release process. This could be quantified below in Table 2 on the study premise.

**Table 2**. Risk & mitigation factors of Software Release at Various Phases

| SR Activity | Risk Factor | Likeli-hood | Mitigation |
|---|---|---|---|
| Release planning | Produce the accurate schedule of various phases and baseline results. Release does not work as the customer expects. Due to extended timeline, requirements changes lead to problem in understanding the customer requirements. | 80% | Acceptance criteria linked to requirements assessment. Increase customer involvement throughout use version control tools. |
| Designing and building a release | Release design validation against the requirement for the new or changed service offering. Selection of a suitable release mechanism for the change. Prioritize the issues and actions to ensure that they can be resolved in a timely manner test where the release package delivers the change effectively in line with requirements. | 65% | Aligned with change and configuration management. Use of automation tools. Increased stakeholder interaction through involvement or feedback. |
| Release acceptance | Release meets the requirements in regard to operability, service and product. | 63% | User acceptance tests aligned with change management. |
| Rollout planning | Staff reluctance to adapt changes. Less weight age over the documentation. | 30% | Sign-off documentation for each phase. Software traceability. Use of automation tools. |
| Communication, preparation and training | Lack of timely training, poor & inaccurate communication. Change in business processes is not completely tended to by user training bring on unsuccessful execution. | 40% | Provide training prior to implementation. Remove employee reluctance to adapt new system by making them aware of the need of change. |
| Distribution and deployment | Timely deployment. | 55% | Ensure the acceptance testing before installation. Recording any incidents, unexpected events, issues or deviations from the plans. Ready the backup plan in case emergency. |

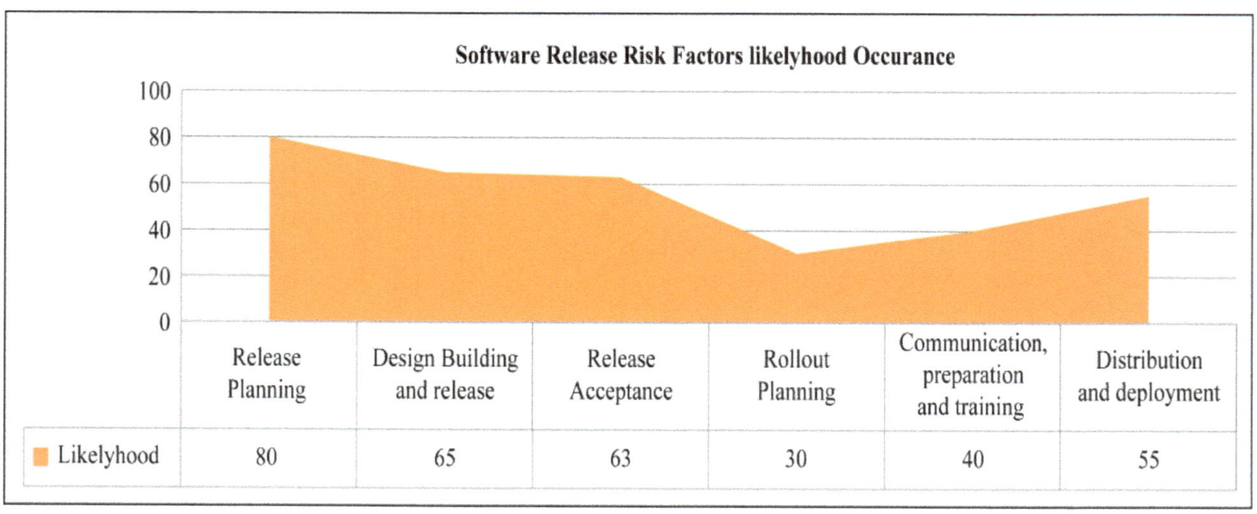


**Graph 1.** Software Release Risks Representation.

## CONCLUSION & FUTURE SCOPE

Arti Rana, S. P. Singh, Rachna Soni, Ashish Jolly Change management plays a vital role in handling the rework requests at any arbitrary point in time as the software development processes generally cannot handle it. The software developmental processes are exposed to certain risks which may hamper the end result. Here common software release activities and their associated risks while exploring mitigation strategies in controlling or reducing those risks are stressed upon. The risk in release planning and release acceptance is high as shown in Graph 1, so the user confidence is built though mitigation strategies. It is observed that change management is aligned with configuration management for better release building. Further release risk mitigation contingency plan can be developed for the cost effectiveness using stochastic system modeling.

## REFERENCES


1. Penny, D.A. (2002) An Estimation-Based Management Framework for Enhance Maintenance in Commercial Software Product. Proceedings of the international Conference on Software Maintenance (ICSM 02), Washington DC, 2002, 122-130.
2. IBM Software Thought Leadership (2013) 7 Proven Practices to Strengthen Release Management. IBM Corporation, USA.
3. Greer, D. and Ruhe, G. (2004) Software Release Planning Software Release Planning: An Evolutionary and Iterative Approach. Information &software Technology, 46, 243-253.
4. Ruhe, G. and Sailu, M.O. (2005) Art and Science of Software Release Planning. IEEE Software, 22, 47-53. http://dx.doi.org/10.1109/MS.2005.164
5. Sailu, M.O. and Ruhe, G. (2005) Supporting Release Planning Decision for Evolving Systems. Proceedings of 29th Annual NASA Software Engineering Workshop, Washington DC, 6-7 April 2005, 14-26.
6. Curtis, P. and Carey, M., Thought Leadership in ERM (2012) Risk Assessment in Practice. The Committee of Sponsoring Organizations of the Treadway Commission (COSO), USA.
7. Shahzad, B. and Al-Mudimigh, A.S. (2010) Risk Identification, Mitigation and Avoidance Model for Handling Software Risk. 2010 Second International Conference on Computational Intelligence, Communication Systems and Networks (CICSyN), Liverpool, 28-30 July 2010, 191-196,
8. Karlsson, J. and Ryan, K. (1997) A Cost-Value Approach for Prioritize Requirements. IEEE Software, 14, 67-74. http://dx.doi.org/10.1109/52.605933
9. Carlshamre, P., Sandahl, K., Lindvall, M., Rengnell, B. and Noch Dag, J. (2001) An Industrial Survey of Requirements Interdependencies in Software Product Release Planning. 5th IEEE International Symposium on Requirements Engineering, Toronto, 27-31 August 2001, 84-91.
10. Jung, H.W. (1998) Optimizing Value and Cost in Requirements Analysis. IEEE Software, 15, 74-78. http://dx.doi.org/10.1109/52.687950
11. Lindren, M., Nordstrom, C., Wall, A. and Land, R. (2008) Importance of Software Architecture during Release Planning. Seventh Working IEEE/IFIP Conference on Software Architecture, Vancouver, 18-21 February 2008, 253-256.
12. Wohlin, C. and Aurum, A. (2005) What Is Important When Deciding to Include a Software Requirement in a Project or Release? 2005 International Symposium on Empirical Software Engineering, Queensland, 17-18 November 2005, 10.
13. Li, Q., Yang, Y., Li, M.S., Wang, Q., Boehm, B.W. and Hu, C.Y. (2010) Improving Software Testing Process: Feature Prioritization to Make Winners of Success-Critical Stakeholders. Journal of Software: Evolution and Process, 24, 783- 801.
14. Wall, A. (2008) Key Aspects of Software Release Planning in Industry. 19th Australian Conference on Software Engineering, Perth, 26-28 March 2008, 320-329.
15. Lu, Y.K. (2012) An Information Systems Design Product Theory for Integrated Requirements, Test and Defect Management Systems. 47th Hawaii International Conference on System Sciences, Maui, 4-7 January 2012, 5516-5525.

CHAPTER 18

# USING RISK APPETITE AND RISK ATTITUDE TO SUPPORT APPROPRIATE RISK TAKING: A NEW TAXONOMY AND MODEL

David Hillson[1] and Ruth Murray-Webster[2]

[1]Risk Doctor & Partners, UK
[2]Lucidus Consulting, UK

## ABSTRACT

**The term 'risk appetite' is used widely and increasingly, but there is no commonly accepted definition for it. This situation is exacerbated by confusion between risk appetite and other risk-related terms, especially risk attitude.**

**This paper offers a consistent and coherent taxonomy of these terms, showing how they relate to one another. This allows development of a rich model to explain the complementary and central roles of both risk appetite and risk attitude when individuals or organizations decide how much risk can be taken in a risky and important situation.**

**By progressively deconstructing the full model, we conclude that the key step is to set risk thresholds. We derive a three-stage approach to setting risk thresholds that ensures that the outcomes properly reflect organizational risk culture and the individual risk propensities of key stakeholders, and also clarifies the essential role of risk attitude as a control point. This enables individuals and organizations to choose the appropriate risk attitude in order to influence the amount of risk that is taken in any given situation, so that the achievement of objectives is optimized.**

## Defining Risk Appetite

Senior management teams and boards are constantly confronted with the need to answer one key question: 'How much risk is too much risk?'. This has led in the past decade to an emergent and extensive interest in the idea of risk appetite and its influence on organizational decision-making at all levels from the strategic to the tactical.

Recent research on risk appetite (Association of Insurance and Risk Managers 2009) has identified four ways in which an understanding and expression of risk appetite can be used within organizations:

- To support strategy-setting, leading to a balanced risk profile and identification of which risks to avoid and which to take
- To support effective management of risk, by ensuring that risk management resources are allocated optimally, and fostering a risk-aware culture across the organization
- To set appropriate boundaries for risk taking, by motivating decision makers to make better and more consistent decisions
- To maximize stakeholder value, by enhancing organizational performance and delivery.

**Citation:** David Hillson and Ruth Murray-Webster, "Using risk appetite and risk attitude to support appropriate risk-taking: a new taxonomy and model," ISSN: 1838-7845.

But what exactly is risk appetite? There have been a number of recent attempts to define risk appetite and outline its practical significance to business:

- International standard ISO Guide 73:2009 includes a normative definition of risk app • etite as 'amount and type of risk that an organization is prepared to seek, accept or tolerate'. This is reflected in other risk standards such as ISO31000:2009, BS31100:2011 and the UK Office of Government Commerce 'Management of Risk' (M_o_R) guidance (OGC 2010).
- Professional risk bodies such as the UK Association of Insurance and Risk Managers (AIRMIC), the Institute of Operational Risk (IOR) and the Institute of Risk Management (IRM) have each issued advice to their members aiming to clarify the meaning of the term and how it should be used in practice (AIRMIC 2009; IOR 2009; IRM 2011).
- Corporate governance guidelines refer to the need for organizations to define and communicate their risk appetite, with the new UK Corporate Governance Code stating that: 'The board is responsible for determining the nature and extent of the significant risk it is willing to take in achieving its strategic objectives' (Financial Reporting Council, 2010). Similarly, the US National Association of Corporate Directors (NACD) Blue Ribbon Commission issued their 'Report on Risk Governance: Balancing Risk and Reward' in October 2009, stating that 'The Board of Directors need to understand the organization's risk appetite and level of risk tolerance. The assessment of the company's risk appetite should be an ongoing process, considering that risks facing the company are constantly changing' (NACD 2009).
- Consultancy firms have undertaken research and offered guidance to clients on the subject (PricewaterhouseCoopers 2008; KPMG 2008; Towers Perrin 2009), perhaps seeing a new business opportunity to provide advice and support.

Academics have also been considering the topic, mostly in journals dedicated to economics and investment theory (see, for example, Kumar & Persaud 2002). This work builds on a rich vein of research from risk psychology and behavioral economics, to address the influence of risk perception on decision choices under uncertainty (for example, Kahneman & Tversky 1979; Tversky & Kahnemann 1981; Sitkin & Pablo 1992; Sitkin & Weingart 1995; Weber & Milliman 1997).

Despite the growing and continuing interest in the subject of risk appetite, there is still no consensus on its meaning or practical application. The situation is made worse by the loose use of other risk-related terms, some of which are used interchangeably with risk appetite. These include: risk attitude, risk capacity, risk culture, risk exposure, risk perception, risk preference, risk propensity, risk threshold and risk tolerance. Existing academic and practitioner sources do not clearly define how these terms might differ, overlap, replace or relate to each other.

This paper dispels the confusion by providing a clear definition of risk appetite and distinguishing it from related terms. We also have a broader reason for considering risk appetite, namely, to explore how it influences decision-making in situations perceived as risky and important. Our previous work has addressed the role of risk attitude in such decision-making (Hillson & Murray-Webster 2007; Murray-Webster & Hillson 2008).

In this paper, we propose a new model in which both risk appetite and risk attitude act as mediating factors between a wide range of inputs and key outcomes. The model is supported by a consistent and coherent taxonomy of risk-related terms, and clarifies how these relate to each other. We also suggest practical ways in which people and organizations can work with these concepts to ensure that they make appropriate decisions in risky and important situations.

## The Centrality of Risk Appetite and Risk Attitude

There is one key decision to make in risky and important situations, namely, how much risk to take. This deceptively simple question is actually very complex to answer. It depends on a wide range of related factors, some of which are internal to the decision makers as individuals and groups, and others that exist externally and independently of people. In addition, some of those factors can be influenced or determined by the choices of the people involved, whereas others exist independent of human choice.

Within this complex set of interacting factors, our contention is that two play a key central role, namely risk appetite and risk attitude. We propose a model showing the central importance of risk appetite and risk attitude, the 'RARA Model', presented in Figure 1, which also illustrates the relationships between the other risk-related concepts in this space. This model is supported by a taxonomy of terms in the Appendix, which describes the key relationships between these concepts. The following sections detail our explanation of the RARA Model, including the implications for appropriate risk taking.

## Introducing the RARA Model

The RARA Model in Figure 1 is centered on the two key concepts of risk appetite and risk attitude. The left-hand side shows a range of inputs to these two central items, with outcomes shown on the right-hand side. Risk appetite and risk attitude appear as mediating factors between inputs and outcomes.

We distinguish in the model between factors that are held internally within people (shaded in Figure 1) and those that exist externally to people and can therefore be more easily observed and measured (unshaded).

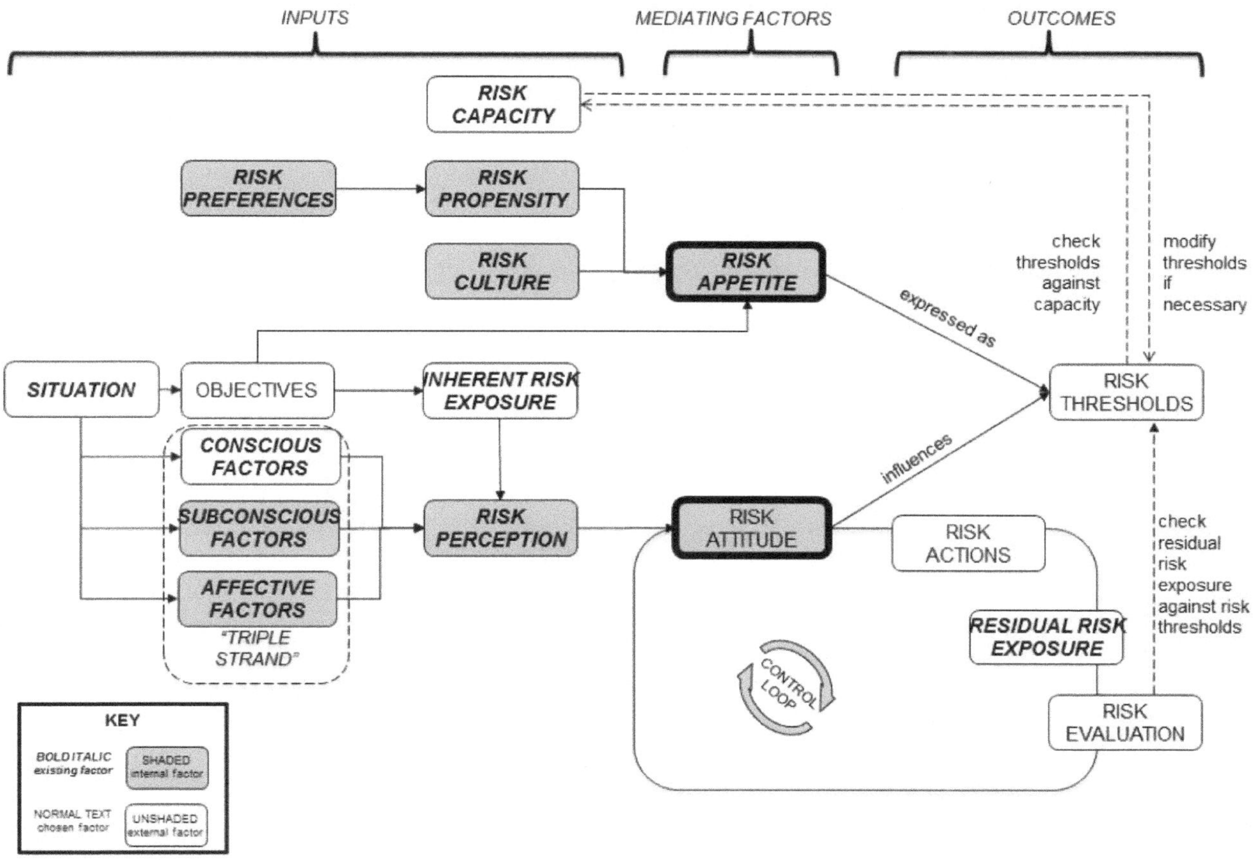


**Figure 1.** The Risk Appetite — Risk Attitude (RARA) Model

The RARA Model also separates factors that exist independently of human choice or decision (shown in bold italic text in Figure 1) and those that are (explicitly or implicitly) chosen (normal text). These distinctions are clarified in Figure 2.

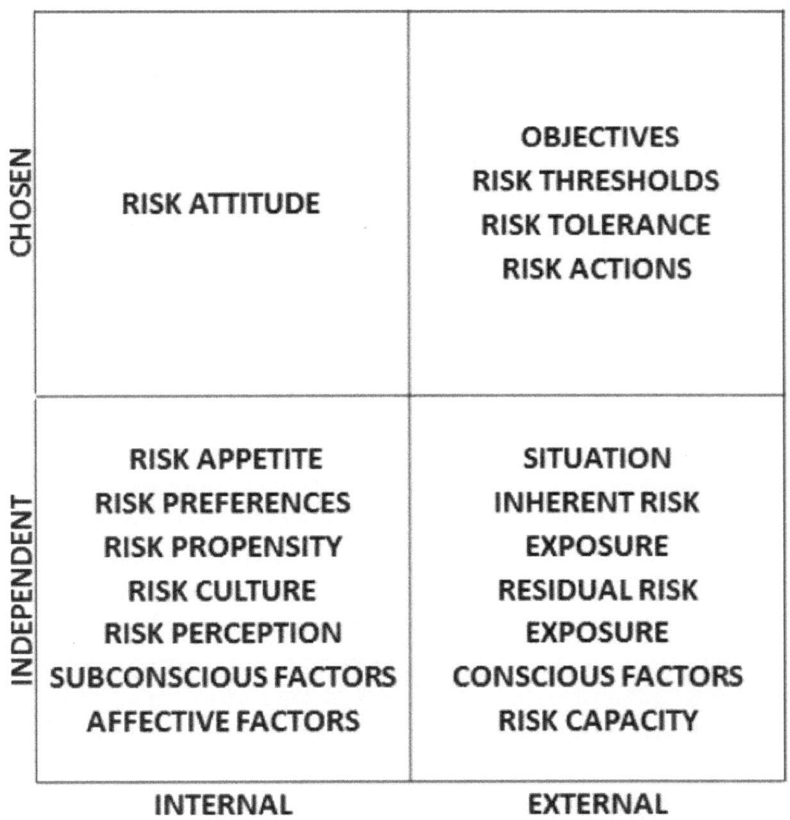


**Figure 2.** RARA Model concepts.

To understand the RARA Model, it is necessary to start with risk appetite and risk attitude. These two concepts are often confused and seen as overlapping or even synonymous, but we argue that they are essentially different in nature. Both risk appetite and risk attitude are internal factors, i.e. they are held within people and can only be seen through some external expression or behavior.

However, the fundamental difference is that the risk appetite of an individual or group exists as a tendency independently of human choice, but that the risk attitude of an individual or group is a chosen response.

It is important to remember that risk appetite and risk attitude do not and cannot exist in isolation. They both only exist in relation to an external situation, which is perceived as both risky and important, and which demands some sort of response by individuals and/or groups. As a result, the situation appears as the initiating trigger on the left-hand side of the RARA Model. The situation usually gives rise to a set of chosen objectives that an individual or group wish to achieve in that situation, although these objectives may be more or less well-defined or expressed. The inherent risk exposure associated with the situation and its objectives also exists independently of people; in other words, risk exists in the situation irrespective of whether anyone is aware of it or not.

The left-hand side of Figure 1 describes the input factors to risk appetite and risk attitude. All these input factors exist independent of human choice or decision, with the exception of the objectives to be achieved in a given situation, which are typically chosen consciously by individuals or a group.

Risk appetite is influenced by the external objectives of the situation in combination with two other factors. The first is the propensity of individuals to act in a certain way in the face of risk (risk propensity), driven by their risk-related personality traits (risk preferences). The second factor is the culture of the group or organization in relation to risk (risk culture). Because all of these factors are pre-existing and uninfluenced, risk appetite arises inherently within an individual or group, without conscious intervention or choice, which is why we describe it as a tendency.

In contrast, risk attitude is a chosen response to the situation and its objectives, influenced by perception of the inherent risk exposure (risk perception) that, in turn, is influenced by a wide range of factors. The choice of risk attitude may be made consciously/explicitly or subconsciously/implicitly, but the ability to choose a different risk attitude always remains a possibility. In our earlier work (Hillson & Murray-Webster 2007; Murray-Webster & Hillson 2008), we categorized the influences on risk perception into three groups:

- Conscious situational factors;
- Subconscious mental shortcuts;
- Affective feelings and emotions.

These three groups of factors are tightly interwoven in practice, forming a 'triple strand' of influences that takes conscious effort and awareness to untangle. Without awareness, the perception of the risky situation will lead to an implicit or tacit choice of risk attitude that might generate inappropriate actions. Awareness of the triple strand, on the other hand, can produce an appropriate chosen risk attitude that properly reflects the perceived level of risk and leads to suitable actions. In either case, risk attitude is a choice. This is a vital feature of the RARA Model, since it represents the first place in the model where conscious intervention is possible. We will return to this feature later to explore its significance for decision-making in risky and important situations.

The right-hand side of the RARA Model in Figure 1 presents outcomes that explain how risk appetite and risk attitude come together in practice as mediating factors to influence the decision on how much risk to accept in risky and important situations. We should note that all of the outcomes on the right-hand side are external factors (unshaded) that can, therefore, be observed and measured.

It is important to recognize that risk appetite is intangible and cannot be measured directly. It is, therefore, necessary to have some proxy by which this intangible tendency can be expressed. This is illustrated by the analogy of physical appetite or hunger, which cannot be directly quantified. Instead, we use figures of speech to express physical appetite. In response to the question 'How hungry are you?' we might answer, 'I could eat a horse' or perhaps 'I fancy a doughnut'. These quantified expressions are not direct statements of appetite, but instead allow us to assess it through a measurable proxy.

In the same way, risk appetite requires a proxy measure. The RARA Model gives this role to risk thresholds, which are the expression of a risk appetite in ways that can be measured externally and objectively. The RARA Model also indicates that risk thresholds are the point at which risk appetite meets risk attitude. This is an important intersection that we will return to below.

We define risk thresholds as the quantified measures that represent upper and lower limits of acceptable tolerance around objectives. Some organizations choose to use the term risk tolerance as an alternative to risk thresholds. Either is acceptable in our view, since risk tolerance indicates upper and lower limits of variability around a risk threshold.

We suggest that risk thresholds are derived from risk appetite (the tendency to take risk in the situation) and are influenced by the chosen risk attitudes of stakeholders (the chosen positioning in relation to the risk exposure inherent in that situation). For risk thresholds to be appropriate in a situation, they should be validated against risk capacity, which we define as the ability of an entity to bear risk, quantified against objectives.

The ideal situation is for risk thresholds to be set that properly reflect both the inherent risk appetite of the organization and the chosen risk attitude in a given situation. This alignment will maximize the chances for the organization to achieve its objectives by taking the right amount of risk consistent with the desired outcomes. What happens if risk appetite and risk attitude are not aligned? We argue that in these circumstances a control loop is required in order to support the necessary corrective behavior. Lack of alignment will lead to inappropriate risk thresholds, with the organization eventually taking on too much or too little risk. This, in turn, is likely to lead to unacceptable risk exposure or inadequate performance because actions are inconsistent with the objectives of the situation. But where can remedial control be exercised within the RARA Model presented in Figure 1?

There is only one control point in the model, which is to modify risk attitude. This is because risk attitude is chosen and that choice leads to action. Therefore, the control mechanism to judge whether the chosen risk attitude is appropriate in a situation is to check the effect of risk actions and the residual risk exposure against the risk thresholds and then to adjust the choice of risk attitude as necessary to create the necessary alignment for the action to lead to appropriate outcomes in the situation.

## Risk Appetite and Risk Attitude in Action

In this section, we demonstrate how risk appetite and risk attitude function within the RARA Model. They can be considered as separate constructs since each has a particular influence on the final outcomes, yet they must be addressed in combination if they are to have a positive effect on individual and organizational decision-making in risky and important situations. The best way to illustrate the contribution of risk appetite or risk attitude is to consider how the RARA Model might work in their absence. In particular, we explore how an organization might set its risk thresholds in three different scenarios:

- Unmanaged, where risk thresholds are set by the organization with no reference to risk appetite or risk attitude.
- Constrained, where risk thresholds are consciously modified by the inherent risk appetite.
- Informed, taking account of the chosen risk attitudes of key stakeholders as well as wider organizational factors when setting risk thresholds.

These three scenarios are outlined below, together with an illustrative example that is based on a real case but one that has been modified for simplicity.

### *The Unmanaged Scenario*

Figure 3 shows what happens when both risk appetite and risk attitude are removed from the RARA Model, which we call the Unmanaged Scenario. A situation arises that is perceived as risky and important and, from this situation, one or more objectives are derived by key individuals, or by a decision-making group. There is, of course, a certain level of inherent risk exposure associated with this situation, but this is not explicitly considered in the Unmanaged Scenario. Having set objectives, the organization then proceeds to set risk thresholds to quantify how much risk is acceptable in the given situation in order to optimize the chances of achieving the objectives. These risk thresholds are validated against the overall risk capacity of the organization and modified if necessary. Risk actions may be implemented to control the perceived level of residual risk exposure, and the results of these actions are compared with the risk thresholds to determine whether they are working adequately.

At first sight, there appears to be nothing wrong with the sequence of events in the Unmanaged Scenario. It describes a set of actions that most decision-making groups would recognize as familiar. However, there is a problem with following this scenario to set risk thresholds. Since inherent risk exposure is not explicitly considered in the Unmanaged Scenario, there is no way of determining whether the selected risk thresholds are appropriate. The organization recognizes that it needs to set risk thresholds in order to indicate how much risk the organization is prepared to accept in the given situation, and so they are set somehow, perhaps intuitively. But it is not possible to know if the chosen risk thresholds are appropriate, without considering the wider context of the decision. It is possible that the unmanaged approach might result in suitable risk thresholds being set, but this outcome would be more the result of good luck than good judgment, and is not guaranteed.

In Figure 3 all the boxes are unshaded, indicating that these are external factors that exist independent of people. In the Unmanaged Scenario, inputs result in outcomes, but without the mediating factors that take explicit account of the internal workings of individuals or groups. Instead, this approach is only influenced by what can be seen and measured.

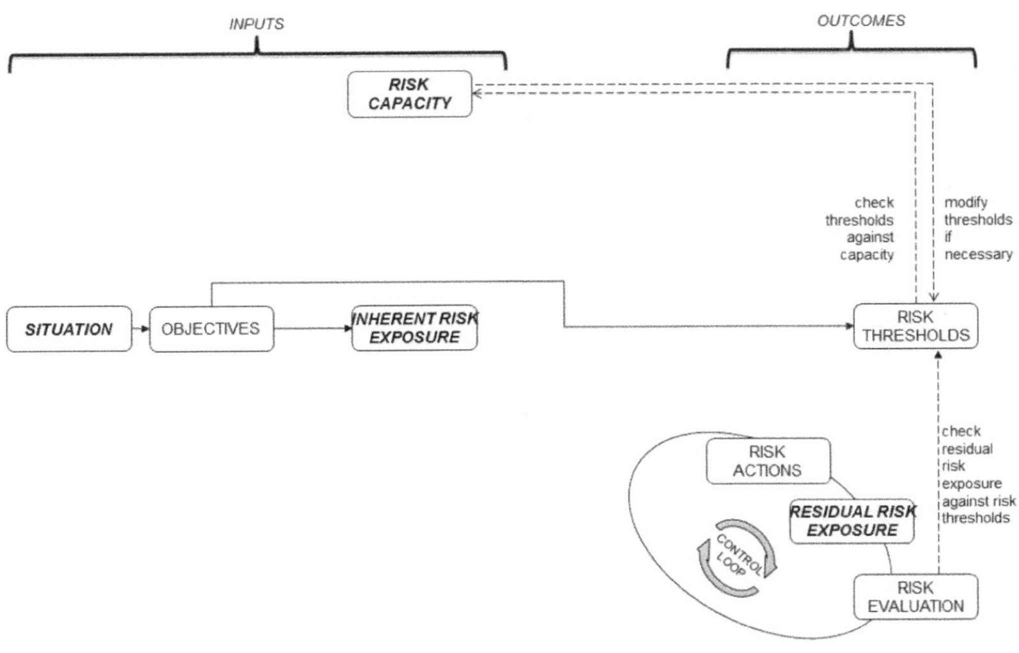


**Figure 3.** The Unmanaged Scenario.

As an example of this scenario, consider the behavior of an analyst who recently joined a leading oil company to conduct economic appraisals. The analyst developed an economic value model for a new exploration prospect using current industry norms and established algorithms, and the model returned a positive result that exceeded all the company's hurdle rates. As a result, the analyst recommended that the company should proceed with the investment. The analyst proposed risk thresholds set at the standard values used for previous similar prospects, and suggested a routine and proven development strategy that was expected to maintain an acceptable level of risk exposure.

The analyst's recommendations were submitted to an investment appraisal panel for approval. We might expect that they would be accepted, since due process was followed in a transparent and traceable manner. However, there is no guarantee that simply following a proven analytical approach produced the right outcome. Other factors need to be considered if the optimal result is to be achieved.

## The Constrained Scenario

This scenario is shown in Figure 4, which adds risk appetite back into the picture, together with its influencing inputs.

In the Constrained Scenario it is clear that risk thresholds are not just choices made in isolation from their context, determined only by the desired objectives in a given situation. Instead, there is a range of internal factors that should influence the chosen risk thresholds. These are required to ensure that the amount of risk considered acceptable by the organization properly reflects both the risk culture of the organization and the risk propensity of key stakeholders. Both risk culture and risk propensity come together in the internal tendency that we call risk appetite. As an internal factor, risk appetite is intangible and cannot be measured explicitly, unless and until it is expressed via risk thresholds.

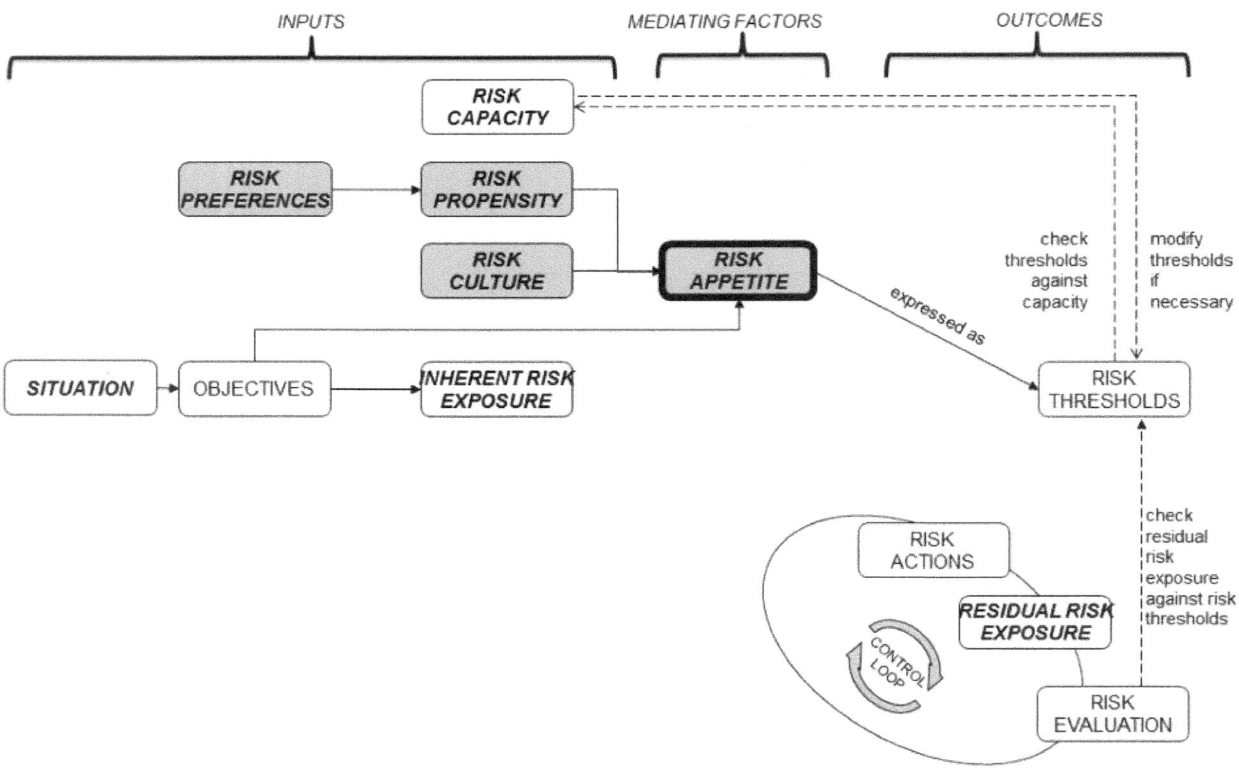


**Figure 4.** The Constrained Scenario.

We can illustrate this by returning to our oil company analyst's recommendations for the exploration prospect. When these were submitted to the investment appraisal panel, the panel members challenged the risk thresholds that had arisen from the analysis. On closer inspection, it appeared that these failed to take account of the company's position on safety and environmental issues, and consequently the risk thresholds were too high. These issues were the result of previous incidents in the company's history that had led to changes in company culture of which the newly appointed analyst was unaware.

Simple analysis of a situation in isolation is not sufficient to determine how much risk should be taken by an organization in a given situation that is risky and important. Instead, it is necessary to take account of organizational risk culture and personal risk propensities, which shape the risk appetite of the decision-making group. These are commonly expressed as 'The way we do things here', and they form an important overlay to the unmanaged calculation of risk thresholds.

The explicit inclusion of risk appetite in the process of determining risk thresholds avoids the problem of setting levels of acceptable risk that are inconsistent with company values, history or norms and which are, therefore, inappropriate in the organizational context. It does not, however, take account of the desire of the organization or key stakeholders to take risk, since risk appetite is an internal tendency driven by other intangible factors. As a result, the setting of risk thresholds is still intuitive and unmanaged. In the Constrained Scenario, risk thresholds are influenced by risk appetite, and can later be modified consciously by reference to risk capacity, but there is no point in Figure 4 at which intervention is possible to influence where the risk thresholds are initially set. Something else is required.

## *The Informed Scenario*

It is clearly important to take proper account of risk appetite when setting risk thresholds, which the Constrained Scenario does, but this is not the whole story. In every case, it is people who take decisions on what level of risk exposure is appropriate, working either as individuals or in groups. Despite claims to the contrary, people are not dispassionate rational actors who make decisions based on perfect economic utility calculations. Instead we bring a range of overt and hidden influences to our decision-making, including subconscious cognitive biases and psychological heuristics, as well as affective emotional factors. It is not possible to set appropriate risk thresholds without considering these influences on our perception of risk that, in turn, affect individual and group risk attitude. It is, therefore, necessary to add risk attitude back into the picture, producing the Informed Scenario, which brings us back to the full RARA Model (see Figure 4, repeating Figure 1).

In the case of our oil company example, the exploration and development opportunity was pursued following the investment appraisal panel, and a project team was appointed with clear objectives and a set of well-defined risk thresholds. However, as the project proceeded, it became clear that the team's actions were in danger of breaching the risk thresholds. On investigation, a range of subtle influences were uncovered that led to risk-taking behavior, including the previous experience of key team members, peer pressure to perform, the financial incentive of potential bonus payments for successful delivery, and a strong macho, can-do culture among the team. This led to a risky shift in the way the team operated, with an inappropriate level of risk seeking. A new project leader was appointed, who had strong interpersonal skills and well-developed emotional literacy, and who was able to modify the team's attitude and approach to risk taking and bring the project back into line.

This illustrates the importance of hidden sources of bias in this area. If these remain unmanaged, they can lead to adoption of risk attitudes that hinder achievement of the desired objectives. Instead, we need to aim for managed risk attitudes to align behavior and actions with the risk thresholds that have been set for a given situation.

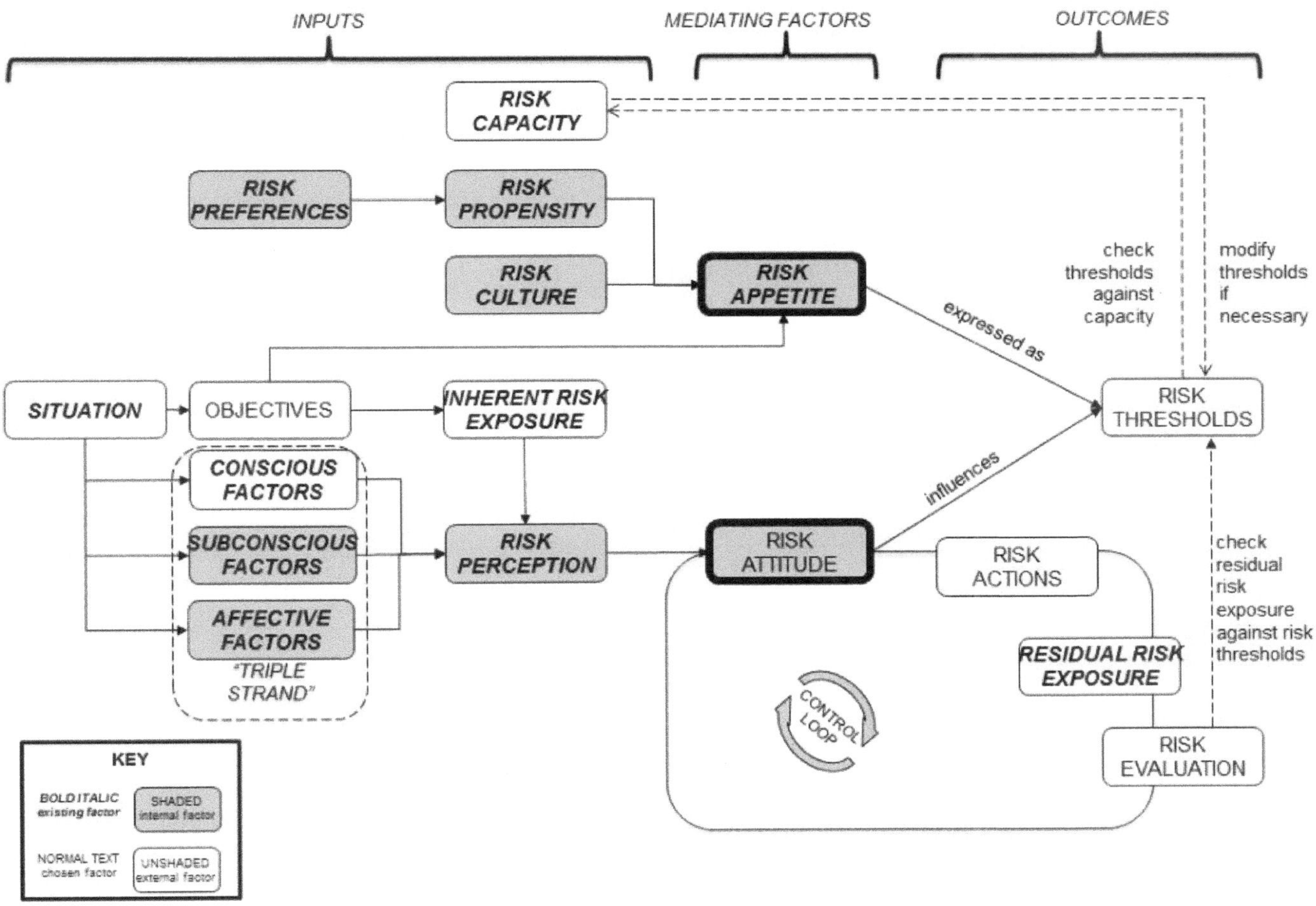


**Figure 5 (repeating Figure 1).** The Informed Scenario.

The Informed Scenario (Figure 5) illustrates the full RARA Model, which includes the influence of risk attitude alongside risk appetite, showing how managed risk attitude offers a point of choice and intervention in the decision-making process. The 'risk attitude–risk actions–risk evaluation' control loop allows the chosen risk attitude to be changed in order to keep actions in line with risk thresholds. As a result, we can reach optimal alignment of risk thresholds with objectives, internal coherence with risk culture and maximum effectiveness of risk actions.

## So What? Implications for Practice

So far in this paper, we have defined a range of risk-related constructs and shown how they relate to each other, as well as describing the part they each play in decision making in risky and important situations. The RARA Model provides a holistic and integrated framework for individuals, teams and organizations to use when answering questions such as 'Is my behavior appropriate in this risky situation?', 'How much risk should we take?' or 'Does our risk culture support our strategy and objectives?'.

This section expands our description of the RARA Model in order to make it useful to practitioners. We particularly elaborate on two key assertions:

- Some risk-related constructs exist independently outside people and in the external environment, and hence can be observed and/or measured.
- Other risk-related constructs are intangible and they cannot be measured directly; they can only be observed through actions or proxy measures.

As above, we achieve this expanded discussion by considering the three possible scenarios in turn, incrementally adding risk appetite and risk attitude back into the unmanaged version of the RARA Model. In doing so, we expose further how the loose use of nomenclature has created confusion in knowing what can be objectively defined and measured, and what cannot.

We then build further on this analysis in the penultimate section by suggesting a practical process for making appropriate risk-informed decisions.

### *The Unmanaged Scenario: Only Tangible Factors*

As shown in Figure 3, all the variables in the Unmanaged Scenario are external factors, existing outside of individual people or a collective group. Some of these are pre-existing un-chosen factors (the situation itself, the risk capacity of the organization and the inherent risk exposure associated with the situation). Others are chosen by people (the objectives in the situation, the risk thresholds and tolerances selected, risk evaluation criteria and risk actions). All the factors in the Unmanaged Scenario can be explicitly observed or articulated. Risk actions can be observed; objectives, risk thresholds, risk tolerances and risk evaluation criteria can be expressed in tangible terms; and risk capacity can be calculated based on the assets of the organization.

Because all the factors in the Unmanaged Scenario are visible and measurable, it appears deceptively simple to set risk thresholds using this approach. However, the failure to take proper account of the other factors in the RARA Model, particularly the central mediating factors of risk appetite and risk attitude, means that the resulting risk thresholds are likely to be flawed. If the 'right result' is achieved, then it probably arose more by good luck than good judgment.

### *The Constrained Scenario: Factors with Proxy Measures*

The Unmanaged Scenario is developed into the Constrained Scenario by the addition of risk appetite and its precedents (risk preferences, risk propensity and risk culture), as described in Figure 4. These factors put the Unmanaged Scenario into its proper context, allowing a link to be made between the risk thresholds and factors that exist independent of the specific situation.

Existing work on risk preferences, risk propensity and risk culture indicate how these might be assessed and/or measured.

Risk preferences of individuals (as innate motivations) can be determined through personality tests, such as the Spony Profiling Model (Spony 2003), or the MyersBriggs Type Indicator (Briggs-Myers 1980). Such instruments allow an individual to diagnose and reflect upon their likely starting point when faced with a risky and important situation. Although some decision scientists argue that risk taking is a rational, economic process, by which human beings are able to compute potential gains and losses and decide objectively (e.g. Dyer & Sarin 1982; Davies 2006), others argue that there are other, more subjective, situational influences on risk propensity (e.g. Sitkin & Pablo 1992; Lopes 1987; Sitkin & Weingart 1995). There is certainly no single, reliable diagnostic that can be used to determine the risk preferences or propensity of individual decision makers; indeed, the fact that these constructs are tendencies should warn us against trying to be overly analytical about them.

Risk preferences and risk propensity apply to individuals, yet individuals rarely make decisions in a vacuum. Individuals form decision-making groups such as families, project teams, company boards, and so on. Groups, particularly long-established ones such as companies, will tend to adopt tendencies of how to respond to risk and this collective tendency is referred to as the group's risk culture. For example, one organization's risk culture might always be to consider how avoid loss, while another might view risk as an opportunity to maximize value. Again, some diagnostics exist that attempt to measure risk culture, although even in the better diagnostics, risk culture is often used interchangeably with risk attitude, incorrectly in our view (e.g. Underwood & Ingram 2010).

Risk preferences, propensity and culture are important influential factors when considering risk appetite, but they are not directly observable. Instead, they are internal tendencies that can be assessed to some degree through the use of diagnostics at an individual or group level. Rather than trying to measure these tendencies per se, it is more important to consider how each may be affecting risk appetite and the resulting risk thresholds.

### *The Informed Scenario: Factors Understood and Controlled with Hindsight*

In the Constrained Scenario, externally measurable factors in the RARA Model are supplemented by an understanding of the factors that influence risk appetite. Although diagnostics exist that seek to evaluate such tendencies, these have use only insofar as they can alert the decision maker. In the Informed Scenario, by contrast, the mediating factor of risk attitude is introduced. We define this term very precisely as a chosen response to risk, influenced by perception. Crucially, risk attitude is a situational phenomenon. It cannot be measured directly, but it can be understood and judged as appropriate or inappropriate during decision-making in a specific, risky and important situation. The triple strand of influences on risk perception and risk attitude shown in Figure 1 can all be reflected upon and understood, either in isolation or, more importantly, as a combined effect, but this is not meaningful out of the context of the specific situation. In a specific situation, risk attitude (how a person or group will respond to the perceived risks) can be evaluated and modified using the Six As model (Murray-Webster & Hillson 2008), shown in Figure 6 below.

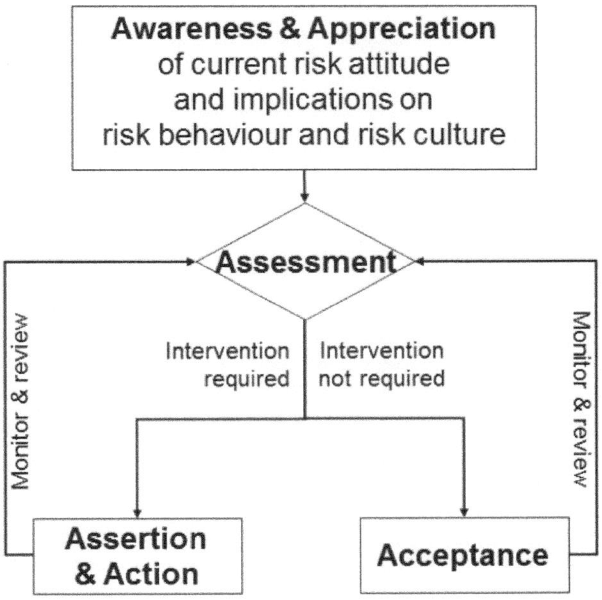


**Figure 6.** The Six As Model.

The Six as model provides a structured framework to help individuals and groups adopt an appropriate risk attitude in any given risky and important situation. The model is described in detail elsewhere (Murray-Webster & Hillson 2008), but it can be summarized as follows:

- First, there is a need for awareness and appreciation of the current risk attitude adopted by an individual or a group, including the 'triple strand' key influences.
- Next comes assessment, to determine whether the unmanaged risk attitude is likely to lead to an acceptable outcome or not.
- Where the assessment step indicates that intervention is required to modify the prevailing risk attitude, assertion and action are employed to make the necessary change.
- If, on the other hand, assessment shows that the existing risk attitude is appropriate, the current risk attitude can be accepted.
- Whether the unmanaged risk attitude is accepted or modified, the ongoing situation must be monitored and reassessed periodically to determine whether intervention may be required at a later time.

Each of these steps involves a range of underlying actions, and this paper cannot cover the full detail. Instead, we have shown how 'chosen risk attitude' works alongside the other risk-related elements of the RARA Model to provide a control loop that can be activated to modify risk attitude where necessary, influencing both the level at which risk thresholds are set and the nature of future risk actions. Since risk appetite is an internal and independent tendency not influenced by human choice, it cannot act in this modifying way, leaving our ability to choose an appropriate risk attitude as the sole control point available to us.

As we have seen, some risk-related constructs exist independently outside people and in the external environment, and hence these can be observed and/or measured. These constructs are those that make up the starting point when considering how much risk is too much risk: the elements of the Unmanaged Scenario. The other risk-related constructs that allow the Unmanaged Scenario to progress through to an informed judgment are intangible and they cannot be measured directly; they can only be observed through actions or proxy measures.

We argue that the control point in the process is achieved by comparing the objective expression of risk thresholds with the evaluation of residual risk, and modifying risk attitude as necessary to ensure that residual risk is matched with thresholds so that the situation poses neither too much nor too little risk.

## Using the RARA Model for Risk-Informed Decisions

This section uses the RARA Model in order to demonstrate how individuals and groups in risky and important situations can make appropriate risk-informed decisions. This is achieved by considering the three possible scenarios in turn, starting with the outcome arising from the unmanaged version of the RARA Model, then incrementally adding risk appetite and risk attitude.

### *Moving through the Scenarios*

There is one key question for any individual, organization or decision-making group facing a risky and important situation. Which is the best approach to adopt in order to determine the 'right' risk thresholds? Clearly, it is not safe to rely on the Unmanaged Scenario (Figure 3), since this produces risk thresholds based on gut reaction and intuition, taking no account of the organizational risk culture or the risk propensities of key stakeholders. As a minimum, we need to consider the norms of 'the way we do things here', as illustrated in the Constrained Scenario (Figure 4). But we have shown that even this is not sufficient to ensure that risk thresholds are set in an appropriate level. Instead, we need to actively adopt a risk attitude that reflects our chosen response to the perceived risk exposure which will, in turn, influence where we decide to set our risk thresholds, as shown in the Informed Scenario (Figure 5).

In order to make this process explicit, we recommend that risk thresholds should be set in a progressive manner, moving through the three scenarios. Initially, risk thresholds are produced and recorded without reference to any factors other than what can be described and measured (Unmanaged). These risk thresholds are then modified to take account of the risk appetite that arises from the organizational risk culture and the risk propensities of key stakeholders (Constrained). A final refinement to the risk thresholds is then made to reflect the chosen risk attitude (Informed). This final step can be achieved by recognizing that risk attitude is a central mediating factor, alongside risk appetite. We have also seen that the ability for individuals and groups to choose a risk attitude provides a vital control point in the process of setting risk thresholds, and the Six As model (Figure 6) provides a practical approach to facilitate the appropriate choice of risk attitude.

## CONCLUSIONS

Our previous work together has focused on the promotion and encouragement of 'appropriate' risk-taking (Hillson & Murray-Webster 2007; Murray-Webster & Hillson 2008). The understanding of what is meant by 'appropriate' is of course both subjective and situational, and it depends on the people involved as well as the circumstances. Behavior towards risk is determined by the underlying risk attitude, which itself is dependent on risk perception, and there is a range of factors that influence perception of risk (the 'triple strand' of conscious, subconscious and affective factors). We have shown previously that risk attitude is a choice, and that it is possible to use a managed approach to choose appropriate risk attitudes in order to optimize both the decision-making process and the decision outcome.

This paper extends our earlier work on risk attitude, to put these ideas of managed choices in risky and important situations into the wider context, particularly in terms of risk appetite. In showing how risk appetite and risk attitude are separate yet complementary ideas, we have also produced a complete and integrated taxonomy and framework of a wider set of risk-related concepts and terms.

Most importantly for practitioners, the RARA Model indicates how both risk appetite and risk attitude influence the setting of risk thresholds. Progressively deconstructing this model has revealed a three-step process that allows informed risk taking when determining what risk thresholds are appropriate in a given situation. This process starts by taking account of external and visible factors to generate an initial set of risk thresholds, without conscious consideration of the hidden influences (the Unmanaged Scenario). This is then augmented and modified by taking account of the pre-existing tendencies of the individual and the organization in relation to risk (risk propensities and risk culture), which produces an intangible risk appetite that modifies the first-cut risk thresholds (the Constrained Scenario). Finally, a further refinement of risk thresholds is achieved through active adoption of the desirable risk attitude in order to optimize the achievement of objectives given the level of risk exposure (the Informed Scenario), using the Six As framework to manage risk attitude proactively.

Our exploration started by considering the ill-defined concept of risk appetite, but it has led to a framework that clearly defines the different roles of a range of risk-related factors and how they interact. Applying the approach outlined in this paper offers individuals and organizations a practical way of ensuring that they take the right risks safely, setting measurable risk thresholds that reflect the inherent risk appetite while also adopting the most appropriate risk attitude.

## REFERENCES

1. Association of Insurance and Risk Managers 2009, Research into the Definition and Application of the Concept of Risk Appetite, AIRMIC, London, UK.
2. Briggs-Myers, I. & Myers, P.B. 1980, Gifts Differing: Understanding Personality Type, Consulting Psychology Practice, California, USA.
3. British Standard BS 31100:2011 2011, Risk Management — Code of Practice, British Standards Institution, London, UK.
4. Davies, G.B. 2006, Rethinking risk attitude: aspiration as pure risk, Theory and Decision, vol. 61, no. 2, 159-190.
5. Dyer, J.S. & Sarin, R.K. 1982, Relative risk aversion, Management Science, vol. 28, no. 8, 875-886.
6. Financial Reporting Council 2010, UK Corporate Governance Code, Financial Reporting Council, London, UK.
7. Hillson, D.A. & Murray-Webster, R. 2007, Understanding and Managing Risk Attitude, 2nd ed., Gower, Aldershot, UK.
8. Institute of Operational Risk 2009, Operational Risk Sound Practice Guidance Part 1: Risk Appetite (version 1, December 2009). Available at: http://www.ior-institute.org/education/soundpractice-guidance/8-sound-practice-guidance-part-1. Accessed 31 January 201.
9. Institute of Risk Management 2011, Risk Appetite and Risk Tolerance, Institute of Risk Management, London, UK. Available at: http://www.theirm.org/publications/risk_appetite.html
10. International Organization for Standardization Guide 73:2009 2009, Risk Management — Vocabulary,
11. International Organization for Standardization, Geneva, Switzerland.
12. International Organization for Standardization ISO 31000:2009 2009, Risk Management — Principles and Guidelines, International Organization for Standardization, Geneva, Switzerland.
13. Kahneman D. & Tversky A. 1979, Prospect theory: an analysis of decision under risk, Econometrica, vol. 47, no. 2, 263-297.
14. Kahneman, D., Slovic, P. & Tversky, A. (eds) 1986, Judgment Under Uncertainty: Heuristics and Biases, Cambridge University Press, Cambridge, UK.
15. KPMG 2008, Understanding and Articulating Risk Appetite, KPMG, Sydney, Australia.
16. Kumar, S.M. & Persaud, A. 2002, Pure contagion and investors' shifting risk appetite: analytical issues and empirical evidence, International Finance, vol. 5, no. 3, 401-436.
17. Lopes L.L. 1987, Between hope and fear: the psychology of risk, Advances in Experimental Social Psychology, vol. 20, 255-295.
18. Murray-Webster, R. & Hillson, D.A. 2008, Managing Group Risk Attitude, Gower, Aldershot, UK.
19. National Association of Corporate Directors 2009, Report on Risk Governance: Balancing Risk and Reward, NACD, Washington DC, USA.
20. PricewaterhouseCoopers 2008, Risk appetite — how hungry are you? The PwC Journal, Special Risk Management Edition, PwC, London, UK.

21. Sitkin, S.B. & Pablo, A. 1992, Reconceptualizing the determinants of risk behavior, Academy of Management Review, vol. 17, no. 1, 9-38.

22. Sitkin, S.B. & Weingart, L.R. 1995, Determinants of risk decision-making behavior: a test of the mediating role of risk perception and risk propensity, Academy of Management Journal, vol. 38, no. 6, 1573-1592.

23. Spony G. 2003, The development of a work–value model assessing the cumulative impact of individual and cultural differences on managers' work–value systems, International Journal of Human Resource Management, vol. 14, no. 4, 658-679.

24. Towers Perrin 2009, Risk Appetite: The Foundation of Enterprise Risk Management. Towers Perrin, London, UK.

25. Tversky, A. & Kahneman, D. 1981. 'The framing of decisions and the psychology of choice'. Science, 211 (4481), 453-458

26. UK Office of Government Commerce 2010, Management of Risk: Guidance for Practitioners, 3rd ed., The Stationery Office, London, UK.

27. Underwood, A. & Ingram, D. 2010, The full spectrum of risk attitude, The Actuary, vol. 7, no. 4, 26- 32.

28. Weber, E.U. & Milliman, R.A. 1997, Perceived risk attitudes: relating risk perception to risky choice, Management Science, vol. 43, no. 2, 123-144.

# INDEX